THE REPORT.

CANNABIS: THE FACTS, HUMAN RIGHTS AND THE LAW;

— by —

Kenn and Joanna d'Oudney.

VERITAS

COGNITIO · IUSTITIA

LIBERTAS

Academic Publications by

SCORPIO RECORDING COMPANY (PUBLISHING) LTD.,
MONOMARK HOUSE, 27, OLD GLOUCESTER STREET, LONDON WC1N 3XX, ENGLAND.

THE REPORT.
CANNABIS: THE FACTS, HUMAN RIGHTS AND THE LAW
— by —
Kenn and Joanna d'Oudney.
— published by —
Scorpio Recording Company (Publishing) Ltd.,
Monomark House,
27, Old Gloucester Street,
London WC1N 3XX,
England.

A book of — *The Restoration Trilogy* —
A Publication for
The DEMOCRACY DEFINED CAMPAIGN for
RESTORATION and UNIVERSAL ADOPTON of
CONSTITUTIONAL COMMON LAW TRIAL BY JURY.
See campaign website **www.democracydefined.org**

THE REPORT. Exposition on Cannabis in contexts of:
AGRICULTURE (FOOD)/ ALCOHOL/ ALTERNATIVE ENERGY/
CANNABIS BIOMASS ENERGY EQUATION (CBEE)/
CANNABIS BIOMASS RESOURCE & PYROLYSIS FUNCTIONS (CBRPF)/
CANNABIS-METHANOL (RENEWABLE POLLUTION-FREE) FUELTECHNOLOGY/
CLIMATE CHANGE/ CONSTITUTION/ CRIMINOLOGY/
'DECRIMINALISATION' (THE FALLACY OF)/ ECOLOGY/ ECONOMICS/
EMPIRICAL RESEARCH FINDINGS OF FACT, DEFINITIVE/ ENVIRONMENT/
GANJA/ GENERAL KNOWLEDGE/ GLOBAL WARMING/ GREENHOUSE EFFECT/ HEALTH/
HEMP/ HISTORY/ ILLEGALITY OF THE STATUS QUO, THE/ JURY NULLIFICATION/ LAW/
MARIJUANA/ MEDICINE/ NATURAL RESOURCES/ POLITICS/ POT/
PROHIBITION: THE PROGENITOR OF CRIME/ RELEGALISATION/ SATIVA/
SINGLE CONVENTION TREATY/ SOCIOLOGY/ TOBACCO/ TRIAL BY JURY/
UNIVERSAL RE-DEMOCRATISATION OF FUEL-ENERGY PRODUCTION (URFEP)/
WAR ON DRUGS

THE REPORT is available from the Publishers (see above) or from
LULU of North Carolina, book manufacturers and worldwide distributors.
Contacts: scorpiobooks@democracydefined.org
Orders: **http://www.lulu.com/commerce/index.php?fBuyContent=821985**

Tenth edition, revised, published 2007. ISBN: 9781902848204. U.S.$25.90
First edition published on the 1st of October, 1994, by
SCORPIO RECORDING COMPANY (PUBLISHING) LTD.

British Library cataloguing in publication data.
A catalogue record for this book is available from the British Library.
STANDARD ENGLISH SPELLING

IN LOVING MEMORY

OF OUR FATHER (AND FATHER-IN-LAW)

ARTHUR

WHOSE LAST YEARS OF TOTAL BLINDNESS

(GLAUCOMA) COULD ALL HAVE BEEN SO DIFFERENT.

Authors' Preface.

Since the first edition of The Report, to those who have turned to us for counsel, we have pointed out the difficulty of achieving Relegalisation because of the utmost corrupt money-motive behind Cannabis Prohibition controls; and the paradox that the unfounded, unlawful Prohibition is as fragile as a house of cards. If there were no Prohibition, or if cannabis were Relegalised today, it would be prohibited again tomorrow, so great is the scale of monetary interest, and so intense is money-motivation behind Prohibition. Nothing less than RESTORATION of democratic control of governments by re-introduction of the authentic Constitutional Common Law Trial by Jury [1] ensures Relegalisation, and the elimination of the corporate and government crime that are all controls.

Cannabis Prohibition is the greatest fraud of all time: the pernicious effects of this crime are myriad, extreme and ubiquitous. Readers assimilate that Prohibition is the direct cause of: War [2]; Crime [3]; astronomical world energy, resource and food prices, with disastrous and homicidal corollary effects; world poverty; world famine; industrial and automotive emissions poisoning air; photochemical smog and Acid Rain; desertification; the Greenhouse Effect, Global Warming and fatally catastrophic weather; and that RESTORATION is the immediate Scientific Solution [4].

It has been interesting to observe that throughout the West since 1994, Prohibition and official attitudes have not changed, while a marked change in the patience, or rather impatience, of the People developed. Politicians' refusal to effect RESTORATION is evolving this impatience into wrath and an acute desire for just retribution. It could be that only self-interested fear in politicians and those others implicated, for impending condign punitive consequences of their culpable actions, will produce RESTORATION. As with all tyrannies, the duty to extirpate criminal governments devolves upon the People.

The Report is intended for a general readership. All Conclusions and Findings of Fact stated herein are the direct product of and supported by the findings of fact of official empirical research studies. Attribution is given in full. For further perusal of this subject the reader is recommended those works selected for the bibliography which includes the major research extant, some deeply perceptive papers and books, and other pertinent revelation.

K.E.A. and J.R. d'Oudney.

1 How the authentic Constitutional Common Law Trial by Jury is intended to work, democratically to nullify enforcement of bad laws and eliminate tyrannical governments, is explained herein, and with greater detail in 'TRIAL BY JURY: Its History, True Purpose and Modern Relevance,' by Kenn d'Oudney and Lysander Spooner, U.S. lawyer; ISBN: 9781902848723. Readers are invited to join in: The DEMOCRACY DEFINED RESTORATION Campaign expounded on the www.democracydefined.org/ website.
2 & 4 Ref. THE REPORT, Part Two; also see: 'GLOBAL WARMING: The Scientific Green Solution to this World Crisis,' by Kenn d'Oudney; ISBN: 9781902848068.
3 Ref. Part Six, PROHIBITION: THE PROGENITOR OF CRIME.

FOREWORD AND ENDORSEMENT BY

Nobel laureate Professor Milton Friedman:

"You have done a splendid job of producing a comprehensive summary of the evidence documenting that the prohibition of the production, sale, and use of cannabis is utterly unjustified and produces many harmful effects. Any impartial person reading your report will almost certainly end up favouring the relegalisation of cannabis."

**Nobel laureate Professor Milton Friedman;
Author; T.V. series & video writer and presenter;
Economics' Adviser to the U.S. Government;
Senior Research Fellow, Hoover Institution
on War, Revolution and Peace;
Professor Emeritus, University of Chicago.**

— REVIEWS AND ENDORSEMENTS —

"You represent a worthy part of the fight in many countries for the logical and beneficial use of cannabis. I thank you for that."
Professor Patrick D. Wall, Author; Professor of Physiology, UMDS St. Thomas's (Teaching) Hospital, London; Fellow of the Royal Society; DM, FRCP.

"I am totally amazed at THE REPORT's quality and overall goodness."
Dr. Anne Biezanek, Authoress; ChB, BSc, MB, MFHom.

"A fine document."
U.S. Judge's letter to Authors.

"THE REPORT's thesis is sound."
U.K. Judge's letter to Authors.

"I did enjoy reading it. THE REPORT should contribute much."
The Hon. Jonathon Porritt, Bt., Adviser to U.K. government on Environment; Author; Founder, Friends of the Earth; TV series writer and presenter.

SYNOPTICAL REFERENCE PAGES OF

CONTENTS.
—fast fact finder —

- PART ONE -

Studies, Statistics
And
The Supreme Law.

Introduction.

IN a world where in some countries people are routinely executed for mere small-scale possession of cannabis for personal use, and incarceration, fines and forfeitures are widespread, sanctioned in the continuing vain attempt at suppression of activities connected with cannabis, its cultivation, trade, possession and use, it is appropriate to study in depth to evaluate cannabis and the Prohibition itself, as expressed in laws and control regulations, to examine ostensible reasons if any for the said Prohibition and ascertain whether such legislation of Prohibition was originally, or is now, justifiable and founded in fact. To this end, many studies over the years and up to date have been made, including THE REPORT, the product and latest conclusion of such, the publication of which is intended to disperse knowledge on a subject in which, literally, human lives and freedom are daily in the balance.

The authors hereby draw attention to the numerous medico-scientific and sociological reports which have been produced by the most prestigious of academic and research institutions, all supporting the legalisation (or rather, *re*-legalisation) of cannabis.

Authentic statistics and official in-depth clinical studies pertaining to cannabis use and its complete absence of deleterious effect on health, work performance, behaviour and motivation, driving skills, etc., are not only publicly available, but repeatedly published.

To begin with, it should be well noted that in all places and at all times, there has never ensued a single death from cannabis use, it being harmless. This statistic of complete safety, of nought (**0**) deaths, deserves comparison with the great many gruesome deaths and pandemic diseases induced in the population by the use of tobacco, alcohol, etc.; viz: U.S. government's Bureau of Mortality Statistics—see next page.

COMPARISON OF CANNABIS TO OTHER SUBSTANCES BY OFFICIAL MORTALITY STATISTICS.

U.S. federal government Bureau of Mortality Statistics.

SUBSTANCE...NUMBER OF DEATHS PER ANNUM:

TOBACCO..**340,000** to **425,000**

ALCOHOL (Not including 50% of all highway deaths and
                  65% of all murders)….......................................**150,000+**

ASPIRIN (Including deliberate overdose)...............................**180** to **1,000+**

CAFFEINE (From stress, ulcers, triggering irregular
                       heartbeats, etc.)…........**1,000** to **10,000**

LEGAL DRUG OVERDOSE (Deliberate or accidental from legal, prescribed or patent medicines and/or mixing with alcohol —
                e.g. Valium/Alcohol).................................**14,000** to **27,000**

ILLICIT DRUG OVERDOSE (Deliberate or accidental,
                  from all illegal drugs).....................**3,800** to **5,200**

THEOPHYLLINE (Pharmaceutical drug legally prescribed for asthma)…..............**50**
*Theophylline is also responsible for **6,500** Emergency Room admissions and*
***1,000** cases of permanent brain damage each year.*

CANNABIS...0

NOTA BENE:

    The sample year shown is unexceptional for in all the years since collation of figures was commenced by the U.S. Bureau of Mortality Statistics, cannabis has never been attributed as a cause of death, its use being incapable of inducing fatality [1] in humans and animals. In the U.S., there are approximately 25 million regular users [2] of cannabis and many more occasional consumers.

1 For OFFICIAL, QUALIFIED FINDINGS OF FACT on SAFETY, see information to follow in this Part, and subsequent Parts.
2 For official confirmation of numbers of consumers, see Part Four.

EXORDIUM.

Did <u>you</u> know *cannabis is harmless ?*

For example, here is a summary from a top-level medico-scientific enquiry...

"One of our principal objectives was to identify gross or subtle changes in major body or central nervous system functions which could be attributable to marijuana. We failed to do so."

"In the politicized and emotionally charged atmosphere surrounding marijuana use, far too much research has been marred by the predetermined stance of the researchers. Much that claims to be research is barely above polemics."

THE EMPIRICAL STUDY CONTINUES:

"Many of us were frankly surprised that we were unable to uncover any real consequences of prolonged use...some of the physicians on our team were sincerely disappointed...Their first reaction was that they would have nothing to say, and this they found frustrating after the enormous amount of effort and time they had invested."

See U.S. research:
'Cannabis in Costa Rica: A Study of Chronic Marijuana Use.'
ISBN: 0897270088.

And, did <u>you</u> know the empirical research studies concur ? So, *WHY* is harmless cannabis prohibited ?

The reason is uncomplicated; it is exposed in:

THE REPORT.

CANNABIS: THE FACTS, HUMAN RIGHTS AND THE LAW.

'Double-talk'.

A famous and favourite piece of double-talk, the language of lies, is that cannabis "cannot be proved to be harmless," despite the fact that no evidence exists to show harm. Within the context of cannabis as a *consumed personal relaxant*, such 'speculations' are irresponsible and prejudiced evasion of Findings of Clinical Fact which exonerate cannabis. Of course, water too "cannot be proved to be harmless"—one can drown in it. However, it is an empirical fact that water, like cannabis, is safe to consume. As DEA Administrative Law Judge F.L. Young observed in his review of the cannabis data, "about the only danger were if a bale of it were to fall and hit you on the head."

That cannabis is harmless cannot be 'half-stated'. To recommend legality without appropriate accompanying measures or controls of *any* substance which is dangerous, would be unfitting and invite censure. In re cannabis, where not only accepted safety but also benefits from use are confirmed, it is necessary to state unambiguously the fact of the safe nature of cannabis and expose the claims to the contrary, wherever and whenever they appear, for the chicanery and tergiversation that they are.

The basis of any statement must refer to and be founded, not on conjecture, but on *the evidence of expert clinical empirical medico-scientific investigations into people's actual use of the herb.* (Ref. Bibliography.) The official Empirical Studies into long and short-term use of cannabis establish that there is absolutely no 'harm' or 'danger' of any type. **The truth is that cannabis is: "de facto, harmless."** As the empirically-established reality is of harmlessness, *it is one's duty to state it.*

<u>Cannabis Is Not A Drug; Accurate Language.</u>

Cannabis is a herb *benign* in effects and results to humans: in all the long history of cannabis use, of which the written record dates back approximately 5,000 years, cannabis has never been cause to a single fatality.

Although people are revealed by post mortem (autopsy) examination to have cannabis in their system at the time of death, their deaths were induced by causes not associated with cannabis. Medical records and study of worldwide pertinent writings over the millennia show that *at no time has any person died from having smoked or taken any amount of cannabis, ever.*

Cannabis is **NON-TOXIC**: one hundred per cent of the scores of studies by research and university medical facilities show *toxicity does not exist in cannabis.* (U.C.L.A., Harvard, Temple, etc.) Cannabis at any dose or quantity is *incapable* of inducing fatality in humans and animals.

For details of its Safety, e.g. the Therapeutic Ratio (none), Lethal Dose Rating (zero; there is no lethal dose) see the section in Part Four of THE REPORT, entitled "The Judge's Ruling." Cannabis does not, and cannot, do harm to consumers. A harmless substance cannot correctly, truthfully or legally, be included in Prohibition legislation controls based on criteria of harm, danger, abuse, or misuse, etc.

Where cannabis is concerned, the U.K. Misuse of Drugs Act, the U.S. Controlled Substances Act, and all legislation and treaties of control or regulation, are misconstrued and inapplicable.

Studies, Statistics and The Supreme Law.

All the clinical Empirical Studies (for example, the U.S.-Jamaican, U.S.-Costa Rican, LaGuardia, etc.) confirm cannabis contains *no addictive properties* in any part of the plant or in its smoke: **cannabis does not induce psychological or physical dependence**. The medico-scientific aspect shows cannabis is not only *wrongly defined* as a "drug" in any meaningful (semantic) definition of the word, but also, by empirical reality, cannabis is *wrongly proscribed* (prohibited) as a "drug" (or other substance).

Although dictionaries vary slightly in their definitions of "drug,"[1] *virtually all refer to, and rely for definition on, a drug's habit-forming, addictive properties.* Webster's New World Dictionary, for example, defines "drug" as: "a narcotic, hallucinogen, especially one that is habit-forming." **To recapitulate: The medico-scientific empirical research confirms cannabis contains no narcotic, no hallucinogenic and no habit-forming properties, neither in the plant itself nor in its smoke. Evident from the most fundamental and widely inferred meaning,** *by definition based on empirical fact, cannabis is not a drug.*

Most unlike, and in contrast to tobacco, alcohol, tea, coffee, the caffeine-colas, and all legal or illegal 'recreational' substances*, cannabis is both non-habit-forming and non-toxic*. Cannabis is uniquely safe. The word "safe" in the context of cannabis use, by definition, means: "free of danger, risk or injury." Referring to cannabis as a "drug" is misleading, and untruthful. In the context of evidence, where accuracy and veracity are paramount, to do so is both inept and unacceptable. The invalidity of linking cannabis with "drugs" is further demonstrated by the U.S. government's Bureau of Mortality Statistics: the table (see previous page) shows that cannabis by any meaningful definition is not a drug. Cannabis cannot correctly be categorised or referred to as a drug of any type.

To people whose financial interests are served by Prohibition (discussed later in THE REPORT) the incorrect use of the word "drug" where cannabis is concerned, is *premeditated*; a strategy of simple but effective disinformation, associating the harmless herb with addictive toxic drugs. The reality is that cannabis and those potentially pernicious substances, the drugs, are wholly unalike. It is necessary to establish *veracious* vocabulary: the word "drug" is wrong and inapplicable to cannabis.

The biochemistry of cannabis is as follows[2] : molecules of cannabis temporarily attach to compatible receptors on cells such as those situated on the outer surface of the brain, the meninges, this gently bringing about a feeling of well-being. *When the cells' receptors are replete, increasing the amount (dose) of cannabis does not and cannot lead to progressive intensification of the mild sensation of well-being experienced.* Regular users generally smoke decreasing quantities until finding their own level of sufficiency and no 'tolerance syndrome' occurs. [Tolerance syndrome is the term used to denote the body's physical acclimatisation to the ingestion of a drug resulting in larger quantities being required to experience the same subjectively desired effect. Users of the drug alcohol call this learning to "hold your liquor." Drug addicts reach tolerance levels to the degree of craving doses simply to maintain an ability to function.] *Tolerance is a fundamental characteristic of a drug. Cannabis, not being a drug, does not possess this characteristic.*

1 The word 'drug' derives from Old Dutch *droog* meaning dried herbs, as used in food, for healing and in the dyeing of textiles; viz: The Wealth of Nations, 1776, Adam Smith; Book One, Chapter One. There was no connotation of addiction. That meaning was transformed in the Twentieth Century, by the specious pseudo-philosophy of money-motivated Prohibitions.
2 See also: 'THC' Is Not 'Cannabis'.

Airways of the lungs are dilated by smoking cannabis; this ameliorates the pulmonary function of blood oxygenation, constituting a significant benefit to the functioning of the human brain and body, as oxygen is the natural 'food' of the brain and muscles. Thus is explained much of the subjectively perceived pleasant sensation. The effects of smoking cannabis are never harmful, always being beneficial. It helps people to feel well and good; there has never been anything wrong with that.

Cannabis reduces intra-ocular pressure (IOP) by approximately 30 per cent, with beneficial relaxation to the eyes noticed particularly by sufferers of high or increasing IOP (glaucoma). The whites of the eyes can become reddened for a short time as cannabis tends to dilate vessels. This temporary effect occurs to a less noticeable degree than the bloodshot eyes associated with the use of alcohol, chopping onions, crying or a swim in a chlorinated pool. Physical tensions and symptoms of stress are alleviated, generally accompanied by slight dilation of blood vessels lowering blood pressure. These effects are measurably mild and, confirmed by Modern Medical Case Histories, only ever do good to the human being (Judicial Enquiry Data, ref. Part Four).

Although it is sometimes asserted that skills, or using heavy machinery and driving a car would be adversely affected by cannabis use, this is the unscientific voice of prejudice speaking. This damaging fiction about cannabis is a widely promulgated, premeditated calumny, for official tests and studies have demonstrated that, with cannabis use, **no deterioration of manual dexterity or mental adroitness occurs. The *opposite* is established: with the use of cannabis heightened awareness is reported and increase in skills is observed.**

The deleterious progressive intensification-by-quantity which occurs with use of alcohol, tranquillisers and other toxic drugs (whose biological action differs from cannabis) is mendaciously asserted to occur with non-toxic cannabis too, in both official and other propaganda, despite the specific and *complete exoneration of cannabis from all such allegations, by replicable, clinical tests*. Given the brief to discover impairment if any, the Crancer Study from the Washington Department of Motor Vehicles, confirms cannabis has no deleterious effects on driving ability. **Clinically tested, cannabis is shown *not to induce functional impairments*.** Rather the reverse is confirmed: ***improvements* in the ability to concentrate and perform are demonstrated by recorded results. The tests of skills in simulated driving performance of the U.S. official Crancer Studies demonstrate that any quantity of cannabis, even huge amounts consumed by test subjects, is unable to cause the slightest impairment of brain function. Crancer finds:**

"Simulated driving scores for subjects experiencing a normal social marijuana 'high' and the same subjects under control conditions are not significantly different. However, there are significantly more errors for alcohol intoxicated than for control subjects."

Moreover, increased quantity does not have deleterious results. To quote Crancer again, both *regular and novice smokers smoking three times effective dose*:

"showed either no change or negligible improvement in their scores."

Thus, 'acute' effects (i.e., current or short-term use) show no maltreatment, no abuse of the cannabis consumer.

Studies, Statistics and The Supreme Law.

It cannot be discerned by looking at, talking to or testing the abilities of a person that they have taken cannabis. Cannabis has no effect on brain mechanisms controlling consciousness, speech, co-ordination, etc.: a person functions normally. See official empirical research: 'The Effects of Marijuana on Human Beings,' by Professor A.T. Weil, M.D., Arizona College of Medicine and Professor N.E. Zinberg, 'M.D., Harvard. Weil and Zinberg relate how, on occasion, some research subjects enjoying effects, thinking themselves "too stoned" to perform adequately, would ask to be excused the tests, which were nevertheless insisted upon. Then, on testing, subjects were surprised and pleased to find themselves able to perform as well as, or better than without marijuana. This finding proved to be replicable [1].

That users were "surprised" their tests' results confirmed no decrements derive from use of cannabis, indicates they had been prepossessed by false indoctrination.

Cannabis is not a narcotic, and does not induce tiredness, drowsiness, torpor or drugged sleep. Inducement of tiredness and drugged sleep is a function of toxic substances which are fatal at some dose. There is no Lethal Dose Rating for cannabis which is a non-toxic substance incapable of causing death in humans and animals at any dose. Nor does cannabis interfere with rest, for those who are tired or in need of sleep are able to sleep normally. Patients and cannabis users report enjoying sleep of the most restful sort with incremented invigoration and energy on awakening. Accurate language reflects that cannabis may be referred to as: a safe relaxant tonic.

Cannabis is not a hallucinogen. Those parts of the brain including the mind, the psyche, pertaining to consciousness, etc., are not deleteriously interfered with by cannabis. It is *untruthful* then to apply to cannabis terms which are generally used to describe the effects of drugs and substances which *do* adversely affect brain function. In this context, such terminology as 'psychoactive' and 'psychotropic' is inadmissible. These words describe substances which thoroughly change personality and behaviour, measurably impair brain function and/or induce psychical distortions and hallucinations. For example, psychoactive alcohol can cause violent and grievous changes of behaviour, destabilising normal social psychical restraints and inhibitions (ref. 'Harm and Danger in Perspective,' in Part Three). Psychotropic hallucinogen Lioresal and other prescription drugs cause hallucinations (ref. Martha Hirsch, in Administrative Law Judge F.L. Young's review, quoted verbatim in Part Four). Psychotropic/psychoactive lysergic acid diethylamide (LSD) distorts perceptions, and so on. Even in small amounts, psychoactive/psychotropic drugs, such as alcohol, impair performance. Although with alcohol the user may feel invigorated and confident ("Dutch courage") when (clinically) tested the recorded results of mental abilities and physical co-ordination consistently show deterioration.

Objectivity and scruple deny *absolutely* the misapplication to cannabis of words such as narcotic, hallucinogen, psychoactive or psychotropic, for this jargon befits psyche-distorting substances, hallucinogens, narcotics and drugs, with their well-known and measurable mind dysfunctions. **The empirical tests of actual use of cannabis herb clinically confirm (i.e., they are replicable) categorically, cannabis does not induce any adversely altered perceptions or impairments of brain function.**

1 Also see 'Clinical and Psychological Effects of Marijuana in Man,' Science, vol. 162, Dec., 1968, pp. 1234-1242; & 'Cannabis: The First Controlled Experiment,' New Society, 16 Jan., 1969, pp. 85-86, by Professors Weil & Zinberg, et al.

The 'Medical Anthropological Study of Chronic Marijuana Use,' conducted in Jamaica by the U.S. National Institute of Mental Health, Center for Studies of Narcotic and Drug Abuse, revealed that from high frequency, long duration use (subjects averaged over 16 years of such use) of cannabis of greater potency than is generally available elsewhere, there results:

"No impairment of physiological, sensory and perceptual motor performance, tests of concept formation, abstracting ability, and cognitive style, and tests of memory."

Thus, the U.S. National Institute of Mental Health Study, taken together with the comprehensive empirical researches of the U.S.-Costa Rican Study (see EXORDIUM, page 3) confirm long-term cannabis smoking and dietary use also show no abuse, no maltreatment of the cannabis consumer.

Lexicographical Observations.

The same respect for accuracy is needed in Semantics as in Arithmetic. It is easy to see why. The accounts' clerk who transfers a couple of digits from the credit balance shown on a statement of account, adding them instead onto his own statement, makes only a small alteration in the numeric representation of the facts. However, the results from such an activity may not be small. By a simple but unnoticed distortion of the truth he multiplies his own wealth an hundredfold, stealing from those whose trust is invested in him and for whom he may well be setting in train ruinous effects.

In casual conversation the word 'drug' has vague and loose meanings. In legislation or litigation, informal misuse of terms which inevitably convey misunderstandings and untruth, is not acceptable. Generalised, polysemous, semantically misconstrued and/or overtly incorrect definitions are dishonestly employed by Prohibitionists. Use of the word 'drug' in connexion with cannabis is malicious defamation which obscures the plain facts of the safe, harmless and benign nature of the herb. This semantic abuse veils the truth that cannabis is not a drug.

For example, as a definition "medical utility" cannot competently be applied to define a substance as a drug because Accessory Food Factors, vitamins, minerals, etc., which are not drugs, are nonetheless used in specific medical treatments. Bandages too have "use in medicine;" therefore, this attribute does not of itself define a substance as a drug.

Likewise, it is so inaccurate as to be nonsensical to nominate as a 'drug' "any substance which kills or inactivates germs." Dichlorodiphenyltrichloroethane, chlorine, ammonia, numerous chemical herb-, pest- and germicides and even common rock salt, all have this property yet they are not drugs. Nor are they ever alluded to as drugs.

In the same way, it is not correct to define drug as "any substance which affects body functions or organs" because food, water, and the very air we breathe, which are not drugs, all have this property.

Thus is exemplified the absolute necessity for authentic objectivity and uncompromised exactitude when entering the realms of analytical semasiology, in order that truth be conveyed in language. Cannabis is not a drug.

Studies, Statistics and The Supreme Law.

Because many grave syndromes can and do result from drugs, that is to say, from the use of addictive, toxic substances, the Prohibitionists' disinformation tactic is to *associate* cannabis with "drugs" to attempt to make their stories of 'harm' sound believable. If a person is duped into accepting about cannabis, the incorrect and defamatory initial supposition that it could be a "drug," i.e., an addictive substance with death-inducing potential like heroin, alcohol, caffeine, and tobacco, then all manner of completely wrong and thoroughly untruthful allegations strike a note to effect a sympathetic resonance in the non-specialist's mind.

This tactic to sow confusion is most evident in the deliberate misapplication to cannabis by some Prohibitionists of the wrong and nonsensical: "*soft* drug," a contradiction-in-terms.

The Prohibitionists' scheme relied upon people's fears and on keeping them ignorant of the truth. Yet, however 'plausible' allegations of 'harm' are made to sound, the plain fact is that cannabis shares in common with other harmless substances the same statistic of complete safety as orange juice, mother's milk and bread because it is neither toxic nor addictive and is not a drug at all. The Prohibitionists' false message is only credible to those people who read or hear *only* the mendacity which the Prohibitionist-controlled governments and media promulgate.

Where cannabis is concerned, the U.S. Controlled Substances Act, the U.K. Misuse of Drugs Act, and all legislative and regulatory controls worldwide are abrogated by the Findings of Fact and Conclusions of the official medico-scientific clinical studies into the actual smoking and consumption of cannabis, conducted by world-respected U.S. academic and research institutions.

The unprecedented (new) **CANNABIS BIOMASS ENERGY EQUATION (CBEE**; ref. Part Two of THE REPORT) proves the oil-gasoline type fuel Cannabis-Methanol is the *cheapest* fuel-energy known to man. The CBEE establishes cannabis as globally capable of providing, *pollution-free*, *production-cost-free* (i.e., **free**); and *duty-free*, fuel.

The CBEE also shows (with instructions and diagrams) how Cannabis-Methanol can easily be made at home *for free*, achieving the **Universal Re-Democratisation of Fuel-Energy Production (URFEP)**.

Information on The CBEE combines with the Findings of Fact established by the professorial Empirical Studies, viz. the published clinical truths about the health-promoting qualities and the absolute harmlessness of cannabis. Education, truth and understanding expose the 'law' and all controls, i.e., Prohibition, to have been, and to be, a façade, the false front to a destructive and degenerate *money-motive.*

Semantics provides the parameters of meaning, a linguistic matrix from which all philosophy, wisdom and knowledge may flow. Semantics also enables judgements of rationality and discernment to be made between subtle truths, plain facts and nonsense. Obviously, when the precise significations of words are known to all parties in reciprocal communication misunderstandings are reduced. More than this however, as the knowledge and sense imparted in language mould the way individuals and multitudes think, they result in conclusions drawn and give direction to subsequent action. Alcohol is a case in point.

Many responsible people use alcohol and are generally able to control their consumption of it to moderate quantities. It is fair to say that all adults use alcohol if only from time to time, apart from members of particular religions or sects and some few abstemious individuals amounting to a small percentage of the population. Few social gatherings are without alcohol. Weddings, formal and informal receptions, banquets, parties, reunions and most occasions would be deemed inadequately provided for, without it. The use of alcohol varies greatly from seldom to frequent. Alcohol is taken at meals and when people are relaxing from work or off-duty in a variety of settings, such as a whisky and soda with a good book by the fireside, the regular bottle of wine with lunch, to a flagon of ale after a strenuous bout of sport.

Yet, *to drink alcohol is "to take drugs."*

Understanding of the meaning attached to the word 'drug' and an appraisal of the clinically-defined action of alcohol upon the workings of the human mind, brain and body convey the inescapable fact that alcohol, as surely as heroin or crack-cocaine, is a drug. These substances fulfil definition of the word 'drug' by sharing in common the characteristics of the (use of) drugs, such as: tolerance syndrome(1) dependence(2) toxicity(3) mortality(4) 'withdrawal' symptoms(5) abstinence syndrome(6) and especially, addiction(7). This is not to say that all people who use alcohol are drug addicts but long-term indulgence, frequent or heavy use, *inevitably* induce the adverse results in humans in varying degrees.

The phenomena associated with the use of substances establish whereby the term 'drug' becomes applicable. Most politicians and journalists and by far the larger part of the population are wont semantically to confuse the issue by using the misleading and inaccurate vernacular of popular phraseology to speak of "drink and drugs," as if in some way alcohol were not really a drug. The other drugs, opiates, etc., can also be taken orally, like 'drink' does this make them less a drug? When consumed in or as liquid, is heroin then "drink" as opposed to "drugs"? The answer, of course, is in the negative. Likewise, alcohol is nonetheless a drug and its use is drug-taking, whether 'polite' society faces this fact truthfully or not.

What is more, shown by the NIDA statistics quoted later[1], alcohol use burdens society on the huge scale with strife, disease, grave accidents, crime, absenteeism, lost productivity, early death and the euphemistically-termed "alcoholism" that is drug-addiction in the worst degree by another name. By contrast, the excellent uses of cannabis as Preventive Measure to replace use of, and avoid, alcohol, *and* to help in the cure of alcohol addiction, are detailed in clinical studies[2].

Comparison reveals that although cannabis has medical utility and health-giving attributes, as do other non-drugs and Accessory Food Factors such as vitamin-C in treatment of the disease scurvy, the parameters of definition, the *meaning* of the word 'drug' including especially a drug's intrinsic chemically-addictive properties, exclude non-addictive cannabis from such categorisation.

Bearing in mind that cannabis induces none of the damaging phenomena associated with drug use, as mentioned, addiction, tolerance, toxicity, mortality, withdrawal, dependence and abstinence, from an objective standpoint, to equate unique cannabis with "drugs" is scientifically preposterous, and legally malicious.

1 Ref. 'Harm and Danger in Perspective'.   **2 Ref. Part Three.**

Studies, Statistics and The Supreme Law.

Before Prohibition enactment, a loose misuse of the term 'drug' by doctors and lay-people produced little or no apparent ill-effect. Nowadays, however, the situation requires complete accuracy and absolute veracity, as words and semantics mould people's thoughts subsequently to affect their decisions and direct their actions.

Currently, to use the term 'drug' to describe cannabis is not simply untruthful, but worse, it is the premeditated adoption of an unconscionable Prohibitionist tactic of semantic abuse. This devious ploy deliberately associates mild, benign cannabis with potentially dangerous, addictive substances, drugs—of which alcohol is one such—to make cannabis *appear* to be something harmful, which the official empirical researches confirm it is not.

The disparateness of harmless cannabis from toxic drugs is empirically established Fact. Justice compels that the completeness of the disparity be reflected in truthful semantics and complete Relegalisation in law.

Controls of cultivation, trade, possession and use purport to be by legislation based on criteria of 'harm' and 'danger', which do not, and cannot, apply to safe cannabis. Not only is cannabis without harm but also, cannabis promotes good health; ref. Parts Three & Four. Modern Medical Case Histories and the Empirical Studies conducted by teams of eminent clinical physicians, toxicologists, pharmacologists, psychologists, sociologists, psychiatrists, etc., re-establish cannabis as a *profoundly benign* Personal Relaxant with unique effective preventive and curative therapeutic applications; *and as the benevolent alternative* to toxic pathogens of addiction, tobacco and alcohol.

The Relaxant.

The Findings of Fact of the official **empirical** [i.e., *actual use* by test-subjects] **studies** are **definitive**. The Empirical Studies show cannabis merits *distinct* vocabulary which unambiguously represents the empirically established fact of its *benign* nature. To describe it, the words "mild safe relaxant" are appropriate. Taken in food or smoked, cannabis is always safe, ingestion gently producing awareness of a pleasant sense of well-being: no single word need be applied to this, general description conveying the fact more accurately. This lasts two to three hours when smoked, or three to four if taken orally, though slower to commence. **Unlike 'drink' or 'drugs', no 'dependence' ever develops from cannabis use; and there is no 'withdrawal' and no 'hangover' when the effect wears off, no matter how frequent or long-term the use** [1].

The term 'relaxant' is chosen on empirical grounds: 'alpha-wave' is the name given to the rhythm of a specific frequency emitted by the brain during the normal relaxed mental activity associated with cogitative processes of <u>creative thought</u>, as recorded by electroencephalogram [2]. Human intelligence applied to problem-solving, creative writing, theoretical physics, or cave wall painting, engenders <u>alpha-waves</u>. The deep concentration required for satisfactory pursuit of such activities is more easily achieved when the distraction of stress is removed. Cannabis use helps to bring this about and increased occurrence of alpha-waves is recorded, *indicating stress-relief* and greater relaxation.

---

1 N.B. 'Psychological' dependence, so-called, on any <u>non-addictive</u> substance, is the manifestation of an individual's pre-existing psychological derangement; see: Ploys; Part Five.
2 See LaGuardia Studies. (Not to be confused with alpha <u>radiation</u>; see following section on tobacco.)

Whatever purpose individuals attach to their use of cannabis (sacrament, prophylaxis, pain-relief, Preventive Measure, etc.) does not alter the fact of alpha-waves, and thus the applicability of, and definition by, the term relaxant. Relaxation should not be confused with "drowsiness"—as noted, non-toxic cannabis does not induce such effects as tiredness and drowsiness, which come from ingestion of toxic narcotic drugs (cf: Set and Setting, in Part Five). Vigorous physical activities, as well as the hard work of mental creativity, are all associated with use of cannabis, as the clinical Empirical Studies' physicians and researchers point out.

In relation to psychological attributes of personality, the integrated organisation of all the physical, mental and emotional characteristics of an individual as they are presented to others, cannabis does nothing to change its ingestor; a person remains exactly what they are in mental and physical terms and in their nature or personal character. The clever, kind, honest and industrious person stays precisely as they are; likewise, the dull, selfish, unscrupulous and idle individual is unchanged. The physically and/or mentally tired are able to rest; the busy and pressured work as they are wont to do.

The mind, the psyche, the seat of consciousness with its metaphysical subjective contents of thought, volition, feelings, intellectual powers, memory and opinions, is not altered or interfered with. Cannabis improves the capacity to work by removing the distractions of stress. This benefit can manifest itself in either a physical vigour or mental concentration, or both, while not affecting the psyche itself (see Findings of U.S. National Institute of Mental Health Study). Because work, mental concentration, is thus facilitated, the historic and well-documented predisposition for cannabis amongst the studious, musical and artistic, meditative, mentally creative, scientific, inventive, industrious and intellectual segment of the population is explained. These activities, in addition to being performed at the level of professional expertise, are also the basis for most spare-time hobbies. Hence, the widespread use of cannabis is associated with them, and as a 'recreational' substance.

The human brain receives sensory input from touch, taste, smell, hearing, and sight; personal preoccupations, tension and worry distract the mind; memory and thinking processes are engaged in *the routine*. The stress relief people experience from cannabis puts distractions into perspective, allowing, and encouraging, creative thinking. This explains why some consumers describe cannabis as "mind-expanding" or "enlightening". Human beings are born with or without certain abilities, talent, gifts. The individual may or may not develop these according to various socio-economic, educational, environmental and other factors. Users often say that cannabis helps them in the development of their talents. This is not statistically quantifiable, nor is it disputable; it is the expression of a subjective viewpoint.

See CONCLUSIONS & FINDINGS OF FACT from U.S. government researchers' Empirical Studies [1], U.S. National Institute of Mental Health:
1.) short or long-term use of cannabis does not have any adverse effect on mental or physical health;
2.) smoked, eaten, or taken as a beverage, cannabis is non-addictive; cannabis does not induce physical or psychological dependence
3.) "psychosis" is not related to cannabis; pre-existing schizophrenia can occur in a cannabis using population;
1 Note, Empirical: i.e., definitive clinical studies, human test subjects' "hands-on" actual use.

4.) no "amotivational syndrome"; *"heavy use of ganja does not curtail the motivation to work"* [original emphasis]. The contrary is concluded: cannabis has <u>tonic</u> effect, which is conducive to productive work and mental concentration;

5.) investigating any possibility of "linkage" as exists between alcohol, bad behaviour and/or crime*: "No evidence of such causality appeared in the findings of the Jamaica project."* In this context, the evidence is presented that cannabis has a positive influence producing beneficial results: i.e…

6.) cannabis reduces and can preclude the use of drugs, thus mitigating their associated negative effects.

N.B. Such findings are replicated in the other empirical researches.

CLINICAL FINDINGS OF FACT.

The U.S. Judicial Review and other Official Studies show: [1]

a.) cannabis has unique health-promoting, and actually life-saving but prohibited applications in Health, Preventive and Curative;

b.) cannabis has the unique enormous life-saving propensity of replacing or reducing use of addictive pathogens: alcohol, tobacco, opiates and other toxic drugs, i.e., use of Cannabis comprises Preventive Measure/Preventive Medicine. Nota Bene: Cannabis use thus is health-enhancing whether used by the sick or hale: *all such use is medical.* The arbitrary fictitious 'distinction' between 'medical' and 'recreational' use is a fallacious and profoundly damaging deception.

c.) cannabis smoking is the only reliable countermeasure to glaucoma known to Man, consistently reducing intra-ocular pressure, dispelling glaucoma symptoms and *saving eyesight*;

d.) restoring appetite to anorexic, ill, crucially wasting patients is another of *many* ways in which *cannabis smoking saves lives*;

e.) the cannabis well-being effect uplifts the spirit, and is of greatest assistance in general health, and in medicine and convalescence.

f.) cannabis alleviates and *prevents* stress-related, psychosomatically-induced adverse conditions;

g.) cannabis is a health-promoting phenomenon Preventive of, and therapeutic in numerous slight or serious adverse conditions: e.g. menstruation pain and tension, headaches and migraine, asthma, fits, spasm from trauma or epilepsy, multiple sclerosis, back pain, pain from various disorders, pruritis, dermatitis, eczema, rheumatism, arthritis, etc. (the list continues and is extremely long [2]). The herb ingested as smoke or as part of a normal healthy diet is *prophylaxis*, i.e., Preventive Medicine, preventing degeneration of the health of the hale.

Denial of cannabis by Prohibition 'law' premeditatedly inflicts suffering, blindness, and, in many instances, death. Those who maintain any use of life-saving cannabis to be "illegal" should be regarded and treated as perpetrators of the gravest of crimes, and deemed unfit to hold any public office in a democratic society.

---

1 See earlier attribution and following Parts Three, Four & Five of THE REPORT for details.
2 Cannabis is curative treatment for <u>over 100</u> illnesses and adverse conditions. See subsequent Parts.

FINDINGS OF FACT.

Reproduced and collated from the Data and Conclusions of the official Empirical Studies into long and short-term use and smoking of cannabis, the following are: THE FINDINGS OF FACT OF THE REPORT. CANNABIS: THE FACTS, HUMAN RIGHTS AND THE LAW.

Cannabis…

1)—is not toxic in any possible quantity; i.e., is *incapable* itself of inducing fatality in a human;

2)—is not addictive, physically or psychologically; i.e., does not induce physical or psychological dependence;

3)—is not pathogenic, does not cause physical or mental deterioration, has no adverse effect on mental or physical health;

4)—does not cause skill impairments;

5)—is benign;

6)—has no potential for abuse, or maltreatment of the user; cannabis has no potential for harm or danger;

7)—does not cause crime;

8)—does not lead to the use of drugs;

9)—mitigates, reduces, and can preclude the use of drugs;

10)— cannabis as Preventive Measure/Preventive Medicine is health-enhancing: all use of benign cannabis is medical, whether by the sick or hale: the fallacious arbitrary fictitious 'distinction' between 'medical' and 'recreational' use is exceedingly damaging.

Where cannabis is concerned, the legislation of its Prohibition:

1)—is, in its entirety, without factual foundation;

2)—is based on mendacity;

3)—is itself *illegal* on numerous grounds by Common, Substantive and International Law;

4)—is perjurious in prosecution; perjury by the state is both implicit and overt in every cannabis trial.

5)—The acts of its enforcement are crime per se; people persecuted thereby qualify for Amnesty and Restitution (as for other Wrongful Penalisation);

6)—the ignoring of these aforegoing Findings of Fact by courts and legislature is ex parte, the crude and criminal denial of Justice.

7)—In its replacement of the use of drugs alcohol, tobacco, etc., by young people and adults, cannabis promotes health. All private cultivation, trade, possession and uses are vindicated.

8)—In regard to cannabis, legislation of substance control is damaging, lethal and unlawful; all special regulatory control of cannabis produces negative, damaging and/or lethal results, and is per se unlawful.

9)—Cannabis related prosecutions are legally malicious, i.e., premeditated crime against the person.

10)— Cannabis Relegalisation is legally mandatory, that is: legislative amendment for the return to the normal status of cannabis which obtained before the introduction of any controls.

Studies, Statistics and The Supreme Law.

RADIOACTIVITY, FROM FOOD AND OTHER CROPS FED WITH PHOSPHATE 'FERTILISER', *IS PRINCIPAL CARCINOGEN.*

Cannabis Smoke Distinguished from Tobacco Smoke.

The smoke of cannabis is not only *safe*, but the Clinical Studies and Medical Case Histories also show that cannabis is *beneficial* to the lungs in general use and in particular instances, of specific medical value. The reader is referred to the empirical research conducted in both the medical and social contexts, of the actual long-term use of cannabis, such as the U.S.-Jamaican governments' Clinical Studies; U.S.-Costa Rican Clinical Studies; the Clinical Study of the New York Academy of Medicine; all concur with the latter's definitive conclusion that:

"*Regular long-term smoking of cannabis causes no mental or physical deterioration.*" The NYAM Study concluded as Findings of Fact that: cannabis is not addictive; does not induce tolerance syndrome; and, regular long-term cannabis smoking does not induce mental or physical deterioration; see pages 141 and 146 of that Study. **The NYAM Study further stated: cannabis neither leads to the use of drugs nor causes crime**. (Again, see pages 12, 13, 16 & 17.)

Also see the UCLA School of Medicine Pulmonary Studies, 1969-1989 and 1989-1997; Donald P. Tashkin, M.D., reported in Vol. 155, American Journal of Respiratory & Critical Care Medicine, 1997:

"*Findings from the present long-term follow-up study of heavy, habitual marijuana smokers argue against the concept that continuing heavy use of marijuana is a significant risk factor for the development of chronic lung disease. Neither the continuing nor the intermittent marijuana smokers exhibited any significantly different rates of decline in lung function as compared with those who never smoked marijuana. No differences were noted between even quite heavy marijuana smoking and non-smoking of marijuana.*"

It is factually incorrect to say that "all" smoking is unhealthy. Tobacco and its associated dangers have so prejudiced people against "*smoking*" that it is easy to think, to believe, that all smoking is 'unhealthy', whereas this is categorically untrue, as the official clinical Studies quoted above confirm. Neither cannabis nor its smoke contains *nicotine*. Nicotine is the addictive and toxic drug in tobacco which is destructive to human health. Tobacco-nicotine is indicated as a cause to lung cancer, emphysema, cardio-vascular disease (CVD), cancers of the mouth, larynx and oesophagus, bronchitis, pneumonia, and stomach ulcers. Tobacco-nicotine is cause to "smoker's respiratory syndrome," symptoms being frequent respiratory infections, constriction of the pharynx, laboured breathing, wheezing and shortness of breath.

In 1996, the U.S. Food and Drug Administration officially 'accepted' *tobacco is a drug*, demonstrating previous generations' dishonesty. The evidence shows that in the U.S. and U.K. the official dishonesty continues.... Tobacco is the most highly addictive of drugs. People find it harder to stop smoking cigarettes than to give up heroin, crack-cocaine or alcohol. While many people are capable of a non-addictive use of alcohol or heroin, nearly all cigarette smokers are addicts. The people who are able to smoke only two or three cigarettes per day, or per week, over the long-term, are very few. Approximately 75 per cent of tobacco users smoke between twenty and forty cigarettes per day, between 7,000 and 15,000 cigarettes a year.

Unlike and opposite to cannabis, *tobacco smoking* causes constriction of the vascular system (veins and arteries) and narrowing of the airways of the lungs with diminution of oxygen supply to brain and muscles. Nicotine induces Buerger's Disease: the nicotine is cause to constriction of blood vessels sometimes leading to gangrene necessitating the amputation of limbs, most often the legs. Patients suffering from Buerger's Disease who give up smoking usually get better. However, to some people nicotine is so addictive that they continue to smoke tobacco even after their second or third amputation. Many people suffering acutely from the effects of nicotine with heart attack or stroke, who have the life or death choice to give up use, are observed to be so addicted to nicotine as nevertheless to persist in their smoking of tobacco.

In 1990, U.S. Surgeon General C. Everett Koop concurred with published Studies, stating on national television that ***radioactivity in tobacco is source to cancers***, explained as follows [1]. Plant-growth is stimulated by: nitrogen(N); potassium(K); and phosphorus(P) which comprises 30 per cent of rock phosphates—*but, rock phosphates also contain intensely radioactive elements in profusion*. Smoking tobacco cultivated in soil 'fertilised', actually *poisoned*, for many decades with uranium-rich phosphates, and tobacco's characteristic absorption patterns, are concluded to be the cause of lung and other cancers. Metastasis (spreading) causes growth of tumours in other parts of the body. Tobacco in particular requires copious fertiliser because each crop leeches large amounts of nutrition from the ground. Tobacco plants' roots absorb naturally occurring radioactive elements in soil, as well as the radioactive phosphates misused as 'fertiliser'. Also, dangerous elements whipped into the air by breezes and farm equipment attach to sticky resin tips of hairs growing on each tobacco leaf. ***In addition to uranium, tobacco absorbs the following radioactive elements from phosphates***:

radium-226	*radon-222*
polonium-210	*lead-210*

Ionising **alpha radiation** is emitted by tobacco and its airborne particulates (smoke). Radioactivity is long-established as cause to cancers and leukaemia, and afflicts people with great harm in numerous other ways. Tobacco is acutely radioactive. Tobacco is potentially fatal.

Amongst the types of radiation, alpha radiation is especially causative of the deformation of DNA (molecular deoxyribonucleic acid) and resultant cancer. Human and animal bodies are made up of cells which replicate before ageing and dying off. DNA within the nucleus of cells is the genetic information 'blueprint' from which cells replicate. Whereas toxic chemicals from tobacco smoke-tar or elsewhere, can injure or destroy cells, radiation interferes at the nuclear atomic and molecular level, deforming the genetic DNA structure. When genetic information controlling cell replication is deformed, cells can over-replicate and grow into malignant tumours [2]. Radiation produces many grave conditions in the human.

Following the nuclear explosions at Hiroshima, Nagasaki and Chernobyl, the consequential disease of epidemic proportions in the nearby populations, characterised by widespread ill-health and reduced immune-system efficiency, and by leukaemia, mental and physical handicaps and deformities, teratoma (congenital tumour), teratogeny (production of mutant monsters), Siamese (conjoined) twins, birth defects, was (and is) due principally to alpha radiation. Infertility and teratogeny

1 Radioactivity in tobacco was first established and researched by Vilma Hunt at Harvard University, as long ago as 1964.
2 A tumour is any lump, swelling or bruise; malignant (cancerous); benign (non-cancerous).

Studies, Statistics and The Supreme Law.

result from irradiation of DNA within sperm and ova. Unborn infants receive leukaemogenic and carcinogenic doses of radioactivity via the mother's bloodstream. In the examples mentioned, extreme doses of radiation produced immediate overt results. The harm from radiation derived from phosphates, though not so easily understood and obvious as that which is associated with a nuclear explosion, can be nonetheless injurious and fatal. Scientists recognise the danger to living things from beta radiation emitted by lead-210, which has a radioactive half-life of 21 years. Alpha radiation can be twenty times more damaging.

Amongst others, Doctor Edward Martell, a radio-chemist of the U.S. National Center for Atmospheric Research, in his paper published in 1983 in Proceedings of the U.S. National Academy of Science, stated that enough polonium-210 alpha radiation exists in tobacco for the polonium alone to be *cause of at least 95 per cent* of lung cancer in tobacco smokers. (Although tumours can be contrived in laboratory animals with intense concentrations of isolated compounds of toxins, which, incidentally, *do not occur* in that chemical configuration in smoke), in addition to the polonium causing up to, or more than, nine out of ten cases of lung cancer, the evidence demonstrates *radiation* as cause to *all* carcinosis in humans: the death-rate from lung cancer is the same from the smoking of *low-tar* as from *high-tar* cigarettes: [1] thus, *not the chemicals* in vegetative smoke-tar but radioactivity is confirmed as cause of cancers from tobacco. The official clinical Empirical Evidence exonerates cannabis and smoke-tars from carcinosis allegations. (Ref. also, UCLA & Studies quoted previously.) [2]

Note well that, *if* the chemicals in tar produced the cancer, then, the greater the quantity of tar, the more cancers that would result. A recent study, which re-confirmed the death-rate from low-tar and high-tar cigarettes is the same, attempted to obscure radioactivity as the cause to cancer pandemic in the population: this dissimulation was as follows: To compensate for the lesser flavour of low-tar, some (but not all) smokers are observed to inhale more deeply, for longer; and some (but not others) smoke more cigarettes; therefore, goes this deceit, the amount of tar absorbed by *superlight* cigarette smokers is exactly equal to that of low, medium and high-tar smokers, thereby "explaining" why the same death-rate exists amongst all. This is specious, for (within reason) however many cigarettes smoked and however deeply smokers inhale, it is self-evidently *impossible* 'to absorb' tar that is *not present* in low-tar cigarettes; also, some people smoke three full-strength high-tar packs per day; others less than one pack of superlights. There is wide disparity between individuals, in the numbers of cigarettes consumed, and of their tar quantity; and, *no parity at all* in the amount of tar absorbed between superlight, low, medium and high-tar smokers. If tar *were* the culprit, smokers' *varying* intake would be reflected by a *multiplicity* in rates of carcinosis produced, which it is not; and the numbers of cancers *could not be uniform*, which they are. This study *inadvertently* reinforces, and emphasises, that it is not smoke-tar but something else, namely the radioactivity, which induces carcinosis [3].

Approximately 50 per cent of the radiation in tobacco is dispersed into the surrounding air when smoked. A 'passive' smoker is a non-smoker who inevitably inhales the airborne smoke present in the company of smokers. The Study by Dr. Takeshi Hirayama for the Tokyo Institute of Preventive Oncology, indicates that,

1 See: U.S. National Institute of Health Study, Lancet, Sept., 1983.
2 Also see: 'Radioactivity: The New-Found Danger in Cigarettes,' Lowell Ponte, Reader's Digest, March, 1986.
3 The 'findings' are so misconceived and erroneous as inevitably to raise questions as to participants' integrity. This 'research', which received universal publicity, avoided mentioning, let alone researching, radioactivity in tobacco.

17

from the records of over 91,000 women, *the non-smoker wives of heavy smokers of tobacco have a more than doubled risk of early death from lung cancer than non-smoking wives of non-smokers*. Human immune-system cells remove debris, including quantities of the radioactive particulates of tobacco, from within the lungs, radio-isotopes being conveyed by the bloodstream to all parts of the body, accumulating in breasts, prostate and sex glands, liver, bone marrow, kidneys, lymph nodes, pancreas, and thyroid. Research by Beverly Cohen and Naomi Harley, of New York University Medical Center, established that: *tobacco smokers who give up, have five years later almost as much lower lung radioactivity as do active tobacco smokers*. Tobacco literally kills over 1000 people every day in the U.S. alone, afflicting many thousands more with disease. An antipathy to *tobacco* smoking is well founded because of the nicotine content and the insidiously fatal radioactive substances from phosphates.

Radioactive elements within *non-smokers* derive from food crops cultivated in soil poisoned by phosphates. Calcified blood plaques of sufferers of arteriosclerosis (hardened arteries) have been shown to contain polonium-210 and lead-210[1]. While circulating in the bloodstream, *the radiation is further indicated to cause cardio-vascular degeneration and associated disease, coronaries and stroke*[2]. The huge number of people who contract cancers, including those who never smoke, is explicated by the radioactive aspect of phosphates. 'Unaccountable', and much wrongly-attributed, pathogeny results from radioactivity in our food. Significantly, *the most common incidence of tumours and cancer occurs within the bowels and stomach, accounting for 24 per cent of diseased organ location*.

Radioactive phosphates are used to boost crop growth *in commercial food production*, a big-business the greater part of which is controlled by a minority of giant corporations. Food sold as 'ORGANIC' can be intensely radioactive: farmers using rock phosphates duplicitously define themselves as "organic" because rock phosphates come from naturally-occurring rather than manufactured sources[3]. Farmers rely on phosphates to produce crops of pasture and animal *feed*, with the result that: the feed; the subsequent 'manure' derived from the animals; the 'food' (carcasses) of the cows, sheep, chickens, etc.; the milk, cheese and dairy products; contain the deadly radioactive carcinogens and pathogens. Cheap rock phosphates are spread every year onto the food-producing grasslands of Europe, the Steppes of Russia and the Prairies of America, and throughout Asia, Australia, Africa and South America. If the equivalent of only one-hundredth part of one per cent of the radioactivity spread every year onto the Prairies, escaped by accident from a nuclear facility, there would be a resounding hue and cry from the mass media, politicians and parties, and the pseudo-green groups. (Viz: the mishap at Three Mile Island nuclear power station.) There would also be severe crimination of the culprits. Yet, the money-motivated ruin by phosphates of *all* the world's prime farmlands, with many hundreds of thousands of consequential annual human mortalities, has the tacit consent of the press and pretentious 'green' groups, and has been, and is, knowingly permitted and thus *abetted* by politicians. In full knowledge of the radiation in phosphates, with complete impunity, these companies and owned subsidiaries, import the phosphates, own and

1 & 2 See: 'Radioactivity: The New-Found Danger in Cigarettes,' Lowell Ponte, Reader's Digest, March, 1986. Note that <u>radiation</u> (particularly the sun's ultraviolet light), is also cause of <u>skin cancer</u>.

3 Definition. Organic: (i) in Chemistry, the chemistry of carbon compounds; (ii) in horti- and agriculture, crops produced using fertilisers and pesticides exclusively of plant or animal origin. Commercial producers of food mislead their buying public into believing that their food is 'organically' produced. However, <u>genuine</u> organic fertilisers derive from guano, manure, hoof and horn, dried blood, soot, bonemeal, fishmeal, and wood ash—<u>not from rock phosphates</u>.

Studies, Statistics and The Supreme Law.

work the farmland, distribute, market and advertise the produce, and own the hyper- and supermarkets where it is sold. As a result of their motivation to maximise profits, it is a premeditated certainty that radioactivity is inserted into the bodies of the mass urban populations of humans, killing many, and causing grievous harm to innumerable others. However, to provide food for the household of the late billionaire Sir James Goldsmith, 80 *separate* acres were cultivated *using only organic fertilisers.*

"Americans are exposed to far more radiation from tobacco smoke [from phosphates] than from any other source," to quote Dr. R.T. Ravenholt, director of World Health Surveys, Center for Disease Control [1]. Pernicious drug tobacco has not a single redeeming feature. Although cannabis smoke contains some chemicals found in tobacco smoke which are common to many plants, cannabis smoke, being free from nicotine and radioactivity, is radically different from tobacco. Cannabis is not cause to illness of any kind. The radioactivity present in tobacco and food explains why. By a contrast which could not be greater, cannabis is a salugen, a health-promoting herb, which replaces use of addictive drugs, has never caused a single case of cancer, is incapable of causing mortality in humans and animals, and promotes good health.

Governments and "charities" expend countless billions researching a "cure" for cancer, but spend nothing on warning people as to its real, and avoidable, *cause*. Up to the time of this Edition, there has been no mass state education of the life-and-death fact of phosphate 'fertiliser' being source of radioactivity in food; this being the cause of cancer in huge numbers of people. Instead of accepting medico-scientific exoneration of cannabis smoke-tar and relegalising cultivation, trade, possession and use, officials perjuriously promulgate disproven derogatory fictions about "all" smoke-tar, *solely* to maintain controls on cannabis. The vindication of cannabis smoking and publication of its positive benefits has caused governments to promote disinformation, to 'programme' populations to accept controls, i.e., Prohibitions, being introduced on Tobacco (viz. California). In this way, governments intend to make legislation *appear* to be on "health grounds," *to conceal the financial reason* behind Prohibitions on therapeutic herbs, and on cannabis in particular. Evidence presented throughout THE REPORT establishes *money-motivation* as cause to this criminal, homicidal government activity of public malindoctrination.

Important health benefits accrue to cannabis smokers by prevention of adverse conditions and disease [2]; it also has scores of effective modern curative applications without the dangerous toxic side-effects associated with pharmaceutical drugs [3]. Cannabis is of profound *unique* therapeutic value to people with terminal, slight or serious illnesses; and for safe routine alleviation of headache, pain, menstruation tensions, and stress [4]. The health-giving properties of cannabis are empirically established and documented: cannabis continues as the effective treatment of **over 100 conditions** listed in the U.S. and other recent official Pharmacopoeias. Cannabis is a natural healer and safe personal relaxant. Use of benign cannabis is health-promoting; i.e., all use is medical. Cannabis has long been used as tonic personal relaxant medication. Pharmaceuticals do not 'replace' cannabis; ref. Parts Three & Four. Cannabis smoke has good effects upon the lungs: due to dilation of bronchial passages and the relaxation which results from its use, cannabis smoke is beneficial to emphysema, bronchitis and asthma sufferers, in that the action of lungs is improved [5]. Ref. the following quotation from the U.S. and the Costa Rican governments' Study:

1 See Whole Life Times, May, 1985.   2, 3, 4 & 5 Ref. Modern Medical Applications; Parts Three & Four.

19

"Users in our matched-pair sample smoked marihuana in addition* to as many tobacco cigarettes as did their matched nonusing pairs. Yet their small airways were, if anything, a bit healthier than their matches. We must tentatively conclude either that marihuana has no harmful effect on such passages or that it actually offers some slight protection against harmful effects of tobacco smoke."

* Original emphasis. See U.S.-Costa Rican Studies, X:205. Also ref. page 3: EXORDIUM.

The definitive Empirical Studies exonerate cannabis from 'harm', 'impairment' and 'danger'.

Legislation of Prohibition, 1.

Being safe, and free from harm, cannabis cannot *legitimately* be subject to any controls. Being benign, on health grounds cannabis qualifies to be generally available for all private cultivation, trade, possession and use: legislative denial of such has always been illegitimate and grievous. That Prohibitions are not genuinely based on 'harm' and 'danger' is shown by the tobacco issue, amongst others: tobacco is long-demonstrated the drug with the most acute potential for abuse, danger and harm, it being severely pathogenic, intensely addictive and often fatal; tobacco is always unsafe to use, and of no medical use whatsoever. If the 'law' were authentic, phosphates and tobacco production, trade and use would have been proscribed long ago [1]. That tobacco and phosphates were not prohibited, affirms regulatory Schedules' criteria do not exist for health but for other, concealed, reasons. With lethal tobacco legal and salutary cannabis forbidden, legislators are not moved by altruistic considerations of people's health. Driven by ulterior motive (exposed hereinafter), the politician is of criminal intent. Based on the definitive scientific data, such conclusions are inexorable. They are sustained by the ultimate verification that all allegations made against cannabis have been repeatedly investigated, evaluated, and dismissed as the uncorroborable fictions of incompetence or duplicity. Cannabis Prohibition is put into effect by conspiracy, or racket (U.S.).

1 N. B. This is not to say that criminal law is endorsable, or legitimate, as a technique for reducing people's consumption of harmful substances; see later sections, Prohibition: The Progenitor of Crime; on Alcohol; and on Justice.

Cannabis—The Benign Herb.

The official Empirical Studies into actual use of cannabis conclude:

1— **use of cannabis has no adverse effect upon mental or physical health:** *cannabis is harmless*;

2— **use of cannabis does not cause any impairment to mental and physical abilities:** *cannabis is safe*;

3— **modern Medical Case Histories** [2] **show cannabis to have numerous beneficial results to health:** *cannabis is benign.*

The reader of THE REPORT is able to state with the absolute certainty that comes from the knowledge, authority and support of the modern official Empirical Studies into cannabis for the last hundred and fifty years plus—up to the present (since 1839, O'Shaughnessy [3]), that all legislation of cannabis controls is fraudulent: all attendant acts of passive acquiescence or active support, i.e., prosecutions, judicial, police and penal enforcement, are malicious, these comprising crimes of themselves. If not before, from now on readers will be able to discern *the motive* [4] behind calculated miseducation, such as when politicians claim "insufficient" research has been undertaken. The state of knowledge about the herb is replete with medico-scientific investigations, cannabis being the most researched plant known to Mankind.

2, & 3 Ref. Parts Three & Four. 4 Apropos of *motive*, ref. Part Two; & Parts Three, Four & Five.

Studies, Statistics and The Supreme Law.

Rights and the Wronged.

Official empirical researches dismiss all allegations of 'harm': cannabis is exonerated; private Production, Trade, and Uses are vindicated. Because Controls on cannabis are in breach of national laws in every state where such controls exist, *under the law*, cannabis cultivation, trade, possession and uses are de facto legal, *not* illegal.

The failure by governments to acknowledge the illegalities of all controls on cannabis, and their ongoing refusal to effect legislative amendment for Relegalisation, are arbitrary, anti-democratic, inherently criminal acts. Where families and people are interfered with in their private life by enforcement of government statute law, it is an overriding requirement of common law that this intervention be justified. The state-funded Empirical Studies refute ostensible 'reasons' for Prohibition controls as invalid. It is small wonder that persons motivated by gain to prohibit the population from taking benefit from cannabis, find themselves by any means and at all costs, attempting to obscure from general public comprehension the fact that it is the superequiponderant evidence of the official studies themselves which establishes cannabis as safe for use as personal relaxant, and of profound benefits to health.

Mankind has benefited from the entirely safe and unrestricted use of cannabis for many thousands of years. Never has there been anything socially or morally dubious about its smoking or use in food. Enjoying its salubrious and innocuous effects is not and never has been a vice. If there exists in the mind of some people an underworld, 'sleazy' connotation, that is a figment caused solely by the fact of the herb's historically recent and completely unwarranted Prohibition. Not one claim of 'harm' or 'danger', by which the legislation purports to be maintained, has ever withstood scientific and objective scrutiny. No (genuine) evidence exists to support Prohibition.

On perusal of the scientific Empirical Evidence the plain facts about cannabis — impartial investigators are astounded at the extent of the untruthfulness and incorrectness found in the inculcated prevailing social "belief" and widely propagated myth of "harm" regarding cannabis. Media *knowingly* spread anti-cannabis falsehoods. As allegations of 'harm' are groundless, it is necessary to look elsewhere for the real, but covert and thus illegal reason, to explain why the herb remains subject to the ban. THE REPORT is comprised of evidence to this covert reason.

Rather than simply being folly or unfounded, legislation of controls on cannabis is based on money-motivated untruth: perjury by the prosecution is both implicit and overt in every cannabis trial. Moreover, control legislation is abrogated on legal grounds of Justice and Equity; see later sections. All controls are unlawful, in all nation states, by existing Common and Substantive laws; the enforcement of controls is crime per se; persons persecuted thereunder qualify for Amnesty and Restitution.

It is upsetting and provoking in the extreme to observe oppression of citizens by governments' tyrannical abuse of the criminal justice system, under the ignominy of 'politicians' who allow themselves to be compromised, corrupted, and manipulated by the grip of Prohibitionists, whose concealed motives are self-interested. False 'laws' which control private cultivation, trade, possession and uses, are prolonged on the illegitimate basis of Prohibitionists' vested interests....

'THC' Is Not 'Cannabis'.

To equate with cannabis, the natural plant, the findings of research into a laboratory synthesised or isolated, concentrated chemical compound, such as THC (tetrahydrocannabinol), is erroneous, technically impertinent and profoundly misleading. **Properties of compounds** are *unique*, and *are not a sum of the properties of the individual elements and compounds from which they are made*. In the Science of Chemistry, the properties of substances, elemental and compound, are seen to alter, and are affected by interaction and combination. Simply, by the binding of atoms and molecules, one 'thing' can and does become quite another. Completeness of the difference of individual substances from the product of their combination, is exemplified by the elements, explosive when separated, hydrogen and oxygen, which combined give the safe vital liquid water. Hydrogen compounded into water is safe to consume, but hydrogen extracted from water boils at room temperature and is fatal to humans if consumed. Similarly, within cannabis, THC ceases to be only THC, as the THC is compounded into the disparate single entity that is the safe herb. (Like hydrogen, oxygen and water), THC, and all isolated cannabinoid compounds, and the cannabis herb, are *disparates*. (Definition. Disparates: different things or species; things too unalike to be compared.)

The carbon from which a human being is in part constructed is different from the complete being: individual cannabinoids and complete herbal cannabis are different, in the same way. THC in combination with other elements and compounds within the natural plant is 'different' from THC isolated and concentrated, in the same sense that carbon combined with other elements, makes of itself wholly alternative substances with different effects or properties; viz: in addition to human bodies, the bubbles in a 'fizzy' drink, the stem of a cabbage, and diamonds, are all carbon-based.

A cannabinoid is a substance unique to cannabis by which it is differentiated from other plants. If a compound also occurs in other plants (such as cocoa-chocolate) then it is not a cannabinoid. Names of the better-known cannabinoids are cannabidiol, cannabinol, and tetrahydrocannabivarin. There are over sixty other known cannabinoid compounds. In addition to unique characteristics, plants have a wide variety of vegetative matter in common. Cannabis totals over 1000 different known substances, which all combine to make but *one* unique substance that is the cannabis herb, which has evolved in nature a benign and health-giving character of inestimable value to the health and well-being of humans....when they can obtain it.... (Ref. information in following Parts.) Pharmaceutical concentrates of THC are legally available by prescription. If herbal cannabis were the *same* it would not be legally possible to maintain the present Prohibition Schedules and Classifications. The law recognises the obvious differences which exist between THC and the natural herb.

It is '*convenient language*' to refer to cannabis as being "THC-rich" or "THC-free," to denote the quantity of chemical concentrate of THC which can be isolated by laboratory chemical processes out of a particular strain or batch of plants, but, scientifically-speaking, **THC cannot even be said to be present in the herb**, because, when THC is in combination with the other compounds, as it is within the herb, *it ceases to be THC*: nature makes it into an *other* single substance, that is, the herb. And when it is no longer the compound THC, it does not have the characteristics of THC.

Studies, Statistics and The Supreme Law.

The total difference between cannabis and THC is demonstrated by the fact that on its own, THC is a toxic substance causing negative, potentially fatal reactions in laboratory animals such as mice[1]. This is utterly different from herbal cannabis which is non-toxic and is *incapable* of causing fatality in humans and animals at any dose[2].

The completeness of the difference between THC and the cannabis plant is also well demonstrated by the fact that cannabis, the natural herb, so efficacious in prevention of glaucoma blindness, relaxes intra-ocular pressure (IOP) by approximately 30 per cent[3]. After THC is extracted from it, the remaining herb lowers IOP by approximately 10 per cent[4]; but THC, after approximately seven days' use during which fluctuating marginal effects are recorded, *THC does not reduce IOP at all*[5]. Patients' Medical Case Histories record the discomforts to humans caused by THC[6]. No such unfavourable response occurs *in the same patients* when the herb is smoked, taken instead of THC[7]. Whereas smoked cannabis is recorded as effective in treatments and as being health-promoting, the unpleasant characteristics of THC *and its failures as medication*[8], give reasons enough to avoid the pharmaceutical product.

Shown earlier, the official empirical clinical tests confirm (i.e., they are *replicable*) that smoking of natural herb cannabis produces no effect on, or, marginal **improvements** to: mental concentration; abilities and co-ordinative skills; use of machinery; driving a car; tests of memory (short and long-term); concept formation and mental adroitness. By contrast, *doses of disparate-substance pharmaceutical-THC cause impairments to test subjects' performance, by nausea, unpleasant mental effects and headache* (ref. Parts Three & Four).

Confirming the medical uses of cannabis throughout history, time and again, modern uses of cannabis in its raw herbal form prove to be therapeutically effective, without any harmful effect. However, *the naturally produced plant is not patentable*. In 1976, under President Gerald Ford's administration, in response to lobbying by drug firms, American university and independent research into use of natural cannabis for medical potentials was Prohibited. The ban exempted *drug companies*, which were permitted to research cannabis to synthesise, and evolve uses of, THC, *in patentable ways*. This Prohibition was intended to provide Owners with **monopoly**: the method by which populations suffer (ref. Parts Two to Six inclusive) while all the money from permitted trading accrues into the hands of a very few preferred people and the state. Nabilone, Marinol, etc., the tablet and capsule attempts to gain a patented, profitable windfall, are a well-known failure. These troches contain lab-synthesised or extracted THC, refined to 90%+ concentrates. Laboratory-processed THC products have been trial-tested since the 1940's. Contrary to the publicised claims of those with vested interests, far from containing or embodying the "active ingredients" of cannabis, THC is useless when compared to the herb itself. Not only is THC ineffective, but patients who respond well to smoked cannabis, experience adverse reactions to THC[9]. Indeed, studies into these artificial products, i.e., concentrates/THC, including sections of LaGuardia research, record *diametrically opposed results* from those clinical studies into the smoking of natural cannabis. For example, doses of lab-THC can *cause* nausea and headache, two of the many adverse conditions for which the resinous herb in its natural form is renowned as *cure*.

1 & 2 See: Medical Data, U.S. DEA, Administrative Law Judicial investigations.
3, 4 & 5 Ibid.; also: Hepler & Frank, UCLA Coll. of Med. Ref. sections on glaucoma, & Elvy Musikka, in Part Three.
6, 7, 8 & 9 See: Medical Data, U.S. DEA, Admin. Law Judicial investigations; ref. Part Four.

THE REPORT. CANNABIS: THE FACTS, HUMAN RIGHTS AND THE LAW.

Since all research into the use of *natural* cannabis was made illegal (1976 in the U.S. and earlier elsewhere) studies have proliferated into THC. Prohibitionist individuals and organisations, representatives of the drug companies' financial interests, promulgate untruth that "hundreds" and even "thousands" of medical studies *which actually have only investigated THC* were made "on cannabis."

In mendacity intended to mislead, the adverse reactions of patients and test-subjects nauseated and otherwise debilitated by THC, are misquoted as 'indications' for...."cannabis." Government 'Advisers', and others, dupe the trusting public with this disinformation, which is disseminated everywhere as "new findings," by financed Prohibitionist activists, in books, leaflets, and all media. Shown herein, the Empirical Studies explicitly exonerate cannabis from all allegations of 'harm' or 'impairment'. But frightening fictions are implanted into the minds of those of the population who do not read the published empirical researches, and who instead rely on the owned and controlled media and the government for their (mis-) information.

The *failure* of THC to have reliable medical uses is *also* maliciously misattributed as being from "cannabis," which is deceitfully defamed as "medically unpromising." The "flop" of THC is but one of many of the drug companies' futile efforts to make artificial substitutes for *the broad range of health applications for which natural cannabis herb has always been, and remains, the only safe and efficacious option* [1].

Therapeutically-successful herbal cannabis [2] exposes the failures of the modern prescribed 'medicines', which yearly acquire trillions of undeserved dollars, pounds, Euros and yen for the pharmaceutical trade in drugs. Relegalised, *cannabis will replace* many of the lucrative addictive toxic pharmaceutical patent drugs, to the great health benefit of the population [3]. Ergo, despite the failure of THC, the Prohibitionist remains intensely driven to prevent cannabis from being Relegalised.

THC-impairments are malevolently ascribed to "cannabis" as "new findings," by those who represent the financial interests of governments, and state or private companies, whose revenues and profits *depend* on keeping cannabis Prohibited [4]. **Motive** for this behaviour should be noted: self-advancement and gain are observed to accrue to professionals who support Prohibition by spreading disinformation. Methodologically, it is incorrect to mix in extraneous THC findings, or irrelevant data from disparate substances, and then make false claims relating these to "cannabis." Findings on lab-THC are admissible *only* as relevant to *that* substance, lab-THC itself. Such findings cannot truthfully be "extrapolated" as "applicable" to "cannabis." When a qualified expert ascribes THC findings to "cannabis," this is a premeditated act of perjury. Yet, to dupe people and prop up Prohibition, government-appointed 'advisers', drug czars, state employees and others constantly lie, by asserting 'harm' or 'toxicity' where there is none in the natural plant [5].

The gentle effective healing herb enjoys the highest of recommendation from those disinterested people, lay and specialist, whose interests and sympathies reside in common with those who hold the good health of the general populace above the avarice of the malign oligarch.

NOTE: Cannabis resin is comprised of hundreds of compounds. The resin exuded on flowertops is sometimes erroneously referred to as "THC". THC is a laboratory-isolated single chemical compound which does not occur in isolation naturally.
1 Ref. Part Three; & ref. U.S. Judicial Review Findings, quoted in Part Four.
2 & 3 Cannabis as Effective Medication in Patients' Medical Case Histories; ref. Parts Three & Four.
4 & 5 Ref. exposition on ULTERIOR MOTIVE; Parts Two to Seven.

THE SUPREME LAW.

In contravention of the letter and spirit of the United Nations' Declaration of Human Rights, the denial of legality in the use of cannabis is the denial of the Human Right and Liberty to *a private activity harmless to the user and of no consequence to others*. Politicians may pontificate, prosecutors may equivocate, and judges may castigate, but let there be no mistaking this simple Principle: in Mankind's affairs, no nation state signatory to the United Nations' Declaration, and no government nor institution anywhere, has the *legal* authority to deny such inalienable Human Rights and Freedom: **such Prohibition is de jure illegal**. All persons thereunder persecuted are due Amnesty and compensatory Restitution (as for other wrongful penalisation). Cannabis controls are in breach of Articles 1, 2, 3, 7, 8, 9, 10, 12, 16, 18, 21, 25, 26, 28, 29 and 30. The United Nations' Declaration on Human Rights adopted and signed by member states, by which the legislature and judges of states are bound, the laws of any state to the contrary notwithstanding:

"Preamble. Whereas recognition of the inherent dignity and of the equal and inalienable rights of all members of the human family is the foundation of freedom, justice and peace in the world,

Whereas disregard and contempt for Human Rights have resulted in barbarous acts which have outraged the conscience of mankind, and the advent of a world in which human beings shall enjoy freedom of speech and belief and freedom from fear and want has been proclaimed as the highest aspiration of the common people,

Whereas it is essential, if man is not to be compelled to have recourse, as a last resort, to rebellion against tyranny and oppression, that human rights should be protected by the rule of law,

Whereas it is essential to promote the development of friendly relations between nations,

Whereas the peoples of the United Nations have in this Charter reaffirmed their faith in fundamental human rights, in the dignity and worth of the human person and in the equal rights of men and women and have determined to promote social progress and better standards of life in larger freedom,

Whereas member states have pledged themselves to achieve, in co-operation with the United Nations, the promotion of universal respect for and observance of human rights and fundamental freedoms,

Whereas a common understanding of these rights and freedoms is of the greatest importance for the full realisation of this pledge,

Now, therefore, The General Assembly proclaims This Universal Declaration of Human Rights as a common standard of achievement for all peoples and nations, to the end that every individual and every organ of society, keeping this Declaration constantly in mind, shall strive by teaching and education to promote respect for these rights and freedoms and by progressive measures, national and international, to secure their universal and effective recognition and observance, both among the peoples of Member states themselves and among the peoples of territories under their jurisdiction."

THE REPORT. CANNABIS: THE FACTS, HUMAN RIGHTS AND THE LAW.

[All forms of controls on cannabis contravene laws, and Articles of Human Rights. For example, the official exonerative evidence collated and presented in Part One of THE REPORT, demonstrates infraction of the following Articles:]

"Article 1: All human beings are born free and equal in dignity and rights. They are endowed with reason and conscience and should act towards one another in a spirit of brotherhood.

Article 2: Everyone is entitled to all the rights and freedoms set forth in this Declaration, without distinction of any kind, such as race, colour, sex, language, religion, political or other opinion, national or social origin, property, birth or other status.

Article 3: Everyone has the right to life, liberty and security of person.

Article 7: All are equal before the law and are entitled without any discrimination to equal protection of the law. All are entitled to equal protection against any discrimination in violation of this Declaration and against any incitement to such discrimination.

Article 8: Everyone has the right to an effective remedy by the competent national tribunals for acts violating the fundamental rights granted him by the constitution or by law.

Article 9: No one shall be subjected to arbitrary arrest, detention or exile.

Article 10: Everyone is entitled in full equality to a fair and public hearing by an independent and impartial tribunal, in the determination of his rights and obligations and of any criminal charge against him.

Article 12: No one shall be subjected to arbitrary interference with his privacy, family, home or correspondence, nor to attacks upon his honour and reputation. Everyone has the right to the protection of the law against such interference or attacks."

Under The Law.

De jure [i.e., under the law], controls on Cannabis are illegal.

Prejudice, intolerance, ignorance and money-motivated conspiracy are causes of indefensible controls of the harmless benign herb. Cannabis farmers, traders and users are abused and deprived of their Rights, and pursued and persecuted with primitive totalitarian cruelty. Conclusions inferred from the Evidence presented throughout THE REPORT are:

firstly, Prohibition is an unlawful political contrivance;

secondly, all 'laws' and 'regulations' of Prohibition or restriction are abrogated, themselves criminally contravening Human Rights;

thirdly, as further demonstrated hereinafter, wherever emplaced, controls breach national Common and Substantive laws; all controls on cannabis constitute infractions of law by governments; enforcement of controls constitutes crime per se.

26

- PART TWO -
THE CANNABIS BIOMASS ENERGY EQUATION.

WHEREAS there is a plethora of publications and programmes about *the problem* of Global Warming, this book provides *the solution*. To the question, "Scientific Green Solution—why cannabis?" the answer follows:

"For Mankind's macroeconomic requirements, energy derived from cannabis is cheaper than energy from coal, oil, natural gas, uranium, wind and wave power, geo-thermal, pressed-seed vegetable oils, ethanol, hydrogen-from-water electrical separation, etc. Cannabis is the most economical resource to fuel and energy known to Mankind. Cannabis-Methanol provides fuel which is pollution-free."

These statements are established as Fact for the first time on record by THE CANNABIS BIOMASS ENERGY EQUATION (CBEE)[1]. The CBEE formulation demonstrates that the Twentieth Century experience of government-corporate monopoly-control of fuel-energy, and its high cost in economic, social and ecological terms, was a bane for Mankind; and one which should have been easily avoided. Learning to live with the world glut of non-polluting, cheap but superior fuel, energy, food and resources, made immediately available by implementation of The RESTORATION Programme, would be a profound liberation.

GLOBAL WARMING, AND HIDDEN COSTS OF ENERGY PRODUCTION.

It is of primary importance that people understand why fossilised hydrocarbons, coal, oil and natural gas, should not be regarded, nor any longer be allowed to be *misused*, as 'fuel'. Preoccupied as people are with the personally absorbing detail of daily living, it is easy to lose touch with much of the basic reality upon which our human civilisation and very existence depend. The danger and damage from the combustion of fossils, coal, oil, and natural gas, come principally from the release into the atmosphere of the carbon absorbed by (fossilised) plants and animals which lived in much hotter primordial carbon-rich atmospheric conditions in ages past, over thousands upon millions of years, long before humans evolved on the planet. Combustion of fossils releases their *stored* carbon, *increasing the total quantity of carbon dioxide gas* (CO_2) *in the atmosphere*. Earth receives heat and light from the Sun: much of the Sun's radiated heat which arrives on the land and sea, rebounds off the face of the globe as long-wave, dissipated energy. It is safely dispersed into Space. Carbon dioxide has the capacity *to retain this infrared heat*—the more CO_2 in the atmosphere, the hotter it becomes, this being called the 'Greenhouse Effect'[2]. The burning of fossils as 'fuel' gives rise to Global Warming[3].

Carbon dioxide is principally responsible for atmospheric heating, being called the 'Greenhouse Gas'. Not less than 80 per cent of the increase of CO_2 in the atmosphere comes directly from the burning of coal and oil products. Since 1850, at which time accurate records were commenced, CO_2 has increased in the atmosphere from 265 parts per million (ppm) to 378 ppm, to date. Emitted in an historically short period, or, relative to geological time-scales, in the blink of an eye, *this represents a colossal 42 per cent increase of carbon dioxide in the atmosphere*.

1 The CBEE is endorsed by eminent academics, authors, doctors of a variety of disciplines, judges (U.S. & U.K.), and ecology experts. [Ref. Publishers' Title Information, at the end of this book.]
2 The greater the quantity present in our atmosphere of gases such as carbon dioxide, nitrous oxide (i.e., photo-chemical <u>smog</u> from fossil combustion), methane, chloro-fluorocarbons and surface ozone, the more heat is entrapped and retained.
3 Details given herein on Global Warming are confirmed by specialist and by encyclopaedic works.

A single small power station's annual fossil combustion to generate energy for only 4000 households (at a lower average consumption rate than the U.S.) releases pollutants: 88 tons of sulphur dioxide; 66 tons of nitrous oxide; 10 tons of flying ash; **and 13,750 tons (*thirteen thousand, seven hundred and fifty tons*) of carbon dioxide.** Statistiken; Bundesregierung Deutschland.

Hegemony, in the physical rather than moral sense, that is, politico-military power and leadership, derives from *ownership and control* of the means of production and distribution of wealth. Appropriation, or misappropriation, of the sources of fuel-energy became crucial to those with commercial interest and/or political ambition. Acquisition of Ownership of subterranean minerals was facilitated by the expedient of government legislation, and by **monopoly**: the licensing of preferred (state or private) corporations to exclusive trade in the invaluable energy resources. Thus, the People are forced to pay *two* 'Owners' for fuel. Governments' *fiscal interventions* (exorbitant duties and taxation) have led to fuel-energy becoming *the principal component* in the industrial production of wealth, today accounting for not less than four-fifths (4/5) of the Cost of Production of Gross World Product: all extracted resources, commercial goods, food and services.

From the early hunter-gatherer, nomadic, and tribal agrarian forms of human organisation, to the establishment of permanent urban communities, through the Ancient and Medieval Eras, the small numbers of people on our planet relied principally for their energy supplies upon the abundance of trees and firewood. Demand for fuel-energy was limited and easily satisfied. Fuel was a trifling factor in the Cost of Production of artefacts. In the Modern Era, local forests having been felled, growing populations availed themselves of coal, oil, natural gas and, eventually, uranium. The disadvantages of nuclear fission, not least of which involves the inevitable proliferation of plutonium availability (the matter of hydrogen fusion bombs) swiftly made themselves evident. Not so obvious, at first, was the danger from the *misuse* of fossils as '*fuel*', which has given rise to the destructive phenomenon, Global Warming, a threat of gravest potential to the ecosphere [1].

Misuse of coal, natural gas, oil and uranium as 'fuel' now poses perhaps the single greatest immediate hazard to planetary well-being and human survival. The price of energy from petroleum hydrocarbons and uranium is high, but the ultimate cost is unknown in view of their actual and further inevitable damage. The greatest cost might be hidden, yet to be paid in full [2]. Global Warming has already had mortal, disastrous results: 10.4 per cent (15,600,000 square kilometres) of the Earth's surface is covered with permanent ice contained in ice sheets, the ice caps and glaciers. Total meltdown would provide a vertical rise in eustacy (world shoreline) of c. 70 metres, i.e., 230 feet. Global Warming of 2° to 3°C is likely to result by the year 2030 with a partial meltdown of permanent ice, yielding an increase in Mean Sea Level (MSL) of c. 8 to 12 inches (20-30 cms.) and 24 to 40 inches (60-100 cms.) by 2100. The trend of Global Warming to date remarked since 1850 is 0.7°C (or 1.26°F). The rate of increase over recent years is faster than at any recorded time past. Without accounting for future increments in CO_2 emissions from ongoing misuse of fossils to supply fuel-energy requirements of increasing world populations, indications are that between 1850 and 2050, an average global temperature increase of not less than 2½°C will have resulted, with the attendant increase in MSL. There are no causes for assuming, moreover, that this heating trend now well under way is not continuous thereafter.

1 The 'ecosphere' is the atmospheric, terrestrial and aquatic environment, the condition of which is vital to life on Earth.
2 In Moses' book of Genesis, the rainbow symbolises God's promise not to destroy the Earth again by flood; but this time Man is doing it himself....

The Cannabis Biomass Energy Equation.

The IPCC group of international scientists investigating climate change on behalf of the United Nations concluded in 2000 that the Earth's atmosphere is warming at a quicker rate than previously realised, and that average global temperature will rise by 6° centigrade in the next hundred years, by 2100. There is no permanence or 'guarantee' on the existing healthy environs, given the addition of CO_2 from the activities of an intemperate species deficient of foresight. Climatic equability is fragile and susceptible even at the best of times. Venus, our nearest planetary neighbour in orbit at an average of 25,718,200 miles from Earth's circuitous path, is hostess to the 'greenhouse effect' and has reached the average atmospheric temperature of 464°C, with planet-wide gales constantly raging at hundreds of miles per hour. It is not herein suggested that Venusian conditions will suddenly be arrived at overnight but, the sounding of a warning note is most assuredly called for in the circumstances whereby the results of this generation's mistakes will be visited upon the next.

Heat is the generator by which our weather systems are activated [1]. In addition to *raised sea levels*, the danger and damage to life, property, agricultural production and civilised order, caused by Global Warming, arise from:
floods; temperature increase enables prevailing currents of air to carry more moisture, precipitating as increased rainfall upon the land. Warming of only a small fraction of 1°C can result in many more inches of rain trillions of tons of catastrophic floodwater, viz. floods virtually simultaneously in England, France, Germany, Northern Italy, New South Wales, Cambodia, Vietnam, Texas, Minnesota, Iowa, Florida, South Africa, Siberia, Chile, Bangladesh, Taiwan and Mozambique; *and,*
from turbulent airstreams, storms, gales, cyclones, hurricanes and tornadoes, viz. life-destroying, devastating Hurricane Mitch in the Caribbean and Central America.

Numerous mortalities have resulted from Global Warming. *Based on death and destruction already perpetrated, Global Warming represents no less a threat to the people of the world than World War*. THE CANNABIS BIOMASS ENERGY EQUATION has shown that the threat and damage from Global Warming by emissions from the combustion of fossils are totally needless, and inexcusable.

Increase in atmospheric temperature is sometimes nonchalantly dismissed as "normal intermittent fluctuations." These conspiratorial statements are neither backed by the indications, nor by impartial scientific studies. This verbal shrug by representatives of coal and oil interests is the money-motivated, predictable attempted obscuration of the fact that government and corporate Owners of coal and oil would prefer the industrial world, ruinously and homicidally, *to continue to consume* their fossil material. 'Fluctuations' do not satisfy these data. While the incaution of foolishness is to be regretted, the dissemination of falsehoods for short-term monetary gain is to be condemned. Serious change in composition of the atmosphere, notably the CO_2 increase, renders Global Warming to have resulted from the misuse of fossils as 'fuel'. Unless immediate responsible legislation emplaces RESTORATION, the indications are that Global Warming will continue [2].

1 The <u>Gulf Stream</u> circulates equatorial Atlantic Ocean water, keeping north-west Europe relatively warm; but, from Global Warming's reduction of the Polar Icecap, quantities of extremely cold meltwater pushing southwards are preventing the Gulf Stream from reaching northerly latitudes. So, paradoxically, Western Europe is to receive generally longer winters and cooler, wetter summers from Global Warming, interspersed with intrusive fronts of warmer, moist air expanding from the South, frequently generating storms.
2 The RESTORATION Program would simultaneously enable eradication of World Famine and World Poverty.

Concerning fuel for world generation of electricity and modern transportation,

The Cannabis Biomass Energy Equation Demonstrates:

1.) cannabis provides **ample and prolific** World Resource to Fuel-Energy;

2.) fuel from cannabis is **non-polluting**.

Combustion of cannabis-sourced fuel emits only water H_2O (as steam) and CO_2. Regarding CO_2 emission: during growth, plants absorb carbon from carbon dioxide in the air. The carbon forms part of plants' biomass, which is pyrolytically convertible into gasoline-type hydro-carbon fuel. On combustion, carbon bonds with oxygen: CO_2 is released back into the atmosphere; ***but**, an equivalent quantity of carbon is absorbed by the next fuel-crop in cultivation*: this is termed a **'closed-cycle'** to signify **no net increase** of atmospheric CO_2 is produced by the use of cannabis for fuels.

Cannabis thus has an enormous immediate stabilising effect on Global Warming.

3.) The cannabis *resource* to fuel-energy is ***production-cost-free*** (ref. sections on Economics of The CBEE, which follow), and,

4.) unlike the high-cost capital-intensive equipment, refinement and production processes necessary with fossils, the *process* of pyrolysis, of producing high-octane methanol-fuel, gases, and lubricants from cannabis, is **also production-cost-free**. To recapitulate: following low-cost investment into simple hardware of the cast-iron Pyrolysis Still, the superior pollution-free liquid **Cannabis-Methanol fuel** for all world industrial and domestic energy requirements, produced in accord with The Cannabis Biomass Energy Equation, **is free**, i.e., nota bene: of no cash cost.

5.) Cannabis utilised for its many *non-combusted* purposes, such as superior but cheap concrete building materials (see Isochanvre), absorbs atmospheric carbon which is **stored**, not re-released. Cannabis used in this way, permanently subtracts from the quantity of carbon dioxide in the atmosphere, ***further reducing*** Global Warming.

6.) If **reversal** of Global Warming has become advisable or imperative, mass-production of cost-free crops of cannabis hurds compacted and stored (e.g. in disused fossil-coal and other mines) forms a strategic energy reserve, and a biological 'sink', **extracting macro-tonnage of CO_2 (carbon) from the atmosphere.**

7.) Agricultural crop resources are *renewable*, not finite in quantity as are the fossils misused as 'fuel'.

8.) The replacement for fossils and uranium is not only already *discovered*, it is also cheap and safe: the technical, economic and resource conundrum of world requirements is resolved by The Cannabis Biomass Energy Equation.

9.) Where fuel and energy-generation are concerned, the practical solution is at hand: immediate rectification of Global Warming is commenced by implementation of The Cannabis Biomass Energy Equation.

10.) If the CBEE were now mandated to a level of priority commensurate with its self-evident importance, suitable measures would ensure its immediate worldwide adoption. Tax, financial incentives, government loans and international technical pyrolysis assistance, would ameliorate the global atmospheric environment *and*, stimulate performance of the world economy by vast provision of cheap Fuel-Energy.

~

The Cannabis Biomass Energy Equation.

When the danger from combustion of fossils remained unrealised, their misuse as 'fuel' was purblind and unfortunate. However, *since* the danger was recognised, *and since* the Scientific Solution to Global Warming was published and has circulated since 1994, the protracted misuse of fossils as 'fuel' *by the failure of governments* to implement The CBEE Solution, has been the wilful premeditated committing of a political act in which large-scale homicide is implicated; an act for which individuals of government and corporate institutions are accountable.

Politicians remain recalcitrant: none are so blind as those who **will not** see. This book explains how magnates of corporations, and governments, comprised of the executive, the legislature and the judiciary, amongst whom some persons are more culpable than others, succumb to a corrupt money-motive to wage this World War of Global Warming upon the people of the planet, **by choice**. Global Warming is a catastrophe for which politicians have made themselves accountable. Allowing continued build-up of atmospheric CO_2 by emissions from consumption of coal and oil is the indictable act of: Crime against Humanity; Crime against Peace; Betrayal; Criminal Dereliction; and Conspiracy (Racket; U.S.). By not adopting The CBEE, politicians endanger **All**.

NO further increases in atmospheric CO_2 from fuel-combustion are acceptable; human lives continue to be taken and the world population remains at risk: **misuse of fossils as 'fuel' must be stopped at once**. In delaying implementation of The Cannabis Biomass Energy Equation, governments become culpable for Homicide and Genocide; individuals who comprise these governments represent legitimate targets of public wrath and just retribution. Global CO_2 emissions are attributed as follows:

North America	28%	East European countries	25%
Western European countries. . . .	15%	China	9%

There is now no serious dissent to the postulation that it is as certain as it is possible to be that continued misuse of fossils as 'fuels', of coal, natural gas and oil, threatens great and continually increasing detriment to the planetary environment. Only the degree of the damage and the speed at which it can occur are in debate. Taking the aforementioned *most conservative* consensual estimate of 2½°C average Global Warming with attendant MSL increase of approximately 12 inches in 30 years and 40 inches by 2100, large areas of land, productive coastal and low-lying plains, scores of major cities and densely populated regions will be invaded by the sea. *Unless RESTORATION is implemented forthwith*, to give but a very few examples, significant portions of Holland, Germany, Florida, the Great Chinese River Basin, Bangladesh, East Anglia, New York, London, Tokyo and Venice, can expect inundative obliteration within decades.

***Prohibition* of Cannabis stands in the way of a safe ecological future for Mankind.**

RESPONSIBLE LEGISLATION.
The following legislation is immediately requisite worldwide:

1.— Misuse of fossils as 'fuel' requires to be terminated with all celerity.

2.— RESTORATION requires adoption and implementation: Relegalisation of Cannabis is indispensable. (Item 2 enables Item 1 to be effectively achieved.)

THE CANNABIS BIOMASS ENERGY EQUATION:

SCIENTIFIC SOLUTION TO THE WORLD CRISIS.
Modern Uses of Cannabis.

For Mankind's macroeconomic requirements, energy derived from cannabis is cheaper than energy from coal, oil, natural gas, uranium, wind and wave power, geo-thermal, pressed-seed vegetable oils, hydrogen-from-water electrical separation, etc. Cannabis is the most economical resource to fuel and energy known to Mankind. Cannabis-Methanol provides fuel which is pollution-free. These statements are demonstrated as fact in the ensuing pages, for the first time on record, by the analysis given which comprises The Cannabis Biomass Energy Equation (CBEE).

The Cannabis Biomass Resource and Pyrolysis Functions (CBRPF).

The best explanation of how cannabis can replace Mankind's misuse of fossils as 'fuel', and uranium, is contained in the following axiom:

"Everything which is derived from hydrocarbons can also be derived from carbohydrates."

Carbohydrates are the basis of *biomass*; that is, organic material, plants and organisms. Oil and coal are fossilised biomass. All are carbon-based matter. All commercial goods (plastics, man-made fibres, products, paints, chemicals, etc.) fuel, and energy now extracted from oil and coal can equally be produced from *fresh*, recently grown biomass. The technical viability of biomass as a resource to fuel and energy is well established and demonstrated. See the following bibliography:

'Methanol Plantations in Hawaii,' Hawaii Natural Energy Institute.
'Chemicals from Biomass: Petrochemical Substitution Options,' E. S. Lipinski, Batelle Columbus Laboratories, Ohio.
'Pyrolysis of Wood Residues with a Vertical Bed Reactor,' J. A. Knight in 'Progress in Biomass Conversion' Vol. 1, Academic Press, N. Y.
'Comparative Yield Trials with Tree and Grass Energy Crops' R. V. Osgood & N. S. Dudley, Second Pacific Biofuels Workshop, University of Hawaii.
'Thermochemical Production of Methanol from Biomass in Hawaii,' V. D. Philips, C. M. Kinoshita, D. R. Neill & P. K. Takahashi, Hawaii Integrated Biofuels Research Program, Phase 2, Final Report, Hawaii Natural Energy Institute, August, 1990.
Also see: Biomass Technology Investigative Reports of Georgia Institute of Technology, and Stanford Research Institute, Stanford University, California.
NOTA BENE.
1. It is not intended herein to duplicate expositions which confirm the technical feasibility of biomass, but to show how cannabis uniquely comprises the most economical (cheapest) source of fuel-energy known to Mankind. The sheer scale of monetary interest reveals the intensity of the corrupt motive behind unlawful introduction and prolongation of controls on people's traditional private cultivation, trade, possession and uses of cannabis. The ulterior motive is *compounded* with those noted in subsequent Parts.
2. Inexorable legal, social, economic, health and ecological reasons require the Abolition of all controls: The Relegalisation of Cannabis.
3. Knowledge about cannabis and understanding of ulterior inducements expose Cannabis Prohibition (controls) to be grave and mortal crime.
4. The macro-economics of The CANNABIS BIOMASS ENERGY EQUATION lay bare the *mens rea*, and establish the deepest culpability, of individuals, corporations and governments involved.

The Cannabis Biomass Energy Equation.

The Pyrolytic Reactor
A Fractionating Column for the
Destructive Distillation of Biomass
to Obtain Fuel & Products.

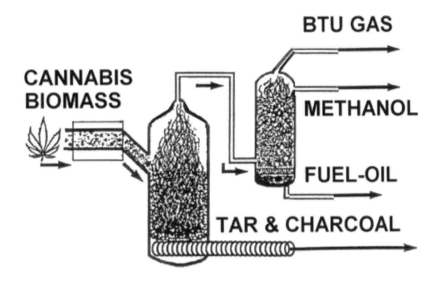

Energy from Biomass: The Concept.

The concept of energy from biomass is as old as Man's pre-historical 'Mastery of Fire'. Firewood for cooking, heating and warding off predatory beasts in the night represents exploitation by humans of biomass for energy. Subterranean coal and oil, high in accumulated sulphurous content, are *fossilised* biomass, the accretion in the Earth over past aeons of concentrations of organic material, plants and organisms.

Cannabis is the most prolific of all low-moisture woody plant species. 77 to 80 per cent of the biomass of cannabis is comprised of **cellulose**, a carbohydrate ideal for conversion into the hydrocarbons of fuel. Improved on by modern techniques to achieve efficient conversion of biomass into fuel, **pyrolysis** is one of Mankind's earliest technologies, an ancient skill used in Pharaonic times to produce oleaginous embalming fluid for mummification. The same process is used today to refine oil.

Pyrolysis *is the decomposing of biomass (fresh or fossil) by the heat of anaerobic (reduced air) combustion which converts organic material into gases and/or fuel oils.*

Fresh biomass is the direct substitute for the fossilised biomass of coal and petroleum., With the hot 'off-gases' collected, which cool to condense into liquid fuels, pyrolysis is known in modern refining as 'thermochemical decomposition' or as 'wood distillation', or as 'destructive distillation'. To achieve an economy based on fresh biomass requires the cultivation of enough suitable biomass to replace coal, oil and uranium, for transportation fuels and electricity generation, to meet domestic and industrial needs. On first impressions, this would seem an ambitious target requiring much land devoted to food production, but, demonstrated as follows by The CBEE, deeper examination reveals that, *firstly*, coal, oil, natural gas and uranium per BTU produced, are *not economic* compared to cannabis as fuel-energy resource. (Prohibition aside) to produce *enough* Cannabis Biomass to power the modern techno-industrial World requires only the fulfilment of the fundamental commercial aspect: the farmer produces that crop which profits him and is in demand. *Secondly*, gross food production is not diminished at all, or will be *increased* by substituting cannabis for present produce.

The Miniature Home Pyrolysis Still.

The Miniature Home Pyrolysis Still is simple to manufacture or make at home from a garbage can, piping and a barrel. It is cheap, portable, and very effective; viz. Southern France in World War II. **Also see Note** [1]. The manufactured version is comprised of iron collars shaped to reduce in size conically, placed atop one another, connected to a metal chimney exit pipe, leading to the familiar coiled distillation cooling pipe (which can be run through a tank to provide warm water). Any closed oven suffices. The coil feeds a barrel. Lit with embers, dry biomass smoulders in the Still, the off-gas condensing to yield methyl alcohol (i.e., methanol) [2]. Only one person is required to move, re-mount or operate the device. Following minimal investment into the purchase of a Pyrolysis Still and the electricity motor-generator, the small-scale production of cannabis crops processed into methanol offers *duty-free fuel and free electricity* to every allotment-using household [3]. After Relegalisation, without a Pyrolysis Still the backyard kitchen-garden, allotment, market-garden, or farm, will be inadequately equipped. From the smallholding's limited acreage, by cannabis cultivation for profitable seed-food, relaxant and fibre crops, the homestead simultaneously becomes *self-sufficient in cost-free* fuel for transport and generation of electricity for cooking, lighting, and heating, *with fuel surplus for sale*. Interestingly, for the last forty years, the Indy series race cars have been fuelled by methanol.

After Cannabis Relegalisation, the Home Pyrolysis Still will be in private use *everywhere*, embodying the **Universal Re-Democratisation of Fuel-Energy Production**. The prospect of fuel-energy again being free to producers, and very cheap and duty-free to customers and people at large, represents liberation from the unnatural enslaving economic domination of Mankind by small numbers of undemocratic individuals, magnates and politicians.

Large Stills are equally simple to construct and run, to process macro-agricultural (large-scale) production of cannabis into fuel, cheaply fulfilling all mass energy needs, electricity power stations, and public and private transport for city populations.

The following reflects upon conspiratorial impedimenta to Cannabis Relegalisation. Purporting to 'educate', the Owned and controlled mass media broadcast 'documentaries' throughout the world, imparting **disinformation** intended to 'dismiss' the viability of methanol, while advocating introduction of exceedingly expensive complicated fuel-technologies, which all pollute at some stage of their energy production, but which yield **control** of energy supplies to their few Owners and government. Methanol is wrongly 'dismissed' as a substitute for fossils on the false notion that its combustion releases CO_2 "like fossils." This is miseducation by omission, for, as mentioned, the equivalent of all CO_2 emitted is re-absorbed by the next fuel crop in production: there is **zero-increase-net** of CO_2 in the atmosphere from the use of methanol derived from fresh cannabis biomass and no pollution whatsoever. Confirmed by the chemical equation of combustion (which follows), Cannabis-Methanol is completely pollution free.

1 Note that, with limited availability of petroleum products brought about by Royal Naval blockade, the motorised blitzkrieg of the German war effort and invasions were fuelled on <u>methanol</u> (also called 'synthetic' fuel and lubricants).

2 Methanol, Fuel Oils and charcoal derived from fresh biomass do not contain the sulphur accumulated by fossils, thereby providing an environmentally clean, i.e., GREEN SOLUTION, the alternative to coal, oil and potentially catastrophic <u>uranium</u> in the generation of electricity; viz. Chernobyl. Sulphur released by fossil combustion is cause to Acid Rain, the dilute sulphuric acid destroyer of fresh water, micro-organisms, fish, wildlife and trees.

3 Duty, i.e., government tax on sale, is largest component in the price of fuel-energy; c 70-80 % in Europe.

The Cannabis Biomass Energy Equation.

Special Attributes of Cannabis:

Of all known plant species, cannabis delivers the most economically efficient biomass fuel-energy as a result of inherent attributes, summarised as follows:-

1. Cannabis is the most prolific of all low-moisture, woody plant species. Cannabis grows well in all climes where Mankind lives. A good crop in sub-tropical Florida produces approximately 18 tons of biomass per acre [≈ 0.4 hectares]. Cannabis grows to full biomass production *in only 4 months* [1].

2. Cannabis is a low-moisture wooden plant. Of other prolific biomass species, sugar cane (tropics only) maize, napier and kanaf, all produce less biomass per 4 months' period (grown in the same soil and climatic conditions). Unlike cannabis, all of those species mentioned are of high moisture content. High moisture plants require pre-drying before pyrolysis, thereby consuming significant quantities of BTU's before delivering them, devaluing the worth of their contribution. Also, by comparison with cannabis, those species are markedly less economical both to cultivate and to process. Seen in Brazil's (Volkswagen) large-scale *ethanol* production to reduce oil imports, high moisture plants lend themselves to the energy production system of bio-chemical (sugar fermentation) conversion to ethanol (ethyl alcohol). This is a very different, energy-consuming and investment-capital-intensive slow procedure. Publicly confirmed by the Vice-President of VW in 1996, ethanol is uneconomical compared to the efficient method of fuel-energy production of methanol by pyrolysis.

3. The internal combustion engine runs well on methanol, without causing any pollution. (See section V of The Economics of The CBRPF.)

4. Cannabis fuel-energy can be made immediately available in all climatic conditions (where Mankind lives).

5. After malt and seedling stage, cannabis requires and retains less water than most plants, and can survive drought.

6. Cannabis survives temporary floods, having deep roots which penetrate 10 to 12 inches in only the first 4-6 weeks. (Grasses generally penetrate 3-6 ins.) Cannabis has an important beneficial effect in reducing topsoil erosion by monsoon and heavy rains.

7. Cannabis survives intermittent frosts, having been observed in the Californian Sierras to tolerate more than 20 degrees of frost, i.e., down to below 12°F (-11°C).

8. Cannabis does not require fertiliser. (It responds, like all plants, to manure and good soil, but does well without.)

9. Cannabis flourishes even on marginal (unproductive) land.

10. Cannabis does not exhaust the fertility [2] of soil on which it grows; and it improves soil by: a.) leaf-shedding throughout the growth cycle, which assists moisture retention in the soil and promotes humus; b.) deep roots which unclog and aerate soil; c.) stands of cannabis hemp grow densely, denying tares, thistles and other weeds the opportunity of growth. Cannabis is found to clear land of persistent recurring weeds. As shown in Kentucky and Wisconsin, after many years of continuous cannabis production (over seven and up to fifteen years) other crops cultivated subsequently on the same land are found to grow well [3].

1 See: 'Fiber Crops,' J.M. Dempsey, University Presses of Florida.
2 See: Yearbook of the United States Department of Agriculture,' 1913, page 321. Also see: USDA Bulletin 404, 1916,' L.H. Dewey, Botanist-in-Charge of Fiber Plant Investigations, & J.L. Merrill, Plant-Chemist, Bureau of Plant Industry.
3 Ibid. Also see: 'The Writings of Thomas Jefferson,' edited by H.A. Washington, Lipincotts, Philadelphia. In addition to law, judicature and Human Rights, the writings of Third U.S. President Thomas Jefferson, author of the Declaration of Independence, have relevance in cannabis cultivation, trade and Agronomics.

Prohibition of Cannabis disallows the most cultivable, optimum dry biomass plant species on Earth, uniquely and immediately capable of the economical (*cheap*) replacement of all Mankind's *misuse* of high-pollutant, costly fossils and uranium, for energy, petro-chemical products, gasoline and plastics.

THE CANNABIS BIOMASS RESOURCE and PYROLYSIS FUNCTIONS:
The CBRPF
versus
FOSSILS & URANIUM

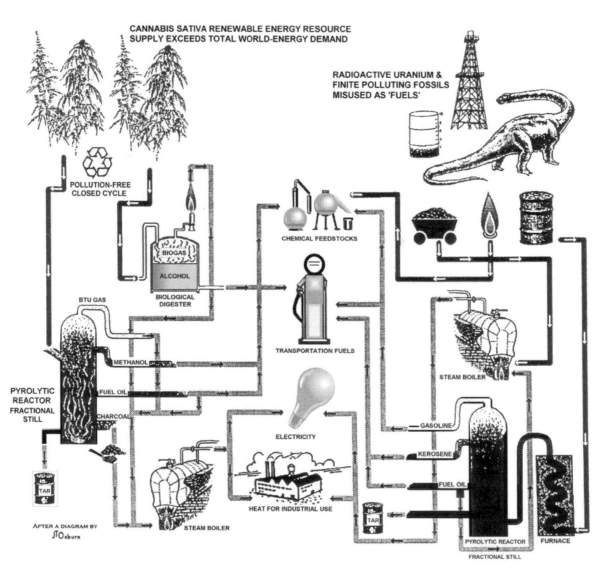

CANNABIS SATIVA RENEWABLE ENERGY RESOURCE
SUPPLY EXCEEDS TOTAL WORLD-ENERGY DEMAND

RADIOACTIVE URANIUM & FINITE POLLUTING FOSSILS MISUSED AS 'FUELS'

POLLUTION-FREE CLOSED CYCLE

BIOGAS

ALCOHOL

CHEMICAL FEEDSTOCKS

BTU GAS

BIOLOGICAL DIGESTER

TRANSPORTATION FUELS

METHANOL

PYROLYTIC REACTOR FRACTIONAL STILL

FUEL OIL

CHARCOAL

STEAM BOILER

ELECTRICITY

GASOLINE

KEROSENE

FUEL OIL

TAR

HEAT FOR INDUSTRIAL USE

AFTER A DIAGRAM BY JTOsburn

STEAM BOILER

TAR

PYROLYTIC REACTOR
FRACTIONAL STILL

FURNACE

THE CANNABIS BIOMASS ENERGY EQUATION cont.

The Cannabis Biomass Energy Equation.

Economics of the Cannabis Biomass Energy Equation;
The Cannabis Biomass Resource and Pyrolysis Functions.

In energy generation, that exigence all-important to Humankind, advantageous properties unique to cannabis render it *commercially superior* to every other resource. There are more ways than one of presenting the esoteric facts and figures of The Cannabis Biomass Energy Equation but, however galling these truths are to the cannabis-Prohibitionist lobby, they amount to the following transfixing conclusions:

1— Cannabis Sativa, the THC-rich full-size variety, is the plant species best adapted to the commercial and other requirements of the Biomass Function.

2— The Cannabis Biomass Resource and Pyrolysis Functions (CBRPF) are available for the efficient, effective total replacement of uranium and fossils misused as 'fuel'.

3— Cannabis produces the BTU's of fuel-energy more economically than coal, oil, natural gas, uranium, wind and wave-power, geo-thermal, and hydrogen-from-water electrical separation, etc.

4— All Mankind's foreseeable fuel and energy requirements can be met by the Cannabis Biomass Resource and Pyrolysis Functions.

5— By the CBRPF, populations everywhere can avail themselves of cheap fuel, staple food, energy and industrial resources, all from cannabis cultivated to supply levels of, or outstrip, demand. Strategic stockpiles can be afforded. The Standard of Living for entire populations, including those now suffering in acute want, may be ameliorated speedily, far beyond the expectations of current economic trends and the inevitably dour forecasts based on present high-cost energy and resources.

6— The commercial superiority of Cannabis the potential death-knell to misuse of fossils and nuclear fission—is demonstrated by the following plain facts:

I. Crops of female cannabis produce abundant seed, a valued traditional staple food [1]. (Seed does not contain relaxant ingredients.) Seed comprises at maturity more than half the total weight of a large plant, which yields more protein-rich food per acre than the grasses (wheat, rice, maize, etc.) and other crops such as potatoes and manioc (tapioca/cassava). *Including income to the farmer, seed profitably covers the cost of producing the crop.*

The trunk and branches of the cannabis plant are comprised of wood (called **hurds**) sheathed in **fibres** which run the length of the plant. 77 to 80 per cent of the wood is comprised of **cellulose**. Farmers sometimes select and uproot young male plants when growing crops for seed, leaving space for the seed-bearing, larger female plant to reach full capacity. These juvenile plants yield hurds (wood) and especially *fine* fibre. Males displaying advantageous propensities are allowed to grow to maturity to pollinate the females. At harvest time, seeds from females with preferred attributes, e.g. relaxant-tonic strength, quantity of biomass (plant size) or seed yield, etc., are selectively retained for next season's planting.

Mild climates provide more than one season's crop in a year, and warmer zones can produce three full crops per year [2].

1 See 'Cannabis Hemp Seeds: The Most Nutritionally Complete Food Source on Earth,' Lynn and Judy Osburn.
2 See USDA Publications listed in bibliography. Also see: Popular Mechanics Magazine, February, 1938.

SEED: -seed, staple food of high protein content, containing the requisite fatty and
      amino acids essential to the efficient working of the human immune system
      -polyunsaturate vegetable oil/margarine/nut-butter (ref. later section: Cannabis
      Resources)
      -pressed seedcake, highly nutritious human food
      -pressed seedcake, high quality feed for livestock
      -seed, food for domestic pets

After harvesting the seed, and then mechanical decortication (fibre separation), the remaining wood **'hurds'** amount to approximately 80 per cent of the plant's biomass. These cellulose-rich bulk residues are a *production-cost-free* by-product.

PRODUCTION-COST-FREE	DISCOVERY AND EXTRACTION	
Hurds = $0	**Coal**	**= $ some**
	Oil	**= $ many**
	Uranium	**= $ great many**

Nota Bene: Whilst growing for profitable, nutritious **seed**, in addition to the **hurds**, the **fibres** from mature plants are *also production-cost-free*, providing the farmer with *another* profitable product. (See III.)

Pyrolysis of Cannabis Biomass, in particular the hurds, yields all the requisite (energy of) fuels and gases, for which coal, natural gas, oil and uranium are at present the pricey source. By comparison, it is seen that:

Cannabis Biomass yields:-   **BTU's cheap; and is *renewable*,
                                     available everywhere, stable supply,
                                     ecologically non-pollutant. . .**

Whereas,
fossils, or nuclear fission yield:- **BTU's of high price; are semi-rare,
                                     finite quantity, unstable prices,
                                     aggravated politics,
                                     strategic dependence,
                                     ecologically destructive. . .**

II. By pyrolysis conversion, biomass delivers 5,000-8,000 BTU's per pound. Approximately 6 per cent of the agricultural land area of the contiguous United States would produce more Cannabis Biomass than is required to supply all current demand for gasoline, diesel and oil for that energy-voracious country. From only 2 crops (8 months, temperate climate) each acre will produce not less than 20 tons of Cannabis Biomass Hurds, which yield 2,000 gallons of methanol. This estimate is minimised: the large 'THC-rich'[1] Sativas yield much more hurds-biomass per acre[2].

Strains of plants vary greatly; e.g. Sativa, Indica, Ruderalis, Americana, etc. The non-relaxant 'low-THC'[3] hybrids grown under license in various countries (France, Germany, Britain, etc.) are also poor in yield of biomass, fibre and cellulose.

1 & 3 THC does not exist *within* cannabis plants, wherein THC combines with other molecules, making it into *another* compound, which is the non-toxic natural herb. Toxic concentrates of laboratory-isolated chemical compound THC have unique attributes which differ widely from cannabis. Ref. Convenient Language, and: 'THC' Is Not 'Cannabis', in Part One.
2 Cf. the large Sativas grown in China, Florida, and at the USDA facility in Mississippi. Ref. USDA Photo shown.

The Cannabis Biomass Energy Equation.

Sufficient acreage is immediately available for Cannabis Biomass production which far exceeds U.S. transportation requirements. The "National Soil Bank's" registered fallow land —(approximately 89 million acres)— can be planted with soil-enriching and non-depletive [1] cannabis as a fallow rotation crop, producing enough methanol, oil and BTU-gas [2] to enable the United States to become a net fuel-energy *exporter*. This is achievable without planting up a single new acre or subtracting land area from current food production. However, noted previously, cannabis grows well on marginal (unproductive) land. Crops therefrom would add value to those acreages of vast total, now considered to be of little or no worth. The enormous quantity of marginal land provides virtually unlimited scope for huge increases in production of the cheap clean fuel-energy of cannabis, far into the future. Cannabis only requires a short growing season (4 months) and can be sown relatively early or late. So, when turning prime land over to cannabis crops and hurds' production, other produce can be grown on the same land in the same year. Farmers will want to cultivate cannabis for its profitability. The plant has multiple valued applications; ref. Traditional Uses.

1 Ref. Special Attributes of Cannabis.
2 This clean-burning product for generators, cookers, heaters, etc., is called BTU-gas to differentiate it from *gas (oline).*

MACRO-AGRICULTURE:

Relegalised Cannabis enters the market in competition with petroleum products, wheat, cotton, lumber, etc., in the large-scale production of fuel-energy, staple seed-food and commercial goods. Many thousands of miles of rolling Steppes, Prairies, Veldt, Savannah, Pampas and nations' agricultural grasslands are covered with cannabis waving in the breeze, absorbing atmospheric carbon.

Where Prohibition only allowed wheat, maize, rice, cotton, etc., now, hundreds of thousands of tons of cannabis foliage, seed, fibre and hurds will also be in fields, in use, in silos, warehouses, factories and power stations, in gardens, homes and shops, and constantly on their way to and fro domestic or commercial processing plants of every type and size, in trailers, trucks and trains from and through every village and town.

III. Cannabis traditionally provides superior fibres for textiles and clothing. Approximately 20 per cent of the hemp stem is comprised of fibre [3]. Again, in this instance the wood-hurds are rendered ***production-cost-free***, as is the seed, being by-products of crops grown for profitable fibre. The educational facts about cannabis fibre which, since introduction of Prohibition have been to date generally suppressed, are that, by a variety of cultivation and/or processing techniques, cannabis comprises:

A.) the most *cultivable* of the fibre-source plant species;
B.) the most *economic* fibre resource known, and
C.) the resource to *every type* of fibre in industrial and domestic use.

Mature and *post-mature* plants (i.e., cropped after seeding) yield long fibres (up to several feet in length) of easily worked, intense strength, and water-rot resistant characteristics. These are source to the traditional canvas products, including sailcloth, carpets, tapestries, etc., and currently provide all the field tents to the Russian Army.

By contrast, juvenile plants yield soft, fine fibres, suited to production of the lighter types of garment now associated with cotton. Still finer fibres are obtained when stands of cannabis are cultivated in extreme density (a seed sown approximately

3 See: Mechanical Engineering Magazine, February, 1937. Also see USDA Publications listed in bibliography.

every two square inches) and then cropped at juvenile stage. These are of similar quality, but superior durability, to the lightest, softest of silks, and cotton-velours, with which they compete. By varying cultivation methods and age at cropping, *every grade of fibre*, and hence of yarn, between these examples is produced from cannabis.

However, cropping *after* seed-production is of economic advantage, because seed provides food vegetable oil of mild flavour suited to cuisine, while the remaining pressed seed is similar to soya in protein, calorific and nutritional value, i.e., *superior* to 'grasses', wheat, barley, maize, rice. Seed-crops render by-products, i.e., the hurds, the relaxant and the fibres, **production-cost-free**. Fibre from mature plants, being subjected to the 1924 patented, Cottonisation or **Dresden Process** (a simple, cheap cold-chlorination technique) is transformed into a level-dyeing, pliable, soft, lustrous fibre, in all physical respects indistinguishable from cotton. *Before* Prohibition, **Dresden 'Cotton'** *came profitably onto the market at considerably less than half the price of the cheapest kinds of cotton* [1]. Without governments' conspiratorial monopoly-control revenue and profit protection-racket by *Prohibition*, to fulfil demand of a normal market, ubiquitous production of Dresden Cotton would eliminate the profitability, and therefore commercial cultivation, of ordinary cotton. *Likewise, cannabis renders all fossil-derived products commercially obsolete*: e.g. Cellulosic Polymerisation of the cellulose-rich production-cost-free cannabis hurds profitably yields: **plastics** (all types) and the **man-made fibres** (e.g. nylons) [2].

The CBEE establishes that, following low-cost investment into the Pyrolysis Still,

♦ Fuel produced from cannabis is <u>free</u>; i.e., of no cash cost. ♦

The Cannabis Biomass Energy Equation shows the farmer's production-cost-free hurds fuel and plastics' resource, profitably undercuts the price of fossils misused as 'resources' or 'fuel'. *In greatest contrast*, the commercially redundant 'fuel', electricity, thermal units and products sourced from fossils and uranium are always more expensive than equivalent products sourced from cannabis. Further, *production costs associated with the fossils and uranium, are enormous*, i.e., of discovery, extraction (viz. drilling; marine oil platforms; coal mines), distribution (e.g. by vulnerable ocean-going tankers), *and* of capital-intensive, energy-consuming *refinement* into usable forms. This polluting and preposterous exercise only remains commercially viable to the minority of countries and corporations involved, for as long as politicians continue to conspire to prohibit cannabis unlawfully. Each continent is capable of producing surplus cannabis-fuel for all energy needs, **which eliminates transport by ocean-going oil-tankers,** *rendering their related environmental disasters a thing of the past*.

Take note! cotton producers, India, Pakistan, Egypt, China, Uzbekistan, and Brazil, of the following **Exemplary Fact of Cannabis Relegalisation:**
Turning the Mississippi Cotton Region over to farm production of profitable Dresden Cotton, also simultaneously produces production-cost-free cannabis grain staple food surplus, and (far more than) enough production-cost-free hurds-sourced fuel-energy to satisfy all U.S. transportation requirements.

Implementation of THE CANNABIS BIOMASS ENERGY EQUATION makes such socio-economic and ecological benefits immediately available from *every* agriculturally productive region, to **all** populations of the World.

1 See Staatliches Material Prüfungsamt, 1924. Also see: Professor Paul Boerman, Manchester Guardian (U.K.) 1924.
2 Plastics derive equally from hydrocarbons or carbohydrates. Cellulosic polymers were invented from vegetative sources.

The Cannabis Biomass Energy Equation.

NOTA BENE: **A**. Implementation of THE CANNABIS BIOMASS ENERGY EQUATION proffers a revolutionarily **ameliorative transformation** to the socio-economic condition of the entire world population.

B. Apropos of GLOBAL WARMING: Replacement of fossils by the cannabis resource makes an immediate reduction of not less than 80 per cent, i.e., an eight-tenths plus *cut* in emissions of Global Warming CO_2 gas; *and,*

C. utilised for its *numerous non-combusted purposes,* cannabis significantly *subtracts* from extant atmospheric CO_2.

IV. Consider an alternative crop: the THC-rich Sativas grow up to and over 15 feet (c. 5 metres) in height, yielding large flowertops for commercial products of the health-improving **relaxant-tonic**. (Ref. Parts One, Three, Four & Five on Health.) Cropped for relaxant, the hurds and fibre are, again, ***production-cost-free*** by-products. (Currently, this traditional industry is under the illegal Prohibition.) Cannabis hurds are the ideal resource to **paper, card products, and newsprint**. Tree wood pulp, thick with lignin (the substance which hardens wood cells enabling trees to stand) requires much costly processing by sulphuric acid to break it down. Chlorine is often resorted to as a 'whitener', deadly dioxins being the inevitable but unwanted consequence of this processing. 'Run-off' has over the years poisoned many lakes and rivers of the E.C., East Europe and the U.S. Even the oceans (e.g. Baltic and North Sea) are susceptible to pollution by these industrial wastes, with adverse effects on wildlife. By contrast, minimal acids are required in the breakdown of cannabis hurds for wood-pulp.

Being *production-cost-free*, the wood-hurds undercut the price of lumber by 100 per cent of the costs of lumber production, rendering trees commercially redundant. Legal cannabis has long been perceived as a 'threat' to the profits of Owners of commercial forestation [1]. Cannabis hurds were confirmed in preference to trees as resource to wood-pulp for production of all paper products, by the U.S. Department of Agriculture, Bulletin 404, in 1916. Publication by Researchers Lyster Dewey and Jason Merrill, of the economic and technical superiority of the cannabis hemp plant over trees, publicly declared the ecologically significant **breakthrough discoveries:**

1. *production confirmed cannabis hemp hurds [2] more economic and easier-worked source of pulp than trees, for all types of paper, newspaper-print, and card*;

2. *the products made from cannabis are of superior quality*;

3. *the crop from 1 acre of cannabis hemp grown to maturity in four months produces as much paper-pulp raw material as 4.1 acres of trees in twelve months' growth [3]* ;

4. *the cannabis resource is available within 4 months (a growth season), but trees require many years' growth before becoming suitable to harvest.*

1 Viz. the instigation of widespread Prohibition disinformation and propaganda by forest and paper-production-mill Owner, the newspaper magnate William Randolph Hearst; ref. section entitled **The Marijuana Tax Act, 1937.**

2 Traditionally, paper was made from cannabis hemp <u>fibre</u> products. (Ref. Traditional Uses.) The sulphuric acid processing of trees came into use during the latter part of the Nineteenth Century, before hurds-from-fibre mechanisation had been developed. Dewey and Merrill foresaw shortages of trees and demonstrated, by use of hurds instead, not only has the wholesale destruction of forests been wanton, but cannabis products are superior, *and* more economic.

3 See Bulletin 404, USDA; 1916. Nota Bene: In some growing areas, a *second*, and the warmer zones a *third*, crop of cannabis hemp can be produced in twelve months, without soil depletion (or other food and cash crops may be cultivated on the same land in the same year, if prime land is used). Cannabis produces good crops even on 'marginal land' where yields of other crops are negligible. Cannabis grown for relaxant-tonic, or cereal-seed plus oil, or fibres, etc., renders the hurds-paper-pulp resource *production-cost-free*, profitably undercutting the price of lumber.

USDA Bulletin 404 stated the deduction that cannabis would become the largest agricultural industry in the United States. It will yet be proved correct...but how much *more* human and ecological damage will this Prohibition wreak before the People are awakened to the truth of its illegality... Since 1937 (instigation of Prohibition in the U.S.*), at least half of the world's trees have been cut down to make paper* [1]. But for the Prohibition, most of these trees would still be standing today, absorbing the carbon of atmospheric CO_2, and oxygenating the atmosphere.

It seems certain that the aware and well-informed citizen-taxpayer would enthusiastically support a state-political policy whereby the public finance the purchase at a full and premium price at once, of some commercial timberland now in private hands, whose owners choose voluntarily to realise their investment by sale, so that these forested areas be protected under suitable designation as public parkland. The trees may then be allowed to stand undiminished by the lumberjack's axe. Further, the re-forestation of great tracts by re-introduced variegated deciduous woodlands (rather than coniferous mono-culture) and the conservation of the few remaining woods, will beautify the countryside, provide wildlife habitat, and make a practical contribution to stabilisation of the Global Warming trend. Such desirable measures only become practicable and economic following complete Cannabis Relegalisation, by which cannabis will replace most demands for commercial timber.

1 See 'Crimping Progress by Banning Hemp,' Alan W. Bock, Orange County Register.

V. Pyrolysis of Cannabis Biomass produces hydro-carbon substitutes; gasoline and kerosene-paraffin jet-fuel substitute methanol, fuel-oils, gases, lubricants, varnishes, bituminous asphalt, tars, charcoal, etc. The thermochemical decomposition can be adjusted to favour production of desired end products. If required, the injection of air (oxygen) consumes residual charcoal releasing its constituents. Used in this 'gasifier' mode, by increasing heat, pressure and adding such catalysts, methanol production is maximised at approximately 100 gallons per ton of biomass [2]. **Methanol** (CH_3OH) has always been the cheap, pollution-free and practical alternative to petrol/gasoline and diesel. The Internal Combustion Engine *receives less wear* from combustion of methanol. By **clean** combustion, continued utility of the powerful Internal Combustion Engine is prolonged by cannabis-methanol, far into the future.

Electricity power generating stations can be run off methanol, or Cannabis Biomass Pyrolysis **fuel-oil**, which is similar to home-heating oil, and/or use compacted charcoal brickettes directly, in place of fossils. (Until the near total removal of many fine forests, e.g. Sherwood and those of the Black Country, the pyrolytic production of charcoal was a large industry. Charcoal was the principal fuel to the early stages of the Industrial Revolution. Coal then replaced dwindling supplies of charcoal.)

In addition to the radically ameliorative economic aspects of production-cost-free fuel-energy, cannabis also yields fuel preferable on ecological grounds—of great importance is the fact that cannabis-methanol combustion releases only CO_2 and H_2O (as steam). (See chemical equation which follows.) City areas would be thus completely relieved from the present foul and unhealthy photo-chemical *smog-pollution from fossil combustion* emissions by cars, trucks, buses, generators, home-heating and power stations. Viz. Paris, Los Angeles, Tokyo, São Paulo, etc.

2 See 'Methanol from Wood: A Critical Assessment,' R.M. Rowell & A.E. Hokanson in 'Progress in Biomass Conversion,' Vol. 1, Academic Press, N.Y.

The Cannabis Biomass Energy Equation.

Cannabis fuel-energy products have further advantages over oil and coal:

A. The considerable and repeated costs of installing mandatory anti-pollution devices in the consumption of fossils for electricity generation by power stations (e.g. smokestack sulphur 'scrubbers') are not incurred when the non-pollutant fuel-energy products of the Cannabis Biomass Resource and Pyrolysis Functions are employed. This renders Cannabis-Methanol and Cannabis Biomass Pyrolysis fuel-oils still more cost-effective.

B. Charcoal, which has the same enthalpic value as coal, is a *production-cost-free by-product* of standard biomass pyrolysis (not gasifier) production of Cannabis-Methanol and fuel oils (see the Pyrolysis Still diagrams). The residual charcoal from cannabis hurds profitably undercuts the price of coal by 100 per cent of the cost of coal's discovery and extraction. Production-cost-free products of CBRPF (methanol, etc.) are always more economical (cheaper) than commercial coal.

C. Cannabis is agriculturally *replaceable*, not a resource of diminishing finite quantity.

D. From the ecological viewpoint, Cannabis-Methanol and Cannabis Biomass Pyrolysis fuel-oils are incomparably preferable to coal, as they are not source to the pollutant sulphur off-gas of fossil combustion, which produces the environmentally damaging sulphuric Acid Rain.

NOTA BENE:

Chemical Equation for complete (i.e., *clean*) combustion of cannabis-methanol:

$$2CH_3OH + 3O_2 \rightarrow 2CO_2 + 4H_2O.$$

Three molecules of oxygen ($3 O_2$) are required for every two molecules of methanol ($2 CH_3OH$) in order that combustion of the latter will be *complete*. Any higher proportion of O_2 will be an excess; combustion will also be complete, and some unused O_2 will remain.

Regarding carbon dioxide released by cannabis-methanol and CBRPF fuel-oil combustion, a ***greater*** quantity of carbon is *re-absorbed* from the atmosphere by growth of the next cannabis crops in cultivation, for: relaxant; *non-combusted* staple seed food; clothing and textiles; paper and newsprint; building-materials (see Isochanvre); timber-substitutes; plastics-resource; etc., *in addition* to cannabis crops produced for the hurds resource to fuels.

Implementation of the Cannabis Biomass Energy Equation initiates a beneficial all-encompassing, immediate stabilising influence on the 'greenhouse effect' of Global Warming:

1.) **by reducing to** zero, **the world fuel-combustion component of overall carbon dioxide atmospheric increase,** *and*

2.) **by subtracting from atmospheric CO_2 whenever cannabis is utilised as resource to non-combusted products (see list in previous paragraph).**

Past and continuing Failure to implement The Cannabis Biomass Energy Equation, implicates politicians in judicable homicide, and indicts politicians' betrayal, dereliction and criminal conspiracy.

OBSERVATIONS ON THE CBEE.

In the last hundred years, there has not been a single ecologically-pertinent fact, theory or postulation embodying practicable potentials as beneficial to the planet and the well-being of its peoples as those of The Cannabis Biomass Energy Equation. This formulation resolves Mankind's most crucial predicament in Economic Affairs *and* Ecology, to have arisen since the incipience of The Industrial Revolution. Abolition of controls on cannabis renders uranium and the fossil pollutants:

A. *commercially obsolete/economically redundant*, and
B. achieves their replacement *without pollution*, while
C. the Economy of the entire world thereby vastly benefits from *significantly reduced energy prices.*

The CBEE establishes for the first time on public record that fuel-energy sourced from the renewable, pollution-free resource of flora in the form of cannabis, achieves *uniquely* economical replacement of fossils and uranium. It is providential that cannabis is ecologically compatible too. There has been no (good) reason to delay implementation of The Cannabis Biomass Energy Equation to power industrial and technological civilisation. Reduced costs of fuel-energy give a boost to every activity of industry, manufacturing and service. At domestic and local level, pyrolysis facilities producing methanol, fuel-oils and lubricants, would provide employment and protect people from the vagaries of petroleum politics, high energy prices and the monopolistic stranglehold of the petro-chemical giant. Small and intermediate communities would enjoy a re-birth of prosperity, initiative and productivity. By implementing The CBEE, *every* village and town has the potential to achieve self-sufficiency in energy, food and resources, *including* those people now suffering deep deprivation across the continents of the Third World. Large-scale industry and cities would all benefit from increased energy supplies at lower prices.

Energy enables all industry (service and manufacturing) and human consumption (heating, cooking, lighting, transport). On a planet-wide average, eight-tenths of the Cost of Living for each person are accounted for by energy related expenditures, resulting from: resource discovery, recovery, supply; transportation; refinery; generation, distribution, retail; *and the largest component*: *government duties* (sale-taxes). Four-fifths of the cost of all commercial goods and services are based on the cost of energy. Over 80 per cent of the value of Stock traded on the Exchanges of the world is in companies involved in the provision of energy. The Economy of the whole World is put on a false-footing by *political* Denial (i.e., Prohibition) of the Cannabis Resource. More pernicious than instability, Prohibition results in an *impoverishment* felt by the majority of the world population, being those people least able to afford the present high cost of energy, food, and services and manufactured goods.

Heightened energy costs cause economic instability, increasing, potentially to socially unendurable levels, unemployment, recession, 'stag-flation' and slump. *Firstly*, this presages economic (trade) and military wars to acquire and/or protect valued resources of all types, and *secondly*, this provides a spur to repeated internal civil strife, which provokes the familiar state enforcement/military response to 'control' emergencies inflicted upon riven populations. *Continuing* failure to relegalise accelerates degeneration, whereby the *total* demise of Democracy becomes likely, perhaps inevitable.

The Cannabis Biomass Energy Equation.

The failure to adopt The CBEE by governments does not simply depress the world economy: far worse, both the socio-economic and climate change aspects of The Cannabis Biomass Energy Equation establish that the politicians' intentional delay is homicidal. It is also already the cause of war (viz. the Iraqi invasion of Kuwait). Oil becomes scarce and of yet higher prices. The permitted energy generation techniques and the so-called 'new alternative' energy sources are relatively unproductive or of increasing industrial complexity and require capital investment of scale. So, governments' know that *procrastination* in implementation of The CBEE works to their financial advantage and increments the hegemony of government and corporate Owners of the fossils. Thus, the failure of governments to implement The CBEE to date is explained.

The politicians' Prohibition installs a racketeering monopolistic profit protection of unnecessarily expensive and otherwise redundant resources and products in the markets and shops of the modern world. At the foundation of what purports to be the Western free enterprise or Free Market system, there is a fundamental destructive lie. At the core of any nation's Economic System wherein Cannabis Prohibition is enacted (Free, or Social-Mixed Market or state-owned) *by political means*, macro-Extortion by Prohibition supervenes as a mechanism of overall economic control and human oppression. Cannabis is banned, not in reality for the given pretexts. Cannabis is banned because, if it were legal, most of its *economic benefits would accrue to the general population*, while business concerns of great scale, comprised of individuals, syndicated financial combines, institutions and states, would find *their* revenues sharply reduced. Returns on their holdings or investment into capital and plant would yield diminished net income. To protect those financial interests preferred of politicians, economic competition from cannabis is eliminated by the felon's methods.

'Prohibition' is imposed not because there is something 'bad' about cannabis, but because of the all-affecting superlative good of cannabis. Magnates of giant companies presume, ad infinitum or until it ceases to suit their purpose, to manipulate politicians and the mentality of the population, into maintaining Prohibition of Cannabis, to the People's certain harm and great disadvantage. At the behest of multi-national corporations whose financial investments and influence interweave through every facet of the socio-economic complex, politicians are not willing to allow the population of the world to acquire and enjoy the boon of a cheap, naturally occurring, beneficent resource. Yet, if the populations of the world but knew it, this providential benefit is there for the asking, and theirs for the taking.

Evidence establishes Cannabis Prohibition as a racket: *the politician* fabricates and perpetuates counterfeit Prohibition controls nationally, and, by fraudulent treaties, e.g. the Single Convention Treaty, worldwide; imposes by force, a set of politically-designed artificial circumstances in support of chosen monetary interests to their undeserved and unearned stupendous financial advantage. To those thus protected, this is an ongoing repeated windfall of a spectacularly huge scale, a 'subsidy' amounting to trillions of dollars/Euros/yen, etc., per annum, paid for entirely out of the pockets of mostly unwitting consumers.

This illegal, unadmitted state-political 'policy' is then compounded by enforcement, with myriad acts of government-by-terror perpetrated upon citizens from all walks of life, for harmless cannabis related activities, in the attempt at political suppression of the herb.

To conceal this conspiracy and the attendant crimes of its enforcement, and to enable the continued illicit protection of the financial gain of some at the expense of others, politicians and their collaborationist administrations resort to use of taxpayers' money to obfuscate the harmless benign nature of cannabis with constant public indoctrination by derogatory fictions. (Ref. Parts One, Three, Four & Five.) In executing this evil scheme, the 'politician' forsakes civilised Principles, such as honesty, truth, justice and liberty, shunning all pretension to democratic legitimacy. Honest evaluation of Cannabis Prohibition shows that the economic precepts and moral philosophy on which the West has long constituted itself, have been abandoned: unprincipled 'politicians' of our self-proclaimed bastions of Democracy, and 'free' and 'mixed market' systems, generate and foster crime (ref. Part Six, Prohibition: The Progenitor of Crime); corruptly practise monopoly duty, tax and profit-protectionism; treacherously usurp the Constitution (ref. Justice and the Constitution); seditiously subvert the democratic rule of law (Part Seven); inflict persecution and suffering; and perpetrate sadistic immolation of personal liberty (all Parts).

Disputes over resources commonly lead to War: Prohibition of the manifold benefits to Mankind of cannabis constitutes criminal infraction of that category of International Law designated: **Crime against Peace**. *Political* denial of the world's most economic energy resource and essential agro-industrial commodity, is an Act of War against the People; consequential suffering and victims are visible everywhere. Cannabis Prohibition is the greatest <u>fraud</u> of all time. Pernicious effects of this crime are myriad, extreme and ubiquitous. Prohibition is the direct cause of: War, e.g. the Iraqi invasion of Kuwait; Crime; astronomical world resource, energy and food prices, with disastrous and homicidal corollary effects; world poverty; world famine; industrial and automotive emissions poisoning air; photochemical smog and Acid Rain; desertification; the greenhouse effect of Global Warming and fatally catastrophic weather. *Had it not been for the obstacle personified by corrupted Owners and politicians, The CBEE would by now have been implemented, and already working its remedy and benefits.*

Oil, coal and uranium are redundant, and destructive. The People of the West and Japan, of Israel, of India, South America, Africa, China and everywhere else, deserve to be freed from dependence on those whose criminal Prohibition scheme gives them control of energy; and from those few who, by geographic chance, happen to inhabit locations above terrestrial minerals. To the detriment of *all*, the tiny group of de facto Owners of the world's Oil want the world population *to continue* using 'their' fossils, regardless of the human, the economic, the environmental, and the other damage this does, and the universal tyranny it inflicts. They require competition from non-polluting Cannabis-Methanol, the world's cheapest (i.e., actually free) fuel, to be *Prohibited* until all the easily recovered oil is consumed. Meantime, in predictable avaricious preparation for when the oil runs out, these same individuals, corporations, institutions and states have been, and are, by 'banking', i.e., mortgage and international loan methods, assuming effective *Ownership*, including in the Third World and former Communist bloc, of the world's agricultural land....the basis of the future world resource to food, fuel and raw materials derived from cannabis.

NO further increases in atmospheric CO_2 from fuel-combustion are acceptable: human lives continue to be taken and the world population remains at risk. The Kyoto Treaty (with its proposed reductions in CO_2 emissions is a destructive elaborate diversion. *All* **misuse of fossils as 'fuel' must be stopped <u>at once</u>.**

The Cannabis Biomass Energy Equation.

In any case, the policies of *increased* fossil exploration and exploitation, and (except for one East European nation) the immediate refusal to ratify the Kyoto Agreement by all countries which participated at that convention, exemplify the criminality and devastation visited by 'politicians' upon apathetic complacent servile populations.

The politicians' energy-monopoly by Prohibition negates the Social-Mixed and/or Free Market, intervening as a macroeconomic tax, duty, and profit protection-mechanism. The manipulations are imposed, by force, on behalf of preferred monetary interests. This Crime is committed against the world's people who (consciously or unwittingly) all endure its extreme consequences. Prohibition imposes worldwide shortages of otherwise prolific availability of (cannabis-derived) food, energy supplies and raw materials. These latter are the essentials of human life. Everywhere, Mankind teeters on the brink of strife, of wars, revolution and armed conflict. This Prohibition visibly exacerbates the problems, while Peace, Prosperity and Progress would be enhanced by the opposite course, that of Relegalisation.

Straightaway, The Cannabis Biomass Energy Equation proffers ameliorative transformation of the world's peoples' Standard of Living, by prolific global provision of very cheap, superior Energy, Food and Resources; The CBEE shows that The Universal Re-Democratisation of Fuel-Energy Production can easily, immediately be realised; *and* implementation of The CBEE simultaneously reduces Global Warming. While all this is acutely desirable to the general population of the world for obvious social, economic and ecological reasons, there exists a major impediment: money-motivated politicians and Owner-magnates; for, although implementation of The CBEE would beneficially transform the status quo for the world and its Peoples, it would effectively pre-empt government collection of the phenomenal duty and revenues on fuel, and everywhere render to individual and small-scale private enterprises, the income and profits which now accrue undeservedly to the Prohibition-monopoly-protected Oil-Producing Countries and giant petroleum corporations.

In clarifying the status quo, consider the scale of money-motivation behind Cannabis Prohibition: Affecting Gross World Product, energy derived from fossils and uranium accounts for not less than eight-tenths of the underlying Cost of Production of all commercial Goods and Services. This four-fifths' (4/5) proportion of the world's peoples' total production of wealth, all duties, taxes and profits therefrom, has been brought by the means of monopoly-control-Prohibition to exclude cannabis, into the hands and under the control of, relatively speaking, a small group of men and women. Owner-magnates, and 'politicians' for whom as a proportion of world population almost nobody has voted, do not relish the prospect of Cannabis Relegalisation, i.e., of having to relinquish the world wealth which they have misappropriated; for the wealth to return to and remain with the People, who create it.

The Cannabis Biomass Energy Equation exposes the utmost money-motive, unmasking deepest criminality behind governments' controls on cannabis [1]. Hegemony, Monopoly, Ownership and/or Control of the multiple trillions involved, comprise the ulterior objects of the minute number of self-serving politicians, bureaucrats and magnates implicated. Financial motive is the reason behind controls on Cannabis. The plant has not been targeted for Prohibition because some people like to smoke it. The racket of tax, duty and profit protection of state-owned and private monopolies trading in the inferior resources and products is the root. However intense the ulterior motive, this does not mitigate the culpability of the culprits, nor the extreme gravitas of the results of their **Crime against Humanity**.

1 This money-motive is *additional* to those in significant economic areas other than energy; ref. Clinical Findings, and Judicial Enquiry Findings, Parts Three & Four.

THE REPORT. CANNABIS: THE FACTS, HUMAN RIGHTS AND THE LAW.

Knowledge and understanding of the evidence of circumstances expose the underlying financial motivation by which a spurious Prohibition is contrived feloniously on a substance that is not only harmless but also health-promoting. Legal availability of, and competition from, cannabis, annihilate duty, taxes and profits in businesses which rely for their income upon sales of inferior products and resources.

So great is the scale of monetary interest behind the criminal intrigue which masquerades as 'Prohibition', that, if there were no Prohibition, or if cannabis were relegalised today, it would be Prohibited again tomorrow. The RESTORATION Programme is indispensable. Nothing less than RESTORATION of the democratic control by citizen-jurors, of every act of enforcement of legislation, **by _re_-introduction** of the *authentic* Common Law Trial by Jury, *ensures elimination* of the corporate and government crime. Exceptional events and measures are required to restore the West to Democracy and legitimacy [1].

Readers having grasped the scale and implications of this government-corporate Crime will appreciate that to date, general public lack of awareness about The CBEE, in the U.K., the U.S. and therefore elsewhere, is attributable to *censorship* and dishonesty in state-controlled and privately-owned information, news and educational mass-media. Editors and reporters employed, and rigidly controlled by state and private Owners of the media, routinely conceal the cardinal truths about cannabis, and propagate lies to dupe the populace, who rely for their information upon the media or the state (rather than the professorial studies which exonerate and extol cannabis). The CBEE has support from our growing number of worthy endorsees and campaigners, including the Nobel laureate former Economic Adviser to the U.S. government who wrote the Foreword; and judges (U.S. and U.K.); doctors (of a variety of disciplines) and academics. At the time of this writing, The CBEE showing cannabis superior to fossils and uranium remains specialist information of which the media have gone out of their way to keep the public in the dark. This duplicates *the silent treatment* [2] by politicians and reporters of the published official empirical clinical investigations conducted by the eminent physicians, psychologists, toxicologists, sociologists, pharmacologists, psychiatrists, of world-respected academic and research institutions, which medico-scientifically exonerate cannabis from all allegations of 'harm' and 'impairment' [3]. Over all the years of Cannabis Prohibition, the published admissible expert evidence of Clinical Findings of Empirical Fact, has always affirmed the complete harmlessness, and benign nature of the herb as personal relaxant. (Ref. bibliography.) For self-advancement and gain, inscrutable professional liars, drug czars, 'advisers', career reporters and others, have actively supported tyranny by dissemination of damaging fictions about cannabis.

Disinformation is constantly spread through financed, organised, manipulated individuals, groups and media, to obtain public acceptance of Cannabis Prohibition. This malevolent mind-manipulation ('brainwashing') for money-motivated social control is intended to forestall a truthfully informed population from bringing appropriate pressure on governments to force Relegalisation. Ambitious Prohibitionist spokespersons and their rapacious leaders, to whom mendacity comes easily, rely on the population remaining insensate passive dupes.

1 Ref. Part Seven. Also see 'TRIAL BY JURY: Its History, True Purpose and Modern Relevance,' ISBN: 9781902848723, for stipulations of the Common Law Trial by Jury, by which democratic control is exerted over arbitrary venal government.
2 Economics' Nobel laureate Professor Milton Friedman coined this expression.
3 Ref. Findings of Fact, in Part One.

The Cannabis Biomass Energy Equation.

The adverse conditions generated by Cannabis Prohibition produce mortal consequences in a variety of ways. For example, in regard to the environment, Global Warming is attributed as cause to the increasingly destructive severity of weather, such as Hurricane Mitch (Dec. '98), the most catastrophic weather on record, the first of more and worse to come. Through the Caribbean and several Central American countries, Mitch wreaked large-scale damage, homelessness—and many thousands of human fatalities. The CBEE has shown that the Global Warming caused by misuse of fossils is totally unnecessary. It is unforgivable for politicians to have *failed* to date to implement The CBEE. Prohibitionists are directly culpable for deaths. The indictment of politicians for exacerbating Global Warming entails their culpability for mortalities and disasters worldwide, constituting crime of global enormity.

So, although liberation of cannabis offers huge benefits to the world and its peoples, which calls for relief and rejoicing, the complete vindication of private citizens' cultivation, trade, possession and use, is galling to media representatives of money-motivated untruth. These latter individuals are but paid henchmen and women. Their longstanding malicious collusion in the deadly criminal political connivance of Prohibition renders such personnel accountable participants in crime. It is small wonder that those *guilty* politicians and reporters give silent treatment to The CBEE and to the government-funded medico-scientific Studies of long-term cannabis smoking, by which cannabis is completely exonerated from all 'harm'. People do not publicise that evidence which incriminates them. . .

Thus, Green Issues constantly on the public agenda receive delusive reportage. There are many *pseudo*-greens, such as nature, wildlife 'conservation' organisations. The Chief Executive of falsely-named 'Greenpeace' claimed to be "too busy" to adopt and campaign for The CBEE. Political parties, including the so-called 'greens', evade The CBEE, because these groups are run by, or receive their funds from, Owners, corporations or organisations who *profit* by Cannabis Prohibition. Compromised and corrupted, their massive mendacity militates *against* environmental improvement.

Political parties vie for and receive funds from corporations whose Owners *profit* from Prohibition. Or, under the Italian system, parties take campaign funding from the state—whose financial motivation for Prohibition is acute. *All* Western political parties adopt money-motivated Prohibitions and/or The Fallacy of 'Decriminalisation'. (Ref. Part Six.) To be selected as a representative, candidates *have* to endorse the party position on cannabis. Hence, when citizens vote, whichever party's representative they choose, it can *only* be for a Prohibitionist. Voting is a delinquent activity which colludes with, and perpetuates, the criminal status quo.

Truth is replacing propaganda: The Scientific Green Solution's glad tidings, expressed in RESTORATION, crucial to every citizen of the World, are spreading.

Nations of the Earth's tropical regions, especially vulnerable to Global Warming, take note ! It is a cruel irony that impoverished populations in countries adversely affected by the high costs of fuel-energy are capable, by adoption of The CBEE, of becoming net energy *exporters*. Three (**3**) full cannabis crops can be grown per year in the world's warmer zones. RESTORATION proffers the immediate affluence of self-sufficiency in food, raw materials, and energy to such countries enjoying the enviable geographic advantage.

THE REPORT. CANNABIS: THE FACTS, HUMAN RIGHTS AND THE LAW.

The THC-rich, large, economically-effective Sativas embody Mankind's ideal crop. Capable of generating the cheap BTU's and virtually unlimited quantities of fuel for transportation and electricity generation, cannabis meanwhile provides food in abundance, a health-promoting personal relaxant tonic restorative, preferred paper-pulp and tree and timber substitutes, and is resource to cellulosic polymers (plastics and man-made fibres). Cannabis also provides superior natural 'breathing' fibres for all types of clothing from hardy water-resistant workwear to light sophisticated finery.

Production-cost-free cannabis hurds also provide quality 'mineralised' concrete: flaked hurds (which contain silica) mixed with lime (crushed calcium carbonate rock with H_2O and CO_2 driven off by heat) react when water is added, creating concrete. Called Isochanvre (French; Registered) this superb building material is of superior strength and sound/heat/damp insulation properties to, but only one-fifth to one-seventh the weight of, cement. Reducing price and weight but increasing strength of building materials challenges the imaginative architect consider, for example, the size made feasible of a building in Isochanvre, the same weight as Sears Tower, Chicago....

Populations resign themselves as passive spectators to their politicians' ravages to, and possible destruction of, the planet's ecosphere, while the fossil economy dangerously pours aeons of accumulated heat-retaining CO_2 into the atmosphere. Responsible citizens' due fury at the politicians' deadly activity is enfeebled by acceptance of Prohibitionists' deceit that pollution by coal and oil is "inevitable" if a high standard of living is to be achieved or maintained. The CBEE exposes politicians' untruth and base motives—there *is* an efficient, incomparably cheaper, clean alternative but, for abject mercenary reasons, it is unlawfully prohibited: cannabis.

Education on the qualities of cannabis and information on the Biomass Function, of which cannabis is the Economic Nonpareil (demonstrated by The CBEE) combine to impart awareness that:

With all cannabis production, trade and uses fully relegalised, worldwide increases in material prosperity are at hand, and international fraternal harmony is enhanced, while simultaneously improving the environment.

Relegalisation of Cannabis today will allow a phased, gradual economic transition governed by market forces, from fossil to CBEE-based techno-industrial civilisation: The Ecological Revolution. Economically outcompeted by cannabis, redundant reserves of pollutant coal, gas, oil and uranium will be left underground.

Prosperity and elusive modernity at last beckon even to those countries where cheap energy and resources have never before been in prospect. Whole populations of hardworking and gifted people, whose national economic development has been seriously impaired or completely retarded by expenditures on high-priced imports of fossil products consuming wholesale their capacity to earn surpluses of foreign and domestic currency, now have the opportunity through The Cannabis Biomass Energy Equation to become *self-sufficient*.

The Cannabis Biomass Energy Equation proffers benefits of historic proportions to the developing world, whose peoples are denied the security, plenty and progress of the Industrial, Technological and Ecological Revolutions, by their governments' compliance with the Western, illegal Prohibition of Cannabis.

The Cannabis Biomass Energy Equation.

All governments of financially straitened countries feel, or are, insecure. To these governments Western economic suzerainty is omnipotent and crucial, under the status quo. The means by which Prohibition of Cannabis is imposed worldwide is by the separate internal legislative enforcement measures taken by nation states to accord with the fabricated 'treaties' on dangerous drugs (e.g. the Single Convention) which fraudulently include cannabis.

The corrupt method by which Prohibitionist politicians and others of the West extract active participation in the felonious enforcement of Cannabis Prohibition from politicians of numerous developing nations, is by a simple but effective pecuniary lever: the granting of Aid and Trade status is tied to the condition that all countries recipient of the said aid and trade participate in the felonious Prohibition Treaties.

While many forms of sorely needed practical international assistance in technical, medical, and educational fields are underfunded, Western Prohibitionists promote the false and damaging idea that throughout the developing world the granting of Western loans and intergovernmental economic 'aid' (cash credit) is the only stabilising factor in a state of constant political flux and economic turmoil. (Routinely expended on weapons and luxury goods for those in power, Inter-Government Cash Credit 'Aid' is not to be confused with charitable emergency aid, such as food and medicine.) In fact, monetary 'aid' conjoined to the corrupting influences and many extreme, negative results of this coerced Prohibition, depresses recipient nations' self-development and prolongs their agonies of financial dependence.

Implementation of the Scientific Solution embodied in Cannabis Biomass Energy Equation offers the dignifying emancipation of economic independence, industrial and agronomical productivity, food and energy self-sufficiency, to affluent and developing nations alike.

For governments of developing nations to delay changeover from fossil and uranium, to Cannabis Biomass based economies, is for them to abet the criminal Western macro-economic Prohibition-racket, to enrich foreigners at the direct expense of their own poorer peoples. The individual politicians responsible commit treacherous repression of their populations' self-development, whilst abetting the aforedescribed Crimes against Peace and Humanity; they actively support economic imperialism, in exchange for cash.

By contrast, those developing nations which now sever the umbilication tying them to the acute debilities of Western cash aid by denouncing the Single Convention and other Prohibition treaties, in order to take up the natural economic bounty of cannabis relaxant-tonics, fibres, food, resources and fuels, will find in this change great relief. The benefits of financial independence securely founded upon self-sufficiency provided by The CBEE, will manifest themselves immediately.

Nations adopting The Cannabis Biomass Energy Equation's Scientific Green Solution will be rendering to Mankind an historic good deed, leading the world into a prosperous New Age of the clean technologies of the Cannabis Biomass Resource and Pyrolysis Functions. The first countries and companies to implement RESTORATION will inherit the Twenty-first Century. . . .

Two-thirds grown cannabis sativa,
pre-efflorescence and before budding stage.
Photo USDA.

The Cannabis Biomass Energy Equation.

CANNABIS: WORLD RESOURCES.

Cannabis remains the world's principal resource. *Many thousands* of commercial products seen in the home, school, office and factory, which now are produced from trees, man-made fibres, plastics, and petro-chemicals, made or processed using energy derived from fossils or uranium, can be produced *more economically* from cannabis itself, or energy derived therefrom. The following are principal categories:

FUEL (FUEL-ENERGY) OIL, LUBRICANTS. (For Electricity-Generation, Transportation, etc.)
PETRO-CHEMICAL, HYDRO-CARBON PRODUCTS.
PLASTICS. All plastic products and the. . . MAN-MADE FIBRES.

The Economics' proposition herein propounded as The Cannabis Biomass Energy Equation, i.e., that Cannabis economically outcompetes and renders commercially redundant the fossils and uranium, was given practical demonstration by Henry Ford: Cellulosic Polymerisation of vegetative matter in the 19th Century gave rise to the invention of plastics. This industry was developed from the use of cellulose in the production of explosives. By the late 1930's, **Henry Ford, the manufacturer**, was displaying a state of the art car [1] with bodywork made of plastic, lighter but "ten times stronger" than steel (safer for occupants) and not prone to oxidisation (rust). At the Ford "cracking" facility (pyrolysis reactor) at Iron Mountain, Michigan, he converted the biomass of (production-cost-free) cannabis hemp into the plastics to make the car and the non-polluting methanol fuel to run it. Prohibition introduced under false pretexts [2], quickly put paid to Ford's ideas which were then unable to progress further than the prototype of the car.

Enormous potentials and benefits to the World and its peoples are embodied in The CBEE—but they all remain conspiratorially repressed in felonious protection of undeserved profits of, amongst others, Owners of oil and petro-chemical corporations. Throughout the Western free-capital-owning democracies, the awareness, impartiality and incorruptibility of the state remain absolutely indispensable to the sustainment of legitimate constitutional democracy and the dispensation of justice. The extreme degree to which these criteria have been neglected by the dissoluteness of those who make pretence of serving the people may be judged by this fact: through Prohibition of Cannabis, the state's criminal protection of the great wealth of a very few, is enforced to the certain destruction of the best interests of the entire community. Examples abound daily—consider two from U.K. newspapers.

1. The European, 21-27 March, 1996: following improved profits, British Petroleum share payout worth nearly £11 million ($16m) to nine Directors.

2. Daily Mail, 23 March, 1996: following Glaxo takeover of Wellcome (pharmaceuticals; ref. Parts Three & Four) job-cuts are indicated of 7,500, while two Directors receive personal payouts worth over £2 million and £7.4 million respectively.

PERSONAL RELAXANT TONIC RESTORATIVE.

Cannabis is out of the ordinary in that it offers special advantages in the food, the economic agro-industrial, *and* the profound Health benefits, which exceed in number and excel in benefaction those of all other known plant species. Ref. Parts One, Three, Four and Five for Health-related issues.

1 See Popular Mechanics, December, 1941.
2 In 1937, the conspiring to eliminate by Prohibition 'law' the economic and other benefits to the masses proffered by cannabis, to protect government taxes and corporations' Owners' profits, was already fait accompli in Europe.

TEXTILES/FABRICS/NATURAL FIBRE: CLOTHING & PRODUCTS.
See The CBEE and Traditional Uses.

PAPER.
Cardboard-packaging, newspapers, journals, books, etc., place an enormous demand for paper products, to which cannabis comprises the ideal, *and production-cost-free*, economical resource. (See The CBEE and Traditional Uses.)

CHIPBOARD, PARTICLE BOARD.
Another replacement for the present costly reliance on trees, cannabis wood hurds are resource to modern furniture materials, and concrete-box template production for the construction industry.

BUILDING MATERIAL. (See Isochanvre in previous section.)

STAPLE FOOD.
(Seed does not contain relaxant ingredients.) Rich in protein and containing the amino acids essential to efficient functioning of the human immune system, seed can be substituted for the flesh of animals in the healthier human diet. It is excellent for milling and baking into bread, cereals, cakes, and in casseroles, (false) 'meat'-loaf, etc. Highly nutritious like soya, cannabis is source of plant milk, cheese, yoghurt curds, and cream. Raw or toasted in salads, the seed can also be ground into butter. The flavour is delicate and delicious. Cold-pressed seed provides polyunsaturated oil suited to cuisine for cooking and salad dressings. **(Also see The CBEE, & Traditional Uses to follow.)**

ERADICATION OF FAMINE
Cannabis, being easy to cultivate even in semi-arid, marginal land, would assist in eradicating world famine thoroughly, and in a way of which none of the other staple food species are capable. (See Special Attributes in The CBEE.)

PREVENTION AND REVERSAL OF DESERTIFICATION.
Seeding from suitable cargo-airplanes' (e.g. Hercules, Galaxy) overflights, will reclaim land suffering from recent and ongoing desertification. (North-East and Central Africa, Central Asia, Australia, etc.)

Variation on a Theme: Another Manifestation of the
Government Tax and Profit Protection Racket by Prohibition Monopoly.
Patented Cannabis Hybrids and Clones; Vegetated Propagation.
Natural plants propagated from seed, such as cannabis, cannot be *patented*. Cannabis also propagates well by cloning. This simple technique familiar to gardeners, eliminates variety produced by sexual reproduction (of male pollen-producing plants fertilising females which produce seed). Cuttings taken and planted quickly produce their own roots and grow into genetically identical copies, or clones, of the donor plant. N.B. Clones are the same **age** as their donor.

Consider the homogeneity (uniformity) of plantation produced tea, camellia sinensis for example, which is *economically* achieved from clones. The tropical tea plant is a tree, pruned for convenience of plucking, into a large flat-bush shape. Tea is a perennial, sprouting profusely all the year round, and living productively for sixty to a hundred years. One tea plant can yield many thousands of clones, which then live on. But none of this applies to cannabis, which lives for but a single season (around four months). Cannabis clones are only satisfactorily taken during the growth cycle (not the flowering cycle).

The Cannabis Biomass Energy Equation.

Young cannabis plants are rich in cannabidiolic acid (CBD) which can be extracted from the plant in inverse ratio to tetrahydrocannabinol (THC). The THC (which is chemically compounded within the plant with the other cannabinoid and vegetative ingredients forming an *other* substance which is cannabis ref. 'THC' Is Not 'Cannabis') can only be extracted in any significant quantity from *mature* plants, particularly from buds and flowertops. So, the plant has to be mature to be of use as a source of relaxant medication. This means the plant, whether propagated from seed or clone, will die shortly thereafter, necessitating the entire process be recommenced.

Clones and hybrids are merely copies or forms of the natural plant. The fact is: *natural cannabis and all related cultivation, trade and use are actually* **legal**: the Prohibition is unfounded, based on mendacity, inequitable and per se, **illegal**. Confirmed by the Empirical Studies and Medical Case Histories, *natural* THC-rich Cannabis Sativa is *the* health-promoting Personal Relaxant, and effective, safe, Preventive and Curative Medicament. (Ref. subsequent Parts.)

In relation to clones, at the time of writing, the British and Dutch governments have a new plot to participate in the "illegal" cannabis trade. By this scheme the state outlaws and punishes everyone, except a few favoured individual Owners, and their backers, who receive a fortune: the state issues preferred companies with lucrative licensed monopoly to cultivate cannabis and confers patents on hybrids and clones, which government designates as the *only* "legal" cannabis for prescription and sale. Special government duty is imposed on top of the exorbitantly priced cannabis. In addition, government skims off 30-40 per cent of profits via Corporation Tax.

This is not to dismiss cloning, selective breeding and experimentation, but the politicians', state-bureaucrats' and corporation Owners' transparent scheme is illegal, conspired from miscreants' greed. It is criminal, for it relies upon continued counterfeit Prohibition of natural cannabis. One does not seek to prohibit those who wish to produce cannabis from clones for commercial purposes from doing so. But on other than the very small scale, cloning is an unnecessary, time-consuming, costly method of producing the harmless plant. With naturally-produced cannabis Relegalised, cloning would be commercially unviable.

All controls on naturally produced cannabis are unlawful, grievous and driven by gain. By Exonerative Evidence, Circumstances and Res Gestæ, under existing national and international laws, all legislation and regulations of restriction are abrogated. All private individuals' normal traditional cannabis Production, Sale and Use are, and always have been, completely legal. State prosecutions of citizens' private cultivation, trade, possession and use are legally malicious; i.e., with pre-determined intent to commit crime, especially against the person.

Licensed Low-Yield Hybrids.

Licensed 'low-THC' strains and hybrids, which yield not more than 60 per cent of the biomass and fibre of the full-blooded 'THC-rich', 20-foot Sativas, constrict for no (*good*) reason the quantity and purposes of crop production of cannabis per acre, to the economic detriment of cultivators, farmers and society. Seen in The CBEE, that variety of cannabis which produces plentiful relaxant-tonic, fibres, seed, and hurds-yielding biomass, being optimised commercially, proffers Mankind the epoch-making benefit of production-cost-free cannabis fuel-energy *replacing* fossils, uranium, and *misuse* of trees as industrial 'resource'. In their paper 'Cultivation, Extraction, and Analysis of Cannabis Sativa L.,' Doorenbos et al observed:

THE REPORT. CANNABIS: THE FACTS, HUMAN RIGHTS AND THE LAW.

"Environmental factors...are not as important as heredity in determining the cannabinoid content of harvested marijuana, contrary to the widespread belief that warmer and sunnier climates produce the most potent marijuana." [1] In cultivation, the soil and climate are relatively minimal factors in influencing inherent traits, such as the relaxant and the biomass (size), these being pre-determined by the Laws of Genetics (cf: Mendel).

1 See Annals of the New York Academy of Sciences, 191, December 31st, 1971, 3-14.

THE TRADITIONAL USES OF CANNABIS.

The official Empirical Studies of long-term, actual human use confirm: cannabis herb-hash has no adverse effect to mental or physical health (is harmless); does not cause skill impairment; does not cause physical or psychological dependence (is non-addictive); is incapable in any quantity of causing fatality to humans and animals (is non-toxic); and has numerous unique good effects on human health (is benign). Prohibitionists *knowingly* spread incorrect derogation about benign cannabis [2].

It is reasonable to assume that since some early prehistoric time when Mankind first found the smoke of burning cannabis plants to be pleasant and recuperative, the 'smoking' of this safe herb became commonplace. It has remained widespread. Hash(ish) consists only of the resin-rich flowers and buds (if the leaves are included the product is considered of lower quality); with twigs removed and when dry, these crumble easily into powder which is lightly baked (warmed) and, with press or rolling-pin, is formed into cakes (slabs). This is then crumbled, and smoked pure in a pipe, or sprinkled in with cannabis foliage and rolled into a pure cannabis herbal cigarette.

Controls and/or rationing, i.e., Prohibition itself, *create* the Black Market, cause scarcity in supply and soaring prices. Prohibition causes unscrupulous Black Market producers and dealers to 'cut' (mix) wholesome cannabis herb and hash with toxic substitutes (datura, grass, henna, glue, etc.) to make supplies go further for increased profit. If hash does not crumble readily at room temperature, it is likely to have been contaminated. Similarly, to render "effects" to consumers, poor quality, inert but harmless herb is systemically 'fed' or sprayed with substances poisonous to humans, or drenched in toxified liquids, then dried before sale. Self-evidently, it is incorrect to ascribe to beneficial cannabis, effects which derive from other substances.

Cannabis was probably the first seed-food plant cultivated (pre-dating the grasses). Professor Carl Sagan proposes in 'The Dragons of Eden' that, long before The Bronze Age and the first use of metals by Man, the cultivation of cannabis may well have developed into the discovery, or 'invention', of (the Science of) Agriculture, giving rise to the first post-nomadic settlements and thence to incipient civilisation.

According to the Science of Archaeology, the earliest examples of woven fabric, which date from Neolithic (Stone Age) times, are made from cannabis fibres [3]. Mummies from Egyptian and other cultures were swathed in cannabis. For all time, most of Mankind's clothing has been of cannabis. Swaddling-clothes were made from cannabis.

Since pre-history until circa 1850, cannabis was the world's principal resource to food, products and artefacts, giving rise to the greater part of human industry, agriculture and employment, comprising the largest single contributor to Gross World Product.

2 Ref. Parts One, Three, Four & Five, for Health-related information.
3 See 'Man and Marijuana,' R. E. Schultes, Harvard University; Natural History, 82, Aug-Sept, 1973.

The Cannabis Biomass Energy Equation.

Cannabis has numerous applications, including the following:

- personal relaxant-medicament

- textiles, from mature and post-mature plants. Dating from the most ancient times, all of history's merchant ships and navies were equipped with cannabis (hemp) fibre sails.

  Hemp and *cannabis* are synonymous, hemp being the ancient Anglo-Saxon word for cannabis.
  (TEXTILES: Also ref. section III of The Economics of The CBEE.)

- fabric, from *densely sown, immature plants*, for all types of garments. Chronicler Herodotus, the Father of History, 490-425 B. C., remarked on the fineness of the hempen raiment the Thracians produced and dressed in. Over the ages, cannabis has provided by far the greater part of Mankind's fibre requirements, cotton and flax contributing a negligible quantity by comparison, to the total, until invention of the labour-saving cotton gin in Victorian times. Hemp fibre-from-woodhurds mechanisation (e.g. Schlichten) was not developed until 1916. According to Encyclopaedia Britannica (1890's, 1910) at least 50 per cent, and more probably, all but a minimal amount of the fabric popularly called 'linen' was not made from flax, but from cannabis (hemp).

  Finest fibres of immature cannabis plants are not less than 4 times stronger than the strongest of cotton. Cannabis is thus proportionately more durable, maintaining its appearance, and is of better value and greater utility to consumers. Levi's Originals (19th Century) and latterly 'denim' from China were/are made from *mature* fibres of cannabis.

  Of all natural fibre sources, cannabis is uniquely water-rot resistant. The superior fibre quality and cultivability of cannabis make it resource to textiles of economic advantage, but when eventually worn out, they were traditionally collected by the "rag-man", or the "rag 'n' bone man", for their re-cycled value as the source of long-lasting *paper* for books and bibles, etc.

- thread, yarn, twine, cordage, rope, cables and matting

- canvas, tarpaulins, art canvas.

  The Dutch word 'canvas' is derived from the Latin, Cannabis, Greek, Kannabis; Sumerian-Babylonian linguistic precursor to the Euro-Semitic-Indo Group languages' Kan-a-ba, i.e.,, the reed, or "*cane-of-two*" (ba or bis) genders. (Cannabis is dioecious, having the male and female sexes on separate plants; hermaphrodites are not usual.)

- carpets, tapestries, curtains

- towelling. Cannabis feels softer, is warmer to the touch, and is more absorbent, than cotton.

- paper. Worn-out sailcloth fulfilled the greater part of paper requirement. Handwritten or printed, medieval books were principally made from cannabis. Extant examples show cannabis-paper (also called India paper) to have a shelf-life of well over a thousand years, ongoing, cannabis thus being incomparably superior paper-resource to the expensive latter-day attempts at alternatives made from trees.
  (PAPER: Also ref. section IV of The Economics of The CBEE.)

- pyrolytic fuel-oil (and vegetable oil) for the lighting of lamps—the fibres of the wick being of cannabis too. Until the relatively recent era of the mass slaughter of oil-yielding whales, followed on by petroleum products, cannabis oils provided the greater part of night light for Mankind throughout history.
  (OIL and PETRO-CHEMICAL PRODUCTS: Also ref. The Cannabis Biomass Energy Equation.)

- oil, tars, pitch, creosote oil, chemicals, paints, resins, protective coatings

- sealant. 'Oakum' is untwisted cannabis fibre rope steeped in tar and hot-pressed, i.e.,, caulked, into seams to render plank-joins watertight on the hulls of ships.

- varnish, preferred by artists for its speedy oxygenation, quick-drying

- linoleum floor covering, i.e.,, hemp fabric impregnated with cannabis oleum (oleum is the Latin word for oil)

- adhesives, glue; embalming fluids (used since Pharaonic times)
  (All the above items obtained by pyrolysis, wood distillation; ref. The CBEE)

- cosmetics, soap; antiseptic ointments, poultices; muscle cream; health-care products

- oleraceous herb, ingredient for cooking. Herbal tea; the decoction 'bhang', made from cannabis, is synonymous with Bengal, Bangalore, Bangkok, etc., and Bang-la-desh, which translates as People of the Land of Cannabis.

- vegetable oil (for cooking and salad dressings)

- seedcake (pressed) and seed. High protein, delectable food for humans. Recipe books are available in good bookshops. [Seed does not contain relaxant ingredients.] 'Seedcake' is the solid food remaining after seed has been cold-pressed to extract the oil. Seeds are achenes, one-seeded fruit.

- seed, seedcake. High quality animal and pet food.

RESTORATIONISTS.

Cannabis is no humble herb. Cannabis is the monarch of vegetative species which has existed in symbiosis with Mankind rendering important benefits at least since the dawn of the cultivation of mental faculties in Homo Sapiens. Accordingly, citizens who demand that the normal, fully-legal status of cannabis be resumed may suitably be referred to as: Restorationists. (Ref. RESTORATION.)

The smoking of cannabis flowers, foliage and hash in bongs and pipes, is described in many cultures in some of Mankind's earliest literature, since which time and up to the present day, cannabis taken in food and by smoking has been recommended as a generally health promoting tonic, and as prophylaxis (i.e.,, preventive medicament); and against malaria, as cure for leprosy, as vermifuge, and as antibiotic topical [i.e.,, local-to-the-injured area] poultice for wounds, amongst numerous other conditions [1].

Cannabis *"stimulates mental powers," "creates energy," "alleviates fatigue,"* is *"refreshing and stimulating," "creates the capacity for hard work and the ability to concentrate," "sharpens the wits,"* and *"sharpens the memory."* [2]

1 Despite Prohibition, Cannabis continues the recommended medical treatment for <u>over 100</u> illnesses and adverse conditions previously listed in the U.S. Pharmacopoeia (and others). Cannabis comprised not less than half of all medication sold. Also see British-Indian Hemp Commission's Report.
2 See British-Indian Hemp Commission's Report. These Findings of Fact are replicated in the official Empirical Studies; e.g. U.S.-Costa Rican, U.S.-Jamaican, etc.

The Cannabis Biomass Energy Equation.

Hindus and Buddhists share respect for cannabis as the Holy Plant given for *"the welfare of Mankind."* Cannabis is praised for its enjoyment, enlightenment, and healing properties, as in the Bhagavad-Gita, and the Sutra Scripts of antiquity regarded by Buddhists as sacred[1]. In his personal writings on the subject of cannabis, George Washington expressed *"a preference for the female flowertops."* (U.S. National Archives.) Flowertops and buds are the most pleasing parts of the cannabis plant for smoking. There is no known use for the flowertops except for smoking or otherwise ingesting them for relaxant/health use.

1 See British-Indian Hemp Commission's Report.

The Way Ahead: RESTORATION.

Education interpreting the Universal Order observes that Mankind's progress from the savage state is marked and facilitated by events such as the Mastery of Fire; by Inventions, of Writing, of Machines such as the Wheel, the Steam and Internal Combustion Engines, the Micro-processor; by Discoveries, of Magnetism, Electricity, Genetics, Radio-Waves, and so on. Invention (or discovery) of the Science of Agriculture and application of production techniques such as the Division of Labour accommodated the requirements of growing populations, and so altered the human modus vivendi as to deserve description by the term 'revolution', as in the Industrial Revolution. RESTORATION proffers a similar departure: The Ecological Revolution.

RESTORATION and Universal Adoption of Constitutional Common Law Trial by Jury [2] assure the Justice of Relegalisation of Cannabis, which secures **abundance** of World Production of Food, Energy and Resources: for the first time in Mankind's history, **scarcity** *is eliminated, and* the Universal Re-Democratisation of Fuel-Energy Production becomes simple and feasible. As staple food is produced everywhere today, so too duty-free Cannabis-Methanol production will be ubiquitous. By RESTORATION, prolific production of cheap high quality food, fuel and raw materials becomes reality; derived essentials, 'luxury' and convenience artefacts realise their true low market price; amelioration of the World Standard of Living is achieved. Elimination of Scarcity and Want actuates a beneficial psychological influence diluting Avarice, dissolving within many individuals their motivation to crime, at all levels. RESTORATION sets in place the basis for *elimination* of *material-acquisition-derived* strife, and the Wars of Aggression: relative Peace on Earth. Given the political intent to achieve these goals of a social order befitting an advancing Human Race, the Elimination of Scarcity is the foundation for a heretofore unrealisable globalised financial security and human Egalitarianism, founded, not on *government* control, but on government *controlled* by citizens' democratic authority Restored, embodied in the *constitutionally explicit intention* of the Common Law Trial by Jury: i.e.,, the democratic **nullification** by jurors of the enforcement of *unjust* laws [3]. Such government cannot but represent and serve the interests of *all* the People.

The indispensable philosophical response to the universal human requirement is embodied in RESTORATION. Material and social benefits to all become practicable by proven measures in RESTORATION: scarcity is eliminated; tyranny is eradicated; democratic control is reaffirmed; and the dispensation of Justice by citizen-Jurors again becomes the Good Way of Life. To achieve RESTORATION, first of all, by any democratic procedures necessary, criminal Prohibitionists must be vanquished.

2 & 3 Throughout the West, this correct form of due process, prescribed by universal Common Law, has been rendered defunct by unlawful and unconstitutional government interventions. Ref. the Constitutional information in Part Seven. Also see: TRIAL BY JURY: Its History, True Purpose and Modern Relevance, ISBN: 9781902848723.

MOTIVE: A Recapitulation.

THE CANNABIS BIOMASS ENERGY EQUATION shows that amelioration of the world's peoples' Standard of Living by global provision of economical (i.e.,, very cheap) superior Energy, Food and Resources (the essentials of human life), and the Universal Re-Democratisation of Fuel-Energy Production can easily, and immediately, be realised. This would yield to domestic, small-scale and localised private enterprises, the profits which currently accrue undeservedly to giant corporations and oil-producing countries; and would render the present arbitrary duties and revenues from fuel, uncollectable.

De facto monopoly on fuel-energy production and provision is obtained solely by the covert conspiratorial means of Prohibition on Cannabis. Fuel-energy for industrial and domestic use at present derives from fossils, uranium and alternatives all significantly expensive compared to the free fuel-energy by-product sourced from cannabis.

As a catastrophic result of Prohibiting cannabis, the world's most prolific and economical fuel-energy resource, fuel-energy presently accounts for not less than four-fifths (4/5) of the Cost of Production of Gross World Product: i.e.,, all commercial Food, Goods and Services. By Cannabis Prohibition, all of the duties, taxes and profits on fuel-energy provision, that is, the four-fifths proportion of the world's peoples' total Production of Wealth, have been brought into the hands and under the control of a small group of men and women. Owner-magnates of oil-producing countries and corporations, and politicians, for whom as a proportion of world population almost nobody has voted, do not intend to relinquish control of the Wealth of the World which they have stealthily misappropriated.

Knowledge and understanding of the evidence of facts and circumstances expose the underlying financial motivation by which a spurious Prohibition is contrived feloniously on a substance that is not only harmless but also health-promoting. Legal availability of, and competition from, cannabis, annihilate duty, taxes and profits in businesses which rely for their income upon sales of inferior products and resources.

THE CANNABIS BIOMASS ENERGY EQUATION exposes and measures the utmost scale of money-motivation behind the illegal controls on cannabis. Regarding fuel-energy, The CBEE reveals the duty, tax and corporate profit-protection racket that is the tyrannical State Crime of Cannabis Prohibition. This is additional to the corrupt money-motives behind Prohibition exposed in other Parts of THE REPORT.

To the mortal detriment of the World and its Peoples, hegemony, control and Monopoly-Ownership of the trillions involved are the ulterior objects of the minute number of self-serving criminal politicians, bureaucrats and magnates implicated.

- PART THREE -

Prevention Is Better Than Cure...
Cannabis as Preventive Measure and Preventive Medicine.

CANNABIS merits complete Relegalisation on grounds of Health. There is no wisdom, nor genuine philanthropy, in the proposals of 'partial' legalisation, that is, only to 'legalise' cannabis for medical purposes restricted to specific applications in curative medicine. There is no consistency in limiting the legal availability of its salutary benefits only to those who are already sick, when one considers the following:

Firstly, the socio-scientific Empirical Studies establish that where cannabis is easily acquired, it often replaces alcohol as the preferred recreational substance, diminishing overall alcohol consumption. In addition to being an *official* Finding of Fact, this Finding is also widely acknowledged by cannabis smokers. Non-addictive, non-toxic **cannabis reduces or *obviates altogether*** the negative results induced by toxic, habit-forming alcohol, including such as: the incidence of alcohol abuse; mortality; crime; alcohol-induced disease; addiction; accidents; murder; rape; child-rape; incest; wife-beating; absenteeism; productivity losses; *and*, the loutish behaviour induced by drunkenness is also mitigated or pre-empted [1]. The Studies also establish that cannabis replaces the use of drugs other than alcohol, i.e., cannabis healthily supplants entirely or partially, the consumption of the addictive substances, *mitigating their associated destructive results* [2].

Profound Findings and Conclusions are inferred by and from Studies such as those of the U.S.-Jamaican [3], and others [4], in which the acute alcohol-related social problem endemic in neighbouring Caribbean islands where cannabis use is unknown does not exist in those nearby regions where cannabis is easily available. The Studies note that when available, ganja [cannabis] largely replaces spirits; for example, rum. Considering the enormous mortality-rate and disease caused by alcohol and tobacco, it is providential that benign cannabis reduces their use and safely replaces them.

Cannabis use is a **measure preventive** of illness and death brought on by drugs. De jure, private cannabis related activities are in all respects legal: recognition of this fact by statutory Cannabis Relegalisation is mandatory. In regard to the use of relaxants by the population, on grounds of public health, **endorsement** of cannabis in preference to tobacco and alcohol, has long been due from state departments; viz: health, education, justice, enforcement; and by politicians. This is substantiated by the state's own publication of statistics (e.g. see page 2) which show the many dread effects of tobacco and alcohol, and which, by comparison, emphasise Absolute Safety of non-drug cannabis for personal use. The perverted character of all who consent to the illegal legislative controls on cannabis is evident.

1 Ref. U.S. National Institute on Drug Abuse Alcohol Statistics in: Harm and Danger in Perspective.
2 Ref. Modern Medical Uses, in Parts Three & Four.
3 'Ganja in Jamaica; A Medical Anthropological Study of Chronic Marijuana Use,' U.S. National Institute of Mental Health.
4 ON: "Reduction of Alcohol Use by Cannabis Smokers" and: "Cannabis, the Benevolent Alternative to Alcohol," see 'Alcoholism and Drinking Practices in a Jamaican Suburb,' Paper delivered by Dr. M.H. Beaubrun to H. Goldman International Lecture, New York City Medical College; and: 'Cannabis or Alcohol: The Jamaican Experience,' by Dr. M.H. Beaubrun in 'Cannabis And Culture,' Ed. Vera Rubin; Mouton de Gruyter Press, The Hague.
Also: 'Cannabis or Alcohol? Observations on Their Use in Jamaica,' by R. Prince, R. Greenfield and J. Marriott, in U.N. Bulletin on Narcotics, 24 (1) Jan-March, 1972, pp. 1-9.
The finding that cannabis smokers consume less alcohol than non-cannabis-smokers, is also reported in 'Drugs and the Public,' by empirical research conductor Professor Norman Zinberg (Harvard University) and John Robertson; New York, Simon and Schuster; and 'Marijuana: The New Prohibition,' by Professor John Kaplan; New York, World.

THE REPORT. CANNABIS: THE FACTS, HUMAN RIGHTS AND THE LAW.

The greater proportion of the population assert their need or preference for legal availability of a 'recreational' substance: it is *deadly* for 'law' to deny people the choice of cannabis, the only one which is safe, and which has the propensity to mitigate, to reduce—and to preclude altogether—people's use of harmful drugs. Cannabis smoking constitutes **Preventive Medicine**. The 'law' and all controls are legally untenable: the fatal 'law' is abrogated.

Nota Bene: Cannabis is only and always benign and conducive to good health. The medico-scientific researches of long-term use conclude cannabis smoking has no adverse effects, and, in particular, cannabis protects the lungs from pollutants such as tobacco smoke (ref. Part One). Also, for example, the U.S. National Institute of Mental Health and Jamaican government empirical investigations of long-term use, with the specific medical brief to find negative results, if any, *conclude that*:

Cannabis smoking has no adverse effect on mental or physical health. Clinical findings throughout the Study support that conclusion. In particular, see pages: 78, 104, 143, 144, 148, 149, 150, 152, 155, 156 & 166.

Secondly (in addition to comprising the aforedescribed Preventive Measure *which is preventive medicine*), the use of cannabis is prophylaxis, i.e., preventive medicine, in that the regular ingestion of cannabis is demonstrated to *prevent* adverse medical conditions from occurring. Cannabis can also prevent the progressive worsening of conditions and diseases. (This is as differentiated from post facto, *curative* medicine; modern uses of cannabis as treatment and curative factor in medicine are considered in more detail hereinafter.)

For example, sufferers of multiple sclerosis have discovered that by the regular use of cannabis they have *prevented* the symptoms of the condition from affecting their normal lives, until the supply stopped. Sufferers from epilepsy, or asthma, arthritis, stress-related psychosomatic conditions, anorexia and anorexia nervosa, acute pruritis, and scores of other afflictions, have had the same experience. Another example: it has never been possible to predict in any particular individual, the incidence of glaucoma, which can cause blindness. Smoking cannabis reduces intra-ocular pressure, effectively *preventing* glaucoma, *and saves eyesight*. The use of cannabis is effective Preventive Medicine. Modern Medical Case Histories confirm the traditional applications: regular cannabis smoking **prevents** the incidence of adverse symptoms and onset of the condition. If cannabis had always been completely legal for any use, and thus the supply unimpeded, these people would not have developed serious symptoms; and they would hardly notice their illness or condition.

There can be few people who could honestly deny benefits from stress-relief. Stress is frequently the precursor to physical and/or mental degeneration, the stress itself being an aetiological (causal) agent in psychosomatically induced, adverse physical conditions, and/or negative behavioural patterns. Cannabis Relegalised as over-the-counter commodity to be freely used as a matter of personal choice, or of medical recommendation, makes available the safe relaxant, effective in relief of stress, and *preventive* of the development of adverse symptoms. Such use of cannabis is prophylaxis, preventive medicine. Cannabis is thus required to be generally available to the public again as a substance of unrestricted cultivation, trade, possession and choice, as smoked tonic-relaxant and for occasional or regular dietary intake.

Prevention Is Better Than Cure

Definitively, personal use of cannabis serves one purpose: **Health**. Cannabis is of great value to Mankind to promote good health. Personal, or 'recreational', use is *concurrently* medical use as Preventive Measure and Preventive Medicine. When all the facts are truthfully confronted, there is only **one** category of cannabis for personal use: all use is medical.

The proposal for selective 'exemption' from the Prohibition is, occasionally, the *emotional* response of sympathetic human beings to the needs of seriously ill or moribund patients. In this instance, proposing 'partial' legalisation derives from ignorance; an impulsive reaction of the heart, not the head. It is spurious on the health grounds on which it purports to be based. To 'legalise' cannabis for *only* the already-sick is inimically discriminatory, because it leaves the other group, who comprise the huge majority, condemned to inevitable deterioration of their health by unmitigated use of alcohol and/or tobacco, until they too fall prey to disease and early death. Catastrophic results to health, now widespread in populations, are inflicted by Prohibition of Cannabis as Preventive Measure and Preventive Medicine. The damage would be mitigated, or avoided entirely, by Relegalised private cultivation and supply.

There are individuals and groups who suggest 'partial' legalisation of cannabis as a regulated prescription-medicine for some of its *curative* applications (such as relief of the chemically-induced nausea of cancer chemotherapies). They concede to the illegal Prohibition of Cannabis as the Personal Relaxant for Preventive Measure: through utmost callousness, these individuals disregard the exonerative Findings of Fact; they ignore the potential for radical improvement in the standard of health and life of huge numbers of people, by voluntary reduction of the use of alcohol and tobacco, i.e.,, **Preventive Measure**; they overlook the need for cannabis of those many people, as previously mentioned, whose health would be maintained *before* getting ill; they ignore those people whose health would be *improved*, and still others whose life would be *saved*, by cannabis as prophylaxis, **Preventive Medicine**. Individuals who propose the selective exemptions from Prohibition, i.e.,, 'partial' legalisation, like to portray themselves as doing 'good', but their idea is far from altruism. It is *unethical*, for it *evades* issues of Human Rights, Justice, Equity, and Common and Substantive law; and it is *malignant*, in that it atrociously disregards some of the most significant medical virtues unique to cannabis: Preventive Measure and Preventive Medicine. **Prevention is better than cure**. Although availability of cannabis as cure is imperative too, the primary health rôle for personal cannabis use is Preventive.

The aware, informed and responsible citizen with a conscience—whether or not they have seen at first hand the Hospice Cancer Ward or the terminal stages of Alcoholism—cannot fail to be incensed by the cruelty and malice aforethought expressed in all the so-called 'legislation' and 'regulations' which control cannabis. Denial of legal availability of life-saving Preventive Cannabis *premeditatedly and maliciously causes early deaths*. By definition and in law, this constitutes murder (U.K.) homicide (U.S.). The need of 'politicians' and others implicated to cover up their wrongdoing and to conceal their culpability for Capital and other Crimes Against Humanity, explains the invention of the derogatory fictions circulated about benign cannabis.

To recapitulate: To both the sick and the hale, cannabis serves but a single purpose: the Health of people; use by all is medical.

The figmental 'division' between 'medical' and 'recreational' use is arbitrary nonsense fabricated for the concealed malevolent purpose behind the 'legislation'. Although the language is convenient, it is actually untruthful to describe Personal Relaxant use of cannabis by the term *recreational*. This misuse of language puts the non-drug cannabis into a fallacious association with the widely used recreational *drugs*. The use, 'recreational' or otherwise, of any substances which are *drugs*, such as heroin, alcohol, tobacco, caffeine, morphine, crack, amphetamines, etc., invites dire effects, addiction, disease and death. (Ref. Mortality Statistics.) By contrast, personal use of cannabis, which is not a drug (ref. definition in Part One), uniquely amongst so-called 'recreational' substances, is always tonic, stress-relieving and good for health. It should be emphasised that even frequent, long-term use of cannabis has no deleterious effect. Note, Merck Manual, Official Field Guide of the U.S. Armed Forces (the most widely sold medical text in the world) states on page 1490:

"Chronic administration [long-term use] of cannabis produces no physical dependence and no evidence of social or psychic dysfunction."

Complete Relegalisation of Cannabis provides the healthy population with the pleasant safe relaxant to use as Preventive Medicine, and, to reduce consumption of malady-causing drugs such as alcohol and tobacco, i.e.,, Preventive Measure. At the same time, Relegalisation makes cannabis available to patients and the medical profession, as *curative* medicine of recommendation and advice. Thus, the aims of the 'partial' legalisation lobbies are simultaneously achieved, without ignoring the equally deserving needs of those of the population whose health requirement for cannabis is as prophylaxis, or to replace noxious alcohol and tobacco.

If cannabis had remained unrestrictedly available for cultivation, trade, possession and use, i.e.,, a substance of legal choice, the multiple millions of deaths from cancers induced by tobacco, could in many, theoretically even all, cases, have been *prevented*. This also applies to alcohol-associated disease. **Prohibitionists** are all those people who accept any controls on cannabis. The men and women who instigate, enforce, or who consent to or permit controls, are instrumental in and culpable for deaths. To consent to any measure is to share responsibility for its results. (Part Six.)

Cannabis is preventive and curative in a wide variety of illnesses and disorders: its legality for all uses must be recognised by rescindment of control legislation. Defence of the People is the foremost duty of all governments, this to include life, health and well-being of the population. At present, those people who wish to use a 'recreational' substance have only the forced choice of the potentially death-inducing *drugs*, such as alcohol and tobacco. Governments' Prohibition of safe non-drug cannabis as alternative relaxant of choice is therefore an especially nefarious crime.

The Prohibition breaches Common Law, Equity, Human Rights, and results in *illegal* arrests, fines, forfeitures and incarceration. The Prohibitionists in some parts of the world execute people for completely harmless cannabis activities. The extreme gravity of the State Crime of Cannabis Prohibition is made evident by consideration of the Health aspects. Cannabis as Preventive Measure and Preventive Medicine could prevent much disease and early death amongst the People. Conversely, the Prohibition controls **cause** the pandemic disease and early deaths. Prohibitionists are guilty of murder.

Prevention Is Better Than Cure

Another Malign Motive behind Cannabis Prohibition; and, The Counterproductive Effects of Pre-Sale Fiscal Measures.

Relegalised availability of cannabis to promote public health by safely replacing consumption of alcohol and tobacco (and other drugs) would have impact on alcohol and tobacco companies' profits, significantly reducing Corporation Tax received by the government therefrom, and diminish the stupendous government revenues from duty on tobacco and alcohol. These factors generate large-scale financial incentive, the malign motive, to prohibit cannabis from the health-promoting voluntary reduction and replacement of social use of pathogenic drugs tobacco and alcohol.

That cannabis is the absolutely safe beneficial substance with which to replace alcohol and tobacco, is an officially-derived, empirically established reality, which the much-publicised derogatory fictions are designed to conceal. In particular, alarming carcinogen allegations are refuted as completely fictitious [1]. Relegalised, Preventive cannabis will assist people to be freed from, or to avoid altogether, their development of dependence on addictive substances, this leading to a healthier society. **The less cannabis is allowed to exert its good influence as Preventive Measure throughout society, the worse the problems associated with drugs become.**

That non-drug cannabis **replaces** the often fatal drugs alcohol and tobacco, and other drugs such as amphetamines, opiates, morphine, codeine, methadone, heroin, tranquillisers, mood- elevators, etc., demonstrates in the most conclusive way that cannabis is no "gateway" and does not "lead" to the use of drugs. The influence of cannabis is towards avoidance and replacement of the use of drugs. The Finding of the New York Academy of Medicine, that cannabis use ***"does not predispose to any crime, even that of using drugs,"*** [2] is unanimously concurred with by the other Empirical Studies.

On health grounds, the production-cost-free [3], inexpensive relaxant flowertops and foliage should always be kept free from duties, sale tax, and trading licenses, etc.: such fiscal measures cannot be justified because they vitiate the herb's life-saving propensity, by regular use, to achieve mitigation, moderation and replacement of both legal and illicit drugs, disease-inducing alcohol, tobacco, heroin, morphine, etc. Sale tax duties are **malignant**, because they result in cannabis becoming *too costly* to consumers for *regular* use, which causes, or forces, people to resort to lethal alcohol. Duty nullifies the essential beneficial attribute of Relegalised cannabis to achieve voluntary reduction in overall public consumption of pernicious drugs, alcohol, etc.

As noted, the profit, duty and tax yielded by alcohol engenders the financial motivation *to prohibit* cannabis from replacing it.... It is often said more in truth than jest that the corporations have the parliamentary and congressional representatives "in their back pocket." **All** fiscal and control measures on cannabis are disguised **monopoly** schemes, intended to protect profits and taxes yielded from trade of other resources and products inferior to cannabis, which cannabis will outcompete and cheaply replace when relegalised; e.g. alcohol, numerous toxic pharmaceuticals, trees for paper, cement, ordinary cotton, coal, oil, uranium, petro-chemicals, man-made fibres, etc. Ref. Part Two. However, *post*-sale income and profits from the cannabis trade may be subjected to tax, as for other produce, such as tomatoes, wheat, tea, etc.

1 Cannabis smoking protects lungs from pernicious effects of tobacco smoke and other pollutants; ref. **Cannabis Smoke Distinguished from Tobacco Smoke; Part One.**

2 See Chapter 1 of the NYAM Empirical Study.

3 Cannabis cultivated for profitable protein-rich staple seed food crops renders all the many by-products, including relaxant flowertops and foliage, production-cost-free. N.B. Seed does not contain relaxant ingredients. Ref. Part Two.

Loss of State Revenues; Prohibition of Alcohol.

Alcohol Prohibition deprived the state of revenues normally levied on commercial alcoholic beverages: before Alcohol Prohibition was enacted (the proposed Constitutional Amendment passed through the Senate in December, 1917) aggregate receipts to the state from internal revenues in fiscal year 1916 were $513 million, with alcohol being the single largest source at $241 million (distilled spirits $153 million, fermented liquors $88 million). By comparison, income tax yielded $68 million. (U.S. government figures.) Prohibition also costs taxpayers increasing sums spent on the general failure of police enforcement, followed by more expenditures on courts, the legal process and prisons, to prosecute citizens accosted for production and/or supply, out of a large alcohol-consuming population. (Alcohol Prohibition was of the intensely crime-producing 'decriminalisation' format.) Governments' *waste* of taxpayers' revenues debilitates states' ability to protect citizens from real crime.

Following Alcohol Relegalisation, tax revenues received from the industry and its normal trade are available for social uses. After Cannabis Relegalisation, post-sale tax levied on income and profits from trade in commercial cannabis products will yield revenues with the whole of society, including non-consumers of cannabis, benefiting. Cannabis Relegalisation could bring about a health-promoting drop in alcohol and tobacco sales. The depletion of revenues from the tobacco and alcohol trades will be compensated for:

firstly, by revenues from profits from the Relegalised trade in cannabis; i.e.,, Income and Corporation Tax on cannabis trade activities will provide ample revenues; and *secondly*, by generating a healthier and more productive society; e.g. Productivity Losses caused by illness and absenteeism induced by Alcohol & Tobacco consumption respectively, average over $100 billion and $52 billion per annum (U.S. government figures); *thirdly*, the healthier society requires less expenditure on socialised medicine; and *fourthly*, by 100 per cent savings on governments' phenomenal Cannabis Prohibition enforcement and propaganda budgets.

NOTA BENE. Despite the above pecuniary advantages, overriding money-motive causes governments to install Cannabis Prohibition **to control energy supplies**, for the hegemony and massive revenues seized therefrom, by which an extreme, but unspoken, oppressive communist status prevails:

Nationalised Ownership of subterranean minerals (coal, oil, uranium, etc.), has long been claimed by the state, by which government today parasitically extracts an overweening excess of money from the population, with gravest results to the people and economies of both the industrialised and developing countries.

First of all, at the great cost of a **monopoly**-license issued by governments, corporations trade in the minerals; the state then also takes significant sale tax/duty; e.g. currently in the U.K., **tax** accounts for **78 per cent** of the **price** of fuels, with similar extortions throughout the E.U. and elsewhere. When fuel commerce passes between companies at any stage of extraction, refinement, transport, marketing and retail, the state takes Value Added Tax; Local Government Taxes are demanded from businesses; *and* the state takes 30-40 per cent of the profits of companies involved, by Corporation Tax. Not fuel itself, but **governments' taxes** render fuel-energy accountable for four-fifths (4/5) of the Cost of Production of Gross World Product, all commercial goods and services, thereby ravaging the global economy and crushing productivity.

Prevention Is Better Than Cure

Wholesome food and commodity *plants*, tomatoes, wheat, cannabis, cotton, *privately grown* in the backyard, the market garden, allotment or farm, cannot, in any ostensibly democratic society, be subject to such State Ownership, controls or claims. Cannabis **hurds** are *production-cost-free by-products* of cannabis cultivated for seed, relaxant, paper, Dresden cotton, etc., and form the resource to virtually *unlimited* pyrolytic, **free** high quality fuel, all hydrocarbon petro-chemical products, and plastics. Cannabis may be grown for the former variety of purposes; the lubricants and fuel can be produced discreetly; ref. the Home Pyrolysis Still, Part Two. By Relegalisation, market forces would encourage achievement of profitable domestic and local private production, and cheap sale, *everywhere* of superior non-polluting cannabis-methanol: the Re-Democratisation of Fuel-Energy Production. Relegalisation would incomparably vitalise the world economy (ref. The CBEE) and, beneficially, would put an end to governments' ability to charge duty arbitrarily on fuel. Hence, utmost money-motive corrupts politicians to control cannabis. In re Cannabis Prohibition, over 80 per cent of the world population is excluded from a reasonable Standard of Life *by politicians*.

Unlawful fiscal measures of partial "legalisation" of cannabis production and trade are planned and proposed by those with vested (monetary) interests, namely, magnates, politicians, bureaucrats and others, to enrich the state and some few selected private beneficiaries. (Ref. Patented Cannabis Hybrids and Clones; Part Two.) These criminogenic Prohibition schemes include: licenses (limitedly available); Production and Trade permitted only by preferred corporations; controlled supply outlets; re-sale price maintenance; and, pre-sale tax and duties on cannabis similar to those on prescription opiates and alcohol, etc. However, the official Empirical Evidence (summarised herein) exonerates cannabis, and shows *all* state interventions and controls on cannabis are legally untenable: they have damaging, and lethal, effects to individual and society; further, *all* fiscal schemes and state controls on cannabis (i.e.,, Prohibitions) *create* a criminal Black Market, and *engender* all associated crimes. To cause crime to occur is a crime per se, and to be accountable for the crime, legally and morally. By common law, the legislation is of itself illegal; and all acts of its enforcement constitute judicable crime per se. (Ref. Parts Six & Seven.)

Stepping Stones; Prohibition of Alcohol.

Alcohol Prohibition is observed to have caused non-criminal citizens who merely wished to indulge their taste for alcohol to have to expose themselves to the compromising company of criminals in its purchase. In order to obtain a Black Market supply many people were routinely obliged by the circumstances of prohibition to have to visit venues where they were simultaneously confronted by and cajoled or seduced into participation in other activities of vice. Other drugs, prostitutes and various modes of sexual diversion, unlicensed gambling and numerous netherworld temptations were provided at the place of alcohol's sale.

Thus, prohibition, *the law itself*, thrust some citizens, however unwillingly initially, on a dismal path of which *the prohibition, being both propellant and stepping stone or bridge*, led people into turpitude. This progression or escalation into enslaving corruption and the use of illegal, addictive recreational substances became for some people a way of life. The removal of prohibition, Relegalisation, was to disassemble the stepping-stone bridge. It is not the proscribed substance, but prohibition itself that propels people into the criminal environment, to the lasting harm of some.

JUSTICE AND LEGAL EQUITY [1].

Just is defined as: fair; righteous; true; equitable; upright; lawful. [From the Latin, iustus—just.]

Justice is the *quality* of being just: integrity; impartiality; retribution. [From the Latin, iustitia.]

Equity is: fairness; moral justice, of which (legitimate) laws are the imperfect expression; the spirit of natural justice which enables the interpretation of laws rightly. [From French, equité and Latin, æquitas, æquus equal.]

The *rule* governing the (judicial) interpretation of statutes and constitutions is that their language shall be construed consistently with Natural Justice, or natural law. The rule assumes: that natural law is a thing certain in itself; that legislators and judges are *incompetent* to make and interpret *the written law* unless they previously understand the natural law; and that the People must understand the natural law before they can understand the written law. The fact that the written law must be interpreted by the natural is a confession of the superiority of the latter. Common Law is the expression of natural justice (e.g. against tyranny, homicide, rape, theft) receiving approbation in all times and places, from all men and women, whether literate or of no education. Understanding of natural justice is acquired by humans at a very young age. Self-evidently, laws which are *against* the spirit of natural justice are unjust, and cannot *legally* be enacted or enforced. However complicated a case may be, where a *law* itself cannot be *uniformly* accepted by adult citizens as being *just*, its enforcement is an illegal act: tyranny. *Equity*, legally enforced, actuates resistance to, and the expunction of, all injustice and unlawful acts by governments. Under national and international law, all 'laws' are illegal which contravene the Standard of Equity, the natural universal common law, and Articles of Human Rights.

SEPARATE GROUNDS GIVING COMPLETE VINDICATION; AND FURTHER EVIDENCE OF CONSPIRACY AND TYRANNY.

In re cannabis, thus far THE REPORT shows how state interference and controls, and their enforcement, constitute crimes per se; but complete vindication of private cultivation, trade, possession and use also derives from other legal considerations: on grounds of Justice and Equity, all controls of cannabis are illegal. To be *legal*, any criterion of 'harm' or 'danger' must be uniformly applied, *without inequity or caprice*. If *harm* were truly the basis for Prohibition, then, under the uncompromising requirements of legal Equity, all substances and activities which do harm people must be subjected to the harm-criteria *equally*, i.e.,, equitably.

Courts everywhere have a bounden duty to uphold the innocent, to prevent malpractice and perjury by the prosecution, and to ensure inequity does not prevail. It is not the job of judges, tribunals and courts to enforce legislation simply because it exists. By moral obligation, and under existing constitutional, civil and Human Rights' laws, national and international, in their supervision of the enforcement of laws, courts, judges, *and* the laws they enforce, must be **fair and just**. De jure, to pick out one activity or group in an unfair way is illegal. In a Democracy, courts have not only the moral human obligation, but also the paramount **duty**, of preventing enforcement of any measure taken by parliamentary or congressional legislation, that is unjust.

In the words of U.S. Chief Justice Harlan F. Stone:

"No one is bound to obey an unjust law." [2]

1 & 2 See: 'TRIAL BY JURY: Its History, True Purpose and Modern Relevance,' ISBN: 9781902848723.

Harm and Danger in Perspective.

Cardio-vascular disease (CVD) and cancer are the most common causes of death in the Western world. CVD accounts for circa 50 per cent of all deaths in the industrialised West. CVD is caused by fatty deposits on the walls of coronary arteries; Saturated Animal Fats promote production of cholesterol in the blood, which in turn encourages the fatty deposits. Consumption of *meat and dairy products* is principally responsible for CVD. Cancers account for circa another 25 per cent of mortality. *Alcohol*, like *meat*, *dairy produce* and *tobacco*, visits death, disease, and its own species of foudroyant destruction upon the population. These extremely harmful, fatal substances are **legal** for unlimited private Production, Sale and Use.

Alcohol is first of all a powerful drug of inescapable physical dependence, inducing degeneration of the physical and mental condition of the user. In addition to damaging health, extreme use of alcohol is so frequent as to be commonplace, causing widespread social problems and grievous behaviour. Tobacco mortalities apart**, of all drug habits alcohol is the worst**, its use being an especial generator of many forms of socially destructive behaviour and results. U.S. statistics on alcohol reflect those of most societies. Consider the following U.S. government statistics provided by the National Institute on Drug Abuse (NIDA).

For the purpose of objective comparison, be it borne in mind that the use of cannabis as a personal relaxant induces no anti-social behaviour and in at least 10,000 years of continuous human use, has not produced so much as a single fatality, it being non-toxic.

U.S. NIDA Statistics on DRUG ALCOHOL. . .

Circa 150,000 (<u>one hundred and fifty thousand</u>) U.S. citizens die each year from diseases related to use of alcohol.

40% to 50% of all murders are alcohol-related.

Alcohol is implicated in 40% to 50% of road accidents in which fatalities occur.

8,000 teenagers are killed each year driving whilst under the influence of alcohol.

40,000 teenagers are maimed each year from accidents which occur in which alcohol was implicated.

Alcohol is indicated in 69% to 80% of child rape.

Alcohol is indicated in 69% to 80% of incest.

Alcohol is indicated in 60% to 80% of wife-beating.

Vide: Sickness does not only manifest itself in the obvious ways, such as in those who are unfortunate enough to become bedridden. Alcohol induces particularly repellent forms of morbidity. *Mild, gentle, safe cannabis gives rise to* **none** *of the above harm.* As a healthy relaxant for personal use which, by Preventive Measure can mitigate or eliminate the bad effects of alcohol, it is incongruous to compare cannabis to alcohol, let alone categorise it with drugs. The comparison herein is requisite because of widespread misconceptions inculcated by perverse miseducation, official and otherwise. The facts produce a clear perspective, *indicting Cannabis Prohibitionists' deception.*

Legislation of Prohibition, 2.

In Legislation of Prohibition, 1, which related to tobacco, it was seen that no authentic health criteria exist (of 'harm', 'danger', etc.) by which substances are objectively judged for legislative Prohibition. Alcohol and tobacco are deadly; toxic; and addictive, capable of inducing acute physical dependence. Alcohol and tobacco are without significant medical, therapeutic use. By any legal, medical, social or logical criteria, **tobacco and alcohol are the most harmful drugs** with the highest potential for abuse and maltreatment of the user, producing large-scale disease and death. *Yet their Production, Sale and Use are legal.* Their legality demonstrates the claim 'Prohibition' is installed to protect health is a **fraud**. "Harm" is not the reason for Prohibitions on selected tradeable substances.

To know the reason for this unjustified Prohibition, one has to see through false arguments; then, Prohibitionists' real purpose becomes apparent. The "health reason," or rather *myth*, is exploded. Official empirical investigations exonerate cannabis from all allegations of 'harm'; and furthermore, modern Medical Case Histories confirm cannabis is of profoundly preventive and remedial benefits to health, and is entirely safe from harm. On Health criteria, cannabis cannot be restricted legitimately. Inspection of the data gives the lie to the Prohibitionists:

Cannabis Prohibition is figmental, a mendacious creation ex nihilo. The Denial by government of private Production, Sale and Use of cannabis, is: corrupt; in breach of laws; and contravenes the Standard of Equity.

Cannabis related prosecutions by the state are malicious and have always constituted serious crime. Most, if not all, of the population consume harmful substances, and the majority, including 'politicians', take drugs, including either or both of the most harmful and the most addictive: alcohol and tobacco. Caffeine (tea, coffee, colas) is a strong stimulant drug and medically recognised as such. "Danger," "harm," "misuse," "abuse" and "health" do not genuinely constitute criteria for the control 'legislation'—*although people motivated by personal gain tell this sanctimonious lie repeatedly to dupe the population.* To reinforce this statement of fact, observe that cannabis is officially recognised by U.S. Judicial Review as being incapable of inducing mortality in humans and animals (i.e.,, cannabis is non-toxic) and official Empirical Studies have *always* exonerated cannabis smoking from all 'harm'.

Prohibition is emplaced on the illegitimate basis of Prohibitionists' personal bias, led by their (unspoken) *money-motive*. The fabrications of 'harm' are a deceit employed to enable Prohibition to be installed and maintained: while people are deluded by the false propaganda of 'harm', or preoccupied with whether or not the 'harm' allegations are true, and to what degree, the debate and people's attention are not focused on the simple straightforward verity that if 'harm to people' were the criterion for Prohibition, then all activities and substances which do harm people must be subject under the law equally and uniformly to the criterion, without inequity or caprice.

The Evidence and the common law render illegal all legislation of control on cannabis production, trade, possession and use. If Justice and Equity were duly respected, judges would never allow cannabis related prosecutions to take place. Instead, however, judges actively abet illegal enforcement, ensuring by their supervision that no process occurs which respects Truth, Evidence, Justice or Equity.

Prohibitions *genuinely* based on harm are unenforceable and risible: saturated-fat-rich foods, delightful Devonshire clotted cream, milk, dairy products, meat, induce cardio-vascular disease and death, CVD being principal cause—*approximately 50 per cent* of all deaths in the West; boxing causes brain damage; yachting, horse-riding, motor sports, mountaineering, Rugby football, indeed most sports, and driving a car, incur serious injuries, have yearly fatalities, and genuine potential for danger; pathogenic addictive alcohol, tobacco, tea, coffee, colas (ref. Mortality Statistics on caffeine) ***all*** qualify for harm-based Prohibition. Not so cannabis, which: ***"cannot induce a lethal response,"*** and, ***"in strict medical terms is far safer than many foods we commonly consume,"*** to quote Findings of Fact of the U.S. Judicial Review (ref. Part Four). Even if all the above harmful, dangerous substances and activities were *prohibited*, note that, whereas the harm inflicted by them is recognised by official publications, in stark contrast cannabis is exonerated from all 'harm' by the official Empirical Studies.

Legal Equity makes the *selecting* of cannabis for control illegal. In any case, the Empirical Studies show cannabis to be harmless and benign. With harm and danger in perspective, the undisclosed prime causation behind Prohibition, i.e.,, the ulterior motive, explains **all**. It is unlawful to control individuals' uses of cannabis. Justice is self-evident in laws against murder, rape, robbery, fraud, theft and so on. However, where the state permits production/cultivation, trade, possession and use of alcohol, tobacco, coffee, tea, orange juice and bread, the 'justice' of a law to suppress cannabis is non-existent.

It is shameful, but it is the truth that substances are controlled, not because they are 'harmful', but because of corrupt money-motive. With the safe, benign aspects of cannabis in mind, comparison with dangerous activities and substances reveals the extreme extent to which people have succumbed to the lie that "Prohibition" is for their "benefit." [1] Note that the carcinogenic radioactivity from phosphate 'fertiliser', in food and legal tobacco has been known about in government circles for decades. But when 'prohibition' is eventually introduced on tobacco, *putatively* on a basis of "harm," it will *actually* be: to obscure the definitive medico-scientific exoneration of cannabis smoke-tar; to obfuscate the modern confirmation of the health-benefits yielded from smoked cannabis; to save government expenditures on socialised medicine; and to conceal the criminal political status quo revealed by THE REPORT. Universal Common Law, Justice and Legal Equity mandate **just** treatment of citizens, *whether or not* substances are "harmful." All *selective* Prohibitions, including on tobacco, alcohol, opiates and coca, are *inequitable*, and hence, illegal.

1 One should be reminded that U.S. Alcohol Prohibition, and the more subtle U.K. version, the controls on when premises licensed to sell alcohol were allowed to be open, were introduced with the intention of reducing alcohol-induced drunkenness and absenteeism, to augment productivity of (factory) workers, for increased profit to Owners and magnates.

TYRANNY AND MALFEASANCE IN THE SERVICE OF MAMMON.

Tyranny is defined as: oppressive rule administered with injustice; the cruel and arbitrary use of authority. From this definition flows the corollary that those who perpetrate and passively or actively support tyranny are the enemies of the People and of Democracy.

Cannabis Prohibition Conspiracy relies for its existence on collusion, and illegal use of force by those state functionaries and employees responsible for its judicial, police and penal enforcement. In the service of Mammon, judges' desertion of the ethical standards and impartiality required in judicature, complicitly assists the politicians and bureaucracy to commit the crimes involved in Cannabis Prohibition.

THE REPORT. CANNABIS: THE FACTS, HUMAN RIGHTS AND THE LAW.

Judges' self-interested zeal to co-operate with corrupted politicians' 'laws' against salutary cannabis compounds their obstruction and perversion of justice. Courts which permit prosecution of the subterfuge that is the 'law' embody and abet cruel tyranny of the historical model.

The judicial department of government is not responsible to the People: by dependence for their careers and salaries, and by impeachment, members of the judiciary are responsible to the legislature. Their dependence on the legislators guarantees that judges sanction and execute the laws, whether or not laws are just [1]. Hence, in all enforcement of law, criminal, civil and fiscal, there exists the crucial need for RESTORATION of the genuine Constitutional Common Law Trial by Jury, which **definitively** requires juries to be comprised of indiscriminately chosen adult citizens and, amongst their duties, **to judge**:

firstly **on the justice of the law**: for the Jurors to find their verdict by including judgement on whether the law and enforcement are themselves **Just**; and, to **annul** enforcement of injustices and bad laws by finding the Verdict of **Not Guilty**; and, *secondly*, **on the facts of the case**, for which, *not the judge*, but the Jury alone is responsible for deciding on admissibility of evidence and the calling of witnesses [2].

It does not take great study or much natural human perspicacity to see tyranny for what it is, where and when it occurs. Just as the simple humble person knows and understands Natural Justice, of which the Common Law is the expression, every sane adult human can recognise tyranny and injustice. Elimination of this aggressive form of state-organised misbehaviour, of tyranny, is a fundamental aim of civilisation, and an undertaking to which all nations signatory to The U.N. Declaration of Human Rights, are dedicated. Every democracy has its constitution and law binding judiciary and legislature to act within the Principles of Justice and Equity. Enforcement of *any* control on cannabis puts the government, specifically, the executive, the legislators, and the judiciary involved, in breach of common and substantive laws, and each act of enforcement renders the state-employed personnel implicated, judicable.

The abandonment by the intelligentsia of Principles, of civilised values and a humanitarian predisposition towards fellow citizens, to adopt the coercive barbarism of tyranny for motives of self-interest, has profound social implications and invites the direst retribution. It is incumbent on state functionaries, judges, and the legal profession, more than anyone else in society, to recognise Prohibition for the tyranny it is and to ensure its annulment and retraction. It is their bounden duty above all others, by checking—not appeasing—tyranny, to serve and protect citizens from abuse by state enforcement of injustices which masquerade under the guise of 'law'. Should they fail in this duty and human obligation, their malfeasance is the gravest of crimes which redounds to society by the fracture of civil peace, the fabric of civilisation in a nation, with all manner of attendant crimes and dire consequences unleashed [3].

1 Ref. Justice and The Constitution; Part Seven.
2 NOTA BENE: The above are among the stipulations of the constitutionally-emplaced, irrevocable, legally correct form of due process: the Common Law Trial by Jury. This has been usurped by the illegal interference of judges and politicians. For the stipulations of Common law, ref. 'What Common Law Trial by Jury Is,' in Part Seven.
3 E.g. Riots: Watts, Broadwater Farm, Toxteth, Brixton, Bradford, St. Paul's, Rodney King Riots, etc.

On The Record.

In addition to the surfeit of crime of various categories heretofore digested, this Prohibition is seen to generate still more of an especially reprehensible type. Consider the following: there are judges who have spoken out on the record, making vehement erroneous statements about a "harm" which does not exist in cannabis. Judges' misstatements of fact are made to accompany sentences of harsh punishments for harmless cannabis activities. Trite fictions are declared by courts of "regrets" for the "victims" of the cannabis trade (individual "victims" or "the whole of society"). These empty utterances are so far removed from the realities of long-established repeatedly re-confirmed empirical evidence of the safe nature of cannabis, and the traditional harmless mundane normality of its multiple millennia-long trade, that it is impossibly hard to accept that judges can be so totally ignorant and scordato, unless they make a prejudiced effort to isolate themselves from a glaring truth which they would rather not see or hear.**....**

This conclusion is emphasised by the duty-bound obligation for judges to immerse themselves in scholarship to acquire knowledge on matters pertinent to cases which they try. Only a normal level of perusal and social awareness, as befits a judge, is required to have revealed to the impartial mind that a more than sufficient body of erudite, expert opinion has always existed which endorsed as fact that Prohibition of Cannabis, no matter how powerful or vituperative were its proponents, was never founded in truth. Over the years, judges cannot have avoided being faced with the results of studies which have negated as groundless all allegations of 'harm' upon which the 'law' controlling cannabis purports to be based, unless these judges do so *intentionally*, that is to say, by a premeditated Prohibitionist evasion of deliberate complicity. On this basis, numerous grave inferences are inevitable.

It is noted that some few exceptional judges are vociferous in condemnation of the Prohibition, such as Judge Wolfgang Nescovic of Lübeck, Judge Robert Sweet of Manhattan, Judge James Gray of Santa Ana, Judge James Paine of Miami, et al.

However, the majority of judges are passive or active in support of Prohibition, despite the fact that the 'law' is not only unfounded but also prejudicial. They collude in grievous oppression of harmless citizens for harmless activities. As with Prohibitionist politicians, all possible inducements and motivations leading judges into wrong-headed and illegal abuse of their position are disreputable and self-seeking. It will be hard for these judges ever to admit that, for solely cannabis related activities, their sentences of punishment on their fellow citizens were always wrong, and wholly unjust. Because they have long given their support to the criminal subterfuge and mendacity of Prohibition, that is to say, they have *knowingly* participated in crime, such judges oppose Relegalisation on any spurious grounds.

The Counterbalance.

Over the years at all times since the earliest days of Cannabis Prohibition, even when state and other propaganda against cannabis has been intense, there has always existed a more than equal counterbalance of expert literature, the published products of medico-scientific specialists of prestigious world-respected academic and research institutions, who, upon methodical examination, have refuted every allegation of 'harm' levelled at cannabis, categorically demonstrating that all the premises upon which Prohibition was/is based, are false. Consider the concerned response of New York Mayor Fiorello LaGuardia to the *unqualified* assertions of 'harm' made to legislators who instigated Prohibition. To acquire knowledge on a reliable scientific basis, in 1938, Mayor LaGuardia commissioned a study from the New York Academy of Medicine. The Study was published in 1944, after several years' comprehensive empirical investigations had been conducted by a team, thirty-one strong, including eminent physicians, psychologists, psychiatrists, sociologists and pharmacologists. This report specifically stated Findings that: cannabis is not addictive; does not induce tolerance syndrome; and that regular long-term use does not induce mental or physical deterioration. (See pages 141 and 146 of that report.) The report further stated that: cannabis use neither leads to the use of drugs nor causes crime. (Again, see pages 12, 13, 16 & 17.)

In short, the allegations of 'harm' by which cannabis has been prohibited are, by disinterested scientific scrutiny, not substantiated: the 'harm' has been competently, comprehensively and consistently dismissed. The allegations are nought but figments. The unfounded 'law' has always been false; the Prohibition is an ongoing **fraud**; all cannabis-related prosecutions of citizens are malicious.

The reality is that the 'harm' stories are a deception by which Prohibitionists attempt to disguise the criminality of their mercenary scheme, which is expressed as cannabis control 'legislation'. If harm or danger were truly the basis for Prohibitions, then meat, dairy produce, alcohol and tobacco, amongst many other activities and substances which **really** *do* harm great numbers of people, would be prohibited, a fortiori, all the more so.

Legal Equity requires the just, uniform application of any harm-based criterion: the Rights of all of the People to their own concepts of self-fulfilment are equal. Around the world literally hundreds of millions of vigorously hale, long-term regular partakers of cannabis, competitive, happy and successful in every walk of life, cannot be arbitrarily dismissed or denied.

The 'legislation' is a cold-blooded criminal plot. No civilised court can enforce such a 'law'. To see judges dispense 'punishment' (de facto, persecution) to men and women on the basis of this legislative imposture arouses just indignation in every decent citizen.

In Concert.

It is the duty of every citizen, including *judges*, to uphold the common law and standards of fairness and justice. It is a virtueless abrogate judiciary that does not resist tyranny. The judge who places his or her career above impartiality to become the servant of corruption is a vile species earning an especial loathing, deserving of the jury's ultimate disdain.

Prohibition produces an enormous number of deaths every year by denying cannabis as Preventive Measure and Preventive Medicine; Prohibition withholds cannabis as Curative Medicament, resulting in further inhumanity and mortality; Prohibition promotes Global Warming with fatal results; Prohibition engenders widespread crime: the judiciary share with the Prohibitionist politicians not only the Guilt of Homicide and of Wrongful Penalisation, but also Guilt for a deep grievous ruin of Western society. (Ref. A Closer Look; & Parts Six and Seven.)

The crime committed by Prohibitionists to support the financial gain of a clandestine plutocracy, must be quashed. This tyranny results in the wreck of countless men and women's lives, health and Freedom. To bring about this exigent change, there are numerous legal grounds for judges (and all courts) to dismiss cases against citizens under the infamous legislation of Cannabis Prohibition.

Judges are in a unique position firstly, to face down Prohibitionists with the injustices of the ban, thereby to achieve Relegalisation forthwith; and secondly, to force re-establishment of proper Constitutional Common Law Trial by Jury (ref. Part Seven).

Let there now prevail an ad hoc, concerted stand for **RESTORATION**: **Relegalisation**, **Amnesty and Restitution**, by all those of the judiciary who hold dear the values of Justice. In the eternal good campaign for the preservation of high moral values and protection of precious Rights, the virtues by which civilisation is edified and differentiated from barbarism, let not the judiciary now be found wanting....

JUSTICE IS THE OBJECT OF GOVERNMENT: RIGHTS AND THE LAW.

Provided a moral choice is open to those acting pursuant to the order of government, those involved in tyranny and enforcement of illegal 'law' are not relieved from responsibility for their actions. **All** who serve or work for a state of tyranny, in the act and by definition, are participants in crime, answerable for their actions. No action taken by government or person acting in the name of government may legitimately usurp the Liberty or Rights of any individual. "Ignorance" of involvement, or that the law is being broken by those who work in or for government, does not excuse the culprit in this instance, nor mitigate culpability, for, as *official* empirical researches deny the very grounds on which the Prohibition 'law' claims to be based, the pleading of "ignorance" by implicated persons would be incredible. Regarding a state of tyranny, the Nuremberg and other post-war proceedings set important precedents in International Law.

"Whereas it is essential, if man is not to be compelled to have recourse, as a last resort, to rebellion against tyranny and oppression, that human rights should be protected by the rule of law." United Nations' Universal Declaration on Human Rights [1].

All people of a democratically constituted nation who submit willingly to the authority of their state have the Absolute Right for their voices to be heard, their view to be promulgated, and their interests to be protected in the creation and carrying out of laws. It is the unalterable duty of government to uphold people's sovereign right to seek their own individually-defined self-fulfilment. Where politicians introduce laws which contravene these, or any, stipulations of Human Rights, as do all controls on cannabis, the legislation is tyrannical, and its enforcement is crime per se.

No man or government has the right to deny any other man or government their Right to unmolested tranquillity of existence. Governments do not 'bestow' Rights upon people: governments are comprised of individuals whose Rights are only the equal of all others in society, no more or less. Politicians are bound to represent the Rights and interests of *all* the People; not to exclude representation of the interests of those who wish to cultivate, trade in, possess and to use cannabis. Whether people are aware or ignorant of this fact, money-motive leads those who gain from Cannabis Prohibition to participate in a gross fraud which adversely affects every person on Earth.

Rights are not a luxury; they are the essence and foundation of civilised existence, sine qua non, within a community of humans. The government which abuses, or fails to protect and uphold citizens whose activities fall within their Rights, cannot be defined as civilised or democratic. In such neglect and abuse of its citizens and their Rights, a government commits grave Crimes against Humanity.

Within a state, religious or secular, Human Rights confer the only modus vivendi capable of functioning for the enhancement of universal values which benefit and protect all men and women equally. While it is accepted that no state is able to attain the abstract virtue of true perfection in these matters, signatory nations to the Universal Declaration on Human Rights are committed to the sincere attempt at achieving the maximum of all Rightful democratic potentials of which they are capable. This comprises the historic and ongoing endeavour which proffers Humankind the quintessential aspiration and challenge of Civilisation.

1 Controls on Cannabis breach Articles 1, 2, 3, 7, 8, 9, 10, 12, 16, 18, 21, 25, 26, 28, 29 and 30, of The U.N. Declaration on Human Rights; ref. Addendum. This Declaration in honour binds the legislature and judiciary of *signatory nations.*

Traditional and Modern Medical Uses.

Cannabis has been an important commodity since the dawn of History. Its uses as preventive and curative medicament represent some of the benefits it bestows on Mankind.

Long before the graphical science and arts were introduced to the then still-illiterate West, in 2737 B.C. the pharmacology of cannabis was carefully detailed in Chinese writings of which the Emperor Shen Nung is believed to be the author. The Chinese found cannabis to be efficacious and have used it for millennia to date, in a great many remedies, as did Western medical practitioners until Prohibition. Amongst the large number of applications, cannabis was recorded to ease the labour of childbirth, and as being helpful in "female weakness," the Chinese epithet for menstruation and its accompanying tensions, cramps and pain, this being the periodic interval during which Oriental women were less disposed to do household or manual work.

Some of its other uses were for general relief of pain, treatment of gout, malaria and, by its stress-relieving propensity which promotes concentration, to preclude absent-mindedness. Efficacious treatment by cannabis of numerous illnesses and disorders is also recorded in writings in India and the Middle East (viz. Restorationists; Part Two). Cannabis was available to the greater part of Humankind the world over. Effective as medicine and as the only scientifically-confirmed healthy smoked relaxant known to Man, cannabis continues to be taken in most parts of the world, albeit 'illegally' [1].

Reneging on The Teachings of Jesus Christ, in medieval Europe the administration of the Church pursued, and became corrupted by, wealth and power, achieving a position of socio-political hegemony. Using totalitarian *prohibitionist* methods [2], the Church forced the population to adopt a fictitious regressed pseudo-philosophy of flat-Earth-ignorance and far-fetched superstitions. Under the Holy Inquisition's threat and use of imprisonment, torture and execution, the Church forbade all practice and use of medicine in the West for well over a thousand years, excepting only alcohol and the leech, blood-letting.

During the Renaissance, the Reformation and the beginning of the transition to the modern era, the blessings of ancient medical science began to be rediscovered, investigated and applied. Early Western 'Herbals' and pharmacopoeias list multiple uses of cannabis. Mankind's principal cure for headache was cannabis. By the Victorian Age, the longstanding use of cannabis by all the world's populations had been adopted by the modern scientific medical profession in the West, to the benefit of Health and significant enhancement of the quality of life. European doctors of medicine in Victorian times discovered widespread multiple uses of cannabis in the Near, Middle and Far East, with notable contributions to knowledge by Dr., Sir W. B. O'Shaughnessy, of The Royal College of Science. They confirmed cannabis effective in treatment of tetanus, or 'lockjaw', a disease with spasms of the muscles of the jaw and other parts, with prolonged, painful muscular cramps. It was recorded as of great benefit to sufferers of hydrophobia, successfully treated chorea, St. Vitus's Dance, which is a nervous disease causing involuntary spasmodic movements of the face and limbs, and effective antidote to poisoning by strychnine, the product of nux vomica, the Deadly Nightshade or Belladonna plant.

1 N. B. Shown in Part One of THE REPORT, the clinical medico-scientific Empirical Studies (i.e.,, of actual use by test subjects) confirm that, when used on its own, pure, in its natural herbal resinous state, cannabis is not only safe, but also of great value to the health of humans. However, mixed with alcohol and/or other drugs in medicinal use, cannabis, which is not a drug, has been wrongly associated by critics of its use, with other than its own benign effects.
2 Ref. Déjà vu; Part Six.

Prevention Is Better Than Cure

Dr. J. Russell Reynolds described the curative efficacy of cannabis for muscle spasms, fits, epilepsy and spasticity, in a Medical Paper published in Lancet, 1890. He prescribed cannabis for many conditions, writing that cannabis: *"is one of the most valuable medicines we possess."* This statement obtains undiminished by the passage of time. Dr. Reynolds's patients will have received much benefit from prescribed and advised use of cannabis, amongst whose number was the Empress Queen Victoria, Dr. Reynolds being her personal physician.

Between 1840 and 1900, **more than a hundred** medico-scientific expositions were published in the U.S. and the U.K., recommending cannabis as effective treatment in a great variety of specific illnesses and disorders; for prophylaxis; and as health-promoting tonic.

Ubiquitous resource to an innumerable variety of staple nutritional and agro-industrial products (ref. Traditional Uses; Part Two) cannabis was also esteemed for its alleviation of both physical pain and psychological stress, and was in general use as soothing relaxant applicable to trying human circumstances, such as stress, fatigue, depression, nerves, and grief. Cannabis continued to be the most widely employed cure for headache. Cannabis was correctly recognised *everywhere* as being of great advantages, used, valued, and available without any restriction.

Additional to pharmacists' and doctors' medicament, the commercial products, hash, herb, candies, and 'tea', smoked and in food and beverage form, were available from confectioners and cafés as stress-relieving, health-promoting relaxants. At the time of Prohibition's introduction, New York, for example, had over 400 cannabis parlours and cafés. These premises were notably civil; a conspicuous contrast to the troublesome bars and restaurants where alcohol was for sale, a fact acknowledged by the official enquiry and Empirical Studies instituted by Mayor LaGuardia, published in 1944.

Cannabis was a traditional commonplace *conventional* substance, endorsed by alcohol-prohibitionists who regarded the herb as of significant virtue for its alleviation of 'hangover,' withdrawal and abstinence symptoms in the cure of opium and alcohol addicts. Drug addicts, opiate, tobacco and alcohol users, existed independently of cannabis, as they do today. Far from 'introducing' or 'leading' these sorry people into the vice of the use of drugs, cannabis was clinically utilised to help in their cure, assisting and relieving individual and society from the ill-effects of drug addiction.

Cannabis has not lost its therapeutic effectiveness simply because the government and corporate paid representatives of the pharmaceutical companies' vested interests say it has. Cannabis was listed in various official pharmacopoeias until the Nineteen-Fifties (U.S.) and the 'Seventies (U.K.). Then, as pharmaceutical firms produced more and more of their patented, exorbitantly expensive laboratory nostrums, which were falsely claimed to 'replace' cannabis as medication, it was arbitrarily removed on no plausible grounds.

Dietary and smoked herbal cannabis remains *the most*, and in many applications *the only*, efficacious medicament for numerous conditions, while, remarkably and providentially, having *no adverse side-effect or toxic effect in its use*—unlike modern pharmaceutical drugs.

Cannabis is established in modern medicine as safe and therapeutically effective in many conditions, by physicians, nurses, clinicians, researchers, psychologists, oncologists, ophthalmologists, psychiatrists, toxicologists, pharmacologists and sociologists. This is confirmed by scores of thousands of patients and documented Medical Case Histories. Nowadays, cannabis continues to be recommended to abate pre-menstrual tension, menstruation pain, and routinely used as the safe, non-habit-forming analgesic [pain reliever] of headache, pains and strains. Cannabis is in widespread use for alleviation of both physical pain and psychological stress, being the *only* non-addictive relaxant, applicable to stress, fatigue, depression, nerves, and grief. Notwithstanding progress in other fields of medicine, no laboratory-concocted attempts to make substitutes for cannabis approach its superiority in its non-toxic safety and its efficacy.

THE RECENT MODERN ERA—AND THE MOTIVE.

To know the educational facts about the many virtues of cannabis is to perceive the conspiracy behind its Prohibition and to comprehend that corrupt money-motivation is the root of a widely pervasive evil inflicted by a Criminal Prohibition [1]:

Today, the DEA, Home Office, Crown Prosecution Service, and organisations and individuals who support controls which have numerous and far-reaching detrimental effects, perjuriously avoid the definitive Empirical Evidence of the *official* medico-scientific studies of the last hundred and fifty years and right up to date, by which cannabis use as personal relaxant is, and always has been, vindicated. They force-feed the public the contrary lie, but **there are no existing studies into empirical use of cannabis herb which find 'harm'**: Modern Medical Case Histories and the official Empirical Studies' Findings of Fact **unanimously** conclude the wholesomeness of cannabis and its benefits to humans.

Within government, the political parties and other Prohibitionist-led and financed organisations, individuals conceal the expert Evidence by which cannabis is exonerated from all 'harm' allegations. Working from motives of personal gain, they confound their colleagues and the trusting public by substituting the exonerative clinical Empirical Facts with trompe l'oeil writings [2], by persons who have never undertaken empirical research of smoked cannabis herb. These *appear* 'authoritative' to the non-specialist, but are in fact the appalling fictions of varying degrees of 'harm' *actually disproven* by the official Empirical Researches. Compounding their perjury, Prohibitionist activists derogate cannabis by infiltrating into the data on *real* cannabis, 'findings' from inadmissibly disparate chemical extracts and synthetic substances, falsely claiming these to "represent" or be "on cannabis." [3] **There is no health-risk associated with smoking cannabis:** shown in Part One in an emphatic contrast, the Studies into people's long-term use establish cannabis as a safe, health-enhancing, categorically benign herb.

In any case, as shown, on grounds of Justice and Legal Equity the *selecting* of cannabis for Prohibition is also unlawful; *and*, the regulatory Prohibition control 'criteria' are duplicitous, unreasonable, capricious, inequitable, fallacious, and based on mendacity (ref. Part Four). The question inexorably arises as to whether there be an undisclosed, **an *ulterior*, motive** behind this Prohibition...

1 Jesus Christ is credited with having observed that: "The love of money is the root of all evil."
2 Ref. Trompe l'oeil; and following Parts.
3 Ref. 'THC' Is Not 'Cannabis,' in Part One. The Home Office and the DEA continuously employ the mendacity of disproven fictions to miseducate the population.

Prevention Is Better Than Cure

Cannabis is not genuinely prohibited on 'health' criteria. Fictions of 'harm' are a Prohibitionists' stratagem of distraction and diversion. Corrupt individuals conspire and defraud the population of enormous sums of money, preventing the People from taking advantage of cannabis. The amounts of money involved are truly staggering. As noted, Cannabis Prohibition comprises the greatest fraud of all time:

Naturally propagated herbs (reproduction by seed) cannot be patented. That is to say, trade in *natural* cannabis cannot be financially exploited by the monopoly of a patent granted by government to state-owned or private companies, and *natural* cannabis can be produced free or cheaply everywhere....

Since early Victorian Times and before throughout the West, and since much earlier in the Near, Middle and Far East, cannabis was everywhere the principal cure for headache. Shortly after the turn of the Twentieth Century, the *commercial success* of introduction of the pharmaceutical company patent-product, the aspirin tablet, proffered to the shrewd, but unscrupulous, business mind a form of insider information. This comprised a crucial monetary incentive....

.... wherever a use for cannabis was to be found in the medical profession's herbal and patent-medicine options as listed in the official pharmacopoeias, if cannabis could be prohibited, there would appear an opening for spectacular financial opportunism by the concocting of pharmaceutical toxins to purport to have made "replacements" or "substitutes" for safe cannabis.

Easily produced at home, unpatentable and cheap, cannabis was the recommended medication in treatments for **scores of ailments** listed in Pharmacopoeias. Additionally, because it relieves patients from the unpleasant effects of treatments by toxic medications, recuperative cannabis was secondary ingredient in numerous other medicines. **Cannabis comprised over half of all medication sold.**

This constituted and continues to do so, the huge financial invitation, by the conspiring to introduce and maintain fraudulent 'legislation' to prohibit cannabis, to make cash profits from the 'substitutes'—regardless of their inefficacy; and without responsible consideration for Prohibition's numerous other catastrophic results to individuals, to families, to society [1], and to the ecosphere [2].

Openly acknowledged in papers published in the U.N. Bulletin on Narcotics [3], it would be extreme naïveté not to know that natural substances with proven therapeutic efficacy and thus spectacular monetary value, cannabis, opiates, and cocaine, are **selected** for Prohibition: the legislation is a mechanism of fiscal monopoly-control to concentrate the financial activity associated with them (production, marketing and distribution-supply trades, including by doctors' prescriptions) so that corporate profits are protected and the collection of government duty and tax revenues facilitated. This maximises profits to corporations producing laboratory-made, expensive *patented* 'extracts' or 'substitutes' (frequently ineffectual as cures [4]) and yields to governments' state administrations the trillions taken in duty and Corporation Tax throughout the West.

1 Ref. Part Six.
2 Ref. Part Two.
3 For example, see the Benabud Study; U.N. Bulletin on Narcotics, Vol. 9, no. 4, pp. 1-16. Ref. bibliography.
4 Ref. Patients' Medical Case Histories in this Part and Part Four.

Where state-owned, pharmaceutical companies yield 100 per cent of profits to government control; where private, the firms render Corporation and Value Added Taxes. Of every political persuasion, governments have an overriding monetary interest, taking not less than 30-40 per cent of the phenomenal sums of profits. The state *also* collects the stupendous *duties* included in the price of the sold items themselves.

Cannabis Prohibition is different from controls on the other therapeutic substances for the following reasons:

Modern Medical Case Histories, Reviews and Research [1] *confirm cannabis efficaciously replaces numerous existing lines of extremely lucrative pharmaceutical drugs* of little or no curative effectiveness. The healing herb is therapeutically efficacious to a degree which far exceeds in effectiveness, many lines of currently-prescribed pharmaceutical products [2].

Relegalised today, cannabis has the potential to render redundant and effectively replace noxious prescribed pills and potions of dubious or no efficacy, which now accrue literally billions of undeserved dollars, pounds, yen, Euros, etc., of annual profits to the Owners of the drugs' companies, *solely* because of the Prohibition on cannabis.... Viz: toxic addictive benzodiazepines, phenothiazines, 'tranquillisers', barbiturates and hypnotics; habit-forming analgesics; the so-called 'anti-emetics', steroids, and seldom-effective drugs now prescribed for glaucoma, multiple sclerosis, asthma, epilepsy, anorexia, etc. [3]

Consider but one of these many lines of pharmaceutical laboratory poisons, benzodiazepines: The irony is grim in the fact that of all the drugs, after tobacco and alcohol, pharmaceutical tranquilliser benzodiazepines are the single largest drug abuse problem in the West. In the U.S., averaged over recent years, Emergency Room admissions brought on by benzodiazepines have amounted to over 18,500 per annum, the most for any class of drug other than alcohol [4]. Many people are addicted to benzodiazepines and find themselves unable to stop taking them without withdrawal symptoms, extreme nervous agitations, etc. So, these drugs are routinely prescribed long-term, which seriously compounds an already unsatisfactory situation.

Latterly in the U.S., of the highly lucrative lines of benzodiazepines, which are stupefying, addictive, mentally and physically debilitating, mind-altering powerful toxic chemical tranquilliser drugs, Valium has been the most widely sold with an average of 23 million, of a total of 81 million annual benzodiazepine prescriptions [5].

Replacement of toxic pharmaceuticals by cannabis is predictable and, on the medical data, desirable: this would be the **RESTORATION** of the recent status quo in which cannabis was principal medication in treatments of <u>over 100</u> illnesses and conditions listed in the U.S. Pharmacopoeia (and others).

It is cruel irony that the aforementioned addictive, generally useless and actually harmful nostrums brewed up in chemical laboratories of the pharmaceutical firms, are the failed attempt by modern drugs to replace safe, efficacious natural herbal cannabis.

1 Ref. Cannabis Modern Uses and Medical Case Histories, following in this Part; and in the U.S. Judicial Review, quoted in Part Four.
2 & 3 Ditto.
4 See: 'Pills That Don't Work,' and 'Stopping Valium,' Ralph Nader's Health Research Group Publications; Washington, D.C.
5 Ibid.

Prevention Is Better Than Cure

The natural resinous herb can be produced free or cheaply everywhere. Relegalised, the consumer or sick patient benefits from easy access to effective treatment, but *natural herbal cannabis offers no opening for large-scale financial opportunism as with the monopoly-control of patented pharmaceutical products.* **A priori, *money* enters the equation**.

If cannabis were legal and therefore generally available so that people could again grow it in the allotment or kitchen garden, or farm and sell it, cannabis would be cheaper per kilo than tea or sage and onion, and replace the dubious pharmaceuticals immediately. A great deal less profit would accrue to the pharmaceutical corporations, and significantly less duty and tax revenue would be produced. Ipso facto, the motive behind Cannabis Prohibition is revealed.

Amongst those people who have a vested or career interest, intense motivation overcomes integrity. It is predictable human behaviour that some of them attempt to prevent Relegalisation by illegal and untruthful means, and especially so, bearing in mind *the sheer scale of the sums of money, of profits involved.*

Shown by THE CANNABIS BIOMASS ENERGY EQUATION, THE REPORT demonstrates that the drugs' companies' corrupt money-motivation is *additional* to that of numerous other corporate and government vested interests behind the Cannabis Prohibition racket. (Ref. Part Two.)

NOTA BENE: Readers—Beware those individuals and organisations who misapply terms such as "legalisation" to the measures which *they* call for, by which Prohibition is actually entrenched and prolonged. These self-obsessed groups mean *partial* "legalisation" for *their* purpose, and *Prohibition for everyone else*; e.g. anti-emetic in chemotherapy; 'action' for cannabis therapeutics; multiple sclerosis 'societies'; glaucoma relief; cannabis for alleviation of AIDS symptoms; hemp clothing industry, etc. Then, there are similar dishonest organisations funded by pharmaceutical corporations, et al.

The situation is as follows: Any use of cannabis is de facto, legal *now*. *Every* application should and must be available; but these organisations do not pursue the proper course of obtaining full RELEGALISATION—because that does not serve *their* particular self-interest. They evade the Findings of Fact of the exonerative Empirical Studies; they cruelly ignore the inequity and injustice of Prohibition of Cannabis as Personal Relaxant; they conceal the long-established effectiveness and safety of cannabis in its herbal smoked form.

They campaign for *their* exemption from Prohibition, for *their* exclusive 'legal' use of cannabis—usually, as a pill or a spray, to be manufactured under patents, and sold under 'license', at high prices for inordinate profits, duties and tax—while they otherwise consent to the devastation by, and collaborate with, the criminal Prohibition. Again, the money-motive is evident: companies licensed for this trade would receive great sums of money for their less effective and actually ineffective laboratory 'concentrates'. Obsequiously looking up to corrupt politicians in the hope they will accede to their special exemption from Prohibition, these craven people accept, and thereby abet the existing illegal Prohibition controls on the Right of all people to unlimited private cannabis cultivation, trade, possession, and all uses, including for universal availability of cannabis as Personal Relaxant, and as the benign alternative to drugs, including tobacco and alcohol.

These people's acquiescence to Prohibition is flagitious and fatal. Dishonourable self-interest produces their duplicity. They evade the guilt of their position which encourages governments' Prohibition, by which the Owners and politicians cause suffering, incarceration, deaths, and ecological disaster. However, to *consent* to any measure is to share responsibility for its results. The 'law' is not simply "wrong;" it is the subterfuge of criminals. People's intentions, guilty or innocent, are tested by their stance: if individuals be selfish and dishonest, or money-motivated, predictably, they do not support Relegalisation; but the *honest* person supports RESTORATION.

They—and everyone else—have the Right to cannabis. Weak in disunited selfish ambition, if these many splinter groups **come together, uniting with the Democracy Defined Campaign in strength unyieldingly to demand the Justice of RESTORATION, cannabis will be swiftly available to them**.

Most of us, and that must include the huge majority of the population, take our health for granted. Year in, year out, we endure nothing more injurious than the irksome, but trivial, common cold. Our lives and energies are spent in our occupational and leisure-time pursuits, with our attention and imagination quite naturally focused for the most part, upon matters which concern the running of our day-to-day living. Only when our health fails do we turn expectantly to others for help, assuming that they will be there and that they are in possession of the remedy of which we suddenly and bewilderingly find ourselves in deepest need.

To be cured, or at the very least to have the progress of a disease delayed or stopped, is the desire of every patient. Allaying the symptoms of a sickness, giving relief and the improved psychological determination that the patient requires in order to live on, to give time for a cure to 'work', and not to 'give in' to the illness, can be crucial factors in the saving of lives of sick people.

Cannabis is popular for its safe use as a stress-relieving relaxant, and is by happy coincidence, of outstanding medical utility in a number of conditions. (Medical utility does not define a substance as a drug. Ref. definition of 'drug'; Part One.) Rendering to the ingestor a feeling of ease and well-being, yet completely free from toxic or habit-forming characteristics, unsurprisingly, the natural herb cannabis has good effects on people, including those who suffer from adverse conditions. Cannabis is well documented in modern medicine as a safe substance with profound therapeutic efficacity, including in the following applications:

ALLEVIATION OF NAUSEA:
When used by people suffering from nausea, the cannabis health-giving effect alleviates that condition. Nausea can have a number of different causes to all of which smoked cannabis gives effective relief. Sea or car (motion) sickness is the most frequently experienced example. Many medical treatments involving pharmaceutical preparations themselves induce nausea. In combating nausea, cannabis proves to be *the most effective form of treatment.*

Alleviating nausea greatly assists treatments in which otherwise the inability of the patient to take food leads to wasting and death before the treatment or further treatments have had time to 'work' to effect a cure. In cancer and leukaemia chemotherapy, the severity of the nausea itself becomes a life-threatening condition and cannabis proves to be life-prolonging, and literally, *life-saving.*

Prevention Is Better Than Cure

1. The decision to provide cannabis to patients undergoing treatments by toxic medications can be the determining factor between their life and death [1].

2. When it is made in the knowledge that cannabis herb could treat, or help save the life of, a person, every individual decision to withhold cannabis is malicious and premeditated, and constitutes a crime; where death ensues, the decision to withhold cannabis constitutes Capital Crime [2].

3. Provided a moral choice was possible (which in this context it always is) the fact that a person acted pursuant to the order of government does not relieve him or her from responsibility under International Law [3].

4. Further, when that decision to withhold and deny cannabis is also made by *government*, the legislation of Prohibition and its enforcement constitute tyrannical Crime against Humanity.

The anti-emetic property of cannabis is widely acknowledged by numerous specialist oncologists [4], in medical literature and textbooks, including Merck Manual. To quote Dr. Thomas Ungerleider, who headed the State of California's programme of research into cannabis use in cancer therapies:

"Marijuana is the best agent for control of nausea in cancer chemotherapy."

1 Ref. ON: Safe Cannabis Compared to Chemotherapy Drugs; and, ON: 'Relief of Nausea Caused by Chemotherapy,' and ON: Cannabis as Appetite Stimulant, in Admin. Law, Judicial Review Transcripts, in: The Judge's Ruling; Part Four.
2 CAPITAL CRIME: murder (U.K.) homicide (U.S.).
3 Ref. PRINCIPLES; Part Six.
4 Ref. ON: Cannabis Relief of Chemotherapies; Judicial Review Transcripts; Part Four. Also see 'Marijuana as Antiemetic Medicine: A Survey of Oncologists' Experiences and Attitudes,' R.E. Doblin & M.A.R. Kleiman; Journal of Clinical Oncology, Vol. 9, No. 7 (July, 1991) pp. 1314-1319.

**APPETITE STIMULATION;
UPLIFTED SPIRIT:**

The stimulation of appetite, a desire to eat, is separate from alleviation of nausea. Patients who are ill can lose their appetite even at times when they are not feeling the effects of nausea. This can be brought about by the patient's feeling of low morale, of depression. The loss of the will to eat can greatly delay recovery. It also results in patients not recuperating at all, leading to emaciation and their death. Cannabis is non-toxic and has no harmful effect of any kind (neither directly nor as side-effect). Any initial qualms experienced by the novice smoker are allayed by a companionable word of reassurance, or disappear automatically, for *the pleasant gentle sensation of well-being accompanying its use, uplifts the spirit and relieves any such stress.*

Hence, the popularity of the safe herb the world over is explained: this benign amenity, the uplifting of morale even in the most acute depression, is a feeling unique to cannabis. It is completely unlike alcohol and drugs; and cannabis never induces physical or psychological dependence, and no hangover or withdrawal occurs. Cannabis has no such ill-effects because it is a substance in which toxicity does not exist.

It is axiomatic that it is impossible to take a toxic dose from a non-toxic substance. Alarming irrelevant stories of 'toxic overdose' and 'delirium' apply to *THC and toxic pharmaceutical laboratory concentrates of isolated chemical compounds*, the disparate chemistry of which is not remotely similar to cannabis herb [5]. These stories do not relate to smoked cannabis herb-hash which is always uniformly agreeable, mild and safe.
5 Ref. 'THC' Is Not 'Cannabis'; Part One.

Absorption of cannabis into the bloodstream by the alimentary (food) tract is slow, unreliable and not easily titrated. Alternatively, ingestion via the lungs by smoking is the quickest and most efficient means of receiving the beneficial effects of cannabis. Contrary to fictions of Prohibitionist propaganda, the Empirical Clinical Studies show cannabis smoke actually has beneficial effects upon the lungs. (Ref. Part One; & ref. Asthma.) The smoker self-titrates the dose, deciding when or if more is required.

Appetite stimulation is well known in cannabis use, famous as the origination of the widely used expression the 'munchies', a desire for food brought on by cannabis. To the healthy, this is essentially a mild effect and soon passes, but it is of crucial value to those who have lost the will to eat.

The benign, pleasant feeling of well-being brought on by cannabis gives to people and patients *a morale boost, an uplifted spirit* despite their condition, restoring appetite, and is thereby of the greatest help to ill people.

1. Restoring appetite to a wasting patient is *another* way in which *smoking cannabis saves lives*.

2. Wrongly 'illegalised', the salutary herb enhances the Health of the hale, is of greatest assistance in the recovery of the sick, and has *life-saving* potential to replace or reduce the use of often-fatal pathogens alcohol and tobacco, i.e.,, Preventive Measure/Medicine (ref. previous section). The Denial of cannabis inflicts suffering and, in innumerably many instances, death.

3. Those who maintain smoking of life-saving cannabis to be "illegal" should be regarded and treated as perpetrators of the gravest of Crimes, and are unfit to hold any public office in a democratic society.

HELP TO PANCREATIC CANCER PATIENTS:
The ability of cannabis to stimulate the appetite of those who do not respond to pharmaceuticals and who will not otherwise take food is of help to patients with pancreatic cancer.

CURE FOR ANOREXIA & ANOREXIA NERVOSA:
FIGHTS EMACIATION:
Stimulation of the appetite makes cannabis the safest, the natural, and the best restorative for those who suffer from anorexia. Commonly found in convalescence, anorexia is dispelled, and the use of cannabis speeds recovery. Cannabis restores appetite to people even in advanced stages of emaciation, and saves lives.

TREATMENT OF DRUG ADDICTS (OPIATES, ALCOHOL, etc.):
Shown in clinical studies, cannabis is of great help to sufferers of chronic alcohol addiction, and to those people who become dependent upon other drugs of addiction, such as opiates (codeine, heroin, morphine). The Studies confirm human experience as stated in innumerable anecdotal and medical case histories.

Researched by Samuel Allentuck (ref. bibliography), Adams, Bowman, et al, cannabis is shown to alleviate significantly, or completely eliminate, withdrawal symptoms, diminishing the discomfort, frequently acute, which besets the cessation of narcotic indulgence. Modern endorsement is bestowed by the re-affirmation of clinical findings, on this long-established application of cannabis.

Prevention Is Better Than Cure

Despite the publicity given to the 'War on Drugs' creating the false impression that enforced Prohibition is able to do some 'good', U.S. government and other statistics show that use of the illegal, addictive substances prevails. Production [1] and availability of illicit drugs continues (especially opiates, crack-cocaine, and amphetamines) and is at an all-time high, without any evidence to suggest a peak has been reached. Meanwhile, the legal hard drugs alcohol and tobacco continue to wreak death, destruction and disease upon society.

In Holland, cannabis is openly sold and publicly consumed in cafés. Where cannabis use and small-scale possession have been tolerated in recent years, addiction to drugs has not only ceased to increase but has actually declined, with the number of registered heroin and cocaine addicts in Amsterdam falling from over 7,000 to 6,200. This decline in the use of drugs has been achieved with a conspicuous absence, by comparison with the U.S., France, Sweden, the U.K., etc., of coercive policing and social disruption. From the public's personal freedom of choice to use cannabis in the Netherlands, no harm in any form is recorded. However, the *'decriminalised'* form of legislation is dangerously flawed and breaks existing laws [2]. Let the good Dutch now be emboldened to *normalise* the cannabis situation in their country, to Relegalise all private and free market activities of cultivation, trade, possession and uses forthwith [3].

1 Land area of approximately 10-20 square miles is sufficient to produce enough opium to satisfy total world demand (legal and illegal) for opiates, e.g. heroin, morphine, etc. See "The American Disease: Origins of Narcotic Control," by Prof. David F. Musto; Yale University Press. Since crops can be grown in amongst other (legal) farm produce, or easily obscured under trees and woodland, or jungle vegetation, the international 'interdiction' policy by governments was always a predictable and foregone failure. Therefore, this costly waste can only be explained as a public relations' subterfuge, a scheme to give the impression to the credulous that government was "actively doing something about drugs," while actually ensuring that contraband achieved higher Black Market prices. Ref. Part Six.
2 Ref. Justice and Legal Equity; & Part Six.
3 On the fallacies of *'decriminalised* small-scale possession for personal use" types of Prohibition, ref. Part Six.

HELP TO AIDS PATIENTS:

Patients with Acquired Immune Deficiency Syndrome (AIDS) suffer nausea as a symptom of the disease. Acute nausea is further induced as a side-effect of the *costly profitable revenue-yielding* pharmaceutical drugs prescribed, such as AZT, etc. Serious wasting results, which exacerbates the illness. Cannabis can and does help these people in their hundreds of thousands, in significant ways similar to those with cancer and leukaemia. Despite these benefits, the use remains subjected to the immoral illegal Prohibition.

It is relevant to cite the example of a physician afflicted with AIDS, wasting away and rapidly approaching death, who moved to Amsterdam to be able to buy and use cannabis without difficulty. Three or four cannabis cigarettes a day have diminished his diarrhoea and completely eliminated his nausea. With regular use of cannabis his appetite returned. Having gained weight and energy, he describes this experience as "dying with AIDS" in his home country where he could not get cannabis, and now, with the life-giving help of cannabis, as "**living** with AIDS...." [Name withheld.]

ASTHMA RELIEF:

The prejudice against "smoking" which is brought about by the deleterious effects to health from use of tobacco must be understood and put aside[4]. In this context, where **only** cannabis is smoked, the smoke is health-promoting and salubrious, and for asthmatics it is effectively Preventive and/or remedial. Asthma is an adverse condition affecting millions of people, many seriously.

4 Ref. Cannabis Smoke Distinguished from Tobacco Smoke; Part One.

THE REPORT. CANNABIS: THE FACTS, HUMAN RIGHTS AND THE LAW.

Over 15 million people in the U.S., for example, suffer from asthma. The life-shortening effects of childhood asthma are so serious and statistically established, as to affect life insurance rates [1]. The legal medicines are toxic, including those for children; viz: Theophylline; ref. Mortality Statistics, page 2.

Asthma spasmodically closes and narrows the larger and small airways of the lungs (bronchi, bronchia) making breathing difficult and impairing the lungs' vital blood- oxygenation function. Cannabis relaxes muscles and tensions, relieving involuntary muscular spasm and cramps in general, and the spasm in the muscle of the bronchi in particular associated with asthma.

Cannabis smoke is a natural broncho-dilator [2], improving the breathing and blood-oxygenation.

Contrary to unfounded stories (maliciously invented and propagated to derogate herbal cannabis) unique cannabis smoke does not damage or irritate the lungs: rather, asthmatics describe cannabis to have a soothing beneficial effect, and that cannabis smoking entirely prevents the onset of asthma attacks.

Cannabis is clinically observed to be protective [3] of lungs, effectively relieving the swelling of the mucosa of the bronchi experienced by asthma sufferers. Anti-microbial action by cannabis (ref. Anti-Bacterial Action) is Preventive and Curative of bronchitic lung infections.

1 See: Life Insurance Actuarial Rates; 'The Life-Shortening Effects of Childhood Asthma, 1983.'
2 This is the *opposite* of tobacco, which is a broncho-*constrictor*. See U.S. government studies: 'The Therapeutic Potential of Marijuana,' by Sidney Cohen & Richard Stillman.
3 See the U.S.-Costa Rican Clinical Studies. Also note the U.S.-Jamaican Clinical Studies; and the Empirical Clinical Studies of the New York Academy of Medicine definitively conclude that:
"Regular long-term use of cannabis causes no mental or physical deterioration."
See UCLA School of Medicine Pulmonary Studies, 1969-1989 & 1989-1997; Donald P. Tashkin, M.D., reported in Vol. 155, American Journal of Respiratory & Critical Care Medicine, 1997:-
"Findings from the present long-term follow-up study of heavy, habitual marijuana smokers argue against the concept that continuing heavy use of marijuana is a significant risk factor for the development of chronic lung disease. Neither the continuing nor the intermittent marijuana smokers exhibited any significantly different rates of decline in lung function as compared with those who never smoked marijuana. No differences were noted between even quite heavy marijuana smoking and non-smoking of marijuana."

REDUCTION OF I.O.P., GLAUCOMA:
Glaucoma (acute and chronic) is a progressive adverse condition in which increased pressure within the eye (intra-ocular pressure or IOP) causes serious deterioration of vision, damages the optic nerve, and can lead to total blindness. In the U.S., there are over 2,500,000 people who suffer from glaucoma.

Especial note should be taken of the fact that cannabis is effective where modern pharmaceuticals prescribed for glaucoma, at best produce minimal results for a short period of time, but generally are completely useless. Furthermore, cannabis has no harmful effect or side-effect, unlike the drug companies' laboratory-concocted eye-drops which, while not helping the glaucoma sufferer, are *intensely toxic*, doing damage to the liver and kidneys, and are associated with catalepsy and sudden-death syndromes [4].

Glaucoma IOP does not develop in people and populations who are, from time to time, ingestors of cannabis in their food as part of a normal healthy diet, or smoked as sensible relaxant of choice. This is another example of cannabis as efficacious prophylaxis, Preventive Medicine.

4 See Data; Administrative Law Judicial Investigation.

In many different adverse conditions, the futile incapability of pharmaceuticals is constantly evident. The contrast is complete when comparing cannabis. The ophthalmological medical facts [1] are that the relaxant effect of cannabis reduces intra-ocular pressure (IOP) by approximately 30 per cent, bringing glaucoma under control, preventing damage to the eyes, also preventing the condition from worsening. Cannabis smoking is the only reliable countermeasure to glaucoma known to Man, consistently reducing IOP, completely dispelling glaucoma symptoms and saving eyesight [2]. Premeditatedly, Prohibition inflicts blindness. Ref. Déjà vu; Part Six.

1 & 2 See: **Medical College of Georgia Studies; University of North Carolina School of Medicine Studies; Harvard; Hepler & Frank; UCLA.**

Elvy.

In 1988, Elvy Musikka of Hollywood, Florida, became the first American woman (and one of then only fourteen people) to receive legal cannabis from the federal government. Elvy has glaucoma. The following are extracts from her account:

"In 1975 I was diagnosed with glaucoma. I lost so much sight that I couldn't return to work. This began a twelve year period during which I went through every known and experimental treatment for glaucoma. Everything that's been experimented with for glaucoma, I've had it pills, drops, surgery. I was a guinea-pig for anything and everything that was out, including the THC pills [3] which only worked for me for about a week. By 1976, marijuana had been suggested to me by several doctors. I still thought 'pot' [4] [cannabis] was something horrible."

"*A doctor told me that if I did not smoke marijuana I would go blind. **I'd been lied to so much about pot** that I was terrified of it, but I was even more scared of going blind—so I tried it—and it worked. I learned that marijuana, one 'brownie' [chocolate cup cake] every twelve hours with a substantial amount of marijuana in it, kept my eye pressure under control. I didn't have to worry about it at all. One of the nice things I discovered when I smoked marijuana was I didn't find myself consumed with the thought of going blind, which I was most of the time otherwise [5]. Instead, I found myself doing creative things, like writing music.*" The police arrested Elvy for possession and cultivation of cannabis in 1988. She continues:

"Yet, I felt no fear. I knew I was on trial, but so was the obscene and immoral law which demanded blindness of me." The Jury, and Judge Mark Polen acquitted, accepting Elvy's Defence of Medical Necessity[6]. In 1988, Elvy began receiving cannabis from the federal government [7], which continues to this day. By mandatory IND medical monitoring, the most intensive scrutiny confirms only benign effects come from her long term use of cannabis. Elvy controls her glaucoma condition *preventively* [8] and effectively, by smoking five or six cannabis cigarettes every day, and taking a similar amount of cannabis in cookies.

Elvy now campaigns coast-to-coast for Cannabis Relegalisation. The government supplies only the chopped male and female leaves of the plant, which are the lowest quality parts for smoking. With the relaxant-rich flowers and buds of the female plant instead, only a third (1/3) of the amount would be equally effective.

3 Ref. **'THC' Is Not 'Cannabis'; Part One.**
4 **"Pot" is a popularly used abbreviated form of the Central American Indian word for cannabis: potaguaya.**
5 **Note the anti-depressant effect; uplifted spirit.**
6 **Also known as Duress of Circumstance.**
7 **Now only eight people receive 'legal' cannabis supplied under the Investigative New Drug (sic) Program (IND).**
8 Ref. **Cannabis as Preventive Measure and Preventive Medicine; Part Three.**

HELP TO SUFFERERS OF MULTIPLE SCLEROSIS, EPILEPSY, MUSCLE SPASMS, RHEUMATISM, ARTHRITIS, and BACK PAIN:

Cannabis relieves suffering of those with multiple sclerosis, rheumatism, arthritis, epilepsy, spasmodic involuntary muscle cramps, pain, seizures, strains anywhere on the body, pulled muscles, and back pains associated with slipped disc(s). As noted, analgesic (pain-relief) qualities of cannabis are well documented throughout history. The benefits bestowed by cannabis are significantly more therapeutic than merely pain relief. Unlike pharmaceutical drugs used for pain relief, cannabis is not habit-forming, and does not require increased dosage over time (i.e.,, does not induce tolerance syndrome). Unlike pharmaceuticals, replicable empirical tests confirm cannabis does not stupefy or dull the senses in any way, nor interfere with the capacity for work, mental or physical (ref. Part One). Also, cannabis is non-toxic and can thus be taken long-term or indefinitely, without harm to any body organs or function.

Epileptics find that seizures become less frequent and are more manageable, being less intense as a result of the cannabis. In documented cases, severely afflicted sufferers have had their ill-effects from epilepsy so mitigated since taking up regular smoking of cannabis, as to be able to get and keep a job. They find their disorders returning when unable to obtain or use cannabis.

Multiple sclerosis (MS) is a chronic progressive disease which affects the central nervous system, in which there is deterioration of the myelia forming the sheath to nerve-fibres, with various results, such as paralysis in parts of the body, muscle weakness, loss of vision, and nystagmus [1]. (Radioactivity associated cause to sclerosis: viz. arteriosclerosis, hardening of the arteries [2].) The adverse symptoms can be prevented, alleviated, and removed by cannabis smoking. Ref. U.S. Judicial Enquiry Findings on cannabis smoking for MS; The Judge's Ruling, Part Four. The relaxant virtues of cannabis provide relief to those many people who suffer aches and pains from sport, manual labour, or the inevitable physical strains of life. Herbal cannabis, hot cannabis poultices, and ingested cannabis (eaten or smoked) bring relief to the painful joints of rheumatic and arthritis sufferers. Until Prohibition, poultices, muscle cream and ointments to treat muscular strains, fibrosis, and fibrositis, were made from the raw herb cannabis, and cannabis extractums. Cannabis is the most effective, the best, of such poultices and ointments, and has thus been applied for millennia [3].

1 Nystagmus: spasmodic, involuntary lateral oscillatory movement of the eyes.
2 ARTERIOSCLEROSIS: Ref. RADIOACTIVITY from PHOSPHATES MISUSED as "FERTILISER"; Part One.
3 See British-Indian Study.

Gordon.

Gordon Hanson of Minnesota, an accountant in his fifties, is an epileptic who smokes cannabis to alleviate symptoms of his condition. Over the years, Gordon's doctor has prescribed as 'medicines' Phenobarbital, Mysoline, Dilantin, and Valium, which caused unpleasant serious side-effects such as irritability, hyperactivity, fatigue, and violent changes of mood. ***The drugs* did not cure his epilepsy; so, Gordon had to cope with the ill-effects of the pharmaceutical drugs, *in addition to*, the symptoms of his condition.**

Gordon found cannabis herb superior treatment to all medicines of prescription: with cannabis, his epileptic seizures were greatly reduced in frequency, and those that he did have were less intense. Note that ***only*** by using cannabis can Gordon perform all the tasks required of him in his job, and lead a more normal fulfilled life. By using cannabis, Gordon was able to give up the pharmaceutical drugs entirely and all their bad side-effects disappeared.

Seen earlier in this Part, Cannabis Prohibition is *inequitably* [i.e.,, illegally] enforced by courts. *In addition*, trial judges do not allow the good motives for cultivation, trade, possession and use of cannabis, to be presented by defendants or defence attorneys for due consideration by the jury; *nor* do judges allow presentation of the Exonerative Evidence of Findings of Fact if these "dispute the legality of the law." *Further*, in finding the Verdict, under universal common law, *and* under British and U.S. Constitutional laws, the Trial by Jury Justice System (sine qua non) *mandatorily* requires the judgement by jurors on whether the act of enforcement, and the law under which the accused is being tried, are themselves **just**. This correct rôle of the juror in Trial by Jury is *also* circumvented by courts: such illegal tampering by state employees, in the functioning of the Justice System, is detailed in Part Seven.

Most judges consider it their job to enforce Prohibition without regard to law, justice, equity, truth, evidence or suffering. Gordon was arrested for cultivating his own supply of cannabis in his backyard, and he now has a Criminal Record, having received a sentence of imprisonment for a year and a day, of which he served three and a half months. The following are Gordon's own words:

"If the government doesn't think marijuana has any medical use, they should read my log from jail. When I smoke pot I have about ten seizures a year. Without it I had thirty-four seizures over the three and a half months I was in jail. Without marijuana I'm unable to get any stable employment. With marijuana I can lead a regular life."

Without cannabis, Gordon endures eleven to twelve times as many fits, and all the epileptic convulsions are much more severe. Again, it is seen how cannabis is a benign relaxant, not to be confused with drugs. The general smoking of cannabis *prevents* countless people from getting slight or serious, adverse medical conditions. However, governments torment and incarcerate, literally, many hundreds of thousands of good people, for sensibly and justifiably using cannabis. The government does this *in our name*.

We, the citizens, are responsible *for allowing* this ferocious tyranny. We are to blame for *consenting* to criminal enforcement, and *for permitting* the Prohibitionists' vicious 'punishments' (i.e.,, persecution) of innocent people. Only we, the People, by our words, resolve and actions, can ensure that the criminal clique's conspiratorial Prohibition is utterly extirpated.

To do nothing to stop this abhorrent Prohibition is as shameful as instigating or enforcing it.

STRESS RELIEF,
RELAXATION and SLEEP:
Cannabis is a relaxant and is stress relieving. It is not a narcotic, and does not induce torpor or drugged sleep. Nor does it interfere with rest, for those who are tired are able to sleep normally. (Ref. Set and Setting; Part Five.) Where a person is by the course of events ready to rest or in need of sleep, sleep ensues in the natural way. Patients, often perturbed deeply by their afflictions, find cannabis helps them to relax and to become more positive. Cannabis users report enjoying sleep of the most restful sort with incremented invigoration and energy on awakening. The stress-relieving benefits of cannabis have been extolled for millennia. Relegalised, cannabis herb/hash, extractums, tinctures and smoking will be the safe *replacement* for a high proportion of the expensive, noxious, addictive dangerous chemical compounds of the pharmaceutical companies, which are dispensed in their trillions, mostly on prescription, such as toxic, torpor-inducing tranquillisers, hypnotics and sedatives.

Plants such as Deadly Nightshade or Belladonna are the poisonous origin of which 'legal' narcotic sleeping pills of prescription, are synthesised laboratory analogues. These drugs are *dangerous*. By contrast, cannabis, which is not a drug, is always safe.

ANTI-BACTERIAL ACTION:

Cannabidiolic acid (CBD) extracted from cannabis plants provides antibiotics which would be especially useful today, where strains of bacteria show increasing resistance to the presently available antibiotics, penicillin, methicillin, ampicillin, etc. Cannabis poultices and ointments have been effective cures for wounds for millennia [1]. Anti-microbial action was confirmed by research conducted in the 1950's at Palacky University in Olomouc, Czechoslovakia [2], *which concluded*: cannabis treated with a consistently greater degree of success those conditions treated with Terramycin antibiotic; cannabis produces anti-bacterial results on *staphylococcus* and other micro- organisms that resist other antibiotics with fatal results; cannabis lotions and ointments (traditional cures [3]) successfully treated infections; topical (local) application of cannabis relieved pain and prevented infection in second degree burns.

The investigators report that a pathologist injured his thumb in the dissecting room; the resulting infection resisted all treatments. Amputation was being considered, until cannabis was tried and it promptly overcame the infection [4].

N.B. Staphylococcus infections are transmitted in hospitals, causing deaths. Again, in this anti-bacterial aspect, as in others, cannabis has potential *to save lives*; and, *Prohibition causes deaths, rendering the legislation of Prohibition illegal.*

1 & 3 See Report of British-Indian Hemp Commission.
2 See: Cannabis as a Medicament, Bulletin of Narcotics 12, 1960; pages 20-22, J. Kabelik & Z. Krejci & F. Santavy; and, On the Problem of Substances with Antibacterial Action: Cannabis Effect, Casopis Lekaru Ceskych 43, 1961; pages 1351-1354, Z. Krejci.
4 This demonstrates that cannabis should not be the last but the first treatment to be applied. Ref. also the Six Conclusions in: Realities and Responsibilities; Part Four.

RELIEF OF MIGRAINE, MENSTRUATION PAIN, HEADACHE, STRESS and ALLERGY-RELATED SYNDROMES, PRURITIS, ECZEMA, DERMATITIS:

Despite Prohibition, cannabis is widely smoked to relieve menstruation pain and pre-menstrual tension; and remains the pleasant cure for headaches (without poisonous aspirin's dangerous side-effects, including that of thinning the blood). Aspirin is usually ineffective for migraines, whereas cannabis relieves migraines' intense symptoms, such as severe headaches and pain in the eyes, frequently accompanied by nausea and disturbances of vision. Modern Medical Case Histories show cannabis is effective in treatment of the above conditions, even in extreme cases where the modern 'medications' prove completely ineffectual. Non-habit-forming and non-toxic, cannabis is safe to smoke repeatedly, as often as the individual wishes or needs. *Pharmaceuticals*, by contrast, are addictive, have *debilitating toxic side-effects*, and rapidly accumulate *lethal dosages*.

The amenity of cannabis to ease people who wish to be relaxed, and to relieve stress, is widely acknowledged. Stress is the considered cause of many, often severe, psychosomatic conditions. Stress is also regarded as dangerous to sufferers of heart complaints. Whereas powerful toxic, addictive drugs such as Valium, Librium, etc., are prescribed in an attempt to reduce (symptoms of) stress, and large numbers of people use alcohol in a similar way, over the long-term, pharmaceuticals and alcohol cause more problems than they cure [5].

5 Ref. Cannabis as Preventive Measure/Preventive Medicine; The Recent Modern Era—And The Motive; and, Part Four.

TUMOUR RESEARCH:

Clinical evidence exists which indicates that cannabis is effective in the reduction of tumours. Research into cannabis was conducted by the Medical College of Virginia. This study was specifically an attempt to find 'harm', if any, associated with use, and was instigated by the U.S. National Institute of Health (NIH) and the DEA. Instead of harm, researchers discovered the reverse.... In 1975, pursuant to indications that harm does not exist in cannabis, researchers announced *that cannabis had been observed to be successful in reducing tumours, including some of the malignant cancerous type.* The response by the DEA was instantaneous: the DEA instructed the NIH to defund the project and ordered the research be terminated forthwith.

Governments which stop research into frontiers of medical knowledge, affront science and society, and break common law; ref. Part Seven: i.e.,, on substantive legal grounds, the legislative and bureaucratic impedance is illegitimate. The indications are that cannabis is effective in reduction of malignant tumours. Let research be recommended forthwith. It would come as no surprise to those who study the therapeutic blessings of cannabis herb, to find that yet further remedial applications await discovery.

Consider leukaemia and cancer chemotherapies: Predictably, from time to time, drug companies produce some chemical concoction or other for taking orally or via injection, which they tout as being *'the'* effective 'medicine' in overcoming nausea or stimulating appetite. Unfortunately for patients, these all have chemically-inevitable unpleasant side-effects and none of these substances are as effective as cannabis in achieving desired results. 'Medicine-men'—doctors purporting to be 'independent', but actually representing financial interests of the pharmaceutical firms—press claims about the 'effectiveness' of the latest products through the indulgent media. These substances are only partially or temporarily effective, or simply do not work at all. Many patients suffering from cancer, relying on the drug companies' nostrums, lose weight, do not have any appetite, experience nausea without relief, become emaciated, and die. *These patients are not given and are not allowed to try cannabis, which when used has proven its therapeutic excellence.*

Consider two injectable substances: the Glaxo product costs over $200 *per day* (!); while Zofran costs approximately $600 *per day*. To these sums must be added the cost of the patient being obliged to attend the ambulatory care centre throughout the time that these substances are administered by qualified staff, rather than going home or to work. *Then compare the advantages of cannabis*: produced **cost-free** at home, or, even at inflated Black Market prices, the cannabis treatment, which is incomparably superior, costs only a few dollars. *Again, financial facts reveal the motive for hostility to cannabis by those whose revenue derives from inferior products.*

Most pharmaceutical nausea 'control' drugs come in pill form which, because of their acute nausea, patients predictably vomit up. This cannot occur with cannabis ingested as smoke. Furthermore, cannabis is conveniently self-administered wherever and whenever the patient feels the need to overcome the nausea, or other unpleasant effects of illness and toxic medicines. A self-titrated dose by a few puffs on a herbal cigarette of pure cannabis or a hash-pipe suffices, delivering the easiest, the cheapest, the most pleasant, and *the most effective type* of relief.

Applicable in <u>every</u> adverse condition, slight or serious, the recuperative importance of the cannabis well-being-effect cannot be over-emphasised: people suffering are significantly helped; and, many lives will be saved and improved by RESTORATION [1].

So effective is smoked cannabis and so important are the confirmed benefits to health from it, that, at great risk to themselves from the enforcement of this grotesque, illegal Prohibition, some doctors, nurses and hospitals have a patients-come-first policy, turning the proverbial blind-eye to patients' smoking of cannabis, or, they actually encourage their patients to smoke cannabis [2].

1 The RESTORATION Programme comprises Part Seven of THE REPORT.
2 See 'Marijuana as Antiemetic Medicine: A Survey of Oncologists' Experiences and Attitudes,' R.E. Doblin & M.A.R. Kleiman; Journal of Clinical Oncology,' Vol. 9, No.7 (July, 1991) pp. 1314-1319. Also ref. The Judge's Ruling.

Health and Safety Investigations.

Health and Safety Investigations conducted by States' Health Authorities have concluded: cannabis herb is a safe medicament, efficacious in treatment of various conditions. Thirty-five of the United States have unilaterally enacted laws to make cannabis available to patients, albeit under cautious legislative research terms. These States, and hundreds of thousands of seriously ill people for whom cannabis would render definite benefits, are denied cannabis-by-prescription by federal authorities, by the corrupt, unlawful 'decisions' of presidents, politicians, DEA, FDA and collusive federal courts of successive administrations. States subjected thus are as follows:

Alabama, Alaska, Arizona, Arkansas, California,
Colorado, Connecticut, Florida, Georgia, Illinois,
Iowa, Louisiana, Maine, Massachusetts, Michigan,
Minnesota, Montana, Nevada, New Hampshire, New Jersey,
New Mexico, New York, North Carolina, Ohio, Oklahoma,
Oregon, Rhode Island, South Carolina, Tennessee, Texas,
Vermont, Virginia, Washington, West Virginia, Wisconsin.

Temporisation and 'Blind' Studies.

So-called "blind" studies are a standard test method for invented drugs. These involve pharmacologically inactive placebos which are administered without the volunteer's foreknowledge, to differentiate results induced by the substance under test, as distinct from subjective impressions. Because of the pleasant feeling of well-being enjoyed by the consumer, it is *always* discernible to the ingestor whether he or she has smoked cannabis, or some pharmacologically inert alternative. Self-evidently, the "blind-test" method in the cannabis context is inapplicable. Yet, in temporisation to delay Relegalisation, Prohibitionists are even heard calling for "blind" studies !

The real test of this herb as medicine is when it is actually administered to or put into use by the sick. Doctors', nurses', and patients' experiences and observations, the Modern Medical Case Histories, are the crucial test as to whether cannabis is safe and effective in treatment. Historical evidence of millennia and the recent past, and present day medical records and case histories, *the living proof*, all confirm cannabis to be profoundly therapeutic without harmful effect. *The truth, the reality, is a sharp contrast to the mythic derogatory propaganda*. In further confirmation (as if any were needed) the next Part of THE REPORT introduces Judge Francis L. Young's review and Findings of Fact.

~

- PART FOUR -
Further Modern Uses and The Judge's Ruling.

THE reader who has assimilated from previous Parts, facts detailing the many benefits which cannabis renders to healthy and/or ailing people alike, will also have observed the great degree to which cannabis constitutes a superior health product: *a uniquely safe benign relaxant with wide-ranging therapeutic efficacity*. Relegalised, cannabis will **beneficially replace** much present use of numerous toxic pharmaceutical and recreational drugs. This is borne out by Judicial Review. As a result of long-term litigation, i.e.,, petitioning by private organisations and persons, in 1987 and 1988 the U.S. Drug Enforcement Agency Administrative Law Regulations were reviewed by Judge Francis L. Young, who held hearings to oversee medical records, case histories, and take evidence, to ascertain whether cannabis remain in (the American regulatory classification) Schedule 1, under the 1970 Controlled Substances Act. To be in Schedule 1, substances require definition as having "no accepted medical use in treatment in the United States" and being "unsafe for use under medical supervision." (These remain the criteria to date.) Regarding Judge Young's Ruling of the 6th of September, 1988, the following are:

EXCERPTS (Transcript).
ON: Safe Cannabis Compared to Chemotherapy Drugs. . .

"**In strict medical terms marijuana is far safer than many foods we commonly consume.**"

"**Marijuana, in its natural form, is one of the safest therapeutically active substances known to man.**"

[In contrast, consider the following....]

"Some of the drugs most widely used in chemotherapy treatment of cancer have adverse effects as follows:

Cisplatin; one of the most powerful chemotherapeutic agents used on humans may cause deafness, may lead to life-threatening kidney difficulties and kidney failure; adversely affects the body's immune system, suppressing the patient's ability to fight a host of common infections.

Nitrogen Mustard; a drug used in therapy for Hodgkin disease—nauseates; so toxic to the skin that, if dropped on the skin, this chemical literally eats it away along with other tissues it contacts; if this drug gets on or under the skin the patient may suffer serious injury including temporary, and in extreme cases, permanent loss of use of the arm.

Procarbizine; also used for Hodgkin disease, has known psychogenic, i.e.,, emotional, effects.

Cytoxin; also known as *Cyclophosphamide*—suppresses patient's immune system response; results in serious bone marrow depletion; studies indicate this drug may also cause other cancers, including cancers of the bladder.

Adriamycian; has numerous adverse effects and is difficult to employ in long term therapies because it destroys the heart muscle."

"While each of these agents has its particular adverse effects, as indicated above, they also cause a number of similar, disturbing adverse effects. Most of these drugs cause hair loss. Studies increasingly indicate all of these drugs may cause other forms of cancer. Death due to kidney, heart or respiratory failure is a very real possibility with all of these agents and the margin for error is minimal. Similarly, there is a danger of overdosing a patient weakened by his cancer. Put simply, there is very great risk associated with the medical use of these chemical agents. Despite these high risks, all of these drugs are considered "safe" for use under medical supervision and are regularly administered to patients on doctor's orders in the United States today."

"The vomiting induced by chemotherapeutic drugs may last up to four days following the chemotherapy treatment. The vomiting can be intense, protracted and, in some instances, is unendurable. The nausea which follows such vomiting is also deep and prolonged. Nausea may prevent a patient from taking regular food or even much water for periods of weeks at a time."

"Nausea and vomiting of this severity degrades the quality of life for these patients, weakening them physically, and destroying the will to fight the cancer. A desire to end the chemotherapy treatment in order to escape the emesis can supersede the will to live. Thus the emesis, itself, can truly be considered a life-threatening consequence of many cancer treatments. Doctors have known such cases to occur. Doctors have known other cases where marijuana smoking has enabled the patient to endure, and thus continue, chemotherapy treatment with the result that the cancer has gone into remission and the patient has returned to a full, active, satisfying life." [1]

1 **This reinforces conclusions drawn earlier. Decisions to withhold cannabis are <u>premeditated, malicious</u>, and can <u>cause death, constituting homicide</u>. Cannabis Prohibition and its enforcement are Crimes against Humanity. By this time, there can be no honest politician or conscientious media commentator remaining in ignorance of the general Health, particular <u>life-saving</u>, and other important benefits to Mankind from cannabis.**

ON: Relief of Nausea Caused by Chemotherapy. . .

"Beginning in the 1970's there was a considerable doctor-to-doctor communication in the U.S. concerning patients known by their doctors to be surreptitiously using marijuana with notable success to overcome or lessen their nausea and vomiting. In San Francisco chemotherapy patients were surreptitiously using marijuana to control emesis by the early 1970's. By 1976 virtually every young cancer patient receiving chemotherapy at the University of California in San Francisco was using marijuana to control emesis with great success. The use of marijuana for this purpose had become generally accepted by the patients and increasingly by their physicians as a valid and effective form of treatment."

"In about December, 1977, the previously underground patient practice of using marijuana to control emesis burst into the public media in New Mexico. As a result, professionals in the public health sector... more closely examined... what now openly appeared to be a widely recognised patient need."

"By the late 1970's in the Washington, D.C., area there was a growing recognition among health care professionals and the public that marijuana had therapeutic value in reducing the adverse effects of some chemotherapy patients. With this increasing public awareness came increasing pressure from patients and doctors for information about marijuana and its therapeutic uses. Many patients moved into forms of unsupervised self-treatment."

"Every oncologist known to one Washington, D.C., practising internist and board-certified oncologist has had patients who used marijuana with great success to prevent or diminish chemotherapy induced nausea and vomiting. Chemotherapy patients reporting directly to that Washington doctor that they have smoked marijuana medically vomit less and eat better than patients who do not smoke it. By gaining control over their severe nausea and vomiting these patients undergo a change of mood and have a better mental outlook than patients who, using the standard anti-emetic drugs, are unable to gain such control."

"About 50 per cent of the patients seen by one San Francisco oncologist during the year 1987 were smoking marijuana medically."

ON: Cannabis as Appetite Stimulant. . .

"In many cases... in addition to suppressing nausea and vomiting, smoking marijuana is a highly successful appetite stimulant. The importance of appetite stimulation in cancer therapy cannot be overstated. Marijuana smoking induces some patients to eat. The benefits are obvious, doctors have found."

"Synthetic anti-emetic agents have been in existence and utilised for a number of years. But marijuana still is found more effective for this purpose in some people than any of the synthetic agents, even the newer ones."

ON: Cannabis Relief of Chemotherapies. . .

"Voluminous reports filed by the participating physicians [to the State of New Mexico's hospitals' research program to try make marijuana available on prescription to cancer patients subsequently closed down by DEA, federal order] make it clear that marijuana is a highly effective anti-emetic substance. It was found in the New Mexico program to be far superior to the best available conventional anti-emetic drug, Compazine, and clearly superior to synthetic THC pills. More than 90 per cent of the patients who received marijuana within the program reported significant or total relief from nausea and vomiting."

"Before the program... cancer patients were surreptitiously smoking marijuana to control their emesis from chemotherapy treatments. They reported to physicians that it was successful for this purpose. Physicians were aware that this was going on."

"...a nurse in a hospital suggested to a chemotherapy patient, suffering greatly from the therapy and at the point of refusing further treatment, that smoking marijuana might help relieve his nausea and vomiting. The patient's doctor, when asked about it later, stated that many of his younger patients were smoking marijuana. Those who did so seemed to have less trouble with nausea and vomiting. The patient in question obtained some marijuana and smoked it, in the hospital, immediately before his next chemotherapy treatment. Doctors, nurses and orderlies coming into the room as he finished smoking realised what the patient had been doing. None of them made any comment. The marijuana was completely successful with this patient, who accepted it as effective in controlling his nausea and vomiting. Instead of being sick for weeks following chemotherapy, and having trouble going to work, as had been the case, the patient was ready to return to work 48 hours after that chemotherapy treatment. The patient thereafter always smoked marijuana, in the hospital, before chemotherapy. The doctors were aware of it, openly approved of it and encouraged him to continue. The patient resumed eating regular meals and regained lost weight, his mood improved markedly, he became more active and outgoing and began doing things together with his wife that he had not done since beginning chemotherapy."

"A Boston psychiatrist and professor, who travels about the country, has found a minor conspiracy to break the law among oncologists and nurses in every oncology center he has visited to let patients smoke marijuana before and during cancer chemotherapy. He has talked with dozens of these health care oncologists who encourage their patients to do this and who regard this as an accepted medical usage of marijuana."

"He has known nurses who have obtained marijuana for patients unable to obtain it for themselves."

"A cancer patient residing in Beaverton, Michigan, smoked marijuana medically in the nearby hospital where he was undergoing chemotherapy from early 1979 until he died of his cancer in October of that year. He smoked it in his hospital room after his parents made arrangements with the hospital for him to do so. Smoking marijuana controlled his post-chemotherapy nausea and vomiting, enabled him to eat regular meals again with his family, and he became outgoing and talkative. His parents accepted his marijuana smoking as effective and helpful. Two clergymen, among others, brought marijuana to this patient's home. Many people at the hospital supported the patient's marijuana therapy, none doubted its helpfulness or discouraged it. This patient was asked for help by other patients. He taught some who lived nearby how to form the marijuana cigarettes and properly inhale the smoke to obtain relief from nausea and vomiting. When an article about this patient's smoking marijuana appeared in a local newspaper, he and his family heard from many other cancer patients who were doing the same. Most of them made an effort to inform their doctors. Most physicians who knew their patients smoked marijuana medicinally approved, accepting marijuana's therapeutic helpfulness in reducing nausea and vomiting."

"In late 1980 a three-year-old boy was brought by his parents to a hospital in Spokane, Washington. The child was diagnosed as having cancer. Surgery was performed. Chemotherapy was begun. The child became extremely nauseated and vomited for days after each chemotherapy treatment. He could not eat regularly. He lost strength. He lost weight. His body's ability to ward off common infections, other life-threatening infections, significantly decreased. Chemotherapy's after effects caused the child great suffering. They caused his watching parents great suffering. Several standard, available anti-emetic agents were tried by the child's doctors. None of them succeeded in controlling his nausea and vomiting. Learning of the existence of research studies with THC or marijuana the parents asked the child's doctor to arrange for their son to be the subject of such a study so that he might have access to marijuana. The doctor refused, citing the volume of paperwork and record-keeping detail required in such programs and his lack of administrative personnel to handle it."

"The child's mother read an article about marijuana smoking helping chemotherapy patients. She obtained some marijuana from friends. She baked cookies for her child with marijuana in them. She made tea for him with marijuana in it. When the child ate these cookies or drank this tea in connection with his chemotherapy, he did not vomit. His strength returned. He regained lost weight. His spirits revived. The parents told the doctors and nurses at the hospital of their giving marijuana to their child. None objected. They all accepted smoking marijuana as effective in controlling chemotherapy induced nausea and vomiting. They were interested to see the results of the cookies."

Further Modern Uses; and, The Judge's Ruling.

"Soon this child was riding a tricycle in the hallways of the Spokane hospital shortly after his chemotherapy treatments while other children there were still vomiting into pans, tied to intravenous bottles in an attempt to rehydrate them, to replace the liquids they were vomiting up. Parents of some of the other patients asked the parents of this "lively" child how he seemed to tolerate his chemotherapy so well. They told of the marijuana use. Of those parents who began giving marijuana to their children, none ever reported back encountering any adverse side effects."

"In the vast majority of these cases, the other parents reported significant reduction in their children's vomiting and appetite stimulation as the result of the marijuana. The staff, doctors and nurses at the hospital knew of this passing on of information about marijuana to other parents. They approved. They never told the first parents to hide their son's medicinal use of marijuana. They accepted the effectiveness of the cookies and the tea containing marijuana."

"The first child's cancer went into remission. Then it returned and spread. Emotionally drained, the parents moved the family back to San Diego, California, to be near their own parents. Their son was admitted to a hospital in San Diego. The parents informed the doctors, nurses and social workers there of their son's therapeutic use of marijuana. No one objected. The child's doctor in San Diego strongly supported the parents giving marijuana to him. Here in California, as in Spokane, other parents noted the striking difference between their children after chemotherapy and the first child. Other parents asked the parents of the first child about it, were told of the use of marijuana, tried it with their children, and saw dramatic improvement. They accepted its effectiveness. "

"In the words of the mother of the first child: "When your kid is riding a tricycle while his other hospital buddies are hooked up to I. V. [intravenous] needles, their heads hung over vomiting buckets, you don't need a federal agency to tell you marijuana is effective. The evidence is in front of you, so stark it cannot be ignored." "

"From the aforegoing uncontroverted facts it is clear beyond any question that many people find marijuana to have, in the words of the Act, an "accepted medical use in treatment in the United States" in effecting relief for cancer patients. Oncologists, physicians treating cancer patients accept this. Other medical practitioners and researchers accept this. Medical faculty professors accept it. Nurses performing hands-on patient care accept it. Patients accept it... acceptance by the patient is of vital importance. Doctors accept a therapeutic agent or process only if it "works" for the patient. If the patient does not accept, the doctor cannot administer the treatment. The patient's informed consent is vital. The doctor ascertains the patient's acceptance by observing and listening to the patient. Acceptance by the doctor depends on what he sees in the patient and hears from the patient. Unquestionably, patients in large numbers have accepted marijuana as useful in treating their emesis. They have found that it "works". Doctors, evaluating their patients, can have no basis more sound than that for their own acceptance."

"The overwhelming preponderance of the evidence in this record establishes that marijuana has a currently accepted medical use in treatment in the United States for nausea and vomiting resulting from chemotherapy treatments in some cancer patients. To conclude otherwise on this record would be unreasonable, arbitrary and capricious."

ON: Cannabis Use in Treatment of Multiple Sclerosis, Spasticity. . .

"MS is the major cause of neurological disability among young and middle-aged adults in the United States today. It is a life-long disease. It can be extremely debilitating to some of its victims but it does not shorten the life span of most of them. Its cause is yet to be determined. It attacks the myelin sheath, the coating or insulation surrounding the message-carrying nerve fibers in the brain and spinal cord. Once the myelin sheath is destroyed, it is replaced by plaques of hardened tissue known as sclerosis. During the initial stages of the disease nerve impulses are transmitted with only minor interruptions. As the disease progresses, the plaques may completely obstruct the impulses along certain nerve systems. These obstructions produce malfunctions. The effects are sporadic in most individuals and the effects often occur episodically, triggered either by malfunction of the nerve impulses or by external factors."

"Over time many patients develop spasticity, the involuntary and abnormal contraction of muscle or muscle fibers. (Spasticity can also result from serious injuries to the spinal cord, not related to multiple sclerosis.)"

"The symptoms of MS vary according to the area of the nervous system which is affected and according to the severity of the disease. The symptoms can include one or more of the following: weakness, tingling, numbness, impaired sensation, lack of coordination, disturbances in equilibrium, double vision, loss of vision, involuntary rapid movement of the eyes (nystagmus) slurred speech, tremors, stiffness, spasticity, weakness of the limbs, sexual dysfunction, paralysis, and impaired bowel and bladder functions. Each person afflicted by MS is affected differently. In some persons, the symptoms of the disease are barely detectable, even over long periods of time. In these cases, the persons can live their lives as if they did not suffer from the disease. In others, more of the symptoms are present and acute, thereby limiting their physical capabilities. Moreover, others may experience sporadic, but acute, symptoms."

"At this time, there is no known prevention or cure for MS. Instead, there are only treatments for the symptoms of the disease. There are very few drugs specifically designed to treat spasticity. These drugs often cause very serious side effects. At the present time two drugs are approved by FDA [Food & Drug Administration] as "safe" and "effective" for the specific indication of spasticity. These drugs are Dantrium and Lioresal Baclofen."

"Unfortunately, neither Dantrium nor Lioresal is a very effective spasm control drug. Their marginal medical utility, high toxicity and potential for serious side effects make these drugs difficult to use in spasticity therapy."

"As a result many physicians routinely prescribe tranquilisers, muscle relaxants, mood elevators and sedatives such as Valium to patients experiencing spasticity. While these drugs do not directly reduce spasticity, they may weaken the patient's muscle tone, thus making the spasms less noticeable. Alternatively, they may induce sleep or so tranquilise the patient that normal mental or physical functions are impossible."

"A healthy, athletic woman named Valerie Cover was stricken with MS while in her early twenties. She consulted several medical specialists and followed all the customary regimens and prescribed methods for coping with this debilitating disease over a period of several years. None of these proved availing. Two years after first experiencing the symptoms of MS her active productive life—as a Naval officer's wife and mother—was effectively over. The Social Security Administration declared her totally disabled. To move about her home she had to sit on a skateboard and push herself around. She spent most of her time in bed or sitting in a wheelchair."

"An occasional marijuana smoker in her teens, before her marriage, she had not smoked it for five years as of February, 1986. Then a neighbour suggested that marijuana just might help Mrs. Cover's MS, having read that it had helped cancer patients control their emesis. Mrs. Cover acceded to the suggestion."

"Just before smoking the marijuana cigarette produced by her neighbour, Mrs. Cover had been throwing up and suffering from spasms. Within five minutes of her smoking part of the marijuana cigarette she stopped vomiting, no longer felt nauseous and noticed the intensity of her spasms was significantly reduced. She stood up unaided."

"Mrs. Cover began smoking marijuana whenever she felt nauseated. When she did so it controlled her vomiting, stopped the nausea and increased her appetite. It helped ease and control her spasticity. Her limbs were much easier to control. After three months of smoking marijuana she could walk unassisted, had regained all of her lost weight, her seizures became almost nonexistent. She could again care for her children. She could drive an automobile again. She regained the ability to lead a normal life."

"Concerned that her use of this illegal substance might jeopardise the career of her Navy officer husband, Mrs. Cover stopped smoking marijuana several times. Each time she did so, after about a month, she had retrogressed to the point that her MS again had her confined to bed and wheel chair or skateboard. As of the Spring of 1987 Mrs. Cover had resumed smoking marijuana regularly on an "as needed" basis. Her MS symptoms are under excellent control. She has obtained a full-time job. She still needs a wheelchair on rare occasions, but generally has full use of her limbs and can walk around with relative ease."

"Mrs. Cover's doctor has accepted the effectiveness of marijuana in her case. He questioned her closely about her use of it, telling her that it is the most effective drug known in reducing vomiting. Mrs. Cover and her doctor are now in the process of filing an Investigational New Drug [sic] application with FDA so that she can legally obtain the marijuana she needs to lead a reasonably normal life."

"Martha Hirsch is a young woman in her mid-thirties. She first exhibited symptoms of MS at age 19 and it was diagnosed at that time. Her condition has grown progressively worse. She has been under the care of physicians and hospitalised for treatment. Many drugs have been prescribed for her by her doctors. At one point in 1983 she listed the drugs that had been prescribed to her. There were 17 on the list. None of them has given her the relief from her MS symptoms that marijuana has."

"During the early stages in the development of her illness Ms. Hirsch found that smoking marijuana improved the quality of her life, keeping her spasms under control. Her balance improved. She seldom needed to use her cane for support. Her condition lately has deteriorated. As of May, 1987, she was experiencing severe, painful spasms. She had an indwelling catheter in her bladder. She had lost her locomotive abilities and was wheelchair bound. She could seldom find marijuana on the illegal market and, when she did, she often could not afford to purchase it. When she did obtain some, however, and smoked it, her entire body seemed to relax, her spasms decreased or disappeared, she slept better and her dizzy spells vanished. The relaxation of her leg muscles after smoking marijuana has been confirmed by her personal care attendant's examination of them."

"The personal care attendant has told Mrs. Hirsch that she, the attendant, treats a number of patients who smoke marijuana for relief of MS symptoms. In about 1980 another patient told Ms. Hirsch that he knew many patients who smoke marijuana to relieve their spasms. Through him she met other patients and found that marijuana was commonly used by MS patients. Most of these persons had told their doctors about their doing so. None of those doctors advised against the practice and some encouraged it."

"Among the drugs prescribed for Ms. Hirsch was ACTH. This failed to give her any therapeutic benefit or to control her spasticity. It did produce a number of adverse effects, including severe nausea and vomiting which, in turn, were partly controlled by rectally administered anti-emetic drugs."

"Another drug prescribed for her was Lioresal, intended to reduce her spasms. It was not very effective in so doing. But it did cause Ms. Hirsch to have hallucinations. On two occasions, while using this drug, Ms. Hirsch "saw" a large fire in her bedroom and called for help. There was no fire. She stopped using that drug. Ms. Hirsch has experienced no adverse reactions with marijuana."

"Ms. Hirsch's doctor has accepted marijuana as beneficial for her. He agreed to write her a prescription for her, if that would help her obtain it. She has asked him if he would file an IND application with the FDA for her. He replied that the paperwork was "overwhelming". He indicated willingness to help in this undertaking after Ms. Hirsch found someone else willing to put the paperwork together."

"When Greg Paufler was in his early twenties, employed by Prudential Insurance Company, he began to experience the first symptoms of MS. His condition worsened as the disease intensified. He had to be hospitalised. He lost the ability to walk, to stand. Diagnosed as having MS, a doctor prescribed ACTH for him, an intensive form of steroid therapy. He lost all control over his limbs and experienced severe, painful spasms. His arms and legs became numb."

"ACTH had no beneficial effects. The doctor continued to prescribe it over many months. ACTH made Paufler ravenously hungry and he began gaining a great deal of weight. ACTH caused fluid retention and Paufler became bloated, rapidly gaining weight. His doctor thought Paufler should continue this steroid therapy, even though it caused the adverse effects mentioned plus the possibility of sudden heart attack or death due to respiratory failure. Increased dosages of this FDA-approved drug caused fluid to press against Paufler's lungs making it difficult for him to breathe and causing his legs and feet to become swollen. The steroid therapy caused severe, intense depression marked by abrupt mood shifts. Throughout, the spasms continued and Paufler's limbs remained out of control. The doctor insisted that ACTH was the only therapy likely to be of any help with the MS, despite its adverse effects. Another oral steroid was eventually substituted."

Further Modern Uses; and, The Judge's Ruling.

"One day Paufler became semi-catatonic while sitting in his living room at home. He was rushed to the hospital emergency room. He nearly died. Lab reports indicated, among other things, a nearly total lack of potassium in his body. He was given massive injections of potassium in the emergency room and placed on an oral supplement. Paufler resolved to take no more steroids."

"From time to time, prior to this point, Paufler had smoked marijuana socially with visiting friends, seeking some relief from his misery in a temporary "high". He now began smoking marijuana more often. After some weeks he found that he could stand and then walk a bit. His doctor dismissed the idea that marijuana could be helpful with MS, and Paufler, himself, was sceptical at first. He began discontinuing it for a while, then resuming."

"Paufler found that when he did not smoke marijuana his condition worsened, he suffered more intense spasms more frequently. When he smoked marijuana, his condition would stabilise and then improve; spasms were more controlled and less severe; he felt better; he regained control over his limbs and could walk totally unaided. His vision, often blurred and unfocused, improved. Eventually he began smoking marijuana on a daily basis. He ventured outdoors. He was soon walking half a block. His eyesight returned to normal. His central field blindness cleared up. He could focus well enough to read again. One evening he went out with his children and found he could kick a soccer ball again."

"Paufler has smoked marijuana regularly since 1980. Since that time his MS has been well controlled. His doctor has been astonished at Paufler's recovery. Paufler can now run. He can stand on one foot with his eyes closed. The contrast with his condition, several years ago, seems miraculous. Smoking marijuana when Paufler feels an attack coming on shortens the attack. Paufler's doctor has looked Paufler in the eye and told him to keep doing whatever it is he's doing because it works. Paufler and his doctor are exploring the possibility of obtaining a compassionate IND to provide legal access to marijuana for Paufler."

"Paufler learned in about 1980 of the success of one Sam Diana, a multiple sclerosis patient, in asserting the defence of "medical necessity" in court when charged with using or possessing marijuana. He learned that doctors, researchers and other MS patients had supported Diana's position in the court proceeding."

"Irvin Rosenfeld has been diagnosed as having Pseudo Pseudo Hypoparathyroidism. This uncommon disease causes bone spurs to appear and grow all over the body. Over the patient's lifetime hundreds of these spurs can grow, any one of which can become malignant at any time. The resulting cancer would spread quickly and the patient would die."

"Even without the development of a malignancy, the disease causes enormous pain. The spurs press upon adjacent body tissue, nerves and organs. In Rosenfeld's case, he could neither sit still nor lie down, nor could he walk without experiencing pain. Working in his furniture store in Portsmouth, Virginia, Mr. Rosenfeld was on his feet moving furniture all day long. The lifting and walking caused serious problems as muscles and tissues rubbed over the spurs of bone. He tore muscles and haemorrhaged almost daily."

"Rosenfeld's symptoms first appeared about the age of ten, various drugs were prescribed for him for pain relief. He was taking extremely powerful narcotics. By the age of 19 his therapy included 300 mg. of Sopor (a powerful sleeping agent) and very high doses of Dilaudid. He was found to be allergic to barbiturates. Taking massive doses of pain control drugs, as prescribed, made it very difficult for Rosenfeld to function normally. If he took enough of them to control the pain, he could barely concentrate on his schoolwork. By the time he reached his early twenties Rosenfeld's monthly intake was between 120 to 130 Dilaudid tablets, 30 more Sopor sleeping pills and dozens of muscle relaxants."

"At college in Florida Rosenfeld was introduced to marijuana by classmates. He experimented with it recreationally. He never experienced a "high" or "buzz" or "floating sensation" from it. One day he smoked marijuana while playing chess with a friend. It had been very difficult for him to sit for more than five or ten minutes at a time because of tumours in the back of his legs. Suddenly he realised that, absorbed in his chess game, and smoking marijuana, he had remained sitting for over an hour—with no pain. He experimented further and found that his pain was reduced whenever he smoked marijuana."

"Rosenfeld told his doctor of his discovery. The doctor opined that it was possible that the marijuana was relieving the pain. Something certainly was—there was a drastic decrease in Rosenfeld's need for such drugs as Dilaudid and Demerol and for sleeping pills. The quality of pain relief which followed his smoking of marijuana was superior to any he had experienced before. As his dosages of powerful conventional [1] (sic) drugs decreased, Rosenfeld became less withdrawn from the world, more able to interact and function. So he has continued to the present time."

[1 Authors' Note: Regarding Judge Young's use of the word "*conventional*," for more than 4,700 years, the tried and tested analgesic and other qualities of cannabis have reliably benefited Mankind. The *reality* is that cannabis is the *conventional medicine*, accepted across the vista of time by the greater part of humanity. The modern proprietary pharmaceutical toxic chemical concoctions are the *unconventional* (and, by comparison, experimental) inadequate attempts to fill the medicinal gap left by Prohibition of Cannabis.]

"After some time Rosenfeld's doctor accepted the fact that the marijuana was therapeutically helpful to Rosenfeld and submitted an IND application to FDA to obtain supplies of it legally for Rosenfeld. After some effort the IND application was granted. Rosenfeld is receiving supplies of marijuana from NIDA. Rosenfeld testified before a committee of the Virginia Legislature in about 1979 in support of legislation to make marijuana available for therapeutic purposes in that state."

"In 1969, at age 19, David Branstetter dove into the shallow end of a swimming pool and broke his neck. He became a quadriplegic, losing control over the movement of his arms and legs. After being hospitalised for 18 months he returned home. Valium was prescribed for him to reduce the severe spasms associated with his condition. He became mildly addicted to Valium. Although it helped to mask his spasms, it made Branstetter more withdrawn and less able to take care of himself. He stopped taking Valium for fear of the consequences of long-term addiction. His spasms then became uncontrollable, often becoming so bad they would throw him from his wheelchair."

Further Modern Uses; and, The Judge's Ruling.

"In about 1973 Branstetter began smoking marijuana recreationally. He discovered that his severe spasms stopped whenever he smoked marijuana. Unlike Valium, which only masked his symptoms and caused him to feel drunk and out of control, marijuana brought his spasmodic condition under control without impairing his faculties. When he was smoking marijuana regularly he was more active, alert and outgoing."

"Marijuana controlled his spasms so well that Branstetter could go out with friends and he began to play billiards again. The longer he smoked marijuana the more he was able to use his arms and hands. Marijuana also improved his bladder control and bowel movements."

"At times the illegal marijuana Branstetter was smoking became very expensive and sometimes was unavailable. During periods when he did not have marijuana his spasms would return, preventing Branstetter from living a "normal" life. He would begin to shake uncontrollably, his body would feel tense, and his muscles would spasm."

"In 1979 Branstetter was arrested and convicted of possession of marijuana. He was placed on probation for two years. During that period he continued smoking marijuana and truthfully reported this and the reason for it, to his probation officer whenever asked about it. No action was taken against Branstetter by the court or probation authorities because of his continuing use of marijuana, except once in the wake of his publicly testifying about it before the Missouri Legislature. Then, although adverse action was threatened by the judge, nothing was actually done."

"In 1981 Branstetter and a friend, a paraplegic, participated in a research study testing the therapeutic effects of synthetic THC on spasticity. Placed on the THC Branstetter found that it did help control the spasms but appeared to become less effective with repeated use. **Also, unlike marijuana, synthetic THC has a powerful mind-altering effect he found annoying**. [Emphasis added.] When the study ended the researcher strongly suggested that Branstetter continue smoking marijuana to control his spasms."

"None of Branstetter's doctors have told him to stop smoking marijuana while several, directly and indirectly, have encouraged him to continue. Branstetter knows of almost 20 other patients, paraplegics, quadriplegics and MS sufferers, who smoke marijuana to control their spasticity."

"Large numbers of paraplegic and quadriplegic patients, particularly in Veterans' Hospitals, routinely smoke marijuana to reduce spasticity. While this mode of treatment is illegal, it is generally tolerated, if not openly encouraged, by physicians in charge of such wards who accept this practice as being of benefit to their patients."

ON: Cannabis as Safe. . .

"Nearly all medicines have toxic, potentially lethal effects. But marijuana is not such a substance. There is no record in the extensive medical literature describing a proven, documented cannabis-induced fatality."

"This is a remarkable statement. First, the record on marijuana encompasses 5,000 years of human experience. Second, marijuana is now used daily by enormous numbers of people throughout the world. Estimates suggest that from twenty million to fifty million Americans routinely, albeit illegally, smoke marijuana without the benefit of direct medical supervision. Yet, despite this long history of use and the extraordinarily high numbers of social smokers, there are simply no credible medical reports to suggest that consuming marijuana has caused a single death."

"By contrast aspirin, a commonly used, over-the-counter medicine, causes hundreds of deaths a year."

"Drugs used in medicine are routinely given what is called an LD-50. The LD-50 rating indicates at what dosage fifty per cent of test animals receiving a drug will die as a result of drug induced toxicity. A number of researchers have attempted to determine marijuana's LD-50 rating in test animals without success. Simply stated, **researchers have been unable to give animals enough marijuana to induce death**."

[Emphasis added. Authors' Note: The preceding paragraph explains why cannabis is properly referred to as a **non-toxic substance**, or, **as a substance in which toxicity does not exist**. Of further interest in this context: self-evidently, the single chemical compound tetrahydrocannabinol, or THC, in isolated pure form is a chemically *disparate* substance from cannabis herb which is *a single substance compounded from literally hundreds of compounds*. (Ref. 'THC' Is Not 'Cannabis'; Part One.)
One demonstration of disparateness, the extreme difference, between cannabis herb and lab-THC is shown by the adverse effects of THC on mice in extreme doses, which yield an LD-50 rating of from 1 : 20,000 to 1 : 40,000.
By contrast, cannabis can have no LD-50 rating as, in any quantity, it is incapable of inducing death in humans and animals, including mice. That cannabis is NON-TOXIC is established Empirical Fact. Judge Young goes on to point out categorically that cannabis is incapable of inducing a lethal response. Veracity requires that cannabis be universally, unequivocally acknowledged to be what it is: **non-toxic**.]

"In practical terms, **marijuana cannot induce a lethal response** as a result of drug-related toxicity." [Emphasis added.]

"Another common way to determine drug safety is called the therapeutic ratio. This ratio defines the difference between a therapeutically effective dose and a dose which is capable of inducing adverse effects. A commonly used over-the-counter product like aspirin has a therapeutic ratio of around 1 : 20. Two aspirins are the recommended dose for adult patients. Twenty times this dose, forty aspirins, may cause a lethal reaction in some patients, and will almost certainly cause gross injury to the digestive system, including extensive internal bleeding."

"The therapeutic ratio for prescribed drugs is commonly around 1 : 10 or lower. Valium, a commonly used prescriptive drug, may cause very serious biological damage if patients use ten times the recommended (therapeutic) dose."

Further Modern Uses; and, The Judge's Ruling.

"There are, of course, prescriptive drugs which have much lower therapeutic ratios. Many of the drugs used to treat patients with cancer, glaucoma and MS are highly toxic. The therapeutic ratio of some of the drugs used in antineoplastic therapies, for example, are regarded as extremely toxic poisons with therapeutic ratios that may fall below 1 : 1.5. These drugs also have very low LD-50 ratios and can result in toxic, even lethal reactions, while being properly employed."

"By contrast, marijuana's therapeutic ratio, like its LD-50, is impossible to quantify because it is so high."

"**In strict medical terms marijuana is far safer than many foods we commonly consume**. [Emphasis added.] For example, eating ten raw potatoes can result in a toxic response. By comparison, it is physically impossible to eat enough marijuana to induce death. Marijuana, in its natural form, is one of the safest therapeutically active substances known to man."

"Based upon the facts established in this record and set out above one must reasonably conclude that there is accepted safety for use of marijuana under medical supervision. To conclude otherwise, on this record, would be unreasonable, arbitrary and capricious. The Administrative law judge recommends that the Administrator [of the DEA] conclude that the marijuana plant considered as a whole has a currently accepted medical use in treatment in the United States, that there is no lack of accepted safety for use of it under medical supervision and that it may lawfully be transferred from Schedule 1 to Schedule 2. The judge recommends that the Administrator transfer marijuana from Schedule 1 to Schedule 2."

Limited Parameters.

Judge Young ruled that, cannabis being safe and effective medicine, it be made available as such by prescription, as per Schedule 2. Given the limited parameters of Judge Young's brief, he could scarcely have ruled otherwise. Nevertheless, cannabis does not qualify for any restriction or regulation, it being entirely safe.

The Judge's ruling was humiliatingly ignored by an unrepentant DEA. *Before* Judge Young's ruling, the DEA could have claimed (albeit disingenuously) that their classification of cannabis in Schedule 1 was an 'error'. *Since* the Judge's enquiry and ruling, the pretext of error is untenable. The implications of the ignoring of evidence and, the arbitrary overruling of the judge by a politically-appointed police bureaucrat, and subsequently by the appeal court, are grave. All is, however, unsurprising; for it typifies anti-democratic and other criminal aspects of money-motivated Prohibitions. Doing the bidding of their unseen avaricious masters, the DEA, retaining cannabis in the regulatory classification of "danger" and "without medical use" (Schedule 1), adopts mendacity in premeditated acts of consummate inhumanity. By regulations of statute, by courtroom false testimony, and by personal statements, the DEA promulgates *disinformation by lies* to the population at large, which constitutes, and abets, the Fraud which is Prohibition. (Ref. section on Schedule One, which follows.)

The government practice of propagating disinformation is hardly a new phenomenon, but it is invariably an infallible yardstick by which is measured the degree to which democracy has been subverted to promote the corrupt interests of a tyrannical minority.

Schedule One: Career Prohibitionists and Fallacious 'Criteria'.

A. To qualify for *proscription* (i.e.,, the act of dooming to death or outlawry) under Schedule 1 of the regulations (amongst other statutory criteria which follow in items B and C) the drug or substance must have a "high potential for abuse." Abuse is allocated the meaning of *dependence*, psychological and/or physical (addiction). Consider the following three aspects:

Firstly, the DEA perjuriously and subreptitiously overlooks the definitive official empirical researches which exonerate cannabis from all 'harm' allegations:

(i) The Empirical Studies' Findings of Fact (shown in THE REPORT, Part One) are derived from medico-scientific investigations of actual long and short-term use of cannabis herb-hash by human test subjects: these Findings of Fact are **definitive**. The DEA's, and all, allegations of harm and/or impairment are categorically disproven and dismissed by the Empirical Studies' Findings of Fact.

(ii) The DEA presents perjury in the form of inadmissible speculations derived, not from cannabis at all, but from disparate laboratory chemical concoctions.

Secondly, shown in THE REPORT, Parts One to Four, by definition based on the medico-scientifically established empirical facts, there exists **no potential for abuse** in non-addictive, non-toxic herb cannabis. Cannabis is benign, and being non-toxic in any possible dose or quantity, has **no potential for maltreatment** of the consumer:

(i) The bureaucratic criteria of the Schedules assign to 'abuse', the propensity of substances to induce 'dependence'. This is capricious language of inauthentic signification: to show 'abuse', a substance must *maltreat* the consumer in some way.

(ii) Cannabis is not only harmless, but is benign, promoting good health in many ways.

(iii) In specific regard to dependence, the following is Empirical Fact: cannabis is a non-addictive substance, which does not and cannot *induce* physical or psychological dependence; ref. Ploys, in Part Five. The person who becomes psychologically dependent on any *non-addictive* substance is suffering from pre-existing psychological derangement; ref. Parts One & Five.

(iv) Cannabis is of significant benefit to individual and society in helping people avoid and be cured from dependence on alcohol, and other addictive drugs; ref. Cannabis as Preventive Measure and Preventive Medicine; & Modern Uses; Part Three.

Thirdly, where curtailment of citizens' Freedoms could occur, Justice and Legal Equity, i.e.,, grounds of equality and fairness, require (judicial) *comparison* of cannabis to substances which are **legal** for unlimited quantities of Production, Trade and Possession:

(i) The Schedule 'abuse' criterion is not genuine. In the meaningful use of the term 'abuse' (i.e.,, maltreatment), numerous *non-addictive* items have "high potential for abuse;" e.g. dairy products induce CVD, etc. Cannabis has no (such) potential for abuse. Ref. Harm and Danger in Perspective.

(ii) The DEA misapplies its own vacuous criteria: *the DEA gives no consideration to 'danger' of* **real** *harm and abuse done by consumed substances, whether dependence-inducing or not, such as alcohol, tobacco, dairy products, animal flesh (meat) and fats.*

(iii) Use of **tobacco** is invariably abuse: tobacco is addictive, a dependence-inducing, insidious toxic pathogen. (Ref. Part One.) Yet, tobacco is legal, emphasising prejudice behind, and the **illegitimate inequity** of, control of cannabis production, trade and use.

(iv) Toxic, pathogenic, dependence-inducing **Alcohol**: Legal for unlimited production, for trade and use, alcohol has documented potential for abuse, demonstrated by Mortality Statistics and other studies. For cannabis to qualify for proscription on the "abuse" criterion, it would have to 'induce' dependence and maltreat users *more*, i.e.,, to a measurably greater degree, than alcohol, because alcohol was prohibited but subsequently was *relegalised*. As shown, cannabis cannot 'induce' dependence, and being benign, is incapable of maltreating consumers in any way.

(v) No serious proposal exists that cannabis could be harmful to the degree of dairy products, animal fats, meat, caffeine, aspirin, alcohol or tobacco, all legal substances.

Cannabis does not meet criteria for potential of abuse as per the Schedules of Prohibition, and no grounds attach thereto for proscription of cannabis.

B. To qualify for Schedule 1, the drug or other substance is required to show no currently "accepted medical use in treatment in the United States." Judge Young's ruling concluded, on ample evidence, "currently accepted use in treatment in the U.S." does indeed exist. *Nor is the evidence controverted.*

One cannot help but be reminded of the relevance of the historic example of citrus fruit, the Royal Navy and 'limeys'. The biochemistry of vitamin-C was not understood in the days when long sea voyages, especially those given to delay in the doldrums of trans-Atlantic crossings, led to lack of fresh fruit and vegetables inducing scurvy amongst crew members of Royal Naval vessels. The Admiralty issued instructions that citrus fruit be stocked aboard ship, especially limes, when in port in New World colonies where these fruit could be obtained. Limes were observed to be safe to use, and to have a medical application preventive of scurvy. More than a hundred years passed between the time of the *observed* efficacious use of limes and a received understanding of ascorbic (antiscorbutic) acid. Many lives were saved and much illness was prevented by such astute observation. Likewise, cannabis has numerous currently accepted medical uses, whether the DEA and its Administrator care to be honest in acknowledging them or not.

Cannabis is a highly effective, superior medicament in a great many conditions, slight and serious, *and*, can safely reduce or mitigate the harm and mortality of pathogens alcohol and tobacco. While it may be edifying to chemists to give technical explanation by intricate bio-chemistry of how cannabis achieves all its excellent results, given Mankind's limitations, it cannot simply be assumed that such complexities will ever *certainly* be accomplished. Meantime, the deadly illegal Prohibition on Cannabis as Preventive Measure and Preventive Medicine must be repealed. There is no (good) reason whatever to sustain *any* controls on cannabis. The state of knowledge already establishes as fact the definitely benign nature of cannabis, which has no potential for abuse or maltreatment of the user.

Special mention should be made of cannabis as Preventive Medicine in glaucoma. There are over 2,500,000 glaucoma sufferers in the United States. 14 per cent of the totally blind are made so by this affliction. *If cannabis had not been* **Prohibited** *most of these unsighted people would today still be able to see.*

If cannabis had been legally available for private cultivation, trade, possession and as Personal Relaxant, its qualities as Preventive Medicine could have precluded the incidence of glaucoma, *amongst numerous other adverse conditions*. Ref. Déjà Vu; Part Six.

To obstruct the very limited Schedule Two availability recommended by Judge Young (which, incidentally, does not include glaucoma and many other conditions for which the only safe, effective medication is cannabis), the DEA thought up further Prohibition 'criteria', which the Controlled Substances Act does not contain: the DEA requires "scientifically determined and accepted knowledge of the chemistry of a drug or other substance" in order for it to have "accepted use;" and "the chemistry of the substance must be known and reproducible" to demonstrate "accepted safety." Bearing in mind the *real motive* behind Prohibition, the despicable DEA servants of corruption and tyranny are predictable, if unclever, in their duplicity.

In the first place, these 'criteria' are unscientific, vacuous and fallacious in the determination of "safety" and "medical use" of a unified compound herbal plant. Secondly, these 'criteria' are capricious and unreasonable because the federal state through the DEA has itself imposed Prohibition on all research into cannabis in the U.S. Thirdly, the DEA 'criteria' are unrealistic because they are only practicable for drugs man-made in the laboratory. Fourthly, they are capricious and unreasonable, because other herbs are not required to undergo research to establish legality.

So intent are these Prohibitionists on proscribing the plant, they do not realise the transparency of their mens rea (criminal intent). These bureaucrats participate in Fraud, and abet the ongoing despoilment of society, in full knowledge of the mortal damage they inflict. Continuation of Prohibition is the conclusion *intended* to be foregone, not based on characteristics of cannabis, but because no one will do the specified, but irrelevant, research. The DEA intends the 'criteria' to be an insurmountable obstruction to the normal due legality of cannabis; but the 'criteria' are *fallacious and unlawful*.

The career Prohibitionists of the DEA proceed from a false premise: the reality is that the properties of a chemical compound are *unique*, and not a sum of the properties of the different individual elements and compounds from which it is made. For example, common salt, i.e.,, sodium chloride (NaCl) does not have any properties remotely like those of metallic sodium (Na) which catches fire on contact with water, or chlorine (Cl) which is a harmful yellow-green gas. *Cannabis herb in its natural form is the matter under consideration*. The completely dissimilar properties of isolated chemicals found therein, being chemically different from whole-cannabis, i.e.,, disparate [1], are *inadmissible* as to whether cannabis herb has "currently accepted medical uses" and is of "accepted safety," which are the points at issue.

The laboratory-isolated concentrates of individual elements or compounds extracted from the plant are **never** represented by, and do not render the same results as, the nature-compounded total chemical constituents of a herb. *This is an elementary rubric of Chemistry*. For example, extracted from water H_2O, pure liquid hydrogen H, is fatal to consume and becomes explosive gas at room temperature—yet no one would maintain that *water* is unsafe to imbibe or has no use for Mankind**....**

Regarding the whole herb, research chemistry of **extracts** *does not and cannot ascertain its efficacy or* safety. ***That*** requires empirical herbal use, as in patients' Medical Case Histories on which Judge Young relevantly based his appraisal.

1 Ref. 'THC' Is Not 'Cannabis'; Part One.

Further Modern Uses; and, The Judge's Ruling.

Indeed, it is on medical case histories that *every* medication is judged for safety and efficacy *especially* those newly-licensed by the FDA. There is no other test or criterion more germane.

The DEA's delusive 'criteria' comprise prevarication, and illegal Obstruction, which Pervert the Course of Justice and epitomise Contempt of Court. The DEA does not even attempt a veracious definition of "current use" and "accepted safety." With the complicity of the court of appeal it does not have to....

In trying to stop the DEA from ignoring Judge Young's ruling, petitioners to the court of appeal found in that court's subsequent ruling, no contention of the evidence on which Judge Young had ruled, but instead an indefensible "*deference*," in support of the DEA's fallacious criteria.

The false 'criteria' require that each of the many hundreds of chemical constituents of the herb first be researched before consideration be given to modifying its regulatory status; i.e.,, the chemistry must be "known and reproducible." These 'criteria' are only applicable to laboratory-made dangerous toxic chemical concoctions invented by pharmaceutical companies, not to natural herbs. Cannabis is not a synthetic, single-action drug—cannabis is not a *drug* at all. (Ref. Part One.)

New drugs of the single-action type are developed by pharmaceutical companies possessing resources sufficient to bear the enormous cost of testing a new drug to obtain approval of its (purported) efficacy and safety, prior to market success. No pharmaceutical company commits itself to such investment expenditure unless, first, it owns the **patent** on the drug so that it can recoup all development costs, and then make profit. Cannabis, *the natural plant*, cannot be patented. So, no pharmaceutical firm could recoup these research costs.

As noted previously, cannabis is comprised of *many hundreds* of compounds. By these 'proposals', *each* requires a complete research programme. If anyone could be found willing to try, this would cost countless billions and take a lifetime or two. The state would not underwrite the cost—indeed, the state installs the spurious 'criteria' and the Prohibition on research, including by state-funded university medical research institutions.

On the other hand, *private companies* deem such a programme absurd, because it is incapable of ever retrieving investment costs, let alone making profit. Drug firms, unsurprisingly now, are chary of more than minimal investment in tentative studies of one or two synthetic cannabinoid compounds, not *the hundreds* of natural compounds in cannabis. Judging by their fruitless results so far the failed product THC further research is unlikely to produce a marketable product anywhere near as good as the safe, cheap, effective natural herb itself.

The bureaucrats *know*, furthermore, private corporations are not interested in achieving legality for the plant which would then cheaply replace a large proportion of their presently profitable but inferior products.

Most substances ingested by Mankind foods, herbs and constituents of alcoholic beverages are unresearched, or only partially so, whereas the plant most researched by Mankind is cannabis, it being more researched than all these mentioned foodstuffs. The official Empirical Studies confirm cannabis is safe and has effective Preventive and Curative utility.

Thus, if the bureaucrats' 'criteria' were enforced *conscientiously*, most of what we eat and drink would be subject to Prohibition, and 100 per cent of the population, government included, would be incarcerated for incessantly breaking the 'law'; whilst cannabis, having been shown by investigations to be safe, would be legal.

Persons with unbiased judgement discern that controls on cannabis cannot be sustained by any sensible criteria. Under the law, cannabis is, and always has been, **legal**.

The façade of Prohibition is propped up by a bureaucrats' ruleless word-game which ignores truths, evidence and all the pertinent plain facts. Yet this is not a game. *Career* Prohibitionists are without conscience in protection of their monetary interest —*which includes*: jobs and careers derived from Prohibition *enforcement*; *and*, the phenomenally large-scale ill-gotten gain which accrues to the '*legal profession*' from 'representing' defendants, 'due process', i.e.,, prosecutions and feigned 'defences' [1].

Career Prohibitionists are profoundly aware that cannabis is safe, effective, Preventive Measure, Preventive Medicine and Curative Medicament; that **Denial** to the population of uses of cannabis by 'legislation' is money-motivated, based on perjury, crime-producing, and, in numerous instances, **homicidal**. This it is that produces the Prohibitionists' vehement derogation of cannabis, to attempt to cover up the enormity of their crimes.

All such odious duplicity by officials and others is due enforced public rejection. The federal, and all courts should both in Law and Morality uphold the needs of health, over the whims or other interests of politicians, bureaucrats and the duped, organised coteries of the Prohibitionists. Constituting criminal collusion by prolonging illegal controls, the Appeal Court's—and all other courts'—"deference" to Prohibition, comprises desertion of the prerequisite Ethical Standards of judicature; and of Truth, Knowledge, Justice and Liberty.

In any assessment of the law, courts have the bounden duty to apply equitable, fair canons; the exonerative Empirical Findings of Fact; to observe Human Rights; and to represent and uphold the health interests *and* democratic Rights of *the individual* citizen, as opposed to the government-corporate financial interest.

Prohibition legislation is unlawful; but, the legal methods of redress nominally available to citizens are obviated by individuals' and courts' criminal, judicable participation in, and abetment of, tyranny.

C. To be in Schedule 1, there must be "lack of accepted safety for use of the drug or other substance under medical supervision." Judge Young ruled that there **is** safety for use of cannabis under medical supervision, and added: "To conclude otherwise, on this record, would be unreasonable, arbitrary and capricious." THE REPORT concurs; i.e.,, cannabis is safe at all times, *with or without* medical supervision. Cannabis is precluded from being universally accepted as safe, efficacious Preventive and Curative Medicament *only* by the fact of its Prohibition. Cannabis has multiple accepted medical uses in the U.S. and elsewhere, as with Elvy Musikka, Gordon Hanson—and literally millions of other people. *Only* empirical use of the whole-herb is able to establish its attributes; and the requisite investigations have *already* been conducted: the Empirical Studies of the last one hundred and fifty years all vindicate cannabis. Non-toxic cannabis is more researched than toxic substances we commonly consume; cannabis is confirmed to be safe**....**

The Administrator would be unable to name a single consumed drug or substance, Scheduled or otherwise, that is research-demonstrated the equal of cannabis on safety criteria.

1 Cf. The Fallacy of 'Decriminalisation' and: Is Fecit Cui Profuit; Part Six; also see Part Seven.

Beyond Words.

THE REPORT reveals and identifies those with vested interests and criminal intent, who conspire versus the People. The DEA's dismissal of Judge Young's ruling is false: it is manifestly undeniable that there *are* "currently accepted medical uses in treatment in the U.S." The court of appeal's "deference" to the DEA shows that, where cannabis is concerned, the wheels of justice are *incapable* of turning. The impediment responsible for Prohibition manipulates at the highest levels, unseen, but not unfelt. Regarding the brushing aside of Judge Young, the genuine evidence, and patients in deepest need, unqualified, haughty, mendacious pronouncements emanated from the Administrator, as follows:

"Beyond doubt, the claims that marijuana is medicine are false, dangerous and cruel. Sick men, women and children can be fooled by these claims and experiment with the drug [sic]. Instead of being helped, they risk serious side effects."

Such lies are regularly promulgated by Prohibitionist media, uncontested. In the ignorance of the unread or the dupe, many of the population accept them. Some who know them to be fictions which cause death, suffering and damage, shamefully prostrate themselves without resistance before Prohibitionists. Still others commit the crime of *becoming* active, or covert [1], Prohibitionists. People who have studied the data recognise such pronouncements for the unforgivable lies they are. Where lies cause the **denial** of cannabis to prevent illness, *engendering* sickness and death, they are especially atrocious. Elvy Musikka and others receive cannabis as medicament; many thousands of patients, backed up by doctors and nurses, establish cannabis as effective and safe in modern treatments. Inevitably, the *Prohibition* has made cannabis less relied on by physicians, but for literally thousands of years cannabis has been known to be efficacious medicament. However, congress, senate, and judicial system collusively close ranks in abetment of the criminal Prohibition.

What of the sick and dying? *What price, health?*

THE REPORT and Judge Young's summary show that, **Relegalised**, cannabis will effectively replace, and significantly reduce consumption of, numerous profitable but frequently useless and harmful pharmaceutical drugs; *and*, will voluntarily diminish the public's intake of recreational drugs alcohol and tobacco [2]. Prohibition is emplaced as a *monopoly* profit and revenue-protection device, by which trillions of dollars, yen and Euros of *undeserved* profits accrue annually to drugs' companies; governments take 30 to 45 per cent of this enormous sum, in Corporation and Value Added *Taxes*. (Percentages vary nation to nation; nationalised corporations yield 100 per cent of profits to state control.) *Also*, governments take more trillions from *duties* on sales of alcohol and tobacco, *and* further phenomenal trillions from *duties* on the toxic chemical drugs of prescription.

To Prohibitionists, who ban the herb to gain money, revenue, profits, careers, wealth and investment income, the sick and dying people, like so much chaff in the breeze, are dispensable and of no consequence. The evil that active, or passive, supporters of Prohibition do to their fellow men and women, and to Western Civilisation and Culture is beyond words.

1 The "covert" Prohibitionist: ref. Part Five.

2 The reader will bear in mind that the products of the drugs' companies are far from being the only ones which cannabis will beneficially replace when relegalised. Ref. Part Two.

Reality and Responsibilities.

Prohibition has *never* been legal: it is the crooked instrument of ulterior motive. In the teeth of Judge Young's ruling, the U.S. Food and Drug Administration in 1992, perversely retracted their then already-given assurance of IND cannabis supply to the further twenty-eight approved, extremely suffering applicants, for whom *cannabis cures*, and all pharmaceutical 'medications' had *failed*. The announcement accompanying this felonious FDA act asserted that to make cannabis available as medicament would "send the message" to people, that cannabis actually is not the "dangerous drug" which the government would have us all believe. The *unintended* message in that FDA announcement was as follows:

1.) after the failure of every type of treatment by pharmaceutical drugs, patients turning to cannabis instead, demonstrate by its use—the most relevant health test of all—the real relief and *undeniable superiority of efficacity of cannabis*;

2.) that the administration attempt to obscure this fact from general comprehension;

3.) that herbal cannabis, being effective, non-addictive, non-toxic and safe, should not be the last, but the *first* treatment to be applied;

4.) that the demonstration of cannabis efficacy and safety produces in the administration deeper entrenchment of its Prohibition; not, as would be expected by decent people, immediate state-approved availability;

5.) for ulterior motive, continuation of the Prohibition is more important to corporations' Owner-magnate-shareholders, and to politicians and bureaucrats, than the genuine needs of the population whom they claim to represent and serve, even though members of that population are sick, dying and in crying need;

6.) rather than fully Relegalising cannabis, politicians prefer patients and people to suffer and die.

The government which ignores the needs of its people even unto causing them to die is barbaric and brazenly criminal. To understand the actions of the politicians and bureaucrats implicated, one requires only to perceive the underlying **motive**.

Certainly, it does not excuse their deeds, but a mighty influence [1] is brought on them to serve this repulsive Prohibition. The U.S. government, and the others, would not find it easy to admit that under successive administrations they have been in the wrong all along—and know it.

Nevertheless, if governments wish to regain an appearance of legitimacy they must face up to reality and their responsibilities: all controls on cannabis are illegal and must be abolished. Not to do so will increase the momentum behind socially destructive forces which are already set in train [2].

Governments' obligations, legal and moral, include prompt Amnesty and Restitution to all those surviving people seized upon for solely cannabis related activities. People persecuted by unfair 'law' are owed by society full recompense for such oppression.

1 The intensity of this influence can be measured by the sheer scale of the money-motive. Ref. Part Two.
2 Extreme ill-effects of the financially-motivated Prohibitions are shown in PROHIBITION: THE PROGENITOR OF CRIME.

Cannabis and Children.

No report on Cannabis Prohibition, Human Rights and the law, could be considered complete without addressing the issue of cannabis use by young people. The proposal is sometimes heard that cannabis be 'legalised' for *adult* use only, under restrictions similar to those which apply to alcohol. This suggestion is inappropriate in many ways, but at its core lies a misconceived 'belief' in some part or other of the Prohibitionists' 'harm-stories', which official investigations establish as disproven. This wrong 'belief' is the appalling consequence of years of mendacity, and is the expression of ignorant fear, not caution.

On inspection, many every-day activities and consumed substances are seen to entail risk of serious harm, but on which the cumbrance of law is not imposed and cannot be justified; ref. Part Three. By contrast, no such risk exists in cannabis, which is completely safe. Regulation of toxic, addictive drugs such as alcohol is required on several grounds; however, none of these apply to the non-toxic, non-addictive cannabis. Controls of alcohol are emplaced to minimise risks to children. This is wholly proper but incomplete without thorough education to make young people and adults aware of the serious potential for harm which accompanies alcohol use [1].

An additional consideration against the aforesaid proposal of an adults-only restriction, is that, for as long as doctors are disallowed from issuing prescriptions for cannabis as Preventive and Curative Medicament, the 'legalising' of cannabis exclusively for adults, leaves children, parents, doctors, and nurses in the invidious position which obtains today, of having to break the 'law' should the child require to use cannabis for one of its great many health applications. Placing the child and others in this position is, of course, unconscionable.... It is also illegal, grievous and homicidal: on Health Grounds, denial of cannabis to the population by the tyrannical edict of Prohibition 'law' constitutes Crime against Humanity.

Criticism of cannabis is to be firmly rejected. These are the facts: humans receive benefits to health from cannabis; whenever cannabis moderates, reduces or replaces the use of those virulent pathogens of addiction, alcohol and tobacco, *by young people or others*, the use of safe cannabis is to be unequivocally endorsed as sensible, and forthrightly recommended for the health-protecting Preventive Measure that it is. Deprecation of smoking tobacco, which damages health by the effects of nicotine and radioactivity in that plant, is comme il faut. However, clinical Facts (ref. Part One) show smoked cannabis has *only* beneficial results, and any disparagement of its smoking is the invalid opinionated product of people manipulated by ulterior fictions. Further, cannabis mitigates drug use and helps people give up harmful addictions. An inequitable 'law' selecting cannabis from amongst activities and substances, to restrict its use by young people or anyone else is not simply illegal; it is insupportable because *that very denial actively causes ill-health*, by withholding from people the efficacious Preventive benefits of cannabis use. This reveals the reverse of the Prohibitionist's counterfeit coin, in whose obverse is seen that Prohibition can *only* be installed for the purpose of protecting profits, in particular amongst others, of those people who seek to peddle ever greater quantities of their 'pharmaceutical' laboratory-concocted, toxic, addictive, high-priced *drugs*.

The realities enjoin all decent people to confront with unstoppable resolve, the 'politicians' and their indefensible Prohibition. Relentless moral and social pressure must be brought to bear until the legal status of the healing herb is *normalised* by its full RELEGALISATION.

1 ALCOHOL: Ref. Part One: Mortality Statistics & the sections defining 'drug', & The Relaxant; ref. Part Three: Harm and Danger in Perspective, & Legislation of Prohibition.
2 Ref. Part Five: Objective Consideration; and this section.

THE REPORT. CANNABIS: THE FACTS, HUMAN RIGHTS AND THE LAW.

Judged by the mandatory Standards of Rights, ethics, equity, and common sense, the *denial* of cannabis as Preventive Measure, Preventive Medicine and Curative Medicament, at any time to any person of any age, is *criminal*, a manifest barbarity. Moreover, no government or person has the legal right or authority to make such decisions *in loco parentis*. As the counterbalance to prejudices against cannabis which have been instilled by long-term disinformation, and by the spurious 'law' itself, one should bear in the forefront of one's mind, the truth that cannabis is benign and health-promoting, and shares in common with bread and water the same statistic of complete safety. Cannabis is safer than foods which the family commonly, even daily, consumes, e.g. cholesterol-producing animal-fat-rich milk, dairy products, meat; and the beverages containing caffeine: coffee, tea, and colas.

Refer to Judge Young's appraisal of cannabis safety, and in particular, his moving account of the beneficial use of cannabis by a three-year-old boy without a moment's untoward effect of any kind. People need appropriate dietary intake to keep up good health and to forestall numerous adverse conditions, *and* require a *safe* relaxant. Where the 'recreational' substances are concerned, *only* cannabis protects health.

Tea and coffee, for example, are not now subjected to regulatory 'prohibition'. (Ref. Part Five.) Nowadays, such a ban on tea and coffee would be neither justifiable nor possible. *Yet, this is, de facto, the same position as cannabis*. Certainly, out of multiple millions of enthusiastic users it is always possible, at many great costs, to arrest, incarcerate, execute or otherwise abuse a few per cent; but no good has ever come from this tyranny, while much bad does. No compromises can be made with Prohibitionists and their malevolent creed. They have wreaked unspeakable harm for generations. Let all citizens awake to their duty and responsibility, to restore the West to Democracy by permanently deposing, and indicting, the criminal infrahuman Prohibitionist ascendancy now, to bring this wretched epoch to an abrupt end. When the responsible citizen assimilates the Empirical Facts, cannabis is seen not to be a "drug" at all, but a wholesome benefit to individual and society. The real perspective emerges to reveal the Cannabis Prohibition Conspiracy: the criminal fabrications which malign the health-promoting herb also tyrannically usurp constitutional democracy, seditiously pervert the rule of law, malindoctrinate the population, and ruinously damage the world economy and ecology, for the personal gain and anti-democratic hegemony of some few individuals. The false 'law' of Prohibition is deeply criminal.

Nowhere is the need to terminate this Prohibition seen to be more pressing than for its deplorable effects upon children, families, and homelife. A prime purpose of The Democracy Defined Campaign, being family orientated, is to provide the parent and teacher with accurate information by which sound judgements and responsible decisions are reached. Propaganda and lies about cannabis can seriously mislead the parent or legal guardian of nonage persons, with desolate and even heartbreaking consequences.

A sad irony is found in the experience of many families whose unity and happiness have been forever sundered by the course of events following the discovery that a son or daughter has a liking for health-promoting cannabis. Sometimes extreme actions are taken against the child by parents or others, who allow themselves to be led by lying indoctrination into the incorrect attitude that the child is doing something 'harmful' or 'wrong'. In many lamentable instances courts cruelly institutionalise children to undergo a so-called 'cure', wherein habit-forming benzodiazepines or phenothiazines are mandatorily prescribed to them. The health-promoting cannabis pastime is thereby exchanged for an introduction-by-force, to a potentially lifelong morbid reliance on stupefying pharmaceutical tranquilliser drugs, which are addictive, mentally and physically debilitating, mind-altering, powerfully poisonous chemicals.

To exact submission from children (and adults), courts and clinics adopt the identical modus operandi of kidnapper gangs who constrain and inject victims with addictive drugs. Indictment of criminal Prohibitionists extends to include the felonious 'psychiatrists', 'doctors' and 'nurses' implicated, and Owners of profiteering participating clinics.

Truthful teaching of the young, to produce understanding in the individual, from which comes firm belief in trying in all aspects of life to do 'the right thing' simply because it is so, is the only reliable method. This is crucial to the creation of a salubrious crime-free social environment, with the achievement of which all involved in education are tasked, including those employed by the state. Indeed, there is no greater challenge presented to, or duty demanded of, teachers, at all levels.

Few people in the entire West have not at a young age learned the behaviour of breaking the law or rules of 'prohibition' on recreational substances. With or without parental approbation, few could truthfully deny having used alcohol in their teens, before legal majority. Like those of their parents, teenagers' parties are often awash with drink. Responsible use of alcohol by teenager (or parent) may realistically, only be expected from *education* by accurate *empirically-derived* information. Hospital visits to view the anti-social and accident results of alcohol use, combined with statistical and video presentation of the physical pathogeny induced in humans by alcohol, speak volumes, whereas mere threats and application of Prohibitionist punishments deserve and obtain scant respect. To arrive at a 'punishment stage' is *already* to have failed. Yet, although alcohol is ubiquitous, premonitory education of the dire consequences of its use is half-hearted, underfunded and, by contrast, rare.

Education about the gruesome results of tobacco use has in recent years to some extent succeeded, where the Prohibitionist failure of a simplistic coercive approach to the children of earlier generations produced the disastrous consequences of today, witnessed in mass long-term addictions, yielding appalling mortality; cf. Statistics, Part One. The indications are that in the U.S. and U.K., as a percentage of population, fewer people now smoke tobacco. *Education, not 'Prohibition', brought this about.* On every count, 'Prohibition' is a demonstrably failed concept. However, as with alcohol, health-education effort on tobacco is sporadic, while the counters to it— commercial advertising and ready availability—are omnipresent.

Such education as there is on tobacco is untruthful in its most significant aspect: by far the most youngsters, and adults, know nothing about the *ionising radiation absorbed by tobacco and some food plants*, although this deadly fact was established at Harvard University as long ago as 1964 (see Part One). The authors would that this unblissful state of ignorance were otherwise. THE REPORT collates the official Empirical Studies' definitive Findings of Fact on benign cannabis smoke-tar and their total exoneration of cannabis from 'harm'. THE REPORT presents the *real* sources of danger to health from tobacco and food crops, by absorption of radioactive elements present in cheap profitable rock phosphate deposits, which, when *misused* as 'fertiliser', cause pandemic carcinosis, CVD, arterio-sclerosis, etc. (Ref. Part One.)

Officially-recognised by the Empirical Studies, cannabis has the propensity to achieve reductions in drug use, ref. Part Three, and this, *before* Relegalisation, or mass education, and ministerial endorsement of cannabis. Any effort to achieve improved health standards in the population by reductions of use of drugs legal and illegal, that could be said to be *genuine*, would necessarily include and be preceded by **Abolition** of controls on cannabis, to make the herb available as safe alternative and replacement of choice. Without the legal and social reform of making *cannabis the officially endorsed*, sensible substitute and moderator of alcohol and tobacco use, attempts to educate the population into voluntarily adopted healthier ways of living, are invalidated, and rendered impotent, by the overpowering presence of alcohol and tobacco in the Western culture and economy. Veracity mandates that legislative amendment for RELEGALISATION recognise that all private cannabis cultivation, trade, possession and use are, and always have been, legal. It is required that cannabis be publicly endorsed at prime ministerial and presidential level, as the single safe recreational substance of sensible choice. These measures are ineluctably requisite from government where the health of the population is in sincere consideration.

From examination of the many types of documented benefits rendered by cannabis, more is exposed about the invalidity of its Prohibition. A web of disinformation is malevolently woven around cannabis to prevent the beneficent herb from competing in the marketplace with other raw materials and products. As the truth is laid bare, despicable elements of dark conspiracy are revealed as being the hidden incipience of Prohibition. This Prohibition has all the scientific basis of a medieval witch-hunt: it supports itself on disinformation and thrives on bigotry. Its victims are Legion. Prohibition, by its characteristic of brutish intolerance, debases and damages too the civilisation which it inhabits, in insidious but telling ways. Prohibition is, at best, a primitive disciplinary—attitude the societal ethos inculcated where Prohibition is applied as the outwardly appearing collective social response to complex human and social problems, induces grave long-term effects upon the individuals and population who allow or instigate such inadequate, simplistic, failed techniques as 'Prohibition', as an ostensible panacea. In societies where such state-institutionalised *obduracy*, as is embodied in Prohibition, is permitted to prevail, the politics of totalitarian extremism dwell and bourgeon, with continuous erosion to the constitutional, philosophical, and human values upon which democracy relies for its foundation and, indeed, existence.

Prohibition is not simply crime-producing and therefore illegal; or, unlawful only because it is inequitable; or, technically wrong and hence unjustifiable; Prohibition is also the ruin by criminals, of the equable ambiance and amity of Western democracy. Prohibition is the principal, ever-present source of social disharmony and racial friction, engendered by constant police Prohibitionist interventions. Rioting and conflict are misattributed to 'racial tension'. This alienation, misanthropy and strife which have occurred over past decades, actually have money-motivated Prohibitions as their font. In Prohibitionist states the conditions are set for continuous imperilment of public order and civil peace. Failure to return to just, democratic values inevitably causes further progressive collapse of civilised standards, Western societies thereby evolving into autocracy or plutocracy, i.e.,, tyranny, and the demise of democracy altogether. Quite simply, the writing is on the wall. This catastrophic aspect of Prohibition is further considered in subsequent Parts.

To child, to adult or the aged, to the sick or hale, *cannabis is benign*. It is wrong to discuss cannabis in the same context as 'drugs'; this is the result of miseducation. To clarify this incongruity of contextual juxtaposition, one requires only to be reminded by the Mortality Statistics of the completeness of the disparity. Demonstration is also made by comparison of cannabis to substances which share the same statistic of harmlessness; see: A Comparative Example. In the context of government policy and action taken to protect the population, and improve health standards, **RESTORATION** is the measure by which political *sincerity* is calibrated.

***There is no single programme which governments could implement capable of introducing greater benefits to Mankind, in so many ways, than* RESTORATION: The Restoration and Universal Adoption of Constitutional Common Law Trial by Jury; and fully de-regulated Cannabis Relegalisation** [1].

A Comparative Example.

Any comparison of cannabis to alcohol and tobacco made at other than the superficial level of remarking that all can be used in association with recreation, reveals that cannabis is utterly different from drugs. To appreciate the extent to which the Prohibition is a deviant expression in untruthful and inappropriate legislation (itself against the law) one has only to attempt to find, to think of, a substance of equal harmlessness with which to make a fair comparison. Alcohol and tobacco must be discounted because of their toxicity, addictivity and associated pathogeny. Could one perhaps compare cannabis with tea and coffee, the well-known beverages and, in the case of coffee, used in desserts and gâteaux ? Again, comparison to those substances would be wrong—tea, coffee, and colas contain stimulant drug caffeine which has negative potentials to health, reflected by the statistics on mortalities.

Leaving aside the *positive*, the benign aspects *and* the recuperative characteristics of cannabis, to find a comparative example that is non-addictive, is equally non-toxic and not injurious to health, one has to turn to items such as bread and water. *Impartial* people cannot but conclude that Prohibition is not only malignant, but it is also the height of pretentious fatuity. Safely used for millennia, endorsed by countless millions of decent people from all walks of life the world over, confirmed harmless and benign by modern science, cannabis is as safe as *the safest* of food and drink which the family enjoys. In expending taxpayers' resources while defiling democratic principles and perverting the rule of law, in the illegal attempt to control private agricultural and horticultural cultivation, trade, possession and use of cannabis, governments commit multifarious acts of crime and folly of great magnitude.

Decisions.

In assessing Facts with the intention of reaching responsible decisions based on accurate information, The Democracy Defined Campaign maintains a strict neutral objectivism, to arrive at conclusions from an aspect of aloof dissociation. The Campaign concludes it indubitable that legislative restriction of cannabis is unlawful; inequitable; morally reprehensible: and, de jure, all legislation of control of cannabis is abrogate. On grounds of Health, Justice and Legal Equity, The Democracy Defined Campaign stands for RESTORATION [2].

1 & 2 Ref. RESTORATION: Magna Carta (U.K.) and the Constitution of the United States of America; Part Seven.

DEFINITION.

When serious and honest standards of appraisal are applied, the truth emerges: there are no grounds for inclusion of cannabis in any legislative regulatory Schedule or classification of proscription or restriction. Cannabis requires veracious definition for purposes of law and language, and completely de-regulated Relegalisation.

THE REPORT proffers the following definition:

"Cannabis (Sativa and related species, e.g. Americana/Indica/Ruderalis), a dioecious, herbaceous plant remarkable for its swift and prolific growth; a resinous herbal relaxant; an officinal ameliorant tonic; a safe, harmless substance smoked or taken orally, with numerous beneficial results to the enhancement of human health, which are the inseparable concomitant of the mild, pleasant sense of well-being rendered by ingestion; an efficacious therapeutic substance with preventive and curative uses; non-toxic; non-addictive, i.e.,, does not induce physical or psychological dependence;

. . . a substance with a long history of benefits to Mankind; *yielding*: staple seed food [1]; high-grade poly-unsaturate vegetable oil; cannabis tea; bhang; oleraceous herb;

. . . *yielding also*: the world standard fibre of textiles; Dresden Cotton® ; cellulose-rich calorific hurds (i.e.,, the wood bulk residues after fibre decortication) which, by industrial processes (e.g. pulp-paper-making, pyrolysis and/or cellulosic polymerisation, etc.) are resource to: fuel-oil; methanol; gasoline; jet-fuel; lubricants; all types of paper and card products; tree/timber substitutes; charcoal; creosote; paints; varnishes; tars; explosives; cellulosic polymers, i.e.,, all types of plastics; man-made fibres; mineralised concrete building materials; Isochanvre® ;

. . . The Cannabis Biomass Energy Equation (CBEE) establishes as fact, and explains how: cannabis is the *production-cost-free* substitute for natural gas, petroleum (oil) and coal, i.e.,, the fossils misused as 'fuel', and for uranium, in the production of fuel and generation of electricity; pollution-free, ecologically superior; the cheapest resource to fuel and energy known to Mankind;

. . . the herb and its products, cultivated and marketed agricultural and horticultural produce, traded and promoted under market conditions as for other agricultural produce such as tea, coffee, oranges, tomatoes and wheat [2]."

1 Seed does not contain relaxant ingredients.
2 THE REPORT explains how fuel made from cannabis is non-polluting, and THE CANNABIS BIOMASS ENERGY EQUATION establishes as Fact, for the first time on record, how cannabis produces fuel-energy *more economically* than uranium and the fossils misused as 'fuel'. (Note: this formulation should not be confused with the assertion by some writers that cannabis can replace the so-called fossil 'fuels', which is self-evident.) The Ecological, Socio-Political and macro-Economic implications of the aforesaid Equation for global amelioration are of paramount magnitude.

~

- PART FIVE -

Washington, Jefferson, Cannabis and Semantics.

Ploys.

THE bureaucratic invention of a 'category' called 'psychological dependence' (or 'psychological addiction') is adopted by the World Health Organisation (WHO), the U.S. Drug Enforcement Administration (DEA), the British Home Office, etc. This is to enable fraudulent inclusion of benign, non-toxic, non-addictive, non-drug cannabis, in controls (treaties, and national legislation) of dangerous, addictive, narcotic and/or hallucinogenic drugs, such as heroin, LSD, and morphine, while—*and nota bene*—addictive, dangerous, toxic lethal drugs alcohol and tobacco *are not included*. Similarly to the 'criteria' exposed in Part Four, examination shows 'psychological dependence' also to be the invalid fabrication of *mens rea* (criminal intent).

Psychoneurosis or psychosis can result from genetically inherited traits and/or a near infinite variety of circumstantial, familial or social deprivations, suppressed childhood traumas, violence, etc. Serious psychological disturbance is already extant within the sufferer *before* the onset of compulsive behaviour such as psychological dependence and fixation, the fixation being its consequence. Mental illness can find its expression in many forms of compulsive behaviour. Fixations can be upon a wide variety of substances or objects; for example, other human beings, inanimate fetish objects (cf: Freud). To *prohibit* a substance or activity because it *might* become the object of a deranged person's fixation is legally untenable. Where, as with cannabis, the substance is health-promoting, the proscription is also irrational. Thus, it is obligatory to consider *the motivation* behind the formulation of this devious bureaucratic simulacrum.

'Subjective preference' or a 'liking' for something, even when the liking is strong, is not 'dependence' nor is it 'addiction'. Dependence and addiction are words which define and describe the morbid [sick] states *unavoidably induced* in humans by use of particular substances, for which craving and fixation are symptoms. The propensity of a substance's *intrinsic chemical properties to induce* dependence or addiction, contributes to the defining of that substance as a 'drug'. (Ref. Part One.) Whereas repeated indulgence in chemically non-addictive substances, say cornflakes and milk, may be *called* a habit, cornflakes do not *chemically form* the habit: i.e.,, cornflakes are non-habit-forming; the substance of cornflakes is not addictive; they do not and cannot *induce* 'dependence' or craving. For purposes of law or lexicography, a liking for, or regular use of, a non-addictive substance, is not a 'condition' definable as addiction or 'dependence' of any type.

The word 'dependence' indicates *reliance*; only if one cannot lead life without some substance, does one *depend* upon it. The person who is distinctly distressed by having to go to work in the morning without the usual cooked breakfast because of an electrical power-cut [failure] is not suffering from 'psychological dependence'. That is to say, the application of the term in such circumstances would be semantically malapropos and literally incorrect. Although one might *hear* the exasperated "I'm addicted to my boiled egg in the morning," this is casual talk, and on such grounds no one would seriously contemplate the prohibition of eggs (boiled or otherwise).

Similarly, the fact that olives are missing from the pizza menu might make a person who always likes to take olives with a cooked cheese dish dismayed to some degree, but it does not mean that this person is 'psychologically dependent' on olives.

Psychological dependence is not simply a strong liking or marked preference for something. Far from it, *'psychological'* dependence self-evidently denotes a mental condition, the derangement of an individual's normal functioning. *Psychological* dependence is a sickness of the mind.

An uncommon phenomenon sometimes referred to as "addictive personality" is the pathological condition which comes to exist within the mind of a person, characterised by *excessive* subjective preference for a given substance or substances, the object of which might typically be anchovies or ice-cream. The obsessional behaviour of extreme preoccupation with, or inordinate consumption of, *any non-addictive* substance is the outward symptom of an individual's *pre-existing* psychological disturbance, present usually from childhood. This syndrome of 'psychological dependence', is caused by, and product of, a mental foible or aberration within a particular human persona and does not mean that the substances upon which the psychologically fraught person becomes fixated, or 'dependent', are more or less 'addictive' than any other non-addictive substance. Categorically, *the substance* does not 'induce' psychological dependence; rather, the substance, the ice-cream or the anchovies, is the 'innocent bystander' which becomes the object of a mentally sick person's attentions.

For any legislation-framing administration arbitrarily to adopt the wrong proposition that one non-addictive substance is more prone to "induce" or "cause" psychological dependence than any other non-addictive substance, and to prohibit it by law, demonstrates (whatever their motive) the failure by that administration to acknowledge that, in connexion with a physically non-addictive substance, **no** 'dependence' of any type is, or can be, 'induced' by that substance. As found in Prohibition Schedules, the misconception 'psychological dependence' *incorrectly* ascribes to cannabis the propensity of chemically addictive substances *to induce* dependence; that is, to bring on cravings and/or fixation concomitant with use of *physically addictive drugs* such as heroin, morphine, tobacco, alcohol, tranquillisers, amphetamines, etc. Cannabis Prohibition is based on dishonesty: the bureaucrats cannot be accused of *ineptitude*; for they know well what they are doing, and why they are paid to do it. The regulatory category 'psychological dependence' is misconstrued and spurious. Legislation formulated thereunder is legally invalid.

Good people are executed, imprisoned and penalised for no genuine reason. Imposed by nation states, control of cannabis requires premeditated criminal collusion by politicians and state employees, functionaries, 'advisers', drug czars, and others, in active support for, or tacit acceptance of, untruthful 'treaties' and 'statutes'.

Shown in Part One, it is empirically established and repeatedly confirmed by the Empirical Studies, frequent use of cannabis over lifetime periods produces no mental, physical or social dysfunction. Being non-toxic and non-addictive, cannabis can do no harm, not maltreating the ingestor in any way. It is a fact that were cannabis to be the object of a psychologically disturbed person's fixation of 'dependence', the cannabis would do no harm to that individual. On the contrary, being benign, with profoundly salugenic properties and unique advantageous applications, the cannabis would, whilst

120

not incurring the least harm, be of health-giving benefits to the consumer. (Ref. Parts Three & Four.) This extreme irony further reveals the pseudo-medical prohibition category of 'psychological dependence' as specious.

Exhibiting a behaviour pattern of self-compensatory overconsumption of *foodstuffs*, the sufferer of a psychological 'dependence' fixation can become compelled to overuse of substances to the sufferer's detriment. By comparison, the rest of the population not suffering from a psychological compulsion would experience extreme discomfort and nausea from such levels of overindulgence. Conspicuous overeating can result in the accumulation of enormous amounts of bodyfat in the condition termed 'morbid obesity'. Chocolate, cheesecake, fudge and peanut butter, apple-pie and hamburgers, French fries, sugary drinks, maple syrup and waffles, ice-cream, anchovies, and milk-shakes, are well-known substances of 'psychological dependence'.

By their use or overuse, *all these foodstuffs have inherent potential for abuse and maltreatment of the user, even to the point of inducing mortality by, for example, cardiac and vascular disease*. Yet, *they* are not subject to prohibition. It is illogical to the point of absurdity to ban any harmless pleasant substance from the whole population because a few deranged individuals are self-compelled to its overuse.

It is a deception, a ploy, to introduce 'psychological dependence' as a 'criterion' for regulations. The only non-toxic, non-addictive substance to which Prohibitionists apply this sophism is....cannabis. Subject to the rabid, obsessive career, or vested, interest, Prohibitionists go to any extreme to make cannabis *appear* 'illegal'. So baneful are they in demonic pursuit of this goal that they do not see it in themselves even when they are at the extreme of ludicrousness.

Use Is Not Abuse.

With reference to the counterfeit 'criteria' of Prohibition discussed in Part Four, where applications of words and semantics are concerned, the term "abuse" cannot (correctly) be applied to any aspect of cannabis use.

In order to convey truth in this as in all matters, correct use of language is essential. Incompetent use of, and faulty, terminology can lead to misrepresentation and untruth. The use of a substance is not of itself abuse; in the physical reality and by definition, to show abuse requires that the use of a substance *maltreats* the user in some way. Cannabis is not only safe, but is actually beneficial.

The term "abuse" is coined in relation to drugs, legal and illegal, such as heroin, alcohol, amphetamines, tobacco, caffeine, etc., where indulgence or overindulgence manifests itself in drunkenness, alcoholism, addiction, or any effect detrimental to the user. Further, in the sense that human beings occasionally (or in the case of psychologically inconstant individuals, more frequently) are known to overindulge in a pleasant everyday substance, say chocolate or anchovies, then where overindulgence is sufficient to induce harm to the user, it is called "abuse." In the familiar moderate quantities usually taken and enjoyed by people, such substances are to all intents and purposes, harmless. However, overindulgence in them can cause physical discomfort as in, for example, nausea, or over the longer term result in (morbid) obesity with all that condition's attendant problems.

Prohibitionists spread miseducation to make it difficult for the non-specialist to appreciate that any 'recreational' substance exists which can be *entirely* without harmful effect, but this is the definitive categorisation in which cannabis correctly fits. Misinformed members of the population are prejudiced simply by the existence of the groundless 'law' which Prohibits cannabis. With their state of mind thus prepossessed, they are easily misled by further disinformation of disproven 'harm' stories, disseminated by officials and others through Prohibitionist-controlled media. These false allegations are the more readily believed, because people are increasingly informed about the detrimental effects of so-called 'recreational' substances, of "drinking" (alcohol) and "smoking" (tobacco). Yet, the clinically established empirical reality is that cannabis is a relaxant which is not only harmless and safe, but is also only-ever *beneficial*. (Ref. Parts Three & Four for Health benefits.)

Demonstrated by the specific laboratory/clinical research and long-term empirical evidence, no amount of use of cannabis incurs harm to the user, it being both non-addictive and non-toxic. The clinical Empirical Studies and Mankind's experience throughout history confirm cannabis in any quantity for short-term, long-term or lifetime use has no deleterious effect on the user, either directly or as a side-effect. Ref. Part One, Studies, Statistics. Also note, long-term use, "even prolonged and excessive", shows no harm to consumers, as in Reports by Allentuck 1942; Freedman 1946; Chopras 1957. Also ref., U.S.-Jamaican Studies; U.S.-Costa Rican Studies; Study of the New York Academy of Medicine; Merck Manual, etc. Ref. Bibliography.

Perusal of the semantics and applications of the word 'abuse' reveals that, in view of the definitions and connotations widely and commonly applied to that word both by layperson and specialist, the term can neither meaningfully nor correctly be attached to any aspect of cannabis use. Cannabis cannot be 'abused', by any definition of the word; rather, the contrary: the documented evidence shows that cannabis is beneficial to the user. *There exists no potential for abuse in cannabis. It is a misstatement of ignorance or outright calumny to indicate otherwise.*

Cannabis Is Not 'Intoxicant'.

Whilst considering use of language in order that truth be conveyed, it is not only technically incorrect to apply words such as "intoxicant" and "inebriant" to cannabis, but to do so is thoroughly misleading, constituting perjury. Intoxication and toxicity, self-evidently, are not unrelated words: the word 'toxic' derives from *toxikon*, Greek for arrow-poison. Toxicology is the Science of Poisons. As mentioned in Part One, it is empirically established that there is *no toxic amount* for cannabis. Put in everyday language, this means cannabis taken in any quantity is non-poisonous [1].

Prohibitionist tactics of a simple but effective mendacity are those which, by their *abuse and perversion* of the use of words and language, intentionally convey to the non-specialist a false belief in 'harm' where none exists. To use language which implies 'toxicity' in connexion with cannabis is one of these misrepresentations. To describe a substance as "toxic" or "poisonous" requires that substance, at some level or dose, to be capable of inducing death. Veracity denies *absolutely* the loose misuse of language or jargon by which people are led into false 'beliefs'. One sees cannabis referred to as one of the "least toxic of the therapeutic substances," a phrase containing a wholly incorrect imputation. To adopt the language is to endorse the lie.

1 **Ref. Judicial Enquiry Findings of Fact on Safety; Part Four.**

Washington, Jefferson, Cannabis and Semantics.

The effect a substance has cannot be described as "toxic" or having "toxicity" at all, if mortality categorically cannot result from ingestion of the substance from which the effect derives.

In the human or animal context, to attempt to define cannabis as having "toxicity," or as of "non-zero toxicity" (DEA), is to state a falsehood, for, however limited the likelihood of 'damage' to the ingestor which may or may not be intended by such expressions, "toxic" means destructive of health with the potential for fatality, which contradicts the empirical reality and fact: cannabis cannot induce fatality in humans. Cannabis is a non-toxic substance. For example, to quote from DEA Administrative Law Judge, Francis L. Young's review of the cannabis data:

"Researchers have been unable to give animals enough marijuana to induce death," [1] and: "Marijuana cannot induce a lethal response." [2]

Thus, the aforesaid "non-zero" or "least toxic" are contrary to the established fact. In reference to medicine, health, the pharmacopoeia, the lexicon and law, the uncompromising demands of veracity require that natural herb cannabis be only and always referred to as: **non-toxic**.

Seen in Part One, cannabis produces no interference in psychological attributes of character and personality. This is most unlike alcohol's toxic effects and results [3]. Alcohol literally poisons people, and, as it does so, it affects their health, behaviour and judgement. Language such as "intoxication" and "inebriation" are used to describe alcohol-effects, alcohol-associated bad behaviour and crime [4]. Alcohol can be referred to as "inebriating" and "intoxicating" with the meaning that it can excite to behaviour beyond self-control, grievously de-stabilising normal social inhibitions and restraints on personal behaviour. Tobacco and alcohol can be described as "intoxicants" because, toxicologically-speaking, they both are literally poisoning agents which induce disease and death. Tobacco, heroin, caffeine, alcohol, and other legal and illegal recreational substances, are correctly referred to as toxic, and as intoxicant, rendering users intoxicated, but not so cannabis.

Benign cannabis is differentiated by its intrinsically safe characteristics: it merits vocabulary which truthfully reflects and accurately signifies this fundamental disparity from drugs. Inexorable empirically-established clinical facts conduce to terminology and definition [5] such as: "safe, recreational substance" or "benign personal relaxant."

1 & 2 DEA Admin. Law Judge Rulings: Findings of Fact; Accepted Safety, Paragraphs 7 & 9: ref. Part Four.
Also ref. 'THC' Is Not 'Cannabis', in Part One; and, Cannabis Is Sui Generis, in this Part.
3 Ref. alcohol-related statistics (NIDA) in: Harm and Danger in Perspective; Part Three.
4 Nota Bene: Findings of New York Academy of Medicine: "use of marijuana does not predispose to any crime, even that of using drugs." See NYAM Report, pp. 12-17.
5 For a more detailed definition of cannabis, ref. Definition; Part Four.

Set and Setting.

The same dose (quantity) of the same (homogenous, laboratory-calibrated) relaxant [6] cannabis can be described by the same person or people as having "different effects" on different occasions. The converse is also established, i.e.,, differing doses of cannabis of a variety of strengths can be attributed by the ingestor/s as "producing" the "same effects." In fact, the same or different cannabis itself is not inconsistently "producing" a variety of "effects"—the variable is the human factor. Sometimes, test subjects do not comprehend the variables of Set and Setting [7].

6 As pointed out in Part One, note this use of the word relaxant has nothing to do with drowsiness or tiredness; far from it. Being in a relaxed frame of mind can be prerequisite to the concentration required for producing a good performance.
7 Set and Setting was propounded by Professor of Psychiatry Norman Zinberg, M.D., Harvard University School of Medicine.

THE REPORT. CANNABIS: THE FACTS, HUMAN RIGHTS AND THE LAW.

Setting relates to the environment of the person smoking cannabis. Smokers' subjective 'interpretations' as to what cannabis is assumed to 'do' are not to be taken at face value. Given the objectivity of the Clinician and the evidence of empirical tests, widespread misconceptions and confused ideas are dismissed. For example, on one occasion a person takes cannabis in a secure relaxed environment at a late hour during the working week, and reports it as "inducing drowsiness." Next, the same clinically tested cannabis taken in the same quantity by the same person in a busy, noisy, laboratory test environment at a different time of day, reports it as "inducing wakefulness and stimulation." In both settings, the converse can also occur. The cannabis is actually "doing" neither. The same dose of the same cannabis can be misattributed with the same or different results, depending on Set and Setting. [1]

Set relates to the condition, both psychological and physical, of the ingestor. Not only are no two people the same, but it is also true that no one is the same twice. Every few months or so, cells in human bodies have replicated, the old ones dying off. Everything about us changes as we grow up and become older: our mentality evolves. Compare the differences in priorities and outlook of the same person at six, sixteen and sixty. Factors external to us alter over time, having their effect on our: set. Finances cause an ebb and flow of satisfaction or irritation. Our mood changes: grief, nerves, and stress disturb our equanimity. Sometimes we are hungry, tired and sleepy; at other times happy, with 'get up and go'. Set affects how subjects receive cannabis.

Set includes consideration of the following: cannabis is universally reported as increasing *awareness*. Unnoticed subtle effects of other consumed substances are sometimes only perceived, and then misattributed, to cannabis, when the person who has taken cannabis is not distracted by external factors, such as work or play. People's bodies are saturated most or all the time, with harmful substances and drugs, such as: tea, coffee, colas containing stimulant caffeine—ref. Mortality Statistics; alcohol—ref. Statistics, Parts One & Three; cholesterol; nicotine—including passively absorbed; phosphate-'fertiliser' derived and naturally occurring DNA-damaging, radioactive elements in food; milk containing sedative tricalciumphosphate; tranquillising vitamin B riboflavin; prescribed substances; agricultural pesticides; food processing chemicals, steroids, antibiotics, additives. On child, teenager and adult, these all have effects, routinely unnoticed. Breeding has selectively reduced the hallucino-psychogens in tobacco from the New World; this is in varying degrees still intrinsic to tobacco and tobacco-smokers are more receptive to these effects when not distracted by stress. People inhaling smoke of radioactive tobacco-nicotine receive numerous toxic results [2].

Set and Setting affect the way the subject perceives cannabis. When one reads or hears of, on the one hand, "chillout cool smoke" drowsiness, and "speedy high" stimulation on the other, this puerile language is incorrect and misleading [3]. The subject, that is to say, the human, is producing the variables. People wrongly ascribe to cannabis the variables of their own physiology and psychology. People differ from time to time, and from each other. Humans change; cannabis however is a beneficial constant. The mild sense of well-being received from pure cannabis is actually consistently the same.

1 Note that drinkers of <u>caffeine-stimulant</u> tea, sometimes claim tea at bedtime "makes" them "sleepy" !
2 People often pollute mild benign non-drug cannabis by smoking it with the disease-inducing strong drug tobacco.
3 Additional to lack of comprehension of Set and Setting, people confuse and misuse words, rendering description erroneous and invalid. Semantics become unavoidable, and empirical Findings of Fact comprise the essential evidence.

Washington, Jefferson, Cannabis and Semantics.

E Pluribus Unum.

Cannabis Prohibition 'law' is the symptom of an unaware, underdeveloped and malgoverned society in which justice is a luxury unequally available amongst its citizens. The degree of civilisation attained by a society may be measured by the way it treats those whom it incarcerates.

Over the years of Prohibition it has been suggested that cannabis is "alien" to the West, and only with familiarity would come social acceptance and a possibility of "eventual" legality. This apocryphal apologia for an illegal Prohibition is one of a thousand ruses invented to mollify the ingenuous into submission to the secret intentions of the criminal.

In respect to the Rights and Freedoms of others, all citizens of probity demand their legislatures, executive and judiciary abide by Equity, Natural Justice and common law. Cannabis Prohibition is in blatant breach of laws which have been passed in every modern democracy to protect people from acts of personal discrimination or intrusion. There are many people who espouse culture, creeds, and religions which do accept cannabis, and, regardless of where these cultures have originated, the Prohibition breaches these people's Rights and Liberty. In every nation signatory to the Universal Declaration of Human Rights, and any society which claims to be pluralist, treating all races, cultures, religions and groups equally before the law, legislation of Cannabis Prohibition enacted or supported by such a criterion (that cannabis is 'alien' to the West) is illegal discrimination.

Prohibition also breaks the laws passed to protect religious freedoms, such as those of the Coptic Christian Church, Buddhists, Hindus, Rastafarians and other denominations or individuals, for whom cannabis represents a holy sacrament, as wine is to the traditions of Judaistic and Christian ritual. Prohibition is a malign insult to all decent people, whether cannabis users or not.

People who make or endorse such completely incorrect proposals as "cannabis is alien to the West," reveal their racist nature and hostility to others. The same people can rarely, if ever, be heard to advocate prohibition of alcohol for its powerful propensity to induce immorality, mayhem and criminal behaviour into the culture of the West. Their inconsistency exposes racist bias. Such xenophobic tendencies are best brought under self-control and eliminated, for they are contrary to comity, and militate against the fundamental virtues and tenets of democracy itself.

Within a nation or between nations of the world, to strive for a just peace requires an understanding and acceptance of the customs and practices which differentiate people and cultures (where these activities do not interfere with the Rights of others). Only by high principles and charity within, can the concept of a Brotherhood of Man, or "e pluribus unum," come to pass. With our differences mutually accepted as amongst equals we may become one people united or one world at peace.

While persecution and criminalisation of harmless cannabis farmers, gardeners, traders and users continues under the fabricated 'laws', realisation of a civilised society remains remote. Still more distant is a compassionate one. With the gall of the bigoted Prohibitionist ascendant, the possibility of a caring world community being at peace within itself recedes.

THE REPORT. CANNABIS: THE FACTS, HUMAN RIGHTS AND THE LAW.

In the proposition that cannabis is 'new' or 'alien' to the West, there is neither merit nor truth. Cannabis, commonly called *hemp* (the ancient Anglo-Saxon word for cannabis) has been part of Western culture for as long as the West can claim to have had culture. Resource to the health-enhancing relaxant and innumerable industrial products, cannabis has been highly valued by Europeans since antiquity [1].

There is no 'culture shock' in smoking cannabis, for, *at least* since Elizabethan times (1558-1603) in Northern Europe, and earlier everywhere else, the smoking of a variety of plants has been ubiquitous. Since prehistory to the present, people comprising at any moment a significant proportion of the Occidental population (e.g. circa 1 in 3 living Americans) have experienced cannabis and know it to be pleasant. Many people know Prohibition is based on claims of 'harm' that are unfounded, but at the time of writing few people are cognisant of the financial motives and conspiratorial manœuvring which produce the illegal Prohibition.

1 Ref. The Traditional Uses of Cannabis; Part Two.

President Carter.

In a 'Message to Congress', President Jimmy Carter stated that penalties against possession of a drug (sic [2]) should not be more damaging to an individual than use of the drug itself. Thus, on President Carter's criterion, possession of any quantity of harmless cannabis should incur no penalties at all....

The President's Message informed congress that he would support amendment to federal law to eliminate all penalties for possession of up to one ounce of cannabis. The President thereby recognised the Right of personal possession, and use, which is a significant fact. However, such gestures are futile. To begin with, in order to possess an ounce, somebody first has to grow the plant. Young plants are rich in cannabidiolic acid (CBD), which can be extracted from the plant in inverse ratio to tetrahydrocannabinol (THC). As the herb grows, CBD reforms, and the chemical constituents develop from which THC can be isolated by laboratory techniques [3]. Mature plants, particularly buds and flower tops, comprise the smoked or dietary relaxant. As any one plant has to grow to a weight much greater than several ounces long before it can be harvested for use as relaxant—automatically exceeding suggested statutory limits—the proposal was unrealistic and not properly thought out.

Secondly, as with any consumables, a person would not necessarily wish to use immediately what a person might wish to buy. A gentleman's wine cellar is stocked with vintages laid down for future occasions. For friends, guests and family, a drinks' cabinet contains far more than a person could or would ever want for themselves. People buy two or three items of household requirements, e.g. packets of cereal, etc., at one time, rather than putting themselves to the inconvenience of repeated shopping. Coffee and tea in choices of strengths and blends suited to differing moods and meals are kept in one's home, yet one would hardly wish to consume them all at once. The same applies with cannabis.

Thirdly, cannabis requires to be generally available for its wholesome benefits: smoked, cannabis is an effective safe preventive and/or curative medicament in many Health applications, and, cannabis staple seed (not containing relaxant) and the

2 The word 'drug' is incorrect and inapplicable to cannabis — see definition of 'drug' in Part One.
3 It is convenient language to talk of plants being "THC-rich" or "THC-free," to denote the quantity of THC which may be chemically isolated and extracted from plants by laboratory techniques; but, actually, THC does not exist at all within the herb, because in the plant, the THC is chemically-compounded with other cannabinoid and vegetative components comprising a substance which is not THC. Ref. 'THC' Is Not 'Cannabis', in Part One.

relaxant oleraceous herb are taken as part of a normal health-promoting diet, and for delectation in many dishes, e.g. cake, 'meat'-loaf [1], animal-fat-free nut milk, curds, cream, butter, staple cereal, bread, puddings, porridge, etc. Cannabis is nutritionally superior to grasses (wheat, maize, rice) and recipes require more than "one ounce" when preparing food for several people. Punitive controls on harmless activities and substances are always unjustifiable in any society. More than this, however, as shown in Parts One, Two, Three and Four, cannabis food and herb is benign: legislation of control breaks substantive and common laws.

Fourthly, if it be conceded that personal possession and use be allowed, it is then wrong to deny: any individual or farmer their Right to grow it; brokers to import and export it; traders and shops to stock and sell it; citizens their consumer quality-protection under existing legislation; and the Exchequer to receive revenues of taxed income and profits. Traditional trade in cannabis is normal healthy activity, to which people have an inalienable Right without let or interference. Politicians and courts have no valid, no *legal*, authority, in denying people their Right freely to grow, sell, supply, possess and use cannabis, in any amount.

Fifthly, 'law' which allows (depenalises) but rations or limits personal possession to specified quantities (in this instance to the infinitesimal amount of one ounce) is in reality another form of the unfounded Prohibition on private commercial Production, Sale and Uses. Widely misnamed 'decriminalisation' or 'depenalisation', this is the most intensely criminogenic type of legislation ever devised [2], being a lucrative form of Prohibition preferred by black marketeers, smugglers, and dealers. As such, it receives attention elsewhere in THE REPORT [3].

'Decriminalisation' (or 'depenalisation') breaks the law and is unacceptable on Principle:

1.) It is an infraction of Common Law to introduce statute 'law' which invents and attributes as 'crime' acts which are innocent in themselves, are of no criminal intent, and are not crimes (eating, drinking, smoking, cultivation, trade, possession, use, import-export, etc.). Enforcement of such legislation is tyrannical crime per se; the statute is unlawful and abrogated. [4]

2.) The control legislation produces world food, energy and commodity shortages, with fatal results; inflates prices; creates a Black Market and causes crime. To **cause** crime to occur is a crime per se: the legislation is unlawful and abrogated [5].

1 Rich in protein and containing the requisite essential amino acids, cannabis seed can be substituted for the flesh of animals in the healthier human diet. Ref. Traditional Uses; Part Two.
2 'Decriminalisation' was the form of Prohibition applied to Alcohol in the U.S. in the Nineteen-Twenties and 'Thirties.
3 Ref. Part Six.
4 See the view on Prohibitions attributed to Abraham Lincoln, Part Six; & ref. Part Seven.
5 Ref. Parts Two, Six & Seven.

Tea and Coffee.

Tea and coffee contain the drug caffeine, also called théine in connection with tea, a powerful stimulant to the central nervous system. Théism, or cafféism, is a morbid state resulting from taking too much tea and/or coffee. Drinkers of coffee and tea find their demand for regular use so easily gratified by cheap, widespread availability, that the degree of habituation and dependence to which users become subject is seldom noticed. However, regular users, especially long-term, experience distress in varying degrees when the supply is removed. This also applies to users of 'colas' containing caffeine (Coca-Cola, Pepsi-Cola, Virgin Cola, etc.).

Caffeine can have dire effects on users; viz. Mortality Statistics; ref. page 2. By contrast, the smoker/ingestor of cannabis enjoys a safe herb of only benign characteristics. The empirical studies confirm cannabis is free from inducing dependence of any type; no 'hangover', no 'withdrawal', no abstinence syndrome, and no tolerance syndrome occur. This is inevitably so because **cannabis is not a drug**.

Tea and coffee were also once subject to Prohibition. Although they had been put to pleasant use by other civilisations for centuries, when introduced to Europe, tea and coffee were met with hostile reaction, and introduction of inordinate penalties for their trade and use. *Without any empirical evidence*, coffee was said to cause impotence, and tea to degenerate the moral fibre of good character; but the real, as opposed to ostensible, reason behind this antagonism was money-motivated. (Ref. Déjà vu; Part Six.) Gradually, Europe adopted a more enlightened attitude: coffee and tea were RELEGALISED. Today there are specialist tea and coffee shops all over the world, offering numerous varieties, blends, strengths, flavours and prices to connoisseurs of these universally accepted and enthusiastically appreciated substances.

Fully Relegalised, a cheap commodity of agricultural production, distribution, and the existing legislation of consumer protection quality control, cannabis will resume its status of health-promoting utility and other important uses. It is recommended that, like tea and coffee, cannabis will be Relegalised, available officially, unrestrictedly over-the-counter, and sold alongside tea and coffee on the supermarket shelf.

Shafer, LeDain and Wootton.

Those reports usually referred to as Shafer, LeDain and Wootton all have in common the same extreme failings: they—and other 'reports' of similar ilk—do not reflect an accurate overview of cannabis; their conclusions are erroneous and their recommendations are awry. The panels sifted through writings which claim to be "on cannabis." The panels reviewed, *but did no empirical research*. They gave undue consideration to unproven, apparently 'speculative'—but actually fabricated—and subsequently officially investigated and disproven, Prohibitionist assertions of 'harm'.

These panels, in further desertion of standards of exactitude and objectivity (imperative criteria where citizens' Freedoms are in the balance) allowed the warping inclusion of inadmissible evidence on chemically *disparate* THC and cannabinoid 'concentrates', as from LaGuardia research, etc. Shafer, LeDain and Wootton were swayed by untruth (product of ulterior money-motive) away from the only possible finding compatible with the evidence of facts, existing law, and Justice: that of the Abolition of Prohibition by complete de-regulation, The Relegalisation of Cannabis.

In contrast to the incompetence and bias of Shafer, LeDain, Wootton, and others, as seen in Part One, there are the medico-scientific Findings of Empirical Fact compiled by physicians, toxicologists, clinical psychologists, pharmacologists, psychiatrists, etc. These latter are officially funded to find harm, if any, associated with cannabis use. In the Empirical Studies in which research on human beings' use of cannabis was carried out, *no harm to the human subjects was recorded*.

Not only is there not one single indication of 'harm' but physicians observe and record *many positive results to health from the use of cannabis*, which is thus confirmed by modern science to be benign.

Washington, Jefferson, Cannabis and Semantics.

Empirical Studies exclusively comprise the admissible Evidence. By exposing the extreme incorrectness of the Shafer, LeDain, Wootton and other 'reports', and by refuting as false all the allegations of 'harm' or 'danger', 'misuse' or 'abuse', on which Prohibition purports to be based (Schedules, etc.), the expert empirical evidence reveals the grave criminality behind, and of, Cannabis Prohibition. Hitherto, these reports on the empirical good of cannabis have remained ignored, underpublicised and to all intents buried by the Prohibitionist state and others, *an act of mens rea which of itself demonstrates the racket* (criminal conspiracy U.K.).

Objective Consideration.

In addition to confusion sown by incorrect application of words such as 'drug', attention is drawn to another misrepresentation of reality by misuse of language. Accurate language is crucial for the truthful conveyance of information. In perusing reports, books and documents, all too often one encounters sentences describing cannabis in ways similar to the following:

"An objective consideration" shows that "marijuana is responsible for less damage to the individual and to society than alcohol or cigarettes." The aforegoing is a quotation from the State of California's Attorney General's Panel, whose report, published in 1990 after 20 years' continuous review of all cannabis data, concluded and recommended cannabis be Relegalised.

To classify cannabis 'lower' in the scale of risk and danger than alcohol or tobacco is extremely unscientific and completely inaccurate. Whereas alcohol and tobacco are long-established inducers of disease and death, benign cannabis does neither. Confirmed by the researches previously quoted, *cannabis has no harmful or toxic effect; the evidence shows cannabis is a salugen, a health-promoting substance.*

Examining comparisons between cannabis and other substances, the reality avoided and pusillanimously unstated by the A. G's Panel, is that "objective consideration" shows that *'marijuana' has done no damage whatsoever in society, totally unlike* alcohol and tobacco which have done and continue to do enormous damage both at the individual level and to society as a whole. To emphasise this, reference is made to the Mortality Statistics (Part One), and NIDA statistics on drug-alcohol in: Harm and Danger in Perspective; Part Three. Also, note that U.S. government figures on Productivity Losses from *illness and absenteeism* induced by *the use of alcohol and tobacco*, equal on average, more than $100 billion and $52 billion respectively, per annum over recent years.

Furthermore, "objective consideration" shows that while cannabis has done no damage to individual or society, the misbegotten Prohibition 'law' has caused in society, turmoil, heartbreak, and suffering on the grand scale.

Let Us Measure the Intensity of the Tyranny:

The Prohibition has exacted circa 400,000 cannabis arrests every year over recent years in the U.S. alone, a cannabis arrest every few minutes; and circa 80,000 annual arrests are made in the U.K. These are followed by incarceration, and/or punishments such as fines, loss of driving licenses, forfeitures.

Around half of the enormous Western prison population is comprised of people jailed for so-called "drug" (sic) charges, out of which approximately 80 per cent are for cannabis cultivation, trade, possession or use. Solely because of the financial interests of a criminal government-corporate clique (i.e.,, the Owners and politicians), enforcement of controls on cannabis accounts for 40 per cent of all people now imprisoned. These people are innocent of crime. In the light of the medico-scientific, social and legal Evidence given herein, **all** such penalisation is legally *malicious* [1].

In the U.S., there are more Black People in jail than attending college. The U.S. government incarcerates a higher percentage of its population than were imprisoned in South Africa under apartheid, or Soviet Russia under Stalinist Communism [2]. Britain's 'politicians' follow suit.

While escalating budgetary billions are squandered on preoccupying police with Cannabis Prohibition enforcement, *the greater part of serious and real crime goes unsolved and largely unchallenged.* (Ref. FBI and U.K. Crime Statistics.) Despite politicians' hollow public posturing on 'law and order', this socially detrimental policy indicates where governments' priorities actually lie, constituting a visible signal, *a green light* to the *real* villain.

Also, in making evaluative judgements on damage to individual and society, the *crime-producing* aspects of Prohibition per se cannot simply be disregarded [3].

In addition, though a report's emphasis may be placed on health matters, any balanced assessment of damage to society cannot exclude ecological, economic and social issues so all-pervading as The Cannabis Biomass Energy Equation, with especial reference to the fact that cannabis has always proffered the source of clean fuel-energy far cheaper than coal, oil, natural gas and uranium. In this aspect, *damage by Prohibition* to society, peace, prosperity and progress, cannot be overemphasised.

In saying "marijuana is responsible for less damage to individual and to society than alcohol or cigarettes," the Panel's uncertain language *implies* marijuana damages but less so than alcohol or tobacco. A glance at the Official Mortality Statistics shows alcohol and tobacco *literally* kill hundreds of thousands of people every year; alcohol and tobacco strike down further multitudes with excruciating diseases, ruining careers, destroying families, causing suffering and grief where they truly need not be. Cannabis does *none* of these things. The Panel's majority advocated Relegalisation. This REPORT concurs but criticises the Panel's insipid equivocal wording. The truth which the Panel could not bring themselves to articulate openly is empirically established; *it is one's duty to state it*: **cannabis is harmless, cannabis is safe, cannabis is benign.**

Harmless cultivation, trade, possession and use have been prosecuted with Draconian fervour. In the face of the government ferocity, despite the timidity of their wording, it is to their credit that the majority of the California Attorney General's Panel published their recommendation for Relegalisation. The Panel advocated Relegalisation despite the possibility of their having to face criticism, controversy and even hostility, from an Establishment *deeply* implicated in the lucrative crime of Prohibition, and a public saturated with prejudice induced by the widespread disinformation about cannabis. History abounds with governments' persecution of those who seek Truth, Knowledge, Justice and Liberty. The certainty of the correctness of RELEGALISATION derives from knowledge of the definitive empirical Findings of Fact (ref. Part One), on the safe nature of cannabis.

1 **Common Law, Equity and Justice, and Constitutional grounds (Part Seven), all abrogate the control legislation.**
2 **0.4 % of U.S. citizens are jailed; whereas, 0.3 % of S.A citizens were jailed under apartheid, and 0.26 % under Soviet Communism. See: The Bakersfield Californian.**
3 **On prohibition per se as: Progenitor of Crime, ref. Part Six.**

Washington, Jefferson, Cannabis and Semantics.

With regard to socio-scientific analysis, it is incorrect and invidious to "compare" *disparate* cannabis to alcohol and tobacco. Certainly, it is proper to show the unlawful inequity in a 'law' which denies people this wholesome relaxant tonic herb while it allows the ravages to health of alcohol, tobacco, and innumerable other harmful dangerous substances which the family consumes daily [1].

If the control (i.e.,, standard of comparison) were honest and scientifically competent, cannabis bears comparison with other substances.... Comparison of harm*less* cannabis to harm*ful* substances to draw the incorrect, defamatory conclusion that cannabis is "less harmful" than they, is inane. Cannabis is due comparison to substances which give rise to similarly salutary indications, and the same Statistic of complete safety as orange juice, mother's milk and bread. Then, and only then is the comparison fair; and, ipso facto, the extreme untruthfulness of the Prohibition is revealed.

The unfounded nature of the 'law' shows its illegality: persecution of citizens is the Fact, not 'punishment'. All cultivation, possession, trade and use are, de jure, legal. The fraudulent legislation and its unconscionable enforcement are criminal under both National and International Law. Citizens persecuted by this felonious Prohibition are due immediate Amnesty, and full and fair Restitution.

1 Ref. Judicial Review Findings; Part Four.

The 1912 and 1924 Conferences.

In 1912, a first "Opium Conference" was convened at The Hague, Holland. At that time, international codes and standards had not been agreed upon, by which to regulate the flourishing inter-continental trade in addictive substances, i.e.,, drugs. Cultivation, processing, manufacture, marketing and retail had become significantly profitable components of a ubiquitous trade, which was comprised of a great many small-scale localised businesses, with wide distribution amongst the population of the related wealth and economic activity. Coca (cocaine) and opium were unrestrictedly cultivated, bought and sold everywhere, and purveyed in cola drinks (e.g. Coca-Cola) and numerous patent medicines; and, *other than alcohol,* **no crime** was associated with the drugs; ref. Prohibition: The Progenitor of Crime, Part Six.

At the conference, government-appointed delegates, representatives of those with *vested interests* in the drug business, had available to them the variety of alternative regulatory formulæ from which to choose, to modify by debate, and finally to agree upon, to commence regulation of this trade. It is reasonable to assume that all the delegates understood and knew in advance, *yet chose to ignore*, the extreme social havoc 'prohibition' would wreak by proliferating both petty and serious crime on the greatest scale, in first establishing and then encouraging an especially lucrative Black Market in drugs. It would take no little effort—if indeed it were possible at all—to conceive of a scheme capable of producing worse results than that which was decided upon and subsequently enacted: *prohibition.*

To this day, the sensible alternatives to the failed, counter-productive, criminogenic prohibition 'method' chosen continue to await implementation...

At that time, it was widely promulgated and true that agreed standards would help protect the patient and consumer from impure products. Labelling, warnings, dosage instructions (to some extent addressed already in the U.S. by the Pure Food and Drug Act, 1906) were necessary. Evidently, where addictive, noxious substances were concerned, the introduction of standards and regulations was desirable.

While publicly purporting to be motivated by the laudable aims of "health" and "protection" of the population, *delegates contravened these stated aims* by adopting *Prohibition*, an approach with the obvious inherent negative potentials (subsequently consummated) for the deepest social and human devastation.

To Recapitulate on Ulterior Motive:

Bureaucratic desertion of principles and financially motivated criminal opportunism have revealed themselves throughout the History of Cannabis Prohibition. At the time of the 1912 conference, pharmaceutical firms had not yet come up with the majority of their addictive toxic pills and potions in their attempt to concoct 'substitutes' (which frequently prove ineffectual in use; ref. Parts Three & Four) for the many therapeutic applications for which cannabis had long been the efficacious medicament recommended by pharmacopoeias. *But, the more* of the natural substances which have therapeutic applications, notably cannabis, opium and coca, which could be brought under controls by treaty and legislation, *the greater the profit that would accrue to those few companies licensed to exploit them financially; and the greater would be the duty and tax taken by the state.*

Cannabis was the world's longstanding principal cure for headache. Shortly after the turn of the Twentieth Century, the commercial success of the introduction of the pharmaceutical company patent-product, **the aspirin tablet**, proffered to the shrewd, *but unscrupulous*, business mind, a form of *insider information*. This was the crucial monetary incentive: wherever a therapeutic application for cannabis was to be found in the medical profession's herbal and patent-medicine list in the pharmacopoeias, there would be an opening for large-scale financial opportunism by the concocting of pharmaceutical toxins, to purport to have made 'substitutes' for safe cannabis. Produced *everywhere*, unpatentable and inexpensive, cannabis herb and hash were the medication recommended in treatments for **more than one hundred ailments** in the U.S. Pharmacopoeia (and others).

Additionally, because it relieves patients from unpleasant effects of treatments by toxic medicines (ref. Parts Three & Four) recuperative cannabis was secondary ingredient in numerous other medicines, comprising about half of all medication sold. This constituted (and still does) the financial temptation, irresistible to the corrupt few in a position to gain from their crime, to conspire to prohibit cannabis by fraudulent 'legislation'. This enables cash profits and government revenues to be made from the concoction and sale of *monopoly-patented*, exorbitantly costly 'substitutes', regardless of their inefficacy [1]. However, this requires ruthless disregard for: human life and health; Prohibition's tyrannical illegal inequity (ref. Part Three); Prohibition's unique propensity to engender crime on the greatest scale (ref. Part Six); and, Prohibition's other catastrophic results to individual, to society, and ultimately, to the ecosphere.

During the course of discussions in 1912, one delegate proposed that Indian hemp [i.e.,, cannabis] be included within the Opium Agreement. "San Franciscans," asserted U.S. delegate Henry Finger, were "frightened" by the "Hindoo" immigrants, who were introducing "whites" into their "habit." (N.B. Cannabis is physically and

1 After the legally set period of time, when the patent monopoly expires on a modern drug concoction, the pharmaceutical Owner alters the ingredients, registers a new patent, and then promotes the exclusive sale of the new 'wonder', regardless of its ill-effects and incapacity to cure.

Note the speech by French Minister of Health, Mme. Trautmann, publicly criticising French pharmaceutical companies for falling behind the British and Americans in the number of inventions of newly patented drugs, by which the state is enriched with money generated from people's suffering.

Washington, Jefferson, Cannabis and Semantics.

psychologically *non-habit-forming*; ref. Part One.) The duplicity of this early Prohibitionist attempt is revealed by the fact that a thoroughgoing investigation of Indian hemp had recently been conducted by the British in India. In the seven volume report containing over 3000 pages by the Indian Hemp Drugs Commission, published in 1894, and which remains thoroughly modern today, *official conclusions drawn were*: cannabis is of many great benefits; is free from deleterious effects, and did not in any case qualify for legal restriction; cannabis has wide prophylactic and curative Health utility; innumerable industrial and employment applications the world over; and is a food staple of life; no reputable or worthwhile purpose could be served by restrictions; controls would be unjustifiable, and would produce many detrimental results.

Twentieth Century Prohibitions, which continue to date, were introduced for the unspoken money-motive.

At the time of the compilation of the British-Indian report, there was no connotation of addiction or harm to the word 'drug', which had the meaning of useful domestic dried herbs (ref. Part One). In a concerted effort, people were and are indoctrinated into a new fearful transformed *addictive* meaning of the word 'drug', which untruthfully evaded inclusion of dependence-inducing alcohol and tobacco. This stigma was then attached to *herbs which have monetary value from their medicinal applications*, particularly opium, coca and cannabis—despite the fact cannabis is not addictive. This procured a general public acquiescence to prohibitions introduced on the people's traditional responsible private cultivation, trade and uses of the herbs.

Vicious hard drugs alcohol and tobacco, which have no medical use and are *only* lucrative to corporations and state *when they are legal*, were, by dishonest bureaucratic and political manœuvering, excluded from categorisation as prohibited substance or 'drug' [1].

Finger was representing vested interests. This devious delegate would have known cannabis had been in commonplace use throughout the West in the Nineteenth Century—including by San Franciscans—and indeed for centuries before. His introduction of a minority immigrant race element to the debate was a tactic of racialist scapegoatism. This ugly phenomenon was seen again in the Nineteen-twenties and 'Thirties, in the manipulated press campaigns to invent for 'marijuana' some fearsome alien mystique (ref. section entitled The Marijuana Tax Act). At first, Finger's proposal was dismissed out of hand....

Delayed by the dolorous global spasm of a vast war fought by Democracy to resist the ambitions of the militaristic Hohenzollern tyranny, the preliminaries of the first Opium Conference did not see their next phase until a dozen years later in Geneva. The 1924 conference was assigned the status and more portentous nomenclature of 'convention', for its purpose, arranged in advance, was to produce a treaty. This was to be signed by government-appointed delegates with the intention that its contents would be ratified by participating nations, in legislation exacted to conform to its stipulations. Pre-conference communications between departments involved, shared the defined intent to bring into being binding agreements to take control of international opium production and trade.

1 To emphasise this point, cf. Mortality Statistics on the annual sum total of deaths from all 'illegal' drugs, and then compare deaths from Tobacco and Alcohol; ref. Part One. Note that these mortalities associated by Prohibitionists with the illegal drugs, heroin, morphine, etc., are actually caused by impurities added by dealers to 'cut' substances for increased profit, or by dosage strengths of Black Market products being unknown. Legal availability and control of quality and dosages (as with toxic alcohol) would pre-empt the fatalities: these lives are taken by Prohibition.

THE REPORT. CANNABIS: THE FACTS, HUMAN RIGHTS AND THE LAW.

Amongst others, the vested interests of the British colonial and U.S. cotton industry were represented: during the 1924 conference, the delegate from the British Crown Colony of Egypt produced a statement containing absurd allegations against cannabis (ref. Psychosis—The First Ruse). Other representatives, including the British, pointed out that it was inappropriate to introduce cannabis into proceedings, delegates being only prepared, instructed and informed, to devise controls on opium. Piqued by opposition to his rash and wrong proposal of Prohibition of Cannabis, the British-Egyptian delegate replied that the reason these other nations delayed prohibition on cannabis was because cannabis did not affect the safety of Europeans. Indeed, he spoke truly but unintentionally so, for cannabis, being harmless, does not and did not affect the safety of anyone.

At this point a conference stalemate and breakdown impended. None of the delegations were prepared to see the opium treaty founder on a rock of temperament, to return home empty-handed. Egypt's participation was essential. Although at that time not an exporter, as a 'Western' [1] opium growing country with a home market, Egypt's colonial opium traders had the power to disrupt the new market arrangements, rendering them worthless before they had a chance to take hold. Without unanimity, the unregulated trade seemed certain to proliferate in a way that would bring no monopoly concentration and control of its financial activity.

As quid pro quo for his co-operation on opium, the British-Egyptian delegate received what he wanted: cannabis availability was to be restricted like opium, only to "medical and scientific" applications. Overall Prohibition was adopted.

By this unscientific negligent bureaucratic débâcle—on no justifiable grounds whatever—unlawful national and international Cannabis Prohibition was initiated. Regarding the all-explaining ulterior motive behind the flagrantly illicit proceedings, it should not escape attention that at that moment and by this measure, the major American and British-Egyptian foreign currency earning cotton fibre cash crop was secured a future of guaranteed prosperity, free from the competition of much cheaper, but superior products of cannabis hemp—**and Dresden Cotton** [2].

1 As a member of the Empire, Egypt had immediate access through the United Kingdom to all markets available to the British, a quarter of the world's population.
2 See Section III of The Economics of The CBRPF in the Cannabis Biomass Energy Equation, in Part Two. Nota Bene: The Dresden Process; its product-price and patent issue date: 1924.

The Marijuana[3] Tax Act, 1937.

A decade later, Dr. William C. Woodward, a physician and qualified lawyer, the representative of the American Medical Association, giving testimony to the House Ways and Means Committee in hearings for the U.S. version of treaty-derived Prohibition 'legislation', the Marijuana Tax Act, stated *on the record* that there was: **"no evidence"** to support allegations of 'harm'. [4]

It is significant attestation against this Prohibition's benighted proponents that Woodward's, *the only qualified evidence presented*, was truncated, and brushed aside in a clôture characterised by the brusque hostility of the overtly bigoted committee. Perusal of this committee's, and subsequent, proceedings, which led to enactment of cannabis Prohibition 'law', is revealing. It is also shameful and shocking, in that it defies all concept of the processes required by constitutional democracy, sine qua non.

3 'Marijuana' (Mary-Jane) is a Mexican colloquialism for the botanic Cannabis.
4 U.S. Congressional Record Transcripts, House Ways And Means Committee, Hearings on Taxation of Marijuana, 1937.

Washington, Jefferson, Cannabis and Semantics.

In the U.S. as elsewhere, Cannabis Prohibition was a foregone conclusion. It passed through legislative channels as if pushed by an unseen furtive power, without any substantiated grounds. The extensive crime and social damage engendered by Prohibition had then only recently been most profoundly experienced throughout American society, which was relieved to Relegalise Alcohol. So, the *covert motive* felt by those intent on Cannabis Prohibition had to be *prodigious*. Inclusion of cannabis in control legislation contravened Equity, Justice and Common Law, and was *officially known* to rely on mendacity: the wildly fictitious scare-stories of circulation-boosting gutter journalism, *and* the incorrect association of cannabis with addictive substances (morphine, heroin, etc.) had been investigated and, *were not only not endorsed, but were categorically dismissed by extant official studies*. For example, in 1930 the U.S. government instituted enquiries into cannabis. Published in 1933, the Siler Commission reported that cannabis was harmless: empirical use and clinical monitoring of heavy cannabis smoking by U.S. Army personnel (volunteers) produced ***no effect* upon motivation or performance.**

That report, like scores of others in medico-scientific journals of the preceding hundred years, not to mention millennia, which exonerated cannabis and extolled its health-promoting virtues, was utterly disregarded by the instigators of Prohibition. The evidence of circumstances and facts establishes that Cannabis Prohibition was brought about and has remained in place by criminal officials' collaboration.

For decades, magnates pressed at the highest levels to obtain Cannabis Prohibition. Leading the field were: Du Pont [1], Owner of General Motors and nationwide Power Utilities based on coal and oil, 'fixing' the market, as the registered U.S. Owner of the *patent* on newly invented but, compared to hemp-fibre, *extremely pricey*, polymers, nylon and man-made fibres; *and*, the press magnate William Randolph Hearst. Not to be outdone or outsold by Hearst, other publishers, newspapers and mass-media followed. Since before the turn of the Twentieth Century, Hearst's international and national publications had been the product of his own presses, his own paper-making pulp mills and print factories, and of his investment as Owner of vast tracts of forest in three North American countries, the U.S., Mexico and Canada.

Given extreme personal influence which derives from great wealth in a way similar to that which issues from dictatorship, the addition of unrestrained self-interest and vehement bigotry comprises a fylfotic combination in any human being. In the Western, free-capital-owning democracies, the application of Jeffersonian "eternal vigilance" by an aware, impartial, and incorruptible state remains the perpetual imperative. Regrettably, this criterion, absolutely indispensable to the sustainment of legitimate constitutional democracy and the dispensation of justice, has been neglected by the dissoluteness of those who make pretence of serving the People. The fallen Standards of the West may be judged by this fact: through Prohibition of Cannabis, the state's criminal protection of the great wealth of the very few is enforced, to the certain destruction of the best interests of the entire community [2].

1 Over 80 % of the business of polluting giant corporations, e.g. DuPont, ICI, BP, Monsanto, Allied Chemical, Siemens, ThyssenKrupp, Exxon/Esso, Shell, Chevron, et al, is in areas which Relegalised cannabis renders commercially redundant.

2 Examples abound daily consider these from U.K. newspapers (noted in Part Two):

The European, 21-27 March, 1996: following improved profits, British Petroleum share payout worth nearly £11 million ($16m) to nine Directors.

Daily Mail, 23 March, 1996: following Glaxo takeover of Wellcome (pharmaceutical) job-cuts are indicated of 7,500 while two Directors receive personal payouts worth over £2 million and £7.4 million respectively.

THE REPORT. CANNABIS: THE FACTS, HUMAN RIGHTS AND THE LAW.

Seen in the historical context, Hearst has wrought deep social, economic and moral damage to the Western World, by long-term inculcation into the public mind of the Prohibitionist mentality. For many years, Hearst's newspapers gave furious vent to malign figments produced by his own particular vices. Following the Spanish-American War of 1898, Mexicans and Latins, together with their harmless 'marijuana' smoking, were targets of racist abuse for decades. Temporary seizure by Pancho Villa's revolutionary army, of over three-quarters of a million acres of Hearst's prime Mexican timber forest was a severe provocation at the time, but over the years Hearst's corrupt purpose spawned intimate prejudices which were journalistically worked into becoming **The Collective Social Delusion of the Masses**, the indoctrinated deviant Prohibitionist attitude of generations of Westerners.

Rationality and reality were overwhelmed by Prohibition's false dogma. This has subsequently led to the engendure of crime on the largest scale; and of harm of a more penetrating societal perniciousness than any which can come from individuals' indulgence in substances. As a non-drinker, Hearst sought (initially with success, but ultimately in vain) to prohibit others from use of alcohol. Outrageously racist, Hearst's newspapers, in addition to Latins, also defamed persons of Asian and African descent, perpetuating inequalities and fostering strife. Hearst was that kind of Prohibitionist who objected to the practices of others without any compunction about not applying the demands of his bias to himself. For example, he railed at all sexual activity outside marriage, but for most of his married life he indulged in adultery [1].

Every trustless word and unbridled deed of Hearst's was calculated to work for his self-gratification, without scruple, conscience or consideration for others. Not for Hearst was the approach of the sophist, who, by clever but false reasoning, gathers support from those whose sympathies are manipulated but whose intellectual curiosity remains inert. Instead, using the bludgeon of mass propaganda and the weapon of personally wielded influence, Hearst marched roughshod over Rights and reason. To obtain results he desired, Hearst scorned Truth and Science. He was a driving force in the development of a harsh climate of torrid Prohibition against drugs alcohol, cocaine and opiates, which has proved so criminogenic and counter-productive to society ever since. Without the merest scrap of genuine evidence, Hearst's media, avidly followed by competitors, mendaciously associated harmless cannabis with the dangers of addictive toxic substances, the drugs [2].

The publication by two U.S. government Department of Agriculture researchers, Lyster Dewey and Jason Merrill, of the *breakthrough discovery of the economic superiority of cannabis hemp over trees as a source of wood-pulp for paper products* [3] gave Hearst acute motivation to set him bent on a course to have cannabis outlawed. Hearst's investment in trees would become ruinously redundant unless a way could be conspired to prevent cannabis from replacing trees as the cheap source of paper. With heroin and morphine already subject to *prohibition* (Harrison Narcotics Act, 1914) and alcohol well on the way to joining them on the list of proscribed substances, the means—the mechanism of a 'law'— suggested itself.

1 See David Niven's account in 'Bring on the Empty Horses,' Hamish Hamilton.
2 This technique of false indoctrination-by-association is constantly used. For example, see the U.K. Channel Four public 'information' programmes and leaflet, March, 1995, including the blatant misinformation provided by the British state-funded Institute for the Study of Drug Dependence. Presenting the lies by this method is much favoured by press and media, and is observed to continue daily.
3 See Bulletin 404, USDA; October 14, 1916. Cannabis grown for relaxant-tonic, or cereal-seed plus oil, or fibres, renders the hurds-paper-pulp resource <u>production-cost-free</u>, profitably undercutting the price of lumber—ref. The CBEE.

Washington, Jefferson, Cannabis and Semantics.

With pitiless contempt for the fellow humans whose lives were to be ruined, Hearst and unconscionable journalists contrived to produce an atmosphere of public alarm about, and hostility towards, cannabis, by sheer unequivocal lying. The reporters of the mass media, initially from Hearst's scurrilous prompting, but increasingly from their own imaginations, competed with one another in the invention of frightening stories about cannabis. Ignoring published Official Investigations [1] and scores of scholarly Medical Papers [2] which advised on the harmlessness and many benefits of cannabis, these careful esoteric professorial works met with journalists' falsification to be buried under an avalanche of circulation-boosting, malignant fantasy.

In 1937, criminal Prohibitionists corrupted the rule of law for the commercial gain of particular vested interests. A 'law' was contrived so that cannabis was neither permissible nor practicable for *any* of its uses, by compelling all possessors to apply for "*registration*" (automatically denied) for a prohibitive "*tax.*" This type of control had been introduced on the Thompson sub-machine gun, whose 200 rounds per minute capability was much favoured by Black Market *gangs profiting from Prohibition* (on Alcohol). It had been effective in limiting access to the Tommy gun to those who had no criminal inclination, but professional criminals always found ways and means to obtain them.

Democracy is only as strong as the character of those who maintain it. In America, as elsewhere, whole fortunes were at stake and to be made by Prohibiting cannabis. With the public mind prepossessed by Hearst's and others' propaganda, it merely remained to subvert the legislative and bureaucratic personnel and system, to co-opt the rule of law into personal profit protection. *Wherever controls exist* there has had to be complicity by legislators in criminal conspiracy, because the Medical Papers and Official Reports showing the harmlessness and benefits of cannabis exist as a palpable fact. Amongst the marionettes, notable for the zealousness of his perjury, was career Prohibitionist, Harry Anslinger, former Assistant Commissioner to departmental Prohibition of Alcohol, promoted Commissioner of the Federal Bureau of Narcotics [3], who was a self-admittedly biased individual. He perjuriously read word-for-word, the *untrue appalling newspaper scare-stories on the record* to the House Ways and Means Committee, misrepresenting these as "*evidence.*" The fictions themselves, and this deed of Anslinger's, do indeed comprise damning evidence, but it is evidence to the Crimes which took place then, and perseverately recur to this day, by which Prohibition of Cannabis came to be, and has remained, illegally installed.... In the United States, the Tyranny became fact on the First of October, 1937.

1 & 2 **The British-Indian Hemp Commission; the U.S. Siler Commission. Also ref. Part Three.**
3 **Forerunner to the DEA—readers can judge how successors have imitated the mendacity of the Anslinger rôle-model by the fact that this Prohibition legislation still exists. Also ref. Limited Parameters, Schedule One, Beyond Words, and Reality And Responsibilities, in Part Four.**

Trompe l'oeil.

Trompe l'oeil is the architect's or painter's technique to effect a quadratura deceit of the onlooker, to whom distant vistas or impossible constructs seem from sense impressions to be real, but which are illusory depiction by the skilled artist working in two dimensions. What the eye transmits to the brain distracts to convince by the contrivances of perspective and minute attention to detail. *A similar procedure* is adopted by the Prohibitionist in the attempt to allege harm where none actually exists in cannabis. Unlike the artist's, the Prohibitionists' is an ignoble application of craft.

The Prohibitionists' ruse is plain and base: the terminologies of technicality so mingle with false intentions that the ingenuous nature of people succumbs to the deceits of an avaricious design by renegade artifice. Society's objective appraisal is (apparently) overwhelmed by the conspiratorial contrivances of abominable deception. The products of incorrect methodology and deliberate duplicity form the entire basis for courts' and legislatures' 'rulings' and 'decisions' by which the Prohibition was introduced and has been sustained. Derogatory fictions, dressed in all the trompe l'oeil minutiae of pedantry, sometimes with 'readings' or 'experiments' to give the appearance of authenticity, have on subsequent repeated investigations been exposed as completely unreproducible and uncorroborable. (In any case, as seen in Part Three, grounds of Justice and Legal Equity abrogate all controls on cannabis [1].)

Especially since publication and wide circulation of THE RESTORATION TRILOGY books, there can be no *responsible* politician, judge, prosecutor, state bureaucrat, correspondent, or socially aware person, who does not now know of the Empirical Studies which categorically establish the benign nature of cannabis. Prohibition is prolonged and enforced by liars. Hand in criminal hand, private avarice, state tyranny, media propagation of lies, pseudo-science and trompe l'oeil tramp a crooked path.

1 Also, ref. Parts Six & Seven.

<u>'Psychosis'</u> — *The First Ruse*.

To succeed over the competition brings rewards to the diligent and efficient businessman or woman. However, *to eliminate* competition guarantees the income (and other) advantages of **Monopoly**, whereby the accumulation of an industry's entire trade and profits is concentrated into a few Owners' hands. Furthermore, given demand, a *monopoly* on trade enables *prices* to achieve the high levels unrealisable in a competitive free market.

By comparison with cannabis, cotton fibre is of ephemeral fragility, obliging consumers to make repeated purchases of clothing which wears out more quickly. Throughout history, the superior fibres of cannabis occupied the ascendancy in the textiles' market until the invention by Eli Whitney of the cotton 'gin' (or engine) in mid-Nineteenth Century. The gin reduced reliance upon *labour*, greatly increasing cotton productivity and profitability, notably, at a time when unpaid (slave) labour was becoming unavailable. (The cotton gin was not applicable to working with cannabis.) Without the 'decorticator', i.e.,, cannabis fibre-from-hurds separation equipment such as Schlichten's [2] (which awaited the machine developments of the second and third decades of the Twentieth Century) the cannabis fibre industry depended upon large forces of painstaking, and, by comparison with the machine, expensive manual labour.

Steam-powered vessels replaced wind-powered sailing ships, progressively eliminating demand for the uniquely rot-resistant fibres of cannabis in the making of sailcloth, which, when worn-out, had been the principal resource to paper. So, paper manufacturers turned to polluting acid chemistry and the inferior resource of *trees*. With mechanisation suddenly making cotton cheaper than cannabis, market forces predictably reduced demand for cannabis-hemp fibre for clothing and textiles. Quite unexpectedly, cotton became "king"—the inferior but cheap raw material for a booming, modernised Victorian industry.

2 George W. Schlichten; see Appendix in 'The Emperor Wears No Clothes,' by Jack Herer; HEMP/Queen of Clubs Publishing.

Washington, Jefferson, Cannabis and Semantics.

Cotton for textiles responds like all commodities, with supply values incremented proportionally to growth in demand. Owners of colonial Egypt's cotton plantations experienced a growing demand matched by increased income.

But, the newfound profit in cotton was under constant threat from cannabis. Few geographic locations in the world lend themselves well to cotton cultivation. By contrast, cannabis grows abundantly everywhere Mankind lives. If cannabis remained legal, and its fibre could be extracted economically by new machinery, then the special advantage to British-Egypt, Mississippi and cotton would disappear overnight. With the ongoing improvements in machines, which marked the commercial history of the Victorian Era (like Whitney's invention of the cotton gin), cannabis, which produces significantly higher per acre yields of a more durable and hence more easily spun and woven fibre than cotton, always possessed the potential, by developments of suitable agricultural mechanisation, to re-assume its former domination of the fibre market, stripping cotton-producers of their gain.

If some way could be found to proscribe cannabis in Egypt, thereby eliminating its return and competition to the fibres' market, it could also be prohibited throughout the Empire [1], and even perhaps elsewhere.... If market competition from cannabis could not be eliminated by fair means, it would be by foul.

Initiated by the 1912 and 1924 Opium Conferences, colonial Egypt was among the first countries to outlaw cannabis hemp, securing for cotton a firm hold on the local market and the base from which to expand production for export to the mechanised wonders of spinning and weaving 'mills', especially of Lancashire, England. The finished products of this, then the world's largest textiles' industry, were subsequently exported to a ready market in all parts of the Empire, which comprised circa a quarter of the world's population. Exports were also made to most of the developed nations. In 1928, Britain followed Egypt in Cannabis Prohibition by the enactment of apocryphal legislation.

In Egypt then, as always in the History of Cannabis Prohibition, to disguise the money-motive behind controls, fabricated stories of 'harm' were the false 'justification' which enabled its Prohibition; but the fact that the substances which really are harmful were not banned gives the lie to the legislators' pretence that 'protection' of public health is the 'reason' for Prohibitions [2].

Notwithstanding religious abstention from alcohol by Muslims, in Egypt, addictive alcohol and other poisonous consumed items such as the sedative drug datura were not then banned, although their toxic and pathogenic properties were well known. However, *these* substances offer no economic competition to profits and trade in other products; whereas cannabis, the popular relaxant-tonic-medication, and a prolific source of food and oils, was also a direct virile competitor which always possessed (by mechanisation) the potential to eliminate the economic viability of cotton agriculture, which, since the introduction of the cotton gin, had become Egypt's largest industry and most profitable business.

The colonial Egyptian introduction of Cannabis Prohibition is a signal example of the deceitful pattern adopted by all Prohibitionists: Cannabis Prohibition is an

1 **Legislation in the colonies required prior approbation by the Colonial Office in London.**
2 **Ref. Legislation of Prohibition, 1 & 2; &, The Counterbalance.**

illegal racketeering enterprise of duty, tax and profit-protection, which the state actively initiates, abets and enforces. The Prohibitionists' fraud which asserts 'harm' is necessary cozenage, if the taxpayer is also to be swindled into paying for the exorbitant costs of state-organised thuggery: enforcement [1].

The scores of British and American published Medical Papers, and exonerative findings of the British-Indian Hemp Commission's investigations, all authored by the foremost medico-scientific minds, testified to the benefits to health of cannabis, *and* the negative repercussions of Prohibition. These were ignored by Prohibitionists in colonial Egypt, and subsequently universally. Disinterested specialist scientific dissertation then, and always, found Cannabis Prohibition unfounded and wrong, but with the money-power of vested interests behind them, Prohibitionists corrupt and destroy the impartiality of politicians, civil service bureaucrats and the judiciary. Anti-cannabis libels are invented and promulgated in the attempt to camouflage the crimes of the state personnel responsible; while other politicians, functionaries and citizens, who knowingly and tacitly acquiesce to the committing of these conspiratorial felonies, are themselves guilty of the crimes of misprision [2].

Allegations of "induced" insanity, of 'psychosis', were made by pointing at the interned occupants of insane asylums, and at the apathetic inadequacy of indigent slum dwellers of North Africa and India, who smoked cannabis. The Prohibitionist never made or allowed the requisite rational comparison to the apodeictic harmlessness of cannabis to those innumerable long-term cannabis users enjoying the best of health, but who experienced the privilege of a better standard of life. This allegation in particular had already been investigated and was officially dismissed by the British-Indian Commission whose findings concluded cannabis does not induce any untoward results to mental or physical health [3].

Even today, the slums of the Third World are not a prospect for which the Westerner can easily be prepared. Not long ago, Henry Kissinger called Calcutta "the necropolis of the world." To describe real poverty to someone who has never witnessed it at first hand, is not easy. One's first experience of it is a stomach-heaving all-pervading stench.... Mere deprivation of the artefacts and material accoutrements of industrial society is not this poverty. Nor is it sufficiently described as inadequate housing, no employment, no source of social security or income, no clean water, no proper lavatory or sewage system, and no available medical care for endemic maladies, infections and recurring epidemics. It is all this but much more and far worse; for people also find themselves born into the inescapable environment of a *psychical* confinement devoid of learning and books. There is no education, no sport, no inculcation of creative attitudes or personal ambition and social responsibility. In their place is a complete lack of feeling of self-worth, the nihil of life without hope.

To all this is added yet another crucially debilitating factor: the physical facts of a dearth of food, and that food which does intermittently become available is deficient

1 **Word chosen advisedly. Definition:** <u>Thugs</u> **were a class of professional robbers and assassins in India, murdering stealthily by strangling or poisoning with datura, extirpated at the behest of the Colonial Service, 1826-1835; any cut-throat ruffian.**

2 **Definition (***law***) misprision: criminal neglect in respect to the crime of another; serious offence of failure of duty.**

3 **Unanimous exoneration of cannabis from all allegations of 'harm' to mental or physical health is replicated in the empirical clinical researches into long-term use.** <u>Pre-existing</u> **psychosis can occur in a cannabis using population. See: Study of the U.S. National Institute of Mental Health; U.S.-Costa Rican Study; Study of the New York Academy of Medicine, Benabud Study, Siler Commission, Allentuck, Adams, Freedman, K. Bowman, M. Bowman, Chopras, etc. (ref. bibliography).**

in both calorific value and essential nutritive elements. Malnutrition reduces immune system efficiency and affects even those who seem to have 'enough' to eat. The brain is adversely affected: pellagra [1], rickets, and beriberi are diseases from poor diet. Confirmed by U. N. studies, the type and quality of food can determine performance, mental and physical development, and individual achievement. However, a personal visit to the slums and shanties of any Third World country will explain more in the experience than can be derived from a tome of words. To observe the hopelessness of life in listless, glazed eyes, withdrawal and lethargy, interspersed by apparently incoherent thoughts and occasional unpredicted emotional agitations, is not to see the 'inducement' of 'psychosis' by some mild, smoked relaxant. The allegation of 'psychosis' is dismissed by the fact that such extreme mental disorder does not occur with cannabis use in affluent conditions and countries. That is to say, psychotic syndromes occur independently of cannabis, the psychosis being a pre-existing morbid mental condition within the individual. It should be noted that the sane or deranged Third World slum dweller able to obtain some cannabis seed food or foliage for smoking, in that aforedescribed perdition of mental, physical, social and nutritional want, would derive some benefit from the health-giving effects of cannabis. This is borne out by Benabud's 1955 study in Morocco:

A. Benabud has been the oft-cited modern source from which 'psychosis' came erroneously to be 'associated' with cannabis. He observed the number of 'psychoses' to occur per 1000 cannabis users as up to and not more than 5, i.e.,, half a per cent or less, of which an unknown proportion *might* be indicated to be associated with cannabis. However, *among non-consumers of cannabis*, including those of Western countries, psychosis is diagnosed to occur at various rates all higher than 5 per thousand. From Benabud's study, which has long been presented as evidence 'against' cannabis, its readings are irrefutably *for* cannabis. Stable mental health is seen, *in fact*, to be enjoyed at a higher rate amongst the cannabis using population than amongst the non-users. The Benabud study shows that, far from 'inducing' it, smoked relaxant cannabis averts or reduces the incidence of psychosis.

1 Pellagra has various symptoms: chronic mental illness; paralysis; shrivelled skin; wasted body; caused by dietary deficiency of certain vitamin-B2 elements.

Money Motives and Machinations.

Bearing in mind the underlying money-motivation at its root, it is fitting to be aware of the attempted deceptions which are manifest results of ruthless self-interest. Over the years of Prohibitionist disinformation, to the objective onlooker, many of the trumped up fictions are overtly nonsensical scaremongering. Yet even these are still often to be seen in some journalist's column, regurgitated in monotonous conformity with mass Medias' long errant tradition of apostate defection from scruple and impartiality where cannabis is concerned. The latterday truism "don't believe what you read in the 'papers," was never truer than in the subject of cannabis. The authors do not intend to play Prohibitionist-Devils' Advocate by giving undue attention to the Prohibitionists' lies. However, readers deserve to know the truth of the ridiculous and the unconscionable extremes of lying to which Prohibitionists routinely stoop.

In the early 'Seventies, two seemingly respectable U.S. surgeons specialising in illnesses of the breast, released a paper widely publicised for its assertion that cannabis "might" (i.e.,, it was never asserted as fact) be cause to gynaecomastia, the abnormal development of enlarged breasts (of feminine type) in men, complete with milky white discharge. *This very rare condition is actually caused by human hormone imbalances.* As some gynaecomastia patients referred to them had smoked cannabis, they invented, with impunity, this absurdity, which would be *gratefully* received by pharmaceutical corporations, a large part of whose astronomical annual profits *relies* on the health benefits of cannabis being denied to the population. That a great many millions of flat-chested American males also smoked cannabis eluded their attention. Furthermore, in many centuries' cannabis use the world over, this phenomenon had never been produced.

Regarding motivation behind "experts' " fabrication of cannabis derogation, *career progress* for the dissimulators, involving financial participation by the state and/or pharmaceutical corporations, is routinely noted.

The suggestion was, of course, nonsense, that cannabis smoke is identical to œstradiol, the hormone of human females, so as to activate its processes. If so, post-menopausal women who smoked cannabis would find themselves in a permanent state of Hormone Replacement Therapy and even have their climacteric postponed, or menstrual cycle re-activated. For millennia, cannabis would have been hailed by women as the elixir of female youth and fecundity. Also, there would be many millions of men in America walking about with milk-yielding feminine bosoms, not to mention hundreds of millions more, worldwide. Having previously written papers on breast cancer (their actual specialty) this fiction, with its trompe l'oeil 'academic' style, was only beguiling superficially. It was published in the New England Journal of Medicine, which must have known better and begs the suspicious question as to why that journal printed it at all.... Predictably, media publicity given to this disreputable non-science was instantaneous and enormous. Seemingly rational officials purported to be convinced, while the unsophisticated lapped it up.

After a pause for thought, nobody took the surgeons seriously and their silly story died a death. Cannabis turning men into women failed as a scare-story. Indeed, it fared rather better as a source of jocularity, if in somewhat ribald vein. Never mind, the Prohibitionist fiction factory would try again: this time they would try to make men sterile ! In the days before hygiene was a concept for combating germs, of ancient tradition in the Far East, for centuries, and continuing still in many parts of the world, cannabis mixed with natural opium and taken orally, has been the cure for worms, intestinal infections, diarrhoea and stomach upsets. As a result, inevitably perhaps, cannabis sometimes has been incorrectly associated with the effects of opiates. One well-known side-effect of long-term, regular, heavy use of opiates is the gradual reduction of hormone testosterone production in men, and diminished sexual impulse. To ascribe this opiate effect wrongly to cannabis is not new. Published in 1649 and in various forms still in print to this day, amongst useful therapeutic applications of cannabis listed in Culpeper's famous 'Herbal', is found the incorrect assertion "that plant of Saturn...dries up the seed." Similar unfounded modern claims that negative interactions occur with the functions of the reproductive organs have been repeatedly investigated and demonstrated to be erroneous and disproven.

In 1974, this claim was sensationalised by the media when the U.S. National Institute on Drug Abuse, an official Prohibitionist organisation, released a paper entitled 'Marijuana and Health.' Despite the important caution stated therein that the contents were *not confirmed* but merely "*speculative*," since that time politicians and others of the Prohibitionist ilk bear false witness to misquote the fiction as "fact." In utter desertion of truth, and of obligatory professional objectivity, this "speculation" *did not even derive from studies on cannabis at all*—but from research on *mice with concentrates of THC*. (See: 'THC' Is Not 'Cannabis'.) Since 1974, with minimal public recognition and no publicity, six separately conducted state-funded, official medical studies have concluded that natural herb cannabis in single dose, or short-term, or heavy prolonged use, induces *no change* upon human testosterone production, and *no effect* on fertility, nor on any functions of the reproductive system. For example, see: 'A Medical Anthropological Study of Chronic [i.e.,, long-term] Marijuana Use,' by the U.S. National Institute of Mental Health, 1975; or see: 'Cannabis in Costa Rica: A Study of Chronic Marihuana Use,' Philadelphia Institute for the Study of Human Issues, 1982; or see: Report of Iowa State College of Medicine, 1992, etc.

The most devious dishonourable machinations of all are to be observed in those doctors, university professors, authors, government-appointed drug 'advisers', lawyers, et al, whose real intent is to be rewarded for serving the Prohibition, and who *ostensibly* propose types of partial 'legalisation' and 'exemptions' from Prohibition, such as 'adults-only legalisation', 'depenalisation', 'decrim', and 'medical'. One refers to them as "*covert*" Prohibitionists: *covert* Prohibitionists are well-paid representatives of the government-corporate vested interests who gain financially from Prohibition. The high profile *covert* Prohibitionists have not undertaken a single moment's empirical research of actual use of cannabis, but they mislead cannabis consumers by *appearing* to make 'expert' assessment to 'weigh' the 'risks' of 'harm.'

Let it be well noted, cannabis is unanimously confirmed not to cause skill impairments and to be harmless and benign, by the clinical researches of the expert Empirical Studies, quoted in Part One. *Covert* Prohibitionists lull *real* opponents of Prohibition into believing that they are 'on the same side'; that they too are 'against' Prohibition. They operate by 'claiming' the harm-stories are "exaggerated"—while they make concessions to a "belief" (unfounded) in varying degrees of "harm." By this method, on TV, in lectures, books and leaflets, they endorse, thoroughly publicise, and lend false credence to Prohibitionists' frightening fictions described herein, which are the very harm-stories the official Empirical Studies' physicians, toxicologists, psychologists and clinicians have repeatedly examined in detail and dismissed as totally invalid.

For self-interested motive, these corrupted scribes and pharisees [1] perjuriously undermine **the legal correctness of the Abolition of all controls**. They participate in, and delude the population into accepting, the greatest fraud of all time. By the technique of divide and conquer, covert Prohibitionists waylay the genuine opponents of Prohibition, splitting campaigners' support amongst various *sham* 'organisations' and impotent conflicting groups 'proposing' different forms of exemption, but whose organisers and chief representatives *are covert Prohibitionists who consent to overall Prohibition*. It is no coincidence that the Prohibitionist owned and controlled mass media constantly give *the covert* Prohibitionists, amongst the other felonious Prohibitionists, opportunities to voice publicly their divisive 'policies' and nonsense of 'harm'. NOTA BENE: Not only do the definitive Empirical Studies (ref. Part One) vindicate cannabis—they *also* expose the covert Prohibitionists' lies and duplicity.

1 Definition. Pharisee, in religion: any one more careful of the outward forms and appearances than of the spirit of it; in general: a very self-righteous person; a hypocrite.

THE REPORT. CANNABIS: THE FACTS, HUMAN RIGHTS AND THE LAW.

In 1974, when Ronald Reagan was first quoted in the media as having said: "Reliable sources say permanent brain damage is one of the inevitable results of use of marijuana," his source was neither reliable nor scientific. A federally-funded researcher, a qualified doctor, produced atrophied brain cells in *monkeys by oxygen-deprivation*, and then misattributed this damage to "marijuana." The doctor used a procedure (which a high school biology student would recognise as asphyxia) of interfering with respiration to prevent air/oxygen reaching the lungs. Monkeys were immobilised and forced to breathe *only concentrated smoke* pumped through a mask strapped over the face. Daily, the monkeys were asphyxiated for several minutes at a time, sometimes for up to 15 minutes, for several weeks. *Three to five minutes of oxygen deprivation atrophies brain cells causing irreversible brain damage.* This 'researcher' then killed the monkeys and on examining their brains, now inevitably containing quantities of atrophied cells, pronounced marijuana smoke "responsible." Officials and other Prohibitionist spokespersons publicly announced as a 'fact' of marijuana use, the brain damage which had resulted from incompetent, or duplicitous, application of faulty methodology. These lies were added to others, printed up into leaflets and distributed far and wide.

Amazingly (to some people) the state, at the same time as publicising the wrong "conclusions" of this flawed "research," failed to publish an accompanying full report. This queer obstructionism was followed by point-blank refusal to accede to numerous requests to release for public scrutiny, details of the method by which these incredible 'results' had suddenly been obtained, after so many thousands of years of beneficial use of cannabis had been methodically investigated and recorded by a host of qualified researchers and physicians. By the duress of a Court Order granted to petitioners under the Freedom of Information Act, after much litigation, delay and the improper resistance of the state, the cruel pseudo-science was exposed in 1980.

Although the inadmissible 'results' have long since been exposed, *to this day* these and other frightening, false 'allegations' are *continuously* circulated at saturation levels to enforcement departments, media, medical colleges and institutions, academic and public libraries, universities and schools, and to parent associations. Owned and controlled news agencies, television, and press correspondents and editors *know well* that the harmlessness of cannabis is an established published Fact of state-funded medico-scientific studies, but they withhold exonerative evidence, concealing the Findings of Empirical Fact (Part One). Involved with the pecuniary motive from which springs the lies to derogate the health-giving herb, these career-minded cruel participants in crime incessantly disseminate disinformation to sustain Prohibition. Newspapers, magazines and journals boost their sales with sensationalised mendacity.

In the documentation on cannabis use by both the sick and hale, it is repeatedly denoted that the herb helps *concentration*: people's attention is focused. *Concentration depends absolutely upon short-term memory retention.* Seen in Part One, in tests requiring concentration, studies confirm cannabis use has no deleterious effect; rather, *the reverse is established*. Prohibitionist assertions regarding short-term memory loss are delusive fabrications. 'Short-term memory loss' is alarming jargon for what most people call absent-mindedness; *everybody* experiences Einsteinian 'short-term memory loss': "Where did I put that telephone message?" This has nothing to do with cannabis.

Washington, Jefferson, Cannabis and Semantics.

Disinclination towards a task in hand encourages the mind to wander randomly or dwell upon preferred topics, thereby disrupting concentration, with accompanying short-term memory loss adversely affecting the supposed nominal preoccupation. Also, worry, underlying or even unconscious fears and agitations distractingly intrude upon a flow of thought.

The *improvements in concentration as recorded by cannabis users* are not induced in some physiological mechanism acting on memory processes; rather cannabis, by its ability gently to relax users by rendering a sense of well-being, assists normal concentration by removing the psychologically incursive distractions of stress. The empirical clinical tests confirm (i.e.,, they are *replicable*) that cannabis smoking produces no effect on, or marginal *improvements* to, mental concentration, abilities and coordinative skills, use of machinery, driving a car, tests of memory (short and long-term), concept formation, and mental adroitness. (Ref. Part One.)

By contrast, doses of chemically-disparate pharmaceutical-THC concentrates cause impairments to test subjects' performance by nausea, unpleasant mental effects and headache. *THC-impairments* are ascribed to "cannabis" as so-called "new findings," by those representing the financial interests of the drug and other companies, and of governments, for whose revenues and Owners' profits, cannabis is illegally banned.

Cannabis has long been clinically established as effective in alleviation of the problems of drug users, notably, opiate and alcohol addicts, *assisting people in voluntary cessation of harmful indulgences*: cannabis did and does help society by mitigating the harm associated with the use of drugs, legal and illegal (ref. Parts Three & Four).

At present, pharmaceutical drugs are the only legally available substances used in dubious 'treatments', but these have seriously detrimental toxic side-effects and are themselves addictive, e.g. Methadone, Valium, etc. They substitute one addiction to illegally supplied drugs for another, to drugs on prescription, doing little or nothing in the way of cure. Cannabis Relegalisation will enable the healthy replacement of these, giving real help once more to people by alleviating withdrawal from tobacco, opiates, alcohol *and* prescription pharmaceuticals.

Relegalised, cannabis offers a healthy relaxant to hale people who so choose or require, and therapeutic options to patients and doctors (Parts Three & Four). With *reduced reliance* on the many useless, harmful pharmaceutical drugs invented and promoted for profit in the failed attempt to replace the healing herb, cannabis will help sufferers of a great many types of serious affliction or slight ailment, as it has done for thousands of years with great success—hence, the prominent inclusion of cannabis in pharmacopoeias of the recent past. Relegalised, cannabis will again be the bonus to health in general, to preventive and curative medicine, and to productive society. The proprietary pharmaceutical business Owner will see a marked downturn in drug sales, *but such is the inevitable 'cost' of better health in the population* [1].

Thus, by assisting in treatment and avoidance of the use of addictive substances (i.e.,, Preventive Measure/Medicine) the *reverse* of 'escalation' or a 'stepping stone' effect has *always* been the real social influence of cannabis, by which cannabis renders significant benefits to individual and society.

1 See: 'Pills That Don't Work,' Sidney Wolfe, M.D., & Christopher Coley, Public Citizen Health Research Group.

THE REPORT. CANNABIS: THE FACTS, HUMAN RIGHTS AND THE LAW.

Despite these advantages of cannabis protecting society from drugs, a trompe l'oeil fabrication proposed 'causal linkage' to drug use (e.g. Paton [1]; Bayes' theorem [2]). This Prohibitionist plot consisted of a misconstrued equation based on discrepant factors and the necessarily bigoted application of wildly incorrect figures plucked from the air, not resembling officially gathered statistics. Equally false and similarly farcical statistical manipulations can also be contrived to show 'causal linkage' between the use of hamburgers or chocolate and intravenous heroin injections. Prohibitionist politicians eagerly endorsed this malefic exercise in numeric dissimulation, to indoctrinate the public, and to obscure their connivance with harmful Prohibition.

For all the deceptive detail which went to great lengths over the years to attempt to implant into the mind of the undiscerning, the false notion of a 'stepping stone' effect, on detached and rational reflection the claim is, at its very basis, absurd. The plain fact is that there are no two different substances in the known world where the taking of one pharmacologically causes the taking of the other [3].

It is a measure of the Prohibitionists' dishonesty to hear their 'speculations' and scare-stories trotted out: cardiovascular/respiratory/immune systems damage? obesity, infertility, brain damage, cancer, aggression, pacifism, amotivation, paranoia, epilepsy, addiction, 'psychological' dependence, escalation?—no shock or horror fiction is too ridiculous and no trompe l'oeil deceit too low for the morbid obsession of the Prohibitionists' avarice. Harry Anslinger used to say in his unscholarly, rabble-rousing Prohibitionist propaganda tours: "If the hideous monster Frankenstein came face-to-face with the monster marijuana he would drop dead with fright." It would all be risible were it not for *the results* produced by the Prohibitionists' pernicious mentality and their illegal ban on cannabis, which are so destructive to society, and so damaging to the health and lives of good men and women, and to the families of so many people who do no wrong. *In all the behaviour of the cannabis related activities of cultivation, trade, possession and use*, **there is no crime** [4].

In all the recorded history of cannabis use dating back approximately 5,000 years, there exists no proof whatever of so much as one induced illness in a person, not a single medical case history of proven cannabis related pathogeny. 'Speculation' bereft of evidence is figmental and does not constitute responsible testimony. In contrast, by demonstrating that cannabis is actually health-promoting, benign to the individual, and of great societal benefits, all the physical evidence, the facts, res gestæ and the circumstances, show up the Prohibition as being, and always to have been, an unfounded pretence, the malicious whimsy and fiction of financially-motivated conspirators. For any court or tribunal to allow the legislation to stand, let alone to permit prosecution of this figmentally-based, deeply damaging Prohibition, is punishable criminal desertion of the ethics of judicature [5].

1 Sir W.D.M. Paton's damaging anti-cannabis <u>libels</u> received worldwide publicity. Without much public notice, Paton was professionally refuted in publications by professorial and specialist contemporaries, and subsequently. Paton led astray the minds of many, at one time serving on no less than 70 committees. He worked for the Wellcome <u>pharmaceutical</u> Trust...
2 Bayes' is an algebraic theorem conceived to make astronomical calculations.
3 Ref. Stepping Stones; Prohibition of Alcohol, Part Three; & Treatment of Drug Addicts, Modern Uses, Part Three.
4 Ref. The intrinsic truths of the pronouncement attributed to Abraham Lincoln; Part Six.
5 Ref. Parts Three and Seven.

Washington, Jefferson, Cannabis and Semantics.

It is criminal collusion when writers describe Prohibitionists' wild fictions as if they were deserving of impartial presentation. Certainly, one is careful to report the flawed postulations accurately, but this is not a prim 'debate'. Enforcement engenders mortal consequences worldwide, incarceration, human misery, corruption, crime and ecological catastrophe. Words and actions measure every adult citizen and place them on one 'side' or the other. When strife occurs then it is of the tyrants' making. There is no 'abstention' from this issue, for to retreat passively to the 'sidelines', as it were, lends support to the Prohibitionists' criminal status quo. As parent, teacher, politician, or state employee, the citizen is either against the Prohibition and active towards the achievement of its total Abolition, or that citizen is part of the tyranny.

Cannabis Is Sui Generis.

Being a species which is entirely different from substances which embody addictive, disease-inducing and fatal properties, the mild safe herb cannot honestly be categorised with drugs, nor described by the same vocabulary. Because cannabis has been loosely, widely and incorrectly referred to in the past as a 'drug' does not mean that this basic untruth can become acceptable. On the contrary, since the introduction of controls, the legal situation compels veracity and clarity more than ever, for, not to articulate the truth accurately involves perjury. Yet, truthful language, the truth, exposes the Crime that is this Prohibition. To call cannabis a "drug" is supposititious, a lie to trick people into imaginary fear. Cannabis is not a drug (ref. Accurate Language). It is unique, one-of-a-kind: cannabis is sui generis.

Particular of Judge Young's wording in his Ruling as DEA Administrative Law Judge, points up another official perpetration of lies in what might be called the 'ultimate fiction' by those who say, or would have the public believe, that death results from use. As Judge Young put it:

*"There are simply no **credible** medical reports to suggest that consuming marijuana has caused a single death."*

Emphasis is added to the word 'credible' because in certain quarters Prohibitionist mendacity and the state propagation of lies reach their logical and abhorrent nadir. While all stories of 'harm' are dismissed from the body of scientific literature on cannabis by the super equiponderant countervailing empirical evidence which refutes the allegations as disproven, officials of Her Britannic Majesty's Government Ministry of State for Home Affairs (the Home Office or H. O.) and the Crown Prosecution Service blithely commit perjury daily, in general by the state prosecution of Prohibition, and in particular by active circulation of fictitious 'mortality' statistics.

It is officially investigated and replicably demonstrated that, unlike alcohol, **cannabis does not impair driving skills** (Crancer and other Studies, ref. Part One). All allegations to the contrary are thoroughly disproven. **It is perjurious to ascribe cannabis use as an "underlying" cause of death in an auto or other accident**. Evident throughout the Prohibition, empirically reproducible established Facts are substituted in the indoctrination of the public by false assertions and vehement cant.

Enquiries made to the Home Office staff at the relevant Croydon department evoke replies which indicate incompetent coroners are to blame for the erroneous statistics. Perhaps this is the origin of the false figures. Nevertheless, if the H. O. itself were competent and scrupulous, guidelines for collation of statistics would preclude any such bias or ignorance of coroners in their returns, by screening out from inclusion as 'underlying' cause all inadmissible harmless substances such as orange juice, cannabis and bread.

Where cannabis and the Prohibitionist front at the Home Office are concerned, as Judge Young put it, there are no credible medical reports. The falsehoods are still being distributed at this time. The mass of false 'literature' about cannabis distributed everywhere by government intentionally conditions the population to accept and prop up the 'law', by which the People are grievously abused, and defrauded. The general public and jurors are actively manipulated by Home Office calumniation.

The scheme to prohibit cannabis involves officials', politicians', and the other Prohibitionists' seemingly limitless criminal capacity to lie and traduce. While exhibiting malignant and illegal disregard for the Health of the people, for Truth, Knowledge, Justice and Liberty, and for Life itself, *the state prosecutor*, who represents the totality of Prohibitionist mendacity, appears as perjury incarnate.

In addition to the malversatory 'underlying cause' chart, the H.O. distributes a statistical table which names cannabis as "poisoning agent" in 19 deaths in recent years, and this from the safe plant which literally scores of research studies establish and confirm to be non-toxic (UCLA College of Medicine, Harvard, Temple, etc.). Again, to quote Judge Young:

"There are simply no credible medical reports to suggest that consuming marijuana has caused a single death."

Put in plain language, the Home Office 'statistics' and literature are the biased and barefaced lies of the money-motivated Prohibitionist conspiracy of politicians and bureaucrats. When he ruled that the fictions propagandised by Westminster and Whitehall are not "credible," by his choice of words, Judge Young had in mind mendacious people, exemplified by those at the British Home Office. All governments who impose controls on private cultivation, trade, possession and use of cannabis, and who accordingly prosecute citizens, commit with malice aforethought a crime of devastating and deadly outcome.

Crime and Punishment.

For ulterior motive, the 'laws' of Cannabis Prohibition are the criminal execution of a cold calculated plan, by which the rule of law is usurped: judicial punishment is perverted into an instrument of oppression and terror, constituting tyrannical ferocity on a massive scale. In 1948 and subsequently, nations ratified The U.N. Universal Declaration of Human Rights. By so doing, signatory states renounced categorically and precisely all and any deeds, or national legislation, which allow or abet tyranny, of which Cannabis Prohibition is The Paradigm [1].

Under common law, by constitutional law (ref. Part Seven), by international law and Articles of Human Rights, governments are legally bound to engage the forces of law and order in the protection of citizens from intrusions on their privacy, and especially from tyranny. The international cannabis controls, and likewise, the unlawful national measures which appear as the Prohibition 'laws', constitute state-organised criminal intimidation of, and physically enforced attacks on, people.

This Prohibitionist-government system is to be extirpated at all costs. Historical examples show that totalitarian tendencies, once tolerated in any sphere, become entrenched, habitual, and spread in application until tentacular state

1 See: 'The Paradigm of Tyranny,' Chapter Two of Volume One of 'TRIAL BY JURY: Its History, True Purpose and Modern Relevance,' by Kenn d'Oudney & Lysander Spooner, U.S. lawyer. ISBN: 9781902848723.

Washington, Jefferson, Cannabis and Semantics.

suffocation of Freedom [1] cannot be reversed by measures short of outright rebellion and civil war. Recognition to this is given in the U.N. Declaration; ref. Preamble, in Part One.

The mores of societies alter and can then revert over time (examples abound). Generally, the change or repeal of laws does not apply *retroactively*. Enforcement of any former legitimately-derived, democratically-passed law was legal at the time and law-breakers do not qualify for Amnesty (Expunction of Records, etc.) and still less for Restitution. This does not apply in the Criminal Tyranny of Cannabis Prohibition which constitutes Crimes against Humanity and Against Peace, amongst other serious crimes. Those adversely affected are *victims* requiring social, moral and legal **expiation** by retroactive legislation. Amnesty, Restitution, return of costs, fines, forfeitures, and redress by monetary Compensation are due in Malicious Prosecutions and/or Wrongful Penalisation.

The official Empirical Evidence has always exonerated cannabis. Further, selective Prohibition is always unjust, and thus abrogated (ref. Part Three). Collusion was required for the 'law' to have been formed, passed, and prolonged. Daily, the Prosecution commits crimes of Subreption and Perjury, concealing and ignoring exonerative evidence. Compounding perjury by officials and false witnesses, the state infiltrates inadmissible 'testimony' of disparate-substance THC and 'speculations' in place of the exonerative evidence of the Empirical Findings of Fact, Circumstances and Res Gestæ. Ex parte manipulations, tampering, and perjury, are overt and implicit in the prosecution of every cannabis trial (also ref. Parts Six & Seven).

In re Amnesty and Restitution, reparations made under retroactive legislation cannot be disputed by assertions that, when the Prohibition was in force, politicians who supported it thought they were entitled to do so... **no one** 'believes' they may 'legitimately' support the legislation's inequity, mendacity, and its unconstitutional usurpations; or inflict desolation on people and families for their harmless private activities; or that they are entitled to deny others their Rights. Relegalisation, Amnesty and Restitution are legally and morally imperative; *but, reparations made to persecuted individuals do not, and cannot, settle the issue of the commission of the crimes contributory to, and in support of, tyranny.*

The politician or state employee involved in the tyranny is a participant in crime. Ipso facto, under International and National Law, that individual is the personally answerable legitimate target of public wrath and just retribution. There are no difficulties envisaged that are insuperable in the all-important issue of setting matters to Rights, and discouraging any recurrence. However, before criminal Prohibitionists can be tried, they must be vanquished.

Within all nations signatory to the United Nations' Declaration on Human Rights, it is now the principal exigency, Duty, as well as the Right, of all private citizens and all state bodies, to execute due process whereby this Crime of Tyranny be terminated; by which to bring before the public those responsible; and where appropriate, do justice [2].

---

1 Real Freedom, respect for the Rule of Law's enforced protection of Human and Constitutional Rights, genuine Liberty, is not to be confused with *permissiveness*. In place of Freedom, and to gain votes, modern politicians advocate *toleration* for <u>negative</u> natural behaviour. Politicians grant the people *licentiousness* in place of Freedom. Moral behaviour is the constraint of negative natural behaviour; Mankind's self-restraint from crime and vice. Cf: Desmond Morris's excellent anthropological and zoological works.

2 Ref. RESTORATION; Justice and the Constitution; Part Seven.

A *Third* Substance?

One of many senseless 'arguments' heard from Prohibitionists is that, as tobacco and alcohol are already legal, why then add another, "a *third* recreational substance," by Relegalising cannabis ? implying that the total of harm done to the public by their use of such items would be increased. The impartial reader will recognise that this, as with all Prohibitionist views, is sheer ignorance or conspiratorial obstructionism. To begin with, the "why legalise a third substance" argument is not based on facts. Use of non-habit-forming, non-toxic, safe relaxant cannabis is not only without risk, but is actually health-promoting. Certainly, alcohol and tobacco are disease-inducing and potentially deadly. If *any* validity exists in 'prohibitions' to attempt to deny people access to pathogens for protection of their health, then whereas salutary cannabis does not fit the harm criteria of prohibition-categorisation, alcohol and tobacco do. However, these prohibitions create the Black Market, engender crime and are thus themselves illegal: to cause crime to occur is a crime itself. Ref. Part Six.

Secondly, this 'third substance' argument discriminates unfairly against the Rights of others. It is sometimes proposed by persons who do not drink or smoke, and who do not condone in others the use of alcohol or tobacco. Such people tend to be against all recreational substances, for there are those who, in addition to calling for total bans on alcohol and tobacco, would be content to see the family's daily beverages containing the stimulant drug caffeine, i.e.,, tea, coffee and colas, included in new laws of prohibition. Even the ingestion, the taking, of medicines is not acceptable to some sects (e.g. Christian Scientists).

The 'third substance' argument is also put forward by people who *do* use alcohol and/or tobacco. Purporting to be, or actually, in ignorance of the harmlessness and health-promoting virtues of cannabis, they do not feel personally impinged upon by its Prohibition. In utmost selfishness, they could not care less when others have their Rights attenuated illegally. Whether they know it or not, those who give voice to such opinions in support of Cannabis Prohibition, are breaking the law by advocating *discrimination* illegitimate under existing Civil and Human Rights', religious and substantive legislation. (Ref. E Pluribus Unum.)

Rights are instituted as law to prevent misanthropy having adverse effects on, and interfering in, the lives of others. There will always be the raised hypocritical tones of the 'holier-than-thou' element in society, as well as the ignorant selfish. None of these attitudes comprehends the importance to the upholding of Liberty in a democratic state, by people's *awareness*, and their words and actions in civic defence of the Rights of all others, even when one's own Rights seem unaffected. For example, not all people want to become a member of a Christian Church, but all should defend the individual's Right to do so. In suppression by a state of the Rights of some group, or even of one individual, the lack of a feeling of being personally discriminated against, in the uninvolved majority, can very easily render to the public the illusion that their own Rights are not being interfered with, but in fact "the bell tolls for thee." The denial by a prohibition 'law' of any harmless private activity is the denial to the entire population of their Right to engage in that activity if they choose to do so.

It is a mistake to imagine cannabis to be "minority activity": Cannabis Relegalised will resume its many former uses and importance in the home, in health, in the pharmacopoeia, and in industry, thus once more realising its appropriately *conventional character*. Although commonplace like tea and coffee, it will be held in a far greater esteem for its health-promoting virtue.

This salugenic commodity is denied to people for whom occasional, intermittent or regular use would, by Preventive Measure be life-saving on the greatest scale; and, by Preventive Medicine or Curative Medicament, be health-improving, and in many instances, *also* life-saving. The fittest of athletes are known to benefit from cannabis as a relief to aches and pain, strains and stress. Beneficent cannabis reduces or obviates the need to resort to the dangerous debilitating pharmaceutical drugs of high toxicity and potential dependence. *At no cost*, the health advantages of cannabis could be realised by everyone who so chooses, when the herb can again be cultivated without restriction in everybody's home, allotment or backyard kitchen garden.

People's Relegalised access to cannabis for implementation of THE CANNABIS BIOMASS ENERGY EQUATION (ref. Part Two), for personal relaxant-medications, fuel, food, plastics, substitute petro-chemical products, textiles, paper, lumber substitutes and building materials, *will*: 1.) radically reduce the costs of food, energy and resources; 2.) stimulate the world economy; and 3.) exponentially increase Mankind's capacity to mass-produce both the essentials and the luxury artefacts of modern life cheaply, revolutionarily ameliorating the World Standard of Living (notably beneficial for the developing world), while, 4.) arresting Global Warming and stabilising climate. **Macro-agriculture** is required of cannabis, the indispensable principal world-resource. Relegalised large- and small-scale agriculture and trade make nonsense of 'controls' of *quantities* for personal possession, and of proposed 'licenses' or controls for production, or processing, or for wholesale or retail, as they would be nonsense too with wheat and wheat-derived products, or tea, cotton, tomatoes, rice or grapes.

One of the many good reasons for renewed legal availability of cannabis, and one which the drug companies' representatives attempt to cloak from public perception, is that every time a person sensibly chooses to use safe tonic cannabis as a relaxant in preference to, or rather than resorting to, tobacco or alcohol, this person is eliminating potential harm to him- or herself which accompanies use of those drugs. Cannabis has profound utility in curative treatments of diseases, *including* those induced by toxic drugs such as tobacco and alcohol. Cannabis is thereby of benefit to the individuals concerned, and to society as a whole by savings of significant scale on the lost productivity currently resulting from tobacco and alcohol-related disease.

To child, to adult or the aged, to the sick or hale, cannabis is benign. It is completely unsuitable to discuss safe, health-giving cannabis in the same context as "drugs," be they alcohol, heroin, tobacco or crack—but this results from decades of corrupt Prohibitionist miseducation. One requires only to be reminded by the Mortality Statistics of the completeness of the disparity. Another demonstration is made by the comparison of cannabis to substances which share in common with it the same statistic of equal harmlessness; ref. A Comparative Example, in Part Four.

Evidently, cannabis is *not* 'another', a 'third' substance 'like' alcohol or tobacco. This 'third-substance' nonsense is seen to be the same ill-informed speciosity used by Prohibitionists throughout, to attempt to obstruct the Justice of RESTORATION: Relegalisation, Amnesty and Restitution [1].

1 Ref. Part Seven.

CULTIVATION AND TRADE: "GUILTY" OR "NOT GUILTY" ?
WRONGFUL PROSECUTION, AMNESTY & RESTITUTION.

It is an unalterable principle of the People's **common law** (by which the executive, legislature, judiciary, and all citizens including jurors, are legally bound) that there can be no crime without there having been *mens rea*, i.e.,, guilt or criminal intent.

Guilt is a personal attribute or quality of the actor. It might not be involved in the act itself but guilt depends on *the intent or motive* with which the act was committed. The jury (or any tribunal) must find a person acted from a criminal motive in order to find him or her guilty. This is the issue the jury try: "guilt," or "not guilty."

Justice can only demand punishment and the finding of a guilty verdict where there has been criminal intent or motive. There is no moral justice whatsoever, nor political necessity (i.e.,, deterrent value) for punishing where there was no mens rea. (In the case of one person injuring another innocently or accidentally, the civil law suit and the Trial by Jury award appropriate compensation for damages.)

Guilt is an intrinsic attribute of actions and motives by which common law defines 'crime'. Common law Trial by Jury makes criminal intent or guilt a necessity preliminary to conviction. **'Guilt' (or 'crime') cannot be imparted to an action simply by legislation.** This *mechanism* of Trial by Jury protects (is intended to protect) individuals from governments which have *criminal ends* and would seek to further them by making statutory 'offences' out of innocent acts or circumstances which are not crimes. It can be effective only where the law is not broken by courts and government, and the Constitution is faithfully upheld: that is, where Jurors' functions to judge the law, facts, and decide on the admissibility of evidence are fulfilled and are not illegally denied by judges or by politicians' legislative contraventions. (Ref. Part Seven.)

Cultivation, production, trade, sale, import-export, supply, smoking (whatever), eating, drinking, injecting, possession and use are all legal. That is, these acts described are innocent in themselves. (Ask a pharmacist or doctor.) Legislation cannot impute criminal intent or guilt to *the act* itself. Today, however, politicians and judiciary driven by shrouded motive, infract Constitutions and common law, and on a routine basis fabricate 'crimes' out of things such as the aforementioned which are not and never will be 'crimes'. 'Drug' Prohibition legislation is the paradigm (exemplar) of the venal [1] statute fabricated from the mens rea of politicians at the behest of a (generally behind-the-scenes) money-motivated plutocracy [2]. Wayward judges' enforcement of the corrupt 'legislation' then fines, incarcerates and otherwise abuses innumerable innocent citizens where their acts are without guilt and of no criminal intent. The 'legislation' creates the Black Market; progenerates mass crime and is thus inherently illegal. By hugely augmenting the value of the proscribed commodities, enforcement itself engenders the very crime it is purportedly emplaced to deter.

The corruption of the modern judiciary is self-evident in judges' representing criminally arbitrary authority of government, by actively procuring conviction of individuals for acts innocent in themselves, and the commission of which indicates no criminal intent.

In flagrant breach of morality and common law, judges routinely abet persecution of innocent people by permitting and participating in prosecutions of these false 'laws', simply because not to do so would lose them their job. In all these cases, citizens are due Amnesty and Restitution (as for other Wrongful Penalisation). Until the situation is put to rights by RESTORATION (ref. Part Seven.), the word *'democracy'* applied to societies of the West will remain an empty misnomer.

1 *Definition*, venal: corruptly mercenary; (able to be) bought over; open to bribery.
2 *Definition*: Plutocracy, government by the wealthiest members of society; also ref. Part Seven.

Washington, Jefferson, Cannabis and Semantics.

Since the time when the Presidents Washington and Jefferson farmed and traded in cannabis, until Prohibition, nothing intrinsically changed in the symbiosis between cannabis and Man. Jefferson was Founder of the Democratic Party and Author of the Declaration of Independence, that document famous in the annals of Mankind's ongoing struggle against tyranny. The Declaration was written (three drafts) on cannabis (hemp) paper. Jefferson wrote [1] at length of his preference for cannabis to tobacco, and when in France as Envoy, he sent to the Far East for seed of the sought-after Chinese cannabis. Hence, consider the significance of these circumstances:

. . . these Presidents' innocent cannabis activities would be interfered with by modern 'politicians': nowadays, Washington and Jefferson would be incarcerated with long sentences; subjected to fines and forfeiture of domestic and business property (homes, farms, buildings); and forfeiture of vehicles and equipment;

. . . since Bill Clinton's ignominious assent to U.S. federal introduction of the Death Penalty for innocent activities of cannabis cultivation and trade, today George Washington and Thomas Jefferson would be executed. **Contraventions of constitution and common law by modern governments now inflict despotism embodying a far greater evil than that of the crass, detested monarch who Washington and Jefferson so staunchly resisted**.

Note well the flaw in the slogan "*no taxation without representation,*" which inspired British colonists to their War for Independence. The defect has been inadvertently exposed by the Prohibitionists: the greater the taxpayer or corporation, the greater their ability by lobbying and/or surreptitious methods, to achieve representation and protection of their financial interests, to the unlawful negation of the interests of others [2].

Rather than the colonists' fallible slogan, the Guiding Moral and Legal Principle is: **"No taxation without consent;"** for to take a person's property, goods or money without his or her *consent* is **Robbery** [3].

1 See: 'The Writings of Thomas Jefferson,' Edited H.A. Washington; J.P. Lippincotts Co., Philadelphia.
2 Ref. the section entitled Is Fecit Cui Profuit; Part Six.
3 See 'TRIAL BY JURY: Its History, True Purpose and Modern Relevance,' ISBN 9781902848723.

The Relegalisation of Cannabis,
Deletion of Cannabis from the Single Convention, etc.

Amongst other treaties, the Single Convention's *purported* purpose is to regulate *dangerous* drugs. It is an empirically established Fact that cannabis has no potential for 'harm' or 'danger'; and, by definition based on Empirical Fact, cannabis is not a drug; ref. Part One. Cannabis does not belong in this fraudulent Treaty in particular, nor in any legislation or regulation of restriction. The only position for cannabis acceptable to the demands of veracity, equity, and compatible with existing law, is its completely unfettered legality, allowing it full freedom of the market as with other agricultural and horticultural produce; its untrammelled cultivation at any scale; its free trade and advertising; its unrestricted private production, possession, trade and uses.

Giving due notice through the United Nations' Organisation, national legislative measures to repeal cannabis controls require unilateral enactment by U.N. member, and other, states, forthwith [4]. Effective expedients are available for immediate implementation, such as the passing of a simple legislative amendment by which to effect the rescindment of all controls. For example, as follows....

"Cannabis is hereby Relegalised: its legal status is returned to that which obtained before the introduction of any controls; all controls on cannabis are hereby rescinded; cannabis is legal as personal relaxant; cannabis is legal for any private cultivation, trade, possession and uses." [5]

4 By Article 46 of the Single Convention, nation states which give six months' notice may withdraw unilaterally.
5 See: RESTORATION, The Program. Part Seven.

- PART SIX -

PROHIBITION: THE PROGENITOR OF CRIME.

To *cause* crime to occur is to be accountable for the crime, morally and legally. To *consent* to any measure is to share responsibility for its results.

A Political Issue.

THIS Prohibition is inextricably a disputation political in nature. The decision to ban cannabis was made by politicians. Against the advice of impartial specialists, educationalists, scientists, legal and economics' experts, doctors, sociologists, etc., the politicians persist with their modern Prohibition. Although cannabis is not subject to "party" or "left/right" differentiation, the dogma of Prohibition is politically defined. It is hard to conceive of a more political issue, because it is made so by politicians.

It is the brief of the United Nations Organisation, and 'amnesty', and Civil and Human Rights agencies, to monitor governments' treatment of citizens. These agencies shirk their duty apropos of political oppression of citizens by enforced Prohibitions. Upright citizens object on Principle to the abuse by politicians of the Rights of any group or person. All men and women should become indignant in the extreme whenever politicians or state employees interfere with or 'remove' precious hard-won Rights from the People. Taking appropriate action to ensure Rights are fully *restored* is not untoward reaction: it is obligatory; de rigueur**....**

Economic Effects of Prohibition.

Since time immemorial, Humankind has sought a code by which to teach, govern and judge behaviour. Taken at *face value*, 'prohibition' would seem to be an attempt in law to discourage, deter and prevent a particular activity. The Commandments, and *moral prohibitions* on acts of murder, rape, robbery, theft, fraud, and so on, are expressed in natural law, formerly called legem terræ, "the law of the land," now called Common Law, which outlaws acts of injustice, tyranny and crime, to exact universally accepted correct forms of behaviour. In the majority of its criminal law applications the moral need for such law of prohibition is self-evident. However, on closer inspection, prohibition is exposed as '*two-faced*', and is not always so uncomplicated as a first glance would lead an onlooker to believe**...**

There is no justification, morality, nor efficacy, in prohibitions on commodities. This type of 'prohibition' is *intrinsically* criminal; for prohibition on tradeable articles engenders strong economic forces which cause and promote all of those very activities of crime which the Prohibitionist (ostensibly) claims to wish to discourage.

Consider 'rationing', which is prohibition on the supply of a commodity above a certain quantity: during the Second World War, in 1940 and 1941, while Britain and her loyal associated dominions were the sole force remaining at war to resist Nazi ambitions, U-boats strategically positioned in mid-Atlantic were able for a time to sink millions of tons of merchant shipping, bringing about an acute crisis to Britain, a nation dependent upon imports and maritime trade. Laws subsequently passed to alleviate shortages in supplies by the imposition of stringent rationing upon the population, demonstrated *the prohibition-led phenomena* that people will break the law to obtain commodities, and that the most mundane items can command very high cash prices on a Black Market. The prohibition controls on trade activities other than

Prohibition: The Progenitor of Crime.

those authorised and supervised by the state, mandatory price controls and rationing of the market supply, rendered *increased value* to meat, flour, eggs, elastic, petrol-gasoline, clothing, etc. (which were available to all people at fixed prices by rations determined upon exigent criteria, in quantities deemed sufficient for their needs). In scarce supply were 'nylons' (ladies' stockings produced from hydro-carbon based, new man-made fibres), sugar and chocolate. People were prepared to pay highly inflated prices, break the law, and risk severe punishments to sell or obtain such items.

Given Demand, the Value of any Commodity is enhanced as the predicted result of restricting Supply. Its Unit Price is raised in proportion to the reduction in Supply. Thus, 'prohibition' applied to *marketable goods*, as opposed to abstract concepts such as murder, robbery, etc., *brings Economics into play*. Human nature being what it is, Prohibition-incremented values in the proscribed goods make money-motivated activities associated with them inevitable.

The more intense the attempt at police and customs' enforcement, the more Profit accrues to criminals. A prohibition on cannabis bestows on black-marketeers the undue Asset of another substance from which they reap huge profits. The U.S. government estimates the Black Market cannabis trade within that country alone amounts to over $50 billion per annum (i.e.,, fifty thousand million U.S. dollars.)

If the intent to rid society of the unlicensed trade in particular substances were *genuine*, such a counter-productive proposal as 'prohibition' to achieve this end, could only arise, or be endorsed, not from a superiority of reason but from utter destitution of insight and ingenuity.

Prohibition induces the same economic effect upon proscribed commodities as Scarcity, by the 'Risk Factor' on illegal trade [1]. This increases or maintains high Black Market value even when availability of the prohibited commodity is not markedly reduced. Where demand for an article exists, to apply prohibition concentrates value into it by *both* enforced scarcity *and* the risk factor inherent in prohibition, which result in the proscribed object acquiring significantly augmented worth. Prohibition is a misbegotten concept from every point of view—except that of the willing criminal. Prohibition could not benefit criminals more even if it were a legislative device, a 'law', devised by criminals themselves and foisted by them or their representatives upon predictable political simpletons. The wealth, power and influence of Organised Crime are created, and maximised, by Prohibition.

From stark commandments exacting universally accepted correct behaviour, in the context of commodities, 'prohibition' is metamorphosed into a potent catalyst reacting negatively in society to produce all the crime of the Black Market. Prohibitionists cannot evade inculpation: the Prohibitionist politician is accountable for initiating all crimes which the Prohibition legislation engenders.

There are no factors mitigating the negative effects of controls on cannabis. An unwarranted measure which produces criminal results on the great and small scale, the Prohibition, the control 'legislation' itself, constitutes crime per se. As incipient agent, i.e., the de facto perpetrator, ultimate responsibility for the crimes is on the head of the politician. For a person (or people) to cause crime to occur is to be culpable for the crime, legally and morally.

1 See the cogent essay 'Drug Prohibition in the United States: Costs, Consequences and Alternatives,' by Professor Ethan Nadelman, Science, Vol. 245, Sept., 1989.

The Prohibitionist Politician.
Though not of itself dishonourable, the 'money-motive' is usually behind crimes....

Until the Twentieth Century's money-motivated Prohibitions, employment and wealth from production and trade activities associated with relaxants, health-care products and drugs, were distributed throughout society in innumerable small localised businesses. Yet, by the intervention of politicians, magnates and state bureaucrats, *by the contrivances of Prohibition-monopoly controls*, vast vistas of local-to-worldwide wealth and economic expansion have been made available to some few preferred business Owners and syndicated financial combines, who trade, 'licensed', under treaty-derived (Single Convention, etc.) national legislation. To these few, such exclusivity *guarantees* profits, and hence investment too.

All other traders to whom state approbation is denied, are 'prohibited' from trade. In addition to the monetary advantage of monopolistic exclusivity, there is the further economic protection, or guarantee, underwritten by expropriation from the public's purse of an apparently unlimited commitment by the taxpayer to fund prohibition enforcement. Enforcement is financed to assail those who are denied access to trade in this field, from engaging in competition, to try to put them out of business. The stricter the enforcement, the greater is the risk factor augmentation of Black Market *value* of the prohibited item. This enhances *the incentive* to individuals to take part in these activities, *the enforcement itself being the counterproductive factor which engenders the very crime it is claimed to be put in place to eliminate.*

'Prohibition' is the lynchpin upon which the whole fallacious and crime-producing scheme revolves. From this ghastly design the gigantic modern proprietary 'pharmaceutical' business was machinated, and the greater part of all peacetime crime of the Twentieth Century was produced, *this ongoing....* Viz. the relevant observation made by The Economist journal:

"A small group of drug criminals now probably launders tax-free sums of over $180 billion a year, more than the Gross National Products of 150 of the 170 nations of the world." This represents the profitable tip of a vast iceberg of crime which would melt to disappear, were the profit and the monetary incentive to crime removed from Black Market drugs.

Prohibition must be source of endless glee, delight and humour to the organised criminal fraternity, amongst whose number but few are ever brought to book. (Those removed from black marketeering are soon replaced by recruits keen to profit from Prohibition.) To the successful criminal, Prohibition is a very major generator of lucre to whom RELEGALISATION would prove a severe setback. The preponderance of arrests under Cannabis Prohibition are made upon the easy prey of harmless citizens who cultivate or possess on the small-scale for private consumption.

Reported in 'The American Disease; Origins of Narcotic Control,' by <u>Professor David F. Musto</u>, M.D. (Yale and Oxford University Presses): continuously over the last sixty years to date politicians and officials have been wont to say that the *"illegal drugs"* caused most of all crime, and *"caused"* up to *"75 per cent of all crimes in large cities."* This is heard so often that it has taken on the familiarity of a slogan. It is utter mendacity, especially abhorrent in responsible persons, for it is knowingly used to mislead citizens from the realities of a more recondite truth....

Prohibition: The Progenitor of Crime.

Mention should be made in this connexion, of the legal drug alcohol which, in addition to impairment of skills rendered by use, also has the well-known propensity for lowering behavioural inhibitions. This is a particular characteristic of alcohol, which explains its wide social use and popularity. However, seen in all social groups who use alcohol are its associated negative results: disease, death, grievous behaviour and crime; ref. NIDA Statistics; Part Three. *The assertion that drugs cause crime is, in the behavioural sense, applicable only to any significant degree to alcohol, and in the case of alcohol it is extreme* [1]. As alcohol is legal, the politician who claims "drugs" are illegal because they "cause" crime, has already broken the universal law which good men and women call Truth. However, the issue does not stop at that**....**

Given demand, Prohibition has the **economic effect** of causing proscribed or rationed tradeable commodities to acquire greatly increased cash values: *if prohibited, drugs command street prices in excess of 3000 per cent greater than the equivalent already profitably prescribed by the physician* [2]. Prohibition 'legislation' is progenitor of the Black Market, and the cause of unscrupulous or fallible members of society from every stratum, being drawn, *inevitably*, into the illegal drugs' trade, to obtain wealth, 'quick' money. Intensification of prohibition enforcement can to some extent, although by no means consistently, increase **scarcity**; but, correspondingly, this causes proportional **growth** in supply **value**, which produces greater **incentive** to crime and negative net results. The economic effect of increasing scarcity synergistically combines with the effect of the stricter prohibition engendering greater 'risk factor', augmenting cash value of the prohibited article. This greater **incentive** to crime concurrently generates an almost Darwinian survival-efficient response of exacerbated ruthlessness, which is expressed in all manner of violence and crimes.

Where proscribed drugs are concerned, *it is the prohibition itself* which produces all manner of crimes, as the subreptitious Prohibitionist politician well knows. By the Prohibitionist approach of the use of 'law' and enforcement, the politicians of 'prohibition' are, for a variety of inexcusable motives and sorry human failings, directly responsible for bringing about the majority of peacetime crime of the Twentieth Century, this ongoing: *the crime which politicians attribute to "drugs" is actually theirs. The aforementioned politicians' and officials' stated figure of "75 per cent of crimes in large cities" is but one measure of their culpability.* The hollow claim 'drugs cause crime' is a political confidence trick, a criminal scam. This is intended to confer false 'respectability' on legislation of prohibitions to obscure the racket of government revenue and corporate profit-protection, by which 'politicians' forcibly subject the People to methodical plundering.

U.K. police statements indicate seizures worldwide of contraband, amount to approximately 10 per cent interruption of supply. Why, when there is a manned police station within a stone's throw of every dealer and user, does the larger proportion *still* reach the streets ?**....** As noted, when rationed or prohibited, even the most mundane items can command very high cash prices on a Black Market. Prohibition imparts so great a value to proscribed substances that many people, including public officials, find the temptation to criminal involvement irresistible due to the huge financial inducements. *Trafficking has always been generated by, and relied for its long-term viability upon, the corruption of state employees.*

1 See: 'The Limits of the Criminal Sanction,' Herbert L. Packer, Stanford University Press; and: 'Crimes without Victims,' Edwin M. Shur, Prentice-Hall.
2 See: 'Repeal the Drug Laws to Help Fight Crime,' J. Riggenbach. (Ref. Bibliog.)

Prohibition produces **corruption** on the largest scale, engendering deep criminality worldwide amongst those whom states employ in positions of trust. Collusion is rampant between the criminal beyond the law, and officials to whom financial inducements are irresistible. It is constantly catalogued at all levels, including up to the very 'top': viz. Prime Minister Pindling. Such reported instances represent only the incompetent criminals who are caught by far the most, i.e., those associated with the uninterrupted **90 per cent** of the 'illegal' drugs' trade quoted, are never known publicly as the criminals they are. Perpend the politicians' two-faced counterfeit coin: while the unspoken revenue and profit **protection racket** of "legal" trade in "prohibited" drugs by pharmaceutical firms directs the deceitful deeds and words of politicians, concurrently, money-motive also corrupts politicians and officials into becoming compliant conspiratorial cogs in mercenary activities of Organised Crime.

U.S. Federal District Judge, James C. Paine (Miami) in 1991, put his finger on the racing pulse of modern "drugs" crime in a speech to the Florida Bar Association. He proposed "legalisation" of all proscribed substances, to take the profits out of illicit "drugs." He stated that in view of the scale of profits generated by Prohibition, it is not remarkable to find that some people *are* "on the take;" the surprise is to find that there are any state employees remaining at all who are *not* "on the take." The worthy judge's observation infers the Prohibitionist 'politician' invades society with an influence so degenerate, it has the potential to cause a collapse of civilised behaviour by those who govern and enforce which is total and terminal.

Politicians go out of their way to make Prohibition *appear* to be the will of the People because people fear and loathe crime—yet, the very crime to which people's attention is directed in the connexion of proscribed substances is itself progenerated by Prohibition.

The inherently criminal political Prohibitions are actuated worldwide by the Prohibitionists' deceptions that are the Single Convention and other treaties, infecting all signatory nations with Prohibition-produced crime. From the top, Prohibition's intensely degenerative effects proceed through every society insidiously. The dire results reach into countless homes in every hamlet, town and city of the affluent and developing world alike. Havoc engendered by politicians and unleashed all over the world, is totally unnecessary and avoidable. **Abolition** of Prohibition eradicates the chaos and crime *at a stroke*: that is, RELEGALISATION annihilates the monetary incentive to criminal activity by eliminating the undue cash value of the proscribed commodity.

Despite huge increments in Western states' enforcement budgets throughout the 1980s, the '90s, and this century, with additional enormous expenditures on international 'interdiction'—which benefit only the criminals by ensuring raised prices of contraband—the world's most profitable industry of importation (smuggling) and distribution (dealing) continues unabated. Vast trafficking prevails, but could not occur without public officials participating at all levels. The *political* Prohibitions are corrupt, and make crime inevitable: every honest official or citizen would wish to eliminate Prohibition.

George Shultz, former U.S. Secretary of State, co-architect of West-Soviet détente, on the faculty of Stanford University, stated in a paper read to the Business School:

"It seems to me we are not really going to get anywhere until we can take the criminality out of the drug business, and the incentives for criminality out of it. We need at least to consider and examine forms of controlled legalisation of drugs."

Prohibition: The Progenitor of Crime.

Advocating Relegalisation of Cannabis, which is not a drug (ref. Accurate Language), and legalisation of *drugs* with controls similar to alcohol, in his 1989 public statement in New York, U.S. Federal Judge Robert W. Sweet (Manhattan) acknowledged the crime-producing economic effects of prohibition 'laws', when he said:

"I suggest it is time to abolish the prohibition. The result would be the elimination of the profit-motive, the gangs, the drug-dealers. Obviously, the model is the repeal of [alcohol] prohibition and the end of Al Capone and Dutch Schultz."
[Authors' emphasis added.]

Rather than receiving reduction of and protection from crime, the citizen- taxpayer finances a Prohibitionist-politician-produced, ever-growing maelstrom of crime which engulfs the innocent. Civilised values and modern society degenerate visibly and inexorably under the excruciating myth and crude dogma of Prohibitionists. The Prohibitionist politician is a destroyer of civilisation; veritably, the enemy within. It is incumbent on all responsible citizens who deprecate crime, to take appropriate and decisive *actions*, not allowing Prohibitionists to delay or foil the utter Demolition of criminogenic Prohibition. The criminality which derives from corrupted leaders to spread through society, undermines its people and ethos, and obliterates civilised institutions.

In the last four years of Alcohol Prohibition to 1933, *approximately half of all prosecutions failed to produce Guilty verdicts*. This contributed to social pressure for repeal of Alcohol Prohibition legislation. Today, however, judges instruct juries to enforce illegitimate Prohibition 'laws', not permitting acquittals; and deny defence lawyers the presentation of the officially-derived expert exonerative evidence which demonstrates that the 'law' is: figmentally-based; money-motivated; legally untenable; criminogenic; inequitable; deeply injurious to individual, society; and in the case of cannabis, the 'law' also causes Global Warming, and damage to the ecosphere, ref. The CBEE; Part Two.

Under the American and British constitutionally-emplaced, sole *legal* form of due process for *all* criminal, civil, and fiscal causes, i.e., the Common Law Trial by Jury [1], the citizen-juror is duty-bound to judge, not only on the facts of the case, but also on **the justice** of the law, and of every act of enforcement, **to annul** bad or unjust 'law', and all unfair enforcement, by pronouncing the Not Guilty Verdict. *Predictably*, in the society whose 'legislature' functions for vested interests at the behest of criminals, the Common Law Trial by Jury is *now no longer permitted* by unconstitutional and illegal government intervention (ref. Part Seven; Justice and The Constitution).

Legally, the Trial by Jury was *irrevocably* emplaced. This was with the specific intention of protecting society and citizens from *government-produced* crime and injustice; and it is the means by which ordinary citizens could, should and would, have annulled all the crime-producing 'laws' of Prohibition, thereby pre-empting and preventing the mass crime which such Prohibitions engender. The Constitution is contravened, Common Law is broken, and Trial by Jury has been destroyed, by the Prohibitionist politician operating for hidden motive. If this tyranny by corrupt 'politicians' is not extinguished, and Constitutional Trial by Jury is not Restored, the slender vestiges of benevolent Western Democratic Civilisation will suffer final demise early in the New Millennium.

1 **Every single form of due process 'trial' that takes place today is illegal, unjust, and contravenes constitutional law and universal natural and common law. The Justice System is perverted to serve crime. See 'TRIAL BY JURY: Its History, True Purpose and Modern Relevance,' ISBN: 9781902848723. Also ref. Part Seven.**

THE REPORT. CANNABIS: THE FACTS, HUMAN RIGHTS AND THE LAW.

Prohibition is the criminal design of legislative bodies comprised of fallible human beings, politicians. After so many years, in some countries two generations, Prohibition is deeply entrenched. There are many unthinking or corrupted people in the spheres of law, politics and the media who are on the record in their support for Prohibitions. Some politicians' motives would have been to use the "menace of drugs" to enliven their public speeches, to try to promote their 'image' in an attempt to boost 'ballot-box appeal'. However, they lie when they do so, for no menace of any kind exists in cannabis use; and, alcohol and tobacco, the most menacing, damaging drugs of all, as confirmed by the mortality and other statistics, are dishonestly not mentioned in this context.

Other public commentators represent, or have, vested interests, whose value they *protect* from economic competition by cannabis, by giving their support to its Prohibition. (Viz. interests, such as corporations involved in the provision of fuel and energy; and the drugs' companies: tobacco, pharmaceuticals, alcohol, caffeine-colas.) Politicians and parties are manipulated and compromised, owing a debt to magnates and corporations, for campaign and other support received.

Presently active or retired, politicians are unlikely to renounce their calumnies and hostilities against cannabis. It is hard enough to admit that ignorance and prejudice led one into taking a wrong stance on a subject when as an elected politician it is one's bounden duty to investigate the issues thoroughly before making decisions upon which punishments are in the balance. It is another matter bordering on the unthinkable, to admit that one knew all along that one was wrong to support Prohibition, but did so for self-interested motives and personal gain.

The People must involve themselves because.... much the greater part of all peacetime crime committed results from, *and is comprised of*, politicians' Prohibitions. Regarding cannabis, voters are obliged to ensure their representatives endorse Abolition of Controls. It would be better for the state of democracy for people not to vote at all in local or national elections, than for them to give their vote or any electoral support to a Prohibitionist, whatever the party.

The politicians' crimes cause all sorts of other crimes to occur. The Prohibitionist politician serves more than one master, proliferating crime and pervading society with corruption at all levels, while innocent citizens are assailed. Consider the masters of this Crime: on the one hand, there is the latterday Dives, the morally bankrupt magnate who dispassionately watches daily enforcement activities of incarceration and abuse of people by malicious prosecutions. By force and violence, cannabis and its derived products are prevented from competing and undercutting (ref. Parts Two, Three & Four). For hegemony, and for Dives' monetary gain, politicians install the racketeering monopolistic profit-protection of unnecessarily expensive and otherwise redundant products in the shops and markets of the modern world. On the other hand, Prohibition serves the professional criminal, by investing such phenomenal value into common or garden cannabis as to make trafficking inevitable.

Whether or not he or she confesses to these crimes, as the maintainer of crime-producing 'legislation', the Prohibitionist politician actively causes crime, promotes the Black Market, and represents the interests of criminals. With the criminal Prohibitionist politician governing, the potential for Prohibition to produce crimes knows no bounds....

Prohibition: The Progenitor of Crime.

The Prohibitionist Politician Instated Organised Crime.

Alcohol Prohibition demonstrated how political Prohibition is a mechanism abetting crime, which puts into effect the deplorable transfer of billions of dollars to criminals, from the legal, taxed, regulated businesses of commercial production and distribution. Money empowered efficient criminal organisations to become impenetrable. The Twentieth Century event—'prohibition'—installed Organised Crime as it now exists: the 'politician' instated Organised Crime. Over the years of Alcohol Prohibition, politicians obliged the taxpayer to foot the bill for costly enforcement which generally hurt small-time purveyors. In rare instances, well-known criminals were apprehended, but their places were swiftly taken by others anxious to seize the lucrative opportunities offered by prohibition. Then, as now, discreet criminals proved to be beyond the reach of law. So, Prohibition fails in its ostensible purpose, while its 'success' is spectacular in promoting crime. The vast revenues taken from overtaxed citizens and expended on 'enforcement' by the state misgoverned by Prohibitionists, which could have been put to many a good use or not levied at all, are utterly wasted.

Prohibition on Alcohol, unlike the other drugs, yields no revenue to government (because it has no medical applications) but 'prohibitions' on therapeutic herbs have been zealously maintained by 'politicians' for nearly a century. Transnational wealth and power have been accumulated by families, groups and sociopathic individuals, who, to enrich themselves, are prepared to break every law and thus to whom commodity and "drug" Prohibitions represent a special economic advantage. 'Politicians', assiduously serving and representing criminals, subvert the Justice System and manipulate 'law' on their behalf. Control by Organised Crime of whole industries, multi-national corporations, of the banking system, groups and persons, of the political parties and the selection and financial support of candidates and representatives, are everywhere in the West, unseen but not unfelt.

By the late 1960's, the F.B.I. released information indicating that the cash resources annually invested by Organised Crime into the pay-offs of bribery and corruption to state employees, had by then exceeded the sum of gross annual wages of all police in the U.S. The American criminal Black Market is a parallel economy of greater annual turnover, or product, than the legal gross national product of the majority of countries member to the United Nations' Organisation. The criminogenic effects operate in all the nations where 'prohibition' is the official approach. Consider the 'parliamentary democracies', for example, the U.S.A.

Judged in the perspective of History by its Bill of Rights, the Constitution, and the Declaration of Independence, the United States of America were bred in high idealism and born of the struggle to establish a democratic haven to justice, values of fairness, liberty and, where this does not obtrude upon the Rights of others, the Right to the pursuit of individually-defined self-fulfilment. However, within any human being or human society, the existence of a parasitic organism intent at all costs upon its own survival to the detriment of its host, defiles, and can even, if undeterred, eventually destroy the body corporate upon whom it feeds.

Today, Western 'civilisation' is thoroughly riddled by the Prohibitionists who discreetly serve crime. The parasitism of real crime erodes decent societal aspirations, but far more than this, in its most 'successful' degree, the parasite can so enslave as to make its host desist from normal functions, to concentrate instead solely on providing

161

for the satiation of the parasite. In this case, undercover criminals replace good citizens in significant social positions, and the morally-based legal philosophy, law, is infiltrated by practices which operate for the abetment of crime. For example, in recent years government interference in the constitutionally-defined due process has produced a dysfunction which denies the citizen legal access to jury and court protection from enforcement of unjust law, thereby negating centuries of recognised correct court practice. This illegal one-sided support for the prosecution of Prohibition further dilapidates Western civilisation. Stone by stone, case by case, democracy is dismantled and its citizens brutalised by courts, adding momentum to the forces of decline and fall. (Ref. Part Seven.)

Adopted by successive Chancellors, Presidents and Prime Ministers, and ongoing to this day, Richard Nixon's much-vaunted perverted 'War on Drugs' is Prohibition: a war waged by a small minority of criminals against the People, for monetary gain.

A population menaced by the all-pervading, ever-increasing crime produced by Prohibition, is readily misled by state propaganda and disinformation. People intimidated by a violent environment turn credulously, in the absence of leadership of probity, to false notions of "tough enforcement," in the vain hope that Prohibitionists' dogmatic vehemence and cruelty (manifested in fierce punishments of harmless citizens) are some longed-for, vague and inexplicable cure for society's ills of crime and violence. In their bewilderment engendered by Prohibitionist deception, people are manipulated to turn once more to that very measure, Prohibition, which, for now nearly a century (since the Harrison Narcotics Act of 1914) has been The Progenitor of most of all peacetime crime.

Society lurches in purblind befuddlement to perpetuate prohibitions; the People thereby enrich their enemies and create a rod for their own backs. The populations who elect Prohibitionists to govern prolong their own agonies and encourage crime.

With the passage of a new Amendment, legal trade in alcohol was resumed, but the damage done to society by the time Prohibition was repealed was severe. Newly empowered, organisations controlled and manned by ruthless criminals went about the acquisition of outward respectability, a camouflage of 'legitimacy' in worldwide businesses which continuously 'launder' their ill-gotten gains. Prohibition's tares of criminality had been deeply sown. The noxious crop poisons society down the generations. The results of Prohibition are devastating and, as seen in the experience with alcohol, immeasurably outweigh the harm of the behaviour it is ostensibly introduced to curtail. Alcohol is not legal because it is 'less' a drug than heroin or 'less' destructive than cocaine—tobacco-induced fatalities aside, by any measure, the comparisons reveal that alcohol is the most destructive drug to individual and society. (Ref. Part Three.) With money-motivations of officials and others at its root, and because Prohibition 'law' is in every way a flawed concept, drug alcohol is today legal. Also, it is a drug that many people use.

Having pondered the stark fact that alcohol is a hard addictive drug, the reader is invited to apply these realities in a grim but apposite way, to relate to the following analogous scenarios and draw parallels with Cannabis Prohibition:

. . . Consider being arrested at your dinner table for having a glass of wine in your hand and being forcefully removed to the police station where you are compelled to have your photograph and fingerprints taken. Subsequently, you are punished in court with a fine you can ill afford and are placed under a threat of imprisonment if you repeat the behaviour, at which time you will also have your children removed into state 'care'....

... Imagine being stopped and taken to the police cells to be stripped naked, searched and urine tested, for having had some cans of beer found in the trunk of your car on your sober way home from shopping. Subsequently, you receive punishment in court and thus a Criminal Record which not only prevents the progress of your career but results in your being fired from your present employment....

... Think for a moment how it would feel to have your pleasant happy home and belongings tumultuously upended by a ferocious troop of drug-search police, because a neighbour had telephoned in that you were seen taking a gin and tonic at your family backyard barbecue....

... How would the homebrew or home-winemaking expert appreciate having his equipment smashed and burned, and spending several years in jail for his hobby ?...

... The contents of a small drinks' cabinet at home constitute more drink than one can reasonably consume at one time. Consider, therefore, a law which stipulates that the possessor of such a quantity is automatically categorised as a 'trafficker' and is accordingly imprisoned for many years....

Readers, especially those who use alcohol in a responsible way, will draw the conclusion that, as all the aforegoing examples represent grotesque enforcement of a bad law of prohibition, which embodies unacceptable breaches of personal Rights and civil liberty, to every shade of political thought in all sectors of the population including politicians, bureaucrats, judges, and police, so too is Prohibition of Cannabis an illegal, unjust, immoral 'law'. Yet, daily, good people are incarcerated and otherwise abused for harmless cannabis cultivation, trade, and use.

Above all the considerations aforementioned stands paramount the ultimate and ironical fact that cannabis is not a drug. Although cannabis has medical utility and health-giving attributes, as do other non-drugs and Accessory Food Factors, such as vitamin-C in treatment of the disease scurvy, the parameters of definition, the meaning of the word 'drug', including especially a drug's intrinsic chemically-addictive properties, exclude non-addictive cannabis from such categorisation. The official Empirical Studies (ref. Part One) confirm cannabis is benign, and induces none of the defining damaging phenomena associated with drug use, such as tolerance, toxicity, mortality, withdrawal, addiction, dependence and abstinence. Scientifically-speaking, to equate cannabis with 'drugs' is nonsense.

Those who influence politicians to prolong Prohibitions are now deeply ensconced; they will not give up easily but the People do not like being duped by those they elect on trust. The steady scrutiny of the informed citizen perceives the hypocrisy and pierces the platitudes, invoked by the Prohibitionist. Politicians' betrayal of the People is not obscured by the froth of their speechifying; their disinformation and propaganda; their bullying, bluster and downright lies.

The door to Truth is locked by mendacious politicians, but the key, Honesty, is in the hands of the People.

As the Bard observed, "The Truth will out!"

THE FALLACY OF 'DECRIMINALISATION' and of 'dépénalisation'.

'Decriminalisation' is a vicious Prohibitionist scheme foisted by the unscrupulous upon the unthinking or the unfortunate. The following explains the fallacy of, and reveals the corrupt purpose behind, 'decriminalisation' and 'dépénalisation' (French).

Note well that Decriminalisation *is* Prohibition: 'Decrim' replicates the legislation of the Nineteen-twenties' and 'Thirties' Alcohol Prohibition in the U.S. Bitter experience from then, and today from various places in Europe where this legislation has been emplaced, shows not only that "decrim" is the most socially destructive, criminogenic form of Prohibition devised, but also, that decrim is actually a misnomer—it is misnamed—for criminalisation actually continues under this form of legislation.

Decrim is not a 'step' towards Relegalisation. Decriminalisation/ depenalisation is: the *non-prosecution* of possession of a miniscule specified quantity; and continued general Prohibition to the public, of private commercial Production and Trade; *and* (unless granted a trade-license) the continued Prohibition and punishment of possession of more than the tiny 'permitted' amount. Depending on the country, in Canada for example, police confiscate any minute quantity possessed; but not so in Holland where use is accepted. On numerous grounds, this legislation is illegal: for example, it embodies *inequity*; the Prohibitions it continues to impose on cannabis-associated activities are prejudicially selective whilst deadly addictive alcohol remains legal for Production, Trade, Possession and Use.

Under decrim, criminalisation *continues* of cultivation and trade and also for possession of only a very small quantity, but which is above the amount stipulated by law. In the U.S. and U.K., many, perhaps most, of the present malicious prosecutions would *still* be pursued following changeover to decrim. So, let us examine what this rigmarole really is and see the hidden purposes behind it.

First, let us be reminded of the official definitive Findings of Fact by which cannabis qualifies for **exemption** from all legislative controls based on 'harm' criteria. (Parts One, Three, Four and Five). Cannabis qualifies to be more freely available for people to cultivate, to trade in and to use than meat, coffee, wheat, milk and tomatoes. The U.K. Misuse of Drugs Act and the U.S. Controlled Substances Act are abrogated. Evidence demonstrates all cannabis control 'legislation' is the fabrication of a racket. Under the law, cannabis and related activities have always been legal. Decrim is merely a variation of the illegitimate Prohibition, the revenue and profit protection-racket subterfuge. Summarised below, people proposing decriminalisation deceitfully, and unlawfully, **evade**:

1. the inherent illegality of legislation which progenerates Crime (Part Six); and
2. Findings of Fact: medico-scientific exoneration of cannabis from 'impairment' or 'harm' to mental and physical health, which exempts cannabis from all controls (purportedly) on grounds of 'danger' or 'health' (Parts One, Three, Four, Five); and
3. benign aspects of fully Relegalised cannabis, in A.) Preventive Health, B.) in socio-economic, and C.) in ecological terms (Parts One to Six); and
4. commercial facts which establish money-motivated felonious machinations as cause to fabricated derogation of cannabis (Parts One to Six); and
5. the unlawful selective inequity of controls imposed on private commercial Production and Trade (Parts Two to Six; compared with safe cannabis, coffee and dairy products are risky); and,
6. infraction of common law (p. 152) and the despotism of inventing 'crimes' out of activities which are not criminal (ref. statement attributed to Abraham Lincoln, Part Six); and
7. aspects of enforcement which contravene common law and constitutions (Part Seven).

Prohibition: The Progenitor of Crime.

Economics explain why Prohibition and 'decrim' are unlawful and unacceptable to honest people. The legislation allows personal possession of small quantities which *stimulates demand* while continuing to constrict legal *supply*. This engenders the *highest* Black Market *prices*, producing the most intense *incentive* to crime. For example, in 'decriminalised' Holland, Belgium [1] (and Germany) by weight, Black Market cannabis can **exceed the price of gold** and seeds of preferred varieties sell at prices from £14 (≈ $24) to £50 (≈ $80) *each*. Given the monetary incentive, people have always been irresistibly tempted to commit crimes. The advocate, instigator and enforcer of the decrim version of Prohibition are responsible for all those crimes which decrim engenders.

In 1994, Lübeck Judge Wolfgang Nescovic suspended a prosecution of small-scale possession and supply, to apply to the Constitutional Court (Germany's highest court) which subsequently ruled, *while Alcohol is legal it is inequitable and unconstitutional to prosecute cannabis use, small-scale possession or supply.* The legislature failed to ratify: the German state continues to prosecute inequitably, i.e., illegally; tyrannically; and, *ignoring* **the legal obligation** to enforce only those laws which are just, legal (ref. ratified U.N. PRINCIPLES), police perjuriously evade empirical facts which prove cannabis does not cause skill impairment, including specific tests on simulated driving; ref. Part One; they search, test without probable cause, and confiscate licenses, even though **no test exists** which can confirm whether cannabis effects are *current*.

Instead of the beneficial transformation of society by **Relegalised** cannabis being cheap and available on the supermarket shelf next to parsley, tea, and oregano, 'decrim' actually brings increased Black Market prices, more crime, constricted supply, rationing, special duties, extra taxes and controls, familial strife, social turmoil, stop and search, police raids, persecution and, ironically, criminalisation. By contrast, Relegalisation results in mass agricultural production of 'THC-rich' cannabis sativa for fibre, Dresden Cotton, and seed-food, and for the bulk wood-hurds residues, the world-resource to Cannabis-Methanol fuel-energy, plastics, lubricants, paper, card, and building materials. This renders to the unused available macro-tonnage of flowers and foliage, a market value for Personal Relaxant cannabis of a mere few pennies per kilo, cheaper than tea or sage and onion, totally devoid of incentive to Black Market activity or crime. RELEGALISATION eliminates the Black Market and all associated crimes.

Moreover, with controls removed, when produced privately as herb of the kitchen garden or allotment, cannabis is *free*, i.e., of no cash cost. Relegalisation normalises and minimises the price of this inestimable resource, and provides a stable supply basis for all men and women who choose to take benefits from it. When legal, cannabis is *conventional*, a social, tradeable commodity again, like tea and coffee—but safer than those beverages (ref. Mortality Statistics) and of infinitely greater advantages to humanity.

The duplicity of those proposing "decrim," "legalisation" or "reform," as opposed to Relegalisation (i.e., Abolition of controls) is revealed by the following examination of their **ulterior motive**. Meanwhile, notice the important benefits available to the world and its peoples from Relegalisation, which are denied by the "decrim" Prohibitionists.

First of all, consider the improvement to our modern world by the large-scale elimination of crime which only comes from RELEGALISATION.

THE CANNABIS BIOMASS ENERGY EQUATION demonstrates liberation of cannabis offers unprecedented amelioration to Mankind, and rescues the environment.

THE REPORT. CANNABIS: THE FACTS, HUMAN RIGHTS AND THE LAW.

1 In 2001, Belgium's legislature adopted the unlawful 'decrim'.

Relegalisation enables the Universal Re-Democratisation of Fuel-Energy Production; providing free and duty-free clean replacement of fossils and uranium for fuel and energy. Decrim denies availability of cannabis, the world's cheapest fuel and the renewable pollution-free prolific agro-industrial raw material. For hegemony, and to enrich only themselves, Decrim-Prohibitionists premeditatedly impoverish mankind. They produce economic (trade) and military Wars (e.g. the Iraqi invasion of Kuwait; the Gulf War). Their scheme embodies Crimes against Humanity and Peace. Decrim abets continued lethal (thus criminal) misuse of fossils and uranium as 'fuel', ensuring environmental pollution by radiation, and, by the continuing accumulation of carbon dioxide in the atmosphere, the exacerbation of GLOBAL WARMING.

'Decrim' is pushed by representatives of the financial interests of those who receive revenues and profits from drugs, that is, government and Owners of the drug firms, pharmaceuticals, alcohol, tobacco and caffeine colas. Pharmaceutical companies opt for decrim because it produces the highest possible price for cannabis, which prevents the chronic-sick and innumerable others from being able to afford cannabis on a regular basis, to take advantage of its therapeutic effectiveness in literally scores of adverse conditions, enabling them to give up the toxic ineffective pharmaceutical products. Bear in mind that, Relegalised, cannabis offers real benefits at minimal or no cost, while effectively and safely replacing numerous noxious, debilitating, addictive, useless pharmaceutical laboratory-concocted nostrums of prescription (ref. Parts Three & Four.)

These economic facts expose the ruthless hypocrisy in politicians and pharmaceutical corporations' representatives and others who propose decrim. They also give the lie to statements that "decrim" of small-scale possession, or "legally permitted" cultivation of statutorily-limited small numbers of plants, makes cannabis "available for health." In practice, it does not. Cannabis is unrealistically 'expected' to materialise into potentially millions of people's homes whenever they need or want it, even in the depths of winter, which would total hundreds of thousands of kilos at any moment, without (generally legal) private commercial agriculture, transport, marketing or trade. Some unreliable availability is produced by haphazard amateur cultivation of small numbers of plants which may or may not come to a successful fruition, but, under decrim, it remains illegal to grow, crop and store sufficient quantity to secure regular, year-round supply. The rationing (i.e., limited legal possession) imposed by decrim, forces the consumer to rely on a potentially contaminated supply from the Black Market, or to cultivate and store more than the tiny quantity the law permits. The home-cultivator and consumer are denied the possibility of avoiding breaking the law, and are obliged by the decrim-Prohibition "law" to encourage the Black Market. 'Decriminalisation' is the same illegal Prohibition by another name !

Decrim is *also* proposed by those who take profit from drugs alcohol and tobacco. The escalating decrim price increasingly prevents people from choosing to use harmless benign cannabis regularly to moderate or replace their use of those dependence-inducing pathogens, alcohol and tobacco. Decrim thereby protects profits, duties and taxes from alcohol and tobacco whilst also denying the natural life-saving propensity of cannabis to reduce or preclude people's use of those addictive drugs. (Ref. cannabis as Preventive Measure/ Medicine; Part Three.) Thus, decrim-type Prohibition, or rather, *the people advocating it*, cause *increased disease and early death* in the population from the use of drugs alcohol and tobacco.

Prohibition: The Progenitor of Crime.

Because decrim makes cannabis increasingly expensive to consumers, decrim is proposed by people who take profits from those many inferior resources, goods and commodities which relegalised cannabis will cheaply replace. So, decrim is advocated *to protect Owners' profits* derived not only from drugs alcohol, caffeine, tobacco and pharmaceuticals but also Owners' profits from cotton, trees, paper, card, cosmetics, and soap, etc.; and also coal and oil-based products (petrol, lubricants, plastics, man-made fibres, paint, varnish, adhesives, tars); electricity generation; and cereal staple food. Literally scores of thousands of goods on the market today would be replaced by better products more cheaply resourced from cannabis and made with incomparably cheaper energy from cannabis-methanol and cannabis fuel-oil.

Celebrities lead astray the minds of many in their campaign for decrim in Britain and elsewhere. It is extreme naïveté not to understand the *unspoken* money-motive behind their activities. Unconstrained by conscience for the damage they do to people and the environment by their rejecting Relegalisation, and defecting from the normal requirement to be truthful, they propose "reform" or "change" to decrim. This is intended to protect their wealth "in excess" (see Aristotle: Is Fecit Cui Profuit) which is based in Ownership of corporations and/or portfolio of investments in: the pharmaceutical drugs' trade; companies involved in production and/or provision of energy from fossils; petro-chemicals; tobacco and alcohol firms; caffeine-colas; newspapers; advertising; banking, financial services; the leisure industry, publishing, TV and mass media; clothing and textiles; paper production and lumber forests; food production and prime farmland. Money-obsessed billionaire decrim-Prohibitionists mislead unlearned minds and hope to attract enough already-corrupted Prohibitionist politicians to gain the change. Under the guise of decrim, they intend to prolong Cannabis Prohibition for another generation.

The Owners' and politicians' crime-producing Prohibitions of The War on Drugs are the indoctrination-induced Collective Social **Delusion** of the Masses (see W.R. Hearst; The Marijuana Tax Act.) Nowadays, the same crude manipulation is resorted to in the attempt to obtain 'decrim'. As Thucydides pointed out, people generally believe the first story they hear without taking the trouble to discover whether it is true. How history repeats itself!

The (U.S.) National Organisation for Reform of Marijuana Law (NORML) and deceptively-named U.K. government-funded 'Release' operate in effect as commercial agents for lawyers, putting defendants in touch with "professionals" who have no intention of helping with genuine "advice" or conducting truthful "defences." Over years, *literally billions*, mostly in Legal Aid, accrue to law firms' lawyers, attorneys, solicitors and barristers for feigned "defences," and to those engaged in tyrannical malicious prosecution of citizens. Lawyers support 'decrim' because it only removes the less well-paid clutter of trifling small-scale possession cases from consuming their valuable time; but, decrim leaves litigation intact for the phenomenally lucrative paydays of higher court cases for cultivation, trade, and possession of more than the decrim "law's" specified tiny quantities. Decrim prolongs and entrenches Prohibition, to the ill-gotten gain of dishonest members of the legal profession. Financial interest corrupts their integrity to the degree that no veracious defences have been presented. (See Part Seven.) The Not Guilty Verdict would almost always have been obtained by presentation of: the Exonerative Findings of Fact, Circumstances and Res Gestae; by disputing the legality of the 'law'; by obtaining jurors' due judgement on the justice of the 'law'; and by truthful defences which inevitably expose the mendacity and inequity on which prosecution and the 'law' depend. Proper defences would have made the State Crime of Cannabis Prohibition unenforceable: all controls would have been abolished years ago.

Others support decrim with dishonesty because they too profit from the 'law', which produces the lucrative Black Market. Criminals do not want Relegalisation: this is as true for politicians and Owner-magnates, as it is for smugglers and dealers. Willing criminals and the smuggler-dealer-customer contact network organisations of the so-called "legalisation campaign" type, are observed to be keenly active in promoting decrim. Given decrim's economic effect of augmentation in Black Market value of cannabis, this was predicted. Black marketeers intend to fill the gaps in demand left by the licensed traders. These gaps are caused by the legislation which rations, imposes duties and taxes, and makes available inordinately priced cannabis in limited quantities. Following complete Relegalisation, crime and the Black Market disappear: so, to protect their profitable parasitism and to produce higher demand, professional criminals campaign for what they misleadingly call "legalisation" by which they mean non-prosecution of possession of tiny quantities for personal use, with continued prohibition controls on possession of more, and with continued regulations Prohibiting private Production and Sale. This is not true legalisation at all, the **Re**legalisation of Cannabis. It is the Prohibitionists' scheme: "decriminalisation." One observes their efforts in media which give prominence to decrim and disinformation. Mass media dishonestly exclude truthful education, facts and philosophy which unite all *honest* citizens behind RESTORATION.

Untold trillions can be derived from cannabis, the historic benefits of which may freely accrue to the entire population of the World, but, of the trillions at stake, anti-democratic politicians and some few advantaged individuals want Ownership or control. The present and future well-being of citizens does not feature in their reckoning. Criminal magnates and their despicable henchmen and women, the career politicians, the judiciary and state bureaucrats, stop at nothing to acquire position, wealth and power. These were the major peacetime criminals of the Twentieth Century, and, if unimpeached, will remain so for the future. Proponents and supporters of the Prohibitions and of "decriminalisation," are mortal enemies of the world and its peoples.

Prohibition: A View Attributed to Abraham Lincoln.

It is relevant here to ponder the pronouncement attributed to Abraham Lincoln on 'prohibition'. The value of quotations rests in their verity. It is what is said that matters, though naturally it does lend added weight when those quoted are respected for their integrity and wisdom. However, as with all quotations, consider the signification of the words, rather than only who may have said them…

NOTES: 1840 was before debates and speeches in the Illinois legislature were recorded verbatim and complete. Principally, 'motions' were noted down. Lincoln's pronouncement may have been considered as noteworthy in the 'pro' or 'against' categories. Matthew Woll stated as sworn testimony in the 1926 Senate Prohibition Law hearings, the exact place in the records (p. 136) where he had seen Lincoln's famous anti-prohibition statement in the written record of the Illinois House of Representatives. As it was then so easy to verify or disprove Woll's testimony, it beggars belief that he would have simply made it up. Woll's is not the only witness assertion to the quotation, but it is the most recent. The page 136 now extant is bereft of all mention of Lincoln. Woll's and the other witnesses' testimony indicates that, if the motive to a criminal intervention exists, the written record was tampered with at some time around the fevered height of the Alcohol Prohibition era.

Counterfeiting and fraud are frequently resorted to when the motivation for the deed exists. In this instance, the motive is known and intense. Police officers are familiar with this crime which occurs in the moneyed areas. Obvious examples are those such as accounting, coins and medals of antiquity, wills and testaments, banknotes, bonds and fine art. At this point, one bears in mind that Alcohol Prohibition had been continuously mooted by elements in society concerned with the social harm of drug-alcohol use, but these people had been utterly ignored by legislators. However, as the Nineteenth Century progressed and Western societies became more urban and industrialised, the economic effect of the removal of the availability of free labour (Slavery) made a swingeing change to the labour market, in particular to the Cost of Labour, and hence, to the Cost of Production. Productivity and profitability are the obsession of the Owners of large-scale monetary interests.

168

Prohibition: The Progenitor of Crime.

Similarly to today, significant Productivity Losses and workplace accidents were caused by alcohol consumption and consequential absenteeism. The economically-damaging aspect of alcohol consumption among the "working classes" became evident and problematic. This persuaded those whose profits were adversely affected, the factory-Owning class, to lead politicians into prohibiting—not drinking or possessing alcohol, for that could have redounded personally upon them—but to prohibiting commercial activities: Importation, Production, Stock-holding and Sale. (This was the "decriminalisation" form of legislation.) U.S. Alcohol Prohibition and the U.K. version, i.e., of controls on the hours when premises licensed to sell alcohol were allowed to be open, were introduced with the intention of reducing drunkenness and absenteeism, to augment the productivity of (factory) workers, for increased profit to Owners and magnates. In theory (although not in the event), this would also improve governments' tax yield therefrom, compensating for the loss of revenues from the alcohol industry.

Money-motive is always the prime mover behind the political type of Prohibition. It is within the power, and typical of the nature, of those whose interests it serves, to falsify, alter, destroy and otherwise undermine all evidence so crucial. The words embody the understanding of the wise. They reflect a Lincolnesque manner of speech-writing. One shall not and cannot deny the witness statements that the words were spoken by Lincoln, for shame that the words are truly Lincoln's. Abraham Lincoln is such an important figure in World History that his antipathy to Prohibition is enough to remove much public support from Prohibitionists, to the degree that Prohibition would become disreputable to all shades of opinion, and unworkable. The monetary motive was massive; and, as with cannabis nowadays, it existed at the very 'top'. It is relatively simple for the professional fraudster to substitute one page with a counterfeit on which references to Lincoln have been removed.

Consider the profound truth in those words, which were borne out by subsequent events: that Prohibition works against temperance; it invents a 'crime' out of things that are not crimes; and that Prohibition legislation "strikes a blow" against the exemplary U.S. Constitutional moral and democratic principle of responsible individual freedom from state tyranny and government interference. As with the other political Prohibitions today, Prohibition engendered so much crime that even teetotallers came to rage against it; and policemen joined the just crusade to stop Prohibition !

THE TESTIMONY OF MATTHEW WOLL, as follows:

"...Abraham Lincoln, the great emancipator, made a similar statement in the Illinois House of Representatives, December 18, 1840, which can be found on page 136 of the Journal of the House of that date: [Lincoln's words:] **"Prohibition will work great injury to the cause of temperance. It is a species of intemperance within itself, for it goes beyond the bounds of reason in that it attempts to control a man's appetite by legislation and makes a crime out of things that are not crimes. A prohibition law strikes a blow at the very principle upon which our Government was founded. " "**

Abraham Lincoln was a highly principled and deeply moral person. He understood well the issues of Human Rights and Mankind's recurring need to be prepared to fight to assert civilised values. As President of the United States he took his country into the Civil War to establish the Right to Freedom for all individuals. Today, with the knowledge of prohibition's devastatingly crime-generating properties derived from first-hand experience, President Lincoln's mooted view is reinforced. It is reasonable to assume he would have striven to achieve total RELEGALISATION. Today, we elicit his moral support towards the elimination of Prohibitionists' malign influence.

It is inexorably concluded from the facts that control of any type on cannabis, i.e., Prohibition, has not one redeeming feature: the Prohibition is scientifically unfounded, technically inept, acutely criminogenic, conspiratorially counterproductive, socially divisive, ecologically destructive, economically stagnant, politically tyrannical, flagrantly in breach of laws, and contravenes Human Rights. The mass of worthy social, medical, legal, political, ecological, moral and economic reasons requires all nations' assemblies and institutions to enact legislation forthwith for RESTORATION. (Ref. Part Seven.)

<u>Déjà vu.</u>

After the decline of the main Roman Empire and the Fall of Rome (476 A.D.), Europe experienced the regression of an extended interval of strife and instability. The earlier Republic had nurtured what we now acknowledge as civilising influences [1]. These were dissipated, to disappear under the imperial

1 Classical Rome awaited re-discovery during the Renaissance (circa 1450-1550 A.D.) and subsequent eras.

tyranny which replaced them. Even for its citizens (as opposed to its slaves) the Empire of Rome was a tyranny. The Roman Empire inflicted injustices which alienated the People of every surrounding and member nation, and especially inflamed the enmity of, and eventually succumbed to, the Northern Nations, whose love of Liberty, and respect for Natural Justice, Equity and the Common law, had evolved Mankind's model Justice System (ref. Part Seven: Justice and the Constitution).

To perpetuate its socio-political and economic ascendancy, a quasi-religious medieval Church instituted *prohibition* on the enlightening teachings and practices of Medicine and Science. Civilisation and progress were thus stifled and stultified. Personal freedoms were extinguished for more than a millennium. Medieval Europe clad herself with tremulant superstitions, the dread shrouds of a long Dark Age. Using extreme punishments and exploiting people's fear of them, the Holy Inquisition was intolerant to the point of fanaticism. It maintained ruthless hegemony over people's mentality, behaviour and beliefs. Not a few were those who suffered grievous, even mortal, oppression for their religious inclination, harmless activities or natural human quest for knowledge. That demoniac tendency lurking latent in much of Humankind was permitted 'legal' free rein, unleashed in dungeon and torture chamber, in the name of some 'god' and 'law and order'.

To give an appearance of 'legitimacy' to the tyranny of enforced prohibitions—to attempt to excuse the inexculpatory—the governing hierarchy's paid scribes fabricated 'official' tracts of 'theocratic' self-justifications and denunciations, documents of non-evidence and unfounded ideas. These perjuries were unceasingly dispersed into the public consciousness from plume and pulpit, accompanied by the implicit chill menace of force and fear. Until the liberating popular struggle of the Reformation's religious wars (late 15th and 16th Centuries), Western society was gripped and held drowning in backwardness and fearful ignorance, terrorised into bleak conformity with the hateful strictures of a barbarous ruling clique. Perhaps so flawed and fallible a species as Man is ordained interminable wretchedness at the repeated resurgence of brutish individuals whose genes compel them to assume to dominate others without regard to reason, scruple or suffering. Yet History [1], the written word and recorded experiences of Mankind since recent emergence from a half-known bestial evolution, proffers to us the unique key to precious emancipation. An impenetrable curtain veils the future. Although nothing in the realm of human affairs can be predicted with certainty, the future may be ameliorated as the result of planning. To ignore the presentment to the mind of lessons from History is to invite all the folly of cyclical repetitions and bring down upon ourselves the convulsions of a catastrophe strewn past. This inestimable key, History, enables us to unlock the encircling bonds of our physical present and, intellectually, to step outside the limiting perimeter of our time, to view it, ourselves, and our forebears more objectively. To delve into the historical attitudes behind these earlier prohibitions is to be confronted by much the same brutality and self-interested malefaction as imbue the present day Prohibitions. This déjà vu is no illusion—historically-speaking, we have seen it all before. Some of the similarities of the ban on cannabis to the 'prohibitions' of the past are striking and obvious, such as:

. . . the rigorous punitive exaction of conformity to prescribed behaviour and beliefs, regardless of the overtly incorrect, prejudiced and hypocritical aspects of the stricture: today, Prohibition is imposed on production, trade and use of salutary cannabis, while trade in and use of carcinogenic, habit-forming tobacco, and trade and indulgence in pathogenic, addictive alcohol, are permitted. This recalls medieval punishments for trade in and use of tea and coffee, while harmful alcohol was allowed [2];

1 Widely attributed as the greatest historian of all, Edward Gibbon describes History as, "indeed, little more than the register of the crimes, follies, and misfortunes of mankind." See Decline and Fall of the Roman Empire, Chapter III.
2 Alcohol was profitably produced by landowning authorities, was a source of visible trade and hence tax revenues. Tea and coffee from overseas were thought to undermine the alcohol trade (cf: cannabis/alcohol today).

Prohibition: The Progenitor of Crime.

. . . the politician who denies cannabis to the glaucoma sufferer as deliberately inflicts blindness as the medieval torturer who put out eyes [1];

. . . this premeditated Prohibitionist mortal cruelty extends also to the Denial of life-saving Cannabis as Preventive Measure [2] to replace or reduce consumption of lethal drugs tobacco and alcohol;

. . . the forbidden benefits of cannabis herb as a most effective Preventive and Curative [3] Medicament today, correspond to the prohibition by the medieval Church on all medicine (save the use of alcohol or blood-letting by the leech);

. . . despite the indications of new and further benefits to Mankind, the Western control-prohibition on medico-scientific research [4] into use of cannabis herb in these modern times is the insensate repetition of the forbidding in the medieval Dark Age of empirical and theoretical development of Science. Not even the Science of Copernican theory and the empirical evidence of the Galilean telescope could be permitted to challenge, still less to change, the petrification of wrong ideas cruelly enforced upon an indoctrinated populace held in thrall to the prohibitionist-led order.

History shows that the actions of the underlying, instinctive psychic forces which influence and can govern Mankind's behaviour are *incessant*.... While his apparel and surroundings alter over time, in his *nature*, Man remains the same. Let us recognise the Prohibitionists for what they are: by their deeds we know them.

1, 2, & 3 Ref. Parts Three & Four. 4 Ref. Part Three.

A Closer Look.

Behold, the Prohibitionist !

The Prohibitionist has a curious mentality which would comprise an interesting psychological phenomenon were it not so distasteful. Let us take a closer look and observe the over-brimming self-satisfaction derived from fatuous complacence in coercive and fallacious dogma. Note how this combines with real or feigned ignorance as to prohibition's many destructive and deadly results, to erect an indurate barrier resistant to the entreaties of intellect or compassion alike. Such outward behaviour is the expression of inner stubborn perverseness of the underdeveloped, brutish or brutalised psyche.

As shown, 'prohibition' is in every way a socially catastrophic concept produced by and finding favour in the minds of humans distraught with immoderation, the contorted psyche of the extremist. 'Prohibition' on any tradeable substances, expressed in minimal understatement, is a costly, longstanding failure with numerous acutely detrimental, criminogenic and counter-productive results.

As a contrast to brute Prohibition, intelligence and magnanimity are traits with demonstrated functional value. Kindness and understanding are the real and effective means by which to approach analysis of human behaviour, therewith to arrive at the best of possible responses. Kindness and understanding are important stabilising human faculties, which are not sufficiently developed or available within the Prohibitionist's persona to allow balanced ideas and rational formulations to be excogitated and hence, exploited.

171

THE REPORT. CANNABIS: THE FACTS, HUMAN RIGHTS AND THE LAW.

Cannabis being neither addictive nor pathogenic is not a drug. Where the use of drugs, i.e., addictive and toxic substances, gives rise to social concern, to eliminate or mitigate their associated negative effects, it is first necessary to come to terms with their aetiology, i.e., cause. Prohibition makes no such attempt. Seen in the example of Alcohol Prohibition (followed by Relegalisation), the harm wreaked upon individual and society by the application of enforced prohibitions, is greater by far than the legal acceptance of such substances, which then devolves down to a containable, and more easily remedied individual's health concern. Put in other words: to solve this problem, it is first necessary to understand it. Prohibition, in attempting to obliterate certain forms of behaviour, in practice only exacerbates and entrenches them. This is manifest in the entire history of the Twentieth Century's ongoing prohibitions.

'Charitable virtues'—kindness and understanding—are not *understood* by the Prohibitionist for the highly evolved, valid mechanisms of creative social management that they are. The subtle approach is the only one capable of producing good results. The 'deterrent' value of punishments for infractions (murder, theft, etc.) of universally accepted correct behaviour, cannot be claimed as having any positive influence in the context of 'prohibition' of tradeable items. For, synergistically combining with the economic effect of enforced scarcity, this 'risk factor' of punishment so augments the Black Market economic value of the proscribed article as actually to give rise to crime, and promote all the very activities the Prohibitionist claims to wish to discourage.

Prohibition relies on the instilling in people of *fear* of enforcement. Some individuals are not susceptible to such methods, on whom they act as a challenge or provocation, producing crimes of counter-aggression and apolitical urban terrorism.

However, others are cowed by Prohibition-induced fear. Their self-awareness of this fact is often repressed or denied, and accompanied by implausible attempts at self-exculpation from timid acquiescence to criminogenic activities of anti-democratic government. Yet, as noted: to consent to any measure is to share responsibility for its results. Certainly, prohibition-induced fear permeates society, as indeed it is intended so to do, to be 'effective'. Such fear is consciously and/or subliminally assimilated by those susceptible to it, irrespective of whether a 'user' or not. Western society submits to, and finances at many great costs, the Prohibitionist state's corrupt psychological conditioning-by-fear ('brainwashing'). One observes contemptible people who, despite their capacity to discern the premeditated Pavlovian mental conditioning of fellow citizens and themselves, for a 'quiet life', shun their civic duty to resist by all appropriate means and measures the Prohibitionists' ruin of both the social ambiance, and the physical world, in which we live. The faint-heartedness or indifference characterised in *consent* to Prohibitionists' despoilment of society, is an ultimately self-destructive appeasement.... The dark deeds of enforcement are the sowing of the dragon's teeth: barbaric impositions of fear and ferocity predictably exact violent responses. In Prohibitionist societies, the 'quiet life' is inevitably doomed to spasmodic disintegration and eventual total extinction.

With arrest, public humiliation, forfeitures, loss of employment, imprisonment, fines, etc., the threat and use of punishments are ostensibly intended to manipulate entire populations into the behavioural response of abstention from trade in and use of specified substances, yet achieve by this 'prohibition' method, neither. Meanwhile, the Prohibition intimidates many, to mar, and coercively to alter society's prevailing mood and manners. Thus, apart from the powerful influence actuating crime on the greatest scale, Prohibition has a further, deeply penetrating socially corrosive residuum: the alienation by fear, threat and aggression gives widespread effect to mass surliness, seen in the acerbic mélange of the fraught urban social flux. Prohibition by force and fear subjects the people to an unrelenting mental influence, sensed at subconscious level, which gestates attitudes, responses, ways of thinking and modes of behaviour. By use of Damoclean threat over the long term, the tyrannical Prohibitionist state terrorises, brutalises and desensitises the individual psyche, en masse, while adversely transforming the societal ethos. Whereas the revolution in electronic and mass communications would be expected to produce generations displaying more uniformly civilised behaviour, these innovations have been exploited exclusively for Prohibitionists' money-corrupted ends, as state and privately-controlled propaganda instruments. Editors and writers, bidden employees of the omnipresent entertainment and information media, obscure the real motive behind Prohibitions, which is actually their employers' rabid preoccupation with the obtainment of wealth and hegemony, by portraying it, and glamourising it, as the 'War on Drugs'. In the New Millennium, day after day, the population of the whole television-watching world sees the standard of morality of the West misrepresented everywhere by corrupt 'works' authored by the minions of money-fixated tyrants.

The Twentieth Century's corruption and crime, the collapse of traditional values, and the fragmentation of social cohesion, bear trenchant testimony to Prohibition being the psychological mechanism which conscripts mentally-moulded, unwitting recruits to a life of crime. In opposition to civilised values, in the crucible of modern life, Prohibition surrounds the person to incise into the superego and personality from the first impressionable age. As in medieval times (ref. Déjà vu), government-by-Prohibition teaches by example that the use of *fear and force* is the apparently 'correct' and 'rewarding' way of behaving to obtain objectives. This nullifies the attempted teaching and cultivation of worthwhile ethics and the decent social behaviour of stable human beings. The simpleton's cudgel of enforced Prohibition batters down civilised aspirations, and shatters the psychological environs essential to their nurture. Sterling efforts at education, the proper upbringing of generations by the conscientious parent and dedicated teacher, are constantly undermined by the brute crime that is Prohibition. Within this psychological environment so unhealthily transmuted by bad 'government', there can be no surprise that Western society is today riven asunder by unsocial behaviour. Prohibition inculcates alienation in the mass of the population, and awe of the ruthless and the unconscionable, the fear and the force. This ruinously gestates asocial and anti-social human beings, the sociopath and the real criminal, and every varying type and degree of degenerate behaviour.

The Prohibitionist's related offspring is the terrorist, the obdurate foe to civilised values, who seeks to obscure venality by claiming 'political' or 'religious' justification for doing injustice and sin. Terrorists obtain wealth by gun-running, kidnapping, drug-dealing, torture and robbery: the terrorist is the traditional criminal by another name. The criminal Prohibitionist and the terrorist alike pursue *undemocratic* hegemony. The tyrant Prohibitionist Owner-magnate and the government 'politician' have already achieved their ascendancy, and merely have discreetly to pervert society's apparatuses into sustaining them. The terrorist seeks to dispossess the governing Prohibitionists. They all operate by fear and force.

THE REPORT. CANNABIS: THE FACTS, HUMAN RIGHTS AND THE LAW.

Apart from alcohol-related misbehaviour, neither crime nor 'money-motivation' results from the use of a *substance*, whether the substance be prohibited or not. Nor is crime the product of a relaxed and lenient way of life. To a marked degree, crime and criminals are the product of Prohibition: the specious legislation. The violent society or 'urban jungle' is the *inevitable* barbaric social environment produced in the harsh circumstances or backward social group within which the infrahuman notions of Prohibitionists are allowed to prevail. Relegalisation of Alcohol was immediately followed by a *halving of the annual rate of homicides*. Equally significant reductions in numerous categories of serious crime were recorded by the F.B.I., following the overturning of Prohibition legislation. To the lasting shame of the politicians involved, this other Prohibition on cannabis soon replaced that of alcohol.

The *moral* prohibitions of universally understood and enforced natural law and justice, the Commandments of a very different order, have their monumental rôle and primacy of place; but, applied to tradeable commodities, prohibition 'law' generates potent economic effects which initiate and amplify vastly those negative results which legislation is ostensibly enacted to eradicate. With saleable items, it is not merely a matter of 'prohibition does more harm than good': it is not truthfully possible to say that Prohibition does any good at all, due to the negative net result of enforced Prohibition: **the Progeneration of Crime**.

Crime is the antithesis of civilised behaviour. Prohibition which engenders crime is not a legitimate option by which to order affairs within a society of civilised values, standards and beliefs. Such Prohibition is not a measure capable of being endorsed by the cerebral or rational person of probity.

Significant social trends denote continuous long-term deterioration. Such is the scale of Prohibition-generated crime and bad behaviour, engrained by nearly a century of the fear and the force (Harrison Narcotics Act, 1914) that in Western society at some stage, even possibly imminent, terminal cataclysm impends. Criminals' "political" leadership abets: racketeering duty, tax and profit-protection ('policies'); the persecution by the Prohibitionist state of its citizens; and, the long-term dispersion of false propaganda. The results are morale-sapping. Criminals have stunned the conscience and social responsibility of generations to this issue. Prohibitionist damage to the underpinning precepts of a civilised free society accelerates and accumulates, unhindered by legal, moral or social restraints. Prohibition's insidious potentials proliferate unchecked.

The entire Western accomplishment of a multiple-millennia long, painful but successful Ascent is in jeopardy. The breakdown here intimated is a transition from the exemplary, honoured, unique, but now only ostensible **'constitutional democratic civilisation' founded upon the Common Law and citizens' Trial by Jury**, into the overtly undemocratic alternative: tyranny; under the yoke of which, in all times past and present, most of Mankind suffers.

The existence of legislated controls on private Production, Sale and Use of Cannabis is both symptom and evidence of such anti-democratic government as *also destroys or denies* the genuine form of citizens' Common Law Trial by Jury. Prohibitionists obliterate (the course of) justice; Jurors are not permitted to see Exonerative Evidence, still less to judge the criminality of the 'legislation'. Western democracy is overrun by the tiny group of money-corrupted Prohibitionists. Today, not only is cannabis prohibited, but Justice is also prohibited.

174

Prohibition: The Progenitor of Crime.

The misappropriation by Prohibitionists of the Western legislatures is complete. At taxpayers' expense, propaganda provides camouflage for the crime-producing, societally-disintegrative 'legislation'. Meanwhile, Prohibitionists usurp constitutional due process and pervert the rule of law which now serve only to execute their purpose. There is no reason to believe overt totalitarianism would be exempt from implementation by that corrupt segment or clique within whose grasp lies the means of its achievement.

Throughout the greater part of the Twentieth Century and continuing in the New Millennium, Prohibition has wrought a severe societal regression, manifested in successive crime 'waves' and deterioration in standards of personal behaviour. Viewed in the temporal linearity of History, the West is experiencing a Prohibitionist-inflicted 'illucid' period [irrationality] of as yet indeterminate duration. This is a vicious self-destructive paroxysm during which the Common Law Trial by Jury, and traditional virtues have been and continue to be discarded as despised encumbrances, to be replaced by misanthropic extremism observed in, and generated by, Prohibitionist measures and attitudes.

Prohibitionists assert emphatically that enforced Prohibition "sends a message." The nub of the matter at issue is what this message actually, rather than purportedly, means. The Prohibitionist places **a doctrine of *inhumanity*** on the level of a 'principle', whereby all former doctrines and concepts of virtue are subjugated and superseded: the Prohibitionist dogma contains the seed for the destruction of democratic civilisation.

Attempts are made to explain the astonishing Twentieth Century phenomenon of the precipitate collapse within the last two or three generations, of populations' personal standards of behaviour in the great Western democracies. All of the possible negative influences at work upon our civilisation mooted to be responsible causes to the social cynicism and widespread misanthropy witnessed, have essentially, in one form or another, existed for centuries. They have exerted their 'ill' at least since the Renaissance, that is to say, with but the one exception: **Prohibition**.

Negative influences affecting the individual or the many, add to the sum of forces and factors which govern human behaviour. Enforced Prohibition is the one new factor powerful enough to initiate reversal of the civilising process, by reinforcing in deadly synergy the negative influences which had been heretofore generally resistible.

Charitable virtues are the indispensable defricative of all human interaction, without an abundant preponderance of which all possible divisive and mutually antagonistic submerged tendencies can be impelled to erupt. That brutishness which characterises the Prohibitionist-led society, and the Prohibitions themselves, together with Prohibition's ubiquitous criminal results, cannot but be the incipient agent, the prime mover, in the complex of the existing social ethos.

To this lamented general collapse, contemplation remits the recurrent aetiological conclusion that Prohibition is the singular, and removable, causation.

IS FECIT CUI PROFUIT.

Some there are who say that Mankind should not need to use relaxants of any sort. As with most generalisations which have the appearance of a modicum of superficial appeal about them, this assertion has its adherents. It does not, however, comprehend the necessities of facing the world as it really is, and dallies fancifully upon the unreality of life as we perhaps would wish it to be. The moment the psychiatrist or physician reaches for the prescription pad to provide a person with something approaching relief, he or she is making the qualified best of the situation with which one is confronted. Every prescription for stress-relieving tranquillisers, hypnotics (sleeping draughts) mood-elevators, sedatives, etc., bears testimony to the real need which exists in the population for the relaxant which brings relief from stress. Drugs are not the solution but more often than not they are today the only available legal means of alleviating or containing a person's adverse condition.

The relaxant or stress-relieving aspect of the widespread use of the drug alcohol is another manifestation of the need of many people, the majority, to ingest a substance which apparently dissolves for them temporarily the tensions of work or worry. Alcohol is also taken for pleasure. As the term 'drug' denotes, these aforementioned drugs of prescription or recreation are toxic and addictive. All have unwanted side-effects of which some are dangerous to health or debilitating, or both. In the longer term, the use of the drug itself can cause new and worse problems for its ingestor without necessarily having removed, or even mitigated, the cause for which it is taken.

The ideal relaxant would efficaciously fulfil relaxational and stress-relieving requirements while being itself non-addictive and non-toxic, that is to say, wholesome, and not a drug at all. If in the meantime, by its recreational use it could also render the great advantages of prophylaxis, that is, the benefit of being a medicament preventive of numerous adverse conditions, in a way similar to inoculations, then so much the better. Recreational use thus is Preventive Medicine.

Cannabis embodies all the virtues aforedescribed and comprises this superior ideal relaxant. Thus is explained further, the popularity of this entirely safe balm, the mild and healing herb used by people of all ages and from all walks of life the world over. In the context of relaxants and stress-relief, no other relaxant is so appropriate a consummation of a human's requirements.

Needless to say, if the superior relaxant cannabis were Relegalised it would replace much reliance upon, and sales of, both the patented proprietary pharmaceutical drugs and the recreational drugs, in the medical and social relief of stress. Under normal market conditions (i.e., without Prohibition) innumerable inferior products and resources will be rendered *commercially unviable* by cannabis (ref. Parts Two to Four). Amongst the Owner-producers of these Prohibition-protected items are people of great influence and possessing large-scale monetary interests. They perceive correctly the undeserved basis of their fortune. It is predictable human behaviour that some are impelled to take the law into their own hands, to conspire to protect their vested wealth by the prevention of Relegalisation by illegal means. Grasping self-interest is the motivation behind 'political' (de facto, criminal) denial of the population's normal legitimate private Production, Sale and Use of cannabis. This illicit protection of excessive private wealth is gravely detrimental to and in conflict with the greater public interest.

Prohibition: The Progenitor of Crime.

Consider the wisdom of the Greek philosopher Aristotle, writing on Politics over 2,300 years ago:

"It remains true that the greatest injustices proceed from those who pursue excess, not from those who are driven by necessity."

For this avaricious pursuit of excess, the complot, to succeed, its instigators remain remote, covert, while its executors require their actions to be camouflaged under a welter of deceit, the fictitious disinformation provided by their paid scribes. In obsequious compliance, self-seeking members of the legislature bestow a spurious façade of 'legitimacy' to criminal deceit expressed as 'law': the controls on cannabis. Meanwhile, the apparatus of enforcement, staffed by individuals not possessed of conscience, is perverted into oppression of good citizens. This tyranny bears the historically familiar stigma, the malignity of greed and avarice, which imparts to it the underlying degenerate impulsion, and from which it takes on physical expression in the corrupt actions of its servitors: ultimately, it is cruelly enforced on decent people by ruthless unthinking fellow citizens. Nevertheless, the crime that is this 'Prohibition' is exposed. The false accusations of 'harm' of the propaganda, rather than concealing, actually point to the lying politicians, bureaucrats and representatives of the financial interests of the drugs' companies (pharmaceuticals, alcohol, tobacco, caffeine-colas) and others, who would have us believe their nonsense or fear their hegemony. These circumstances call forth the Roman maxim which accuses:

"Is fecit cui profuit;" he did the deed who profited by it. . . .

Disinformation, the lie about cannabis, is distributed within most nations by the government itself and other agencies. Private and state organisations are financed to militate against cannabis on the basis of false information, continuously circulating to homes, schools, libraries, citizens' agencies, hospitals, universities, research, academic and medical libraries, offices and factories, the leaflets and publications containing the frightening falsehoods. Their activities include holding seminars, infiltrating parent-teacher meetings and malindoctrinating children at school, in relentless manipulation of the public. Press, t. v. and radio are exploited to promote the Prohibition on cannabis by the propaganda of abject lies. The public-funded studies which have investigated, categorically exonerated and which extol cannabis, have been and are systematically substituted by derogatory fictions.

The pharmaceutical companies finance printing and distribution activities of the aforesaid anti-cannabis propaganda journals and leaflets, through ironically-named groups such as 'Pharmacists against Drug Abuse'; and through the 'public services' of their commercial advertising agencies. Funding is also provided to anti-cannabis organisations by other companies, with tax-deductible government connivance. 'Front-men' for the manufacturer-producers, cultivators and distributors of the drugs alcohol and tobacco, the public relations and advertising agencies and media, who take money to promote the tobacco and alcohol trades, fulfil definition of the colloquialism 'pusher'.

Money-motivation of utmost scale (ref. Parts Two to Four) produces the scheme to prevent the truth of the health-promoting safe nature of cannabis from becoming public knowledge again. It is accompanied by rancorous speechifying by politicians, state officials, politically-appointed drug 'czars' and other perpetrators of the State Crime. The health-giving harmless herb is maligned as a 'danger' and as a 'drug'.

THE REPORT. CANNABIS: THE FACTS, HUMAN RIGHTS AND THE LAW.

By cliché and platitude, pretentious posturing and outright lies, the population is misled and intimidated to substitute facts with fear, and rationality with emotion. There are few, perhaps none, who escape being exposed to this conditioning. Some who know well the truths about benign cannabis, and who therefore should speak out and resist the tyranny, hold back in tacit timidity. There are others who, despite full knowledge about the herb's beneficence, co-operate with Prohibitionists. Whether by mute acquiescence or active involvement, they become partner to and participant in the state's reign of terror.

However, when the quotidian circumstances of the *non-efficacity of modern drugs* are personally experienced, the tardy realisation of this tyranny's deadly implications dawns on even the most recalcitrant Prohibitionist: when they or their dearest are unexpectedly beset with the progressive blindness of glaucoma, or overtaken by the problems of 'moderate' but long-term alcohol consumption, or suddenly begin to suffer from stress-related afflictions, or any one of numerous debilitating conditions, who will save them then. . . ? Confirmed by the Medical Case Histories, such maladies are cured, or frequently avoided entirely, by smoking cannabis, or by the inclusion of cannabis herb as part of a normal, healthy diet; ref. Parts Three & Four. Too late, they realise *their consent* to Prohibition's denial to the people of general legal access to cannabis, is a criminal, intrinsically homicidal, act.

That all individuals have the Right to make such use of cannabis as they choose is beyond question or compromise. Empirical Facts establish that by regular use of Cannabis as Preventive Measure and Preventive Medicine *anyone* can avoid and prevent adverse and even fatal health conditions from afflicting them in their present or future life.

Certainly, this tyranny is pandemic, and the media are wholly owned. Yet, which journalist, which man or woman, is so base as to remain the muzzled dupe when their loved ones, acquaintances, friends, relatives and neighbourly citizenry are so abused ? Let every individual man and woman who consents to state interference and controls on cannabis be aware of the crime he or she commits against the world and its good souls. Let perfidious reporters beware: they are legitimate targets of righteous wrath and the just retribution of myriad people injured by Prohibition.

All men and women owe a debt of respect and gratitude to the medico-scientific community by whose fine minds, talent and toil such medical developments as antibiotics and wonders as the total eradication of smallpox are achieved, from which we all derive benefit. Yet, these wholehearted and due sentiments of admiration and gratefulness should not misdirect nor cloud judgement upon the issue at hand.

There is a well-known breach between the acrimonious proponents of modern pharmaceutical inventions of 'single-action' drugs and those oncologists, psychiatrists, ophthalmologists, physicians, nurses, and specialists, who, in seeking to promote good health or cure patients, endorse the superior and proven track record of this herbal medicament and relaxant. Nowhere is this attitude of 'rift' between natural herbs and concentrated chemical drugs more visible yet purblind than in the unprincipled rant by which Prohibitionist 'medical' representatives of the pharmaceutical argument support the denial to the general population of the benefits to Health of this non-toxic, non-addictive, safe herbal relaxant.

Prohibition: The Progenitor of Crime.

Following Cannabis Relegalisation, overuse of hyper-profitable toxic nostrums concocted in the laboratories of the pharmaceutical firms will be fittingly reduced. Over-reliance on addictive patent drugs such as the 'tranquillisers', benzodiazepines, phenothiazines, Darvon, Seconal, Tuinol, Thorazine, Stelazine, Chlorpromazine, Librium, Valium, and *scores* of others; aspirin, the barbiturates, hypnotics in addition to habit-forming analgesics, so-called 'anti-emetics', steroids, and the seldom effective drugs such as those now prescribed for glaucoma, asthma, multiple sclerosis, epilepsy, etc., will be diminished. Not being a drug and not inducing tolerance syndrome, cannabis neither loses its therapeutic efficacity nor requires quantitative increases over long-term use, it being providentially the unique, safe natural healer. *Everybody knows people who would benefit from cannabis.* As noted earlier, following Cannabis Relegalisation, Owners of pharmaceutical companies will see a drop in sales of their patent drugs—this being the resultant "cost" of better health in the population.

The implacable drug companies are comprised of the multi-national and national pharmaceutical manufacturers, the alcohol and caffeinated beverage businesses, and tobacco cultivators and traders. Financially linked with multi-national oil and petro-chemical corporations and other manufacturing and service companies, newspapers, publishing, press, radio, television and advertising companies, banks and finance houses, the drug companies now are huge, highly diversified conglomerates with heavily financed effective political lobbies, reaching into and influencing the deliberations of governments. The motivations of a small ruthless Owning clique find expression in the legislative Crime of Prohibition. Drug companies operate within this felonious framework conspired to protect their profits, the ill-gotten gains of their Owners. This system is machinated by a corrupt minority in the financial interests of a numerically miniscule fraction of the population, at the expense, and to the destruction of the Health, Freedom and Rights, of all the rest of the People. Consider but one of the many organisations financed to militate against cannabis, whose malindoctrination is spread by the press in Britain, and throughout Europe and the Americas, namely the Partnership for a Drug-Free America,' whose accounts reveal that its damaging Prohibitionist activities are funded by contributions from the following:

Anheuser-Busch (Budweiser beer) Philip Morris (Miller beer and Marlboro cigarettes)
American Brands (Jim Beam whiskey and Lucky Strike cigarettes)
R. J. Reynolds (Camel and Winston cigarettes); PepsiCo; Coca-Cola;
and the following proprietary pharmaceutical/health care firms and their beneficiaries:
Bristol-Meyers Squibb; Ciba-Geigy; Merck; Dow; Du Pont; Glaxo; Pfizer;
Hoffman-LaRoche; Warner-Lambert; Johnson & Johnson; Procter & Gamble;
Schering-Plough; SmithKlineBeecham; J. Seward Johnson Charitable Trusts;
Robert Wood Johnson Foundation;
and the following publishers: Time Warner; Dow Jones; Reader's Digest.

O tempora ! O mores !

From 1988 to 1991, the 'Partnership for a Drug-Free America' received $5.8 million from their largest 25 contributors, of which pharmaceutical companies and their beneficiaries gave $3,132,000. This pattern is repeated yearly. In addition, ongoing and remorseless, supervised vitiation of the population's mentality by disinformation is abetted by the owned and controlled media on a constant basis.

NOTE: Regarding illicit profit-protection of businesses other than those listed, see Parts Two to Four.

THE REPORT. CANNABIS: THE FACTS, HUMAN RIGHTS AND THE LAW.

The state, an eager accomplice, also participates in malindoctrination of the People through the various government departments of health, law, education, enforcement, etc. This is financed from taxes. The American and other disinformation is spread worldwide by state agencies, quasi-autonomous government institutions, the Home Office, the DEA, the International Organisation of Police Chiefs, while the wrongdoing is also perpetrated by the numerous financed private groups, such as 'National Drug Prevention Alliance,' 'parent' groups, 'Life Education Centres,' and 'Drug Watch' organisations. All these comprise a controlled and manipulated chain of different outlets for the same criminal disinformation activity.

To summarise: good citizens pay taxes which are fraudulently misused to keep them from becoming aware of the criminal subversion of their own constitutional democracy by politicians and others. Consumers and Voters are forced to finance the miseducation by which they are conspiratorially prevented from taking their due benefit from the relaxant, the health, the food, the resource, The CBEE and the ecological virtues of cannabis, to the detriment of the entire world's population, and the ecosphere. Yearly, hundreds of thousands of criminal acts by governments, of persecution of men and women, are paid for by fleeced citizens who certainly would not knowingly finance, still less participate in, tyranny. It is appropriate to repeat that there are circa 400,000 U.S. cannabis arrests per year, one every few minutes; currently, c. 80,000 cannabis arrests per annum in the U.K.; while c. 85 per cent of real crime goes unsolved, and largely unchallenged. Circa half of all prisoners in the West are incarcerated on "drug" [sic] charges, of which about 80 % are for cannabis. That is to say, about 40 per cent of all people imprisoned in the West are there for the corrupt duty, tax and profit-protection of government and Owners. Meantime, 'politicians' wage the World War of Global Warming on the people of the world, *by choice*: people are killed, wildlife, property, and agricultural produce are destroyed, the environment is damaged, and the climate becomes increasingly hostile.

As with all criminals, in the context of this State Crime of controls on cannabis, it is inappropriate to be deferential to its perpetrators, our Western state judiciary, bureaucrats and politicians, local and national, a mixed minority of persons who reflect disgrace upon their rank instead of deriving honour from it. That we are misgoverned by criminals is demonstrated by this epitomic tyranny. It is imperative that nations purge those cankers by which Democracy is attacked and its existence imperilled. Citizens have ultimate authority: misgovernment by the accountable criminal minority remains possible only so long as the People allow it.

Mention must be made of the long Western tradition of Judaeo-Christian morality which teaches that the individual's Human Rights and democratic control of government are to be favoured over the recurrent human tendency of established authority to suppress Freedom. Consider some of the long list of those best of human souls to whom we look for exemplary guidance in the matter of bad oppressive laws:

Was Moses right to dispute the unjust treatment of his people and ultimately to rend society by leading them from tyrannical jurisdiction ? Which secular historian would say Herod's law was right in the slaughter of the Bethlehem boys of two and under ? The martyrs of the Christian religion, looked up to with adoration and esteem by Church and congregation for their selfless moral virtue, were in most cases simply regarded as law-breakers under the doctrines of their contemporaries. To obtain the

Prohibition: The Progenitor of Crime.

vote, so obvious an equal Right, Suffragettes broke the law. Wallenberg, that most righteous of men, broke the law. . . . There is no mitigation available to the Prohibitionist who vacuously proclaims that it is "wrong" to "break" this law—for **to instigate, respect, obey or enforce that law which is wrong is itself the crime.**

Untruthful, corrupted, personally ambitious while ruthlessly inhumane, criminal 'politicians' control every financed party. With their own characters destroyed, they spurn truth, squandering taxpayer-provided state resources at the behest of magnates, to fabricate and propagate their degenerate contagion of delusion, indoctrination and public intimidation. In normal circumstances of party politics, individuals openly seen to support squalid barbarous criminal avarice would be mocked and vilified into correcting their course; but in the criminal pseudo-politics of the racket of Prohibition, there are no correctives such as opposition parties or left/centre/right differentiation. With the denial by governments of the proper function of Jurors to judge the law in Common Law Trial by Jury, there is no unbiased umpire. Enforcement is the mindless tool of the lawless.

This tyranny relies upon those people who execute its malefaction being servitors of unquestioning obedience: It remains an acute failing at all levels of authority, for individuals to operate within an area of immediate preoccupation, neglecting to relate their actions (which contribute to the totality of a corrupted system), to the universal surrounding moral ground. By this crucial shortcoming, as within all tyrannies, the people who perpetrate enforcement of Prohibition divest themselves of the highest human characteristic and principal democratic civic obligation, that of thinking for themselves and making free choices at the individually self-aware responsible level. By such displacement, people make of themselves the tyrant's torturous instrument, the subhuman automaton, the accountable participant in criminal destruction of the lives and freedom of fellow men and women.

To recapitulate: Cannabis Prohibition is the greatest fraud of all time; the pernicious effects of this crime are myriad, extreme and ubiquitous. *Prohibition* is the direct cause of: War (viz. Iraqi invasion of Kuwait; the Gulf War); Crime; astronomical prices of energy, resources and food, with disastrous and homicidal corollary effects; world poverty; world famine; industrial and automotive emissions poisoning air; photochemical smog; Acid Rain; desertification; the greenhouse effect of Global Warming; resultant ever-intensifying catastrophic weather, chaos, human woe, food crop destruction, and worldwide mortalities.

So great is the monetary interest (ref. Parts Two to Five), and so intense is the money-motivation behind Prohibition, that, if there were no Prohibition, or if cannabis were Relegalised today, it would be Prohibited again tomorrow. So acute is the money-motive, that *only* self-interested fear in politicians for impending condign punitive consequences of their culpable actions will produce Relegalisation. Nothing less than **RESTORATION** of constitutional democratic control of governments' modus operandi by the re-introduction of the *authentic* Trial by Jury, ensures Relegalisation, and the elimination of the corporate and government crime that are all Prohibition controls. (Ref. Part Seven.) **RESTORATION** embodies the immediate Scientific Solution.

As with all tyrannies, the duty to extirpate criminal governments devolves upon the People.

181

PRINCIPLES

Be it well understood:

Whether instructed to do so by the judge or not, whenever a juror convicts a person who, according to the juror's conscience has not committed any wrongdoing, that juror thereby commits a crime. The juror abets the Crime of Malicious Prosecution by the state: a criminal injustice occurs (cf. Crime against Humanity). (See section on *conscience*; Part Seven.)

Jurors are ignorant, servile and morally wrong if they convict against their conscience—but, above all, in so doing they strike a blow against democracy and the people; and they defile the Constitutional Trial by Jury Justice System.

To convict someone Not Guilty of any wrongdoing is one of the most serious crimes it is possible to commit. This is the behaviour which drives politicians and judges to become confidently despotic beyond restraint. At all times, every adult person has the moral responsibility to suppress injustice. Every act of injustice is a common law crime, whether committed by private citizens or by the state. Jurors and government employees alike are accountable. See ratified Principles, U.N. Resolution of the 10th of December, 1946:

PRINCIPLE I
Any person who commits an act which constitutes a crime under international law is responsible and liable to punishment.

PRINCIPLE II
The fact that internal law does not impose a penalty for an act which constitutes a crime under international law does not release the person who committed the act from responsibility under international law.

PRINCIPLE III
The fact that a person who committed an act which constitutes a crime under international law acted as Head of State or responsible government official does not relieve him from responsibility under international law.

PRINCIPLE IV
The fact that a person acted pursuant to the order of his government or a superior does not relieve him from responsibility under international law, provided a moral choice was in fact possible to him.

PRINCIPLE V
Any person charged with a crime under international law has a right to a fair trial on the facts and law.

Whether by participation in the enforcement of arbitrary legislation, or from the following of direct orders, being party to the execution of injustice is a criminal offence (cf. Crime against Humanity).

In the Trial by Jury context, the moral choice quoted above is **always** "possible;" it is definitively **obligatory**: the "choice" is **mandatory**. De jure, under pain of penalisation, all those involved at every stage of the creation, maintenance and enforcement of law, including jurors, must make the moral choice and judge the law, and accordingly take the appropriate action or make the apposite decision.

~

- PART SEVEN -

RESTORATION: MAGNA CARTA,
THE GREAT CHARTER OF ENGLISH LIBERTIES, and
THE CONSTITUTION
OF THE UNITED STATES OF AMERICA.
JUSTICE AND THE CONSTITUTION:

THE (*authentic*) Trial by Jury Justice System is revered in Britain and respected abroad as embodying the finest and most democratic form of law enforcement ever devised. This worldwide reputation derives from one phenomenon: Constitutional Law Magna Carta, the Great Charter of English Liberties, first passed in 1215; *for this document sets in place the definitive Trial by Jury*. Trial by Jury is enshrined also within the Constitution of the United States of America, re-affirmed by every president at inauguration by oath to uphold the U.S. Constitution. **Trial by Jury comprises a constitution** [1] per se, for it is intended to curtail despotism and govern the way in which governments themselves may legally operate.

Magna Carta was formed and passed by a legislature of Barons and received Royal Assent in 1215, becoming a written statute of government law, subsequently ratified explicitly a further thirty-five times. Since 1688 (and earlier), monarchs ratify Magna Carta when they swear at coronation to uphold the "statutes of parliament." This includes Head of State Queen Elizabeth II. Magna Carta is law throughout Britain and is emplaced to apply *in perpetuity*.

Trial by Jury embodies the Juror's Right, and Duty, to acquit as Not Guilty (innocent) according to the Juror's **conscience** [2], citizens tried under law which the Juror judges to be oppressive or unfair; *and*: jurors, not judges, are required to review all evidence to decide on its admissibility. The Juror decides the Verdict not simply on whether facts and evidence indicate the Defendant broke the law. In addition, the Juror decides the Verdict by judging whether the law under which the Defendant is being tried, is itself **Just**. *This is the special virtue of Magna Carta: it emplaces Common Law Trial by Jury to protect citizens for all time from tyrannical injustice by governments*, achieved by the **Annulment by Jury (i.e., Jury Nullification)** of the enforcement of unjust laws and injustices, put into practice as the Hung Jury (majority required for guilty not found) or by the pronouncing of the Verdict: Not Guilty.

In this context, U.S. President John Adams, lawyer, said of the Juror:

"It is not only his Right but his Duty to find the verdict according to his own best understanding, judgement and conscience, though in direct opposition to the direction of the court." [3]

A shining example was set for the world by the Trial by Jury which incorporates the Right of the citizen-juror to judge on the justice of the law, this Right being held by all who have adopted the Trial by Jury as *the principal constitutional defence against the enforcement of unjust laws, and arbitrary government*. Prime Minister William Pitt, later Earl of Chatham, aptly described the Petition of Right, 1629, the Bill of Rights, 1689, and Magna Carta, as forming *"the bible of the English Constitution."*

1 *Definitions*, a '*constitution*' is a code of laws and customs established by the government of a nation for its own control and guidance; and, '*government*' is comprised of the executive, the legislature and the judiciary.
2 Explicative information on <u>conscience</u> on pages 195-7.
3 Yale Law Journal.

The Constitutional Common Law Trial by Jury Justice System intentionally takes a person out of the hands of the government (i.e., from judges, prosecutors, police and prison service) and places the accused under the protection of his or her equals and the Common Law alone: Trial by Jury allows no man or woman to be punished unless the indiscriminately chosen equals of the accused (i.e., the jurors) consent to it.

Trial by Jury is so-named, for in democratic societies the trial of a citizen is by fellow citizens who comprise the Jury. Trial is not 'trial-by-government' which could never be seen to be fair where government is also one of the contesting parties. Judges themselves comprise a branch of government, and, they are in the pay of government. Government employees always have a *moral* choice in whether or not to follow government instructions; but those who do not follow orders or serve the interests of their employers, do not remain employees for long. Police, prison service and above all, prosecutors and judges are employed to enforce governments' laws. Such personnel should never be asked, nor relied on, to decide impartially whether laws are just, for they *must* fulfil their task or face the fury of the government, their employer. For these reasons, government and judiciary are incompetent to require the conviction or punishment of any person for any offence whatever.

Neither in Britain nor in the United States have legislatures ever been invested by the People with authority to remove the Right of the accused to a Trial by Jury, to impair the powers, to change the oaths, or abridge the jurisdiction of jurors.

MAGNA CARTA: Articles 39 & 40:

Magna Carta and the Trial by Jury Justice System show *why* all accused men and women *everywhere* have the right to a Trial by a Jury of free equal citizens (not trial by government or its representatives and employees) and *what form* this Trial must take; and *why* no one, no government nor institution anywhere, has any legal or moral right whatever to deny this; and explain *how* such a denial itself transgresses law and morality.

The two most famous Articles of Magna Carta, 39 and 40, give Guarantee to democratic people's most deeply held political beliefs. These and other Articles, lawyers take as legal basis, and recognition, of such fundamental Rights as that of the Juror to judge on the justice of the law itself in finding a verdict in Trial by Jury; the Right of the accused to a Trial by a Jury of one's peers, i.e . equal citizens, not trial by government employees; Habeas Corpus; freedom from arbitrary arrest; and equality before the law. Originally written in Latin, translated, they read as follows:

39. "No free man shall be seized or imprisoned, or stripped of his rights or possessions, or outlawed or exiled, or deprived of his standing in any other way, nor will we proceed with force against him, or send others to do so, except according to the lawful judgement of his equals and according to * the law of the land *."
* **"The law of the land," derived from universal tenets of natural law and justice, is the people's Common Law as it was at the time Magna Carta was first enacted.**

40. "To no one will we sell, to no one deny or delay right or justice."

Until the Latin-derived word 'juror' was adopted, jurors were actually called **the judges**, in recognition of their rôle. All the various presiding convenors of courts, such as justices (who were appointed representatives of the government's, i.e., the monarch's, interests), or stewards, sheriffs and bailiffs, under the common law, were, and, following the written Constitutional Statute (Law) Magna Carta, *are* **prohibited** from interfering in matters of judgement and justice in civil, criminal and fiscal causes (lawsuits). This is the exclusive preserve of the twelve indiscriminately chosen equals of the accused. *"...the judges, for so the jury were called..."* p. 55 of Crabbe's History of the English Law. Also see TRIAL BY JURY.

What Common Law Trial by Jury Is:

See The Form of Trial by Jury prescribed by Common Law and the U.S. Constitution, and defined by Magna Carta, in: 'TRIAL BY JURY: Its History, True Purpose and Modern Relevance,' by Kenn d'Oudney, ALAM (Hons) Dip. GSA and Lysander Spooner, U.S. Lawyer (barrister-at-law); ISBN 9781902848723.

Article 39 of Magna Carta specifically prescribes the definitive Trial by Jury in which jurors include judgement on the justice of the law in finding the Verdict: Trial by Jury was itself at the time of Magna Carta, the central tenet of "the law of the land," now called common law, by which all the people are bound (governments and judges included), and to which they are subject; and, which does not include any statutes or laws passed by government, president, monarch and legislatures. Since Magna Carta, Trial by Jury may be called Constitutional, and/or Common Law Trial by Jury.

According to "legem terræ," the law of the land *requires*: Common Law Trial by Jury to be the sole justice system for all causes, criminal, civil and fiscal; **all** adult citizens (save lunatics and convicted criminals) qualify for jury service; jurors to be drawn indiscriminately by lot from the people (to represent fairly all views held in the country, to protect minorities, and to prevent the government or prosecution from illegally *packing* the jury to try to produce that verdict desired by the prosecution and government); unanimity amongst the jurors to pronounce guilt; jurors to be the equals (peers) of the accused.

Wherever it takes place, be it in the U.S., the U.K., Australia, Canada, New Zealand, and numerous other countries, the simple demands **DEFINITIVE** of the Constitutional Common Law Trial by Jury are that in finding their Verdict, the jurors judge:

on the justice of the law (also see page 182), in addition to

the facts, and

on the admissibility of evidence.

Jurors must judge:

that the accused acted with a malicious motive, criminal intent, i.e., mens rea, to find guilt (also see page 152); and,

where guilt is **unanimously** found, on mitigating circumstances if any; and

set the sentence (with regard to its being fit and just).

For jurors not to do the above, or for someone other than the jurors to make any such decisions, is another process: call it 'trial-by-someone-else' if you will, or 'trial-by-the-judge'—but this travesty cannot be defined as Trial **BY JURY**.

In Constitutional Common Law Trial by Jury:

the jury has the power to call witnesses, advisers and appoint amicus curiæ;

the correct common law rôle of judges is advisory and as a convenor of courts (and for arranging re-trials and appeals if necessitated by circumstances);

(those misnamed) 'justices' or 'judges' are wholly subsidiary to and at the command of the jury and its Foreman or woman;

contempt charges laid on persons by juries or judges have to be tried as for any crime, that is, by jury;

all evidence can be presented, and requires to be considered for its admissibility by the jurors—*especially* if it reveals partiality, injustice, an unfounded nature, or venality in the law.

The Trial by Jury was emplaced constitutionally for the purposes of:

A.) not only ascertaining guilt or innocence of the accused and where necessary for apportioning retribution, but also

B.) of transcendent importance, as **a barrier** to protect the vast mass of innocent citizenry from arbitrary government, i.e., unjust laws, tyranny; and from the prejudices and incompetence of fallible justices (judges). Genuine Trial by Jury enables the people to judge **authoritatively** what their liberties and laws are (as explained hereinafter), so that the people retain all the liberties which they wish to enjoy. This crucial facet of Jury Trials contributes to the establishment and defining of Democracy [1].

Self-evidently, Trial by Jury can *only* achieve these purposes, A and B, when it is executed in its **definitive** form. Constitutional Common Law Trial by Jury *requires*:

— jurors to annul enforcement of law adjudged to be unjust, by pronouncing the verdict of Not Guilty;

— jurors to judge for themselves of their rights and liberties, and to try the accused by their own standards, not those dictated by the government, for there are no oppressions which the government may not authorise by law, viz. Slave Laws; severing of limbs for petty theft; decapitation or lapidation (stoning-to-death) for female adultery; Nürnberg (NAZI) Race Laws; money-motivated Prohibitions, etc.;

— jurors to judge on all aspects of the validity, morality, the present relevance or applicability, of the law;

— judges, i.e., convenors of courts, to be elected locally by the people, and answerable to and replaceable by the people;

— no person appointed by the government may hold or preside at jury trials;

— the jury to be sole judge of the cause;

— the jury, not the judge, to decide on all matters concerning admissibility of evidence and the calling of witnesses;

— juries to have overriding enforced authority;

— restriction of the judge's and the government's powers by subjecting all due process to the rulings of the jury;

— (excepting emergency reaction to contain violence present) the judge's rulings regarding contempt to be enforceable only when concurred with by a jury, after Trial by Jury thereon, the jury confirming, modifying or dismissing such rulings;

— jurors to take account of the defendant's motives, and to judge on incitation, provocation, temptation, and degree of criminal intent (Latin, *mens rea*);

— jurors to bind themselves by oath to: do justice, to try the case, civil, criminal or fiscal, according to their conscience, to convict the guilty and acquit the innocent;

— the jury to decide the sentence.

With the benefits of consultations and advice (from the judge and any other sources it may care to call) in the final analysis, in Trial by Jury—*not* the judge, the government's beholden employee—but, *the jury* is the sole, final, omnipotent judge and arbiter of democratic justice. Anything less than, or different from this, is not Trial by Jury, but trial by someone else.

Readers acquainted with process of law in the United States, Britain and elsewhere today, will see how far removed the practices of courts are from the ideals and legally binding stipulations of those nations' Constitutions.

1 See the Democracy Defined website www.democracydefined.org

186

Restoration…

JUSTICE AND THE CONSTITUTION, cont.

If a juror accepts as the law that which the judge states, then that juror has accepted the exercise of absolute authority of a government employee and has surrendered a power and right that was once the citizen's safeguard of liberty. The saddest epitaph which can be carved in memory of vanished liberty is that it was lost because its possessors failed to stretch forth a saving hand while there was time.

Consider the words of <u>Thomas Jefferson</u> [1], Author of the Declaration of Independence, Founder of the Democratic Party, and Third President of the United States:

"*I consider Trial by Jury as the only anchor yet imagined by man, by which a government can be held to the principles of its constitution.*"

According to <u>Samuel Chase</u> [2], U.S. Supreme Court Chief Justice, 1796, a signatory to the Declaration of Independence:

"*The Jury has the Right to determine both the law and facts.*"

In this matter, good men and women who stand up against tyranny are of one mind.

More recently, according to <u>Chief Justice Oliver Wendell Holmes</u> [3]:

"*The Jury has the power to bring a verdict in the teeth of both law and fact.*"

Consider <u>Harlan F. Stone</u> [4], Chief Justice of the U.S. Supreme Court from 1941 to 1946; writing 'The Common Law in the United States,' Harvard Law Review, 1936:

"*If a juror feels that the statute involved in any criminal offence is <u>unfair</u>, or that it infringes upon the defendant's natural God-given unalienable or Constitutional rights, then it is his <u>duty</u> to affirm that the offending statute is really no law at all and that the violation of it is no crime at all, for no one is bound to obey an unjust law.*"
(Emphases added.)

"*That juror <u>must</u> vote Not Guilty regardless of the pressures or abuses that may be heaped on him by any or all members of the jury with whom he may in good conscience disagree. He is voting on the justice of the law according to his own conscience and convictions and not someone else's. <u>The law itself is on trial quite as much as the cause which is to be decided.</u>*" **(Emphases added.)**

See the ruling of the U.S. 4th Circuit Court of Appeals, 1969:

"*If the jury feels the law is unjust, we recognise the undisputed power of the jury to acquit even if its verdict is contrary to the law as given by the judge, and contrary to the evidence. If the jury feels that the law under which the defendant is accused is unjust, or that exigent circumstances justified the actions of the accused, or for any reason which appeals to their logic or passion, the jury has the power to acquit, and the courts must abide by that decision.*"

Part of the Trial by Jury procedure is for the judge to **educate** jurors of their Right, and to **instruct** them of their Duty to judge on the justice of the law. As the appointed supervisory officer of the court, part of the judge's function is to explain what the law is and instruct jurors in their rôle. As a jury includes people inexpert in legal matters and most only ever serve once or twice on a jury, it is self-explanatory that members of a jury require to be educated and apprised by the judge of their Rights and Duty, especially that of judging on the justice of law. **No individual juror can be expected to know, unless so instructed and taught, that it is his or her duty to nullify unfair persecutory law enforcement**.

1 Letter from Thomas Jefferson to Thomas Paine, 1789. ME 7:408, Papers 15:269. Also see: 'The Writings of Thomas Jefferson,' edited by H.A. Washington; J.P. Lippincotts Co., Philadelphia.
2, 3, 4, & 5 For all references herein to presidents, justices, etc., see Democracy Defined Campaign Essays and Educational Publications.

<u>WHY</u> Is the Citizen-Juror's Judgement on the Law So Important a Part of any Fair and Competent Justice System ?

IS YOUR COUNTRY A DEMOCRACY OR
IS YOUR GOVERNMENT A DESPOTISM ?

In the governance of men and women, few, if any, matters are of greater consequence than the diligence and precision with which the judiciary observes and adheres to the definitive code of Common Law Trial by Jury, long established for the determination of an accused person's guilt or innocence. Some term other than Trial by Jury is necessary to describe a court ritual enacted wherein the jury is not instructed to execute the juror's Right and Duty to judge the law, without which Trial *by Jury* cannot be said to have taken place.

All governments, comprised as they are of human beings, are fallible. Governments are capable of passing bad or oppressive [i.e., illegal] laws, and authorising and organising the enforcement of such bad laws. When jury-trials are disallowed or juries are limited in their rôle to decide guilt or innocence only on the evidence produced by the state prosecutor of whether the accused had broken a law or not, any jury acting in this restricted way would not be able to protect good fellow citizens from unjust laws or the oppressions of the state. These 'show trials' are observed to take place in fascist, communist, and primitive tyrannies of totalitarian dictatorships, in countries which claim to be 'democratic'. They are traditionally scorned for the mockery of justice that they are when compared to the democratic standards of Trial by Jury.

Suffrage does not define **democracy**, for electoral voting takes place in totalitarian states. Having been elected, there is nothing to stop government from imposing control of an upper house, reneging on pledges, nor from adopting any tyrannical measures it chooses. *Etymological derivation*, Greek Demokratia: *demos*, the people; *kratein*, to rule; *kratos*, strength. Democracy is the form of government in which the Supreme Power is vested in the Common People.

Naturally, people have the moral responsibility, the right and the duty to resist and suppress injustice *wherever* it occurs, and by whomsoever it is perpetrated, governments notwithstanding. By definition and in practice, Democracy requires that the People **at all times** retain the Supreme Power to annul injustices and the bad laws made by fallible politicians. This Power is uniquely embodied in the Citizen-Juror's Duty in Trial by Jury to judge the justice of every act of law enforcement, and to render the Not Guilty Verdict whenever conviction or punishment of the accused would be unfair, according to the juror's conscience.

Government which denies its ordinary citizens the right to judge the justice of the laws and the manner of their enforcement *on their fellow citizens at trial*, is a despotism.

Only as long as *juries of ordinary citizens* have the final say, government remains the servant, not the master, of the people. Constitutions and governments which deny the Common Law Trial by Jury Justice System install <u>constitutional despotism</u>. The *denial* of the Common Law Trial by Jury transfers supreme power from the People to a ruling élite: a despotism or oligarchy. The denial of the Juror's rôle and Duty denies Trial by Jury.

Constitutions and governments which may be defined as legal, and as democratic, institute the true Trial by Jury Justice System which embodies the Duty of ordinary citizens as Jurors to acquit as Not Guilty according to the Juror's conscience, all citizens tried under law which the Juror judges to be oppressive or unfair. **It is the presence of constitutional adoption and practical implementation of the Citizen-Juror's Duties in Common Law Trial by Jury, to judge the justice of law and every part of the act of law enforcement, which *defines*, and comprises the basis of, Democracy, sine qua non.**

THE RIGHT OF JURORS TO JUDGE ON THE JUSTICE OF LAW.
The Commemorative Plaque, Old Bailey Law Courts, London.

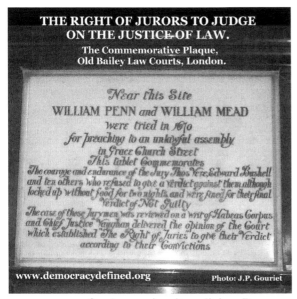

Photo by John Gouriet. For ease of reading, here is a transcription of the Plaque:

"Near this site William Penn and William Mead were tried in 1670 for preaching to an unlawful assembly in Grace Church Street. This tablet commemorates the courage and endurance of the Jury, Thos (Thomas) Vere, Edward Bushell and ten others who refused to give a verdict against them although locked up without food for two nights and were fined for their final Verdict of Not Guilty."

"The case of these Jurymen was reviewed on a writ of Habeas Corpus and Chief Justice Vaughan delivered the opinion of the Court which established The Right of Juries to give their Verdict according to their Conviction."

Quakers: minority religion. Penn was subsequently Founder of Pennsylvania.
N.B. Like the Trial by Jury, this plaque will be removed if the dissolute have their way.

In 1670, <u>Chief Justice Vaughan</u> re-affirmed the then already longstanding Right of Jurors to give their verdict according to their conviction and their conscience. Jurors do not decide the Verdict simply on whether evidence indicates a person "broke the law." Quakers Penn and Mead broke the law in letter and spirit in front of very numerous witnesses. The Penn and Mead infraction was knowing and intentional. The facts of the case were known to all: judge, jury and the public. The evidence against them was incontrovertible. Furthermore, there was no desire in the defendants to deny their brave stand; indeed, rather the converse.

Chief Justice Vaughan upheld the jury's Duty to acquit regardless of the law or the instructions of the judge, if the finding of a verdict of 'guilty' would be unjust to the accused. N.B. Latterday lawyers' erroneous or malindoctrinatory accounts of this case (which are intended to undermine the right of, to efface the value of, and to deny the necessity for, Annulment-by-Jury) evade, or are in ignorance of, the religio-political circumstances surrounding it.

The King was not only Head of State but Supreme Head of the Established Protestant Church of England. Following Europe and England's centuries of 'religious' wars and strife, the Church was in favour of and intended the most extreme castigation (decapitation or auto-da-fé, i.e burning alive at the stake) of adherents such as Quakers to "heretical religions." In religious matters, the Church could not be disputed.

For Chief Justice Vaughan to have made an outright declaration or even an allusion to or recognition of the 'possibility' that the jury in the Penn and Mead case could have annulled the prosecution on the grounds that the law was "*unjust*" would have earned him the executioner's blade. It also would have set back the cause of religious toleration and freedom, which most educated people had at last come to adopt. Yet, in view of the absolute irrefutability of the evidence; the defendants' defiant, declamatory demands from the dock for independence of conscience; and the fatal hostility of the Church to even the slightest dissent, *to allow the acquittal to stand was blatantly to confront the injustice and tyranny of the law.*

Although Penn and Mead had flagrantly broken 'the law', at trial the jurors found not the defendants, but the law wanting. No mens rea, **no criminal intent** could be imputed to the defendants' activities even though they were infractions of "the law." By common law, 'guilt' cannot be imparted to an action simply by passing legislation; see p. 152. Thus, the only just verdict could be that of Not Guilty. Exemplified by this well-known instance, for the trial to be *by jury*, the Jury's Duty and Right to acquit supersedes in authority the government and court; and, to protect citizens against injustices and arbitrary government, Jurors have the Duty to acquit whenever conviction or punishment of the accused would be unfair.

The Chief Justice's upholding of the acquittal was acknowledged throughout the land, the Colonies and elsewhere overseas as a sensational and supremely courageous act, especially given his proximity to the sanguivolent chief representatives of the Church.

People suffering under, or aware of, the threat and cruelty of despotism understand immediately that Jury Nullification is a mechanism *indispensable* to the dispensation of Justice and to the very existence and survival of Democracy. The Penn and Mead case exemplifies how, *for all time*, **Democracy and Justice rely utterly on ordinary citizens having ultimate control of the Justice System**.

The Principle of Jury Nullification confirms in the minds of the discerning that the Trial by Jury, defined and prescribed by England's Constitutional law Magna Carta and likewise Constitutionally enshrined for all (non-impeachable) crimes by the Founding Fathers and originators of the U.S. Constitution, is the finest and most democratic Justice System ever devised. Founded on and resulting from Trial by Jury, this Constitutional Justice System earned respect worldwide and remains the envy and aspiration of tyrannised, suppressed populations everywhere.

In addition to enforcing justice on wrongdoers, it was *precisely* for the purposes of establishing ordinary citizens' control of the Justice System in order that they be enabled to judge *authoritatively of and retain their liberties*, and to confront and eradicate government tyranny, that Trial by Jury was installed by Magna Carta and the U.S. Constitution. Chief Justice Vaughan's ruling sets an example for today, not only to Jurors but also to citizens in judicial and magisterial positions in tribunals *everywhere*: In finding a Verdict, **everyone** is not only morally and duty-bound, but also *legally* bound (see ratified U.N. Principles; p. 182) to judge both the justice of the law, and on whether the behaviour of the accused was of mens rea, i.e., guilt or criminal intention, without which **no crime can have been committed** (see p. 152).

At this point, one of the many aspects of the superiority of the Constitutional Common Law Trial by Jury Justice System is established over the uncouth tyrannical system of enforcement-by-government-judges; which does away with citizens' judgement and the Trial by Jury: As the foremost democratic Safeguard of the ordinary people against those in government who would do injustice, the jury is **the only** *extra*-governmental body [i.e., outside of the government and state employees] constitutionally emplaced to judge the law and every act of enforcement. Bearing in mind that **no government** *ever* conceded that the laws it enforces could be "unjust," this makes the jury's judgement on the justice or otherwise of the law, **the** *only* **true democratic testing** of the law.

To his eternal credit, Chief Justice Vaughan set the example for judges everywhere and in reviewing the case re-confirmed the Right and Duty of Jurors to judge the justice of laws, upholding this Principle as the quintessential **Safeguard of Democracy, intended for all time.**

THE PURPOSE OF TRIAL BY JURY.

People who judge authoritatively for themselves what their liberties are, retain all the liberties which they wish to enjoy. **This is Liberty**. Trial by Jury is a trial by the People of the country, distinguished from a trial by the government. The *intention* of this trial is to enable the People to determine what their liberties are, as opposed to the government making such decisions; because, if the government is the judge of its powers and determines what the People's liberties are, then government has Absolute Power over the People: and this is the definition of **despotism** [1].

In recognition of these immutable facts, Trial by Jury was adopted by the People as part of the law of the land [common law] and installed by written Constitution [Magna Carta; U.S. Constitution] as that tribunal which permanently establishes within the domain of the People, as opposed to the government, supreme judgement by citizen-jurors of the People's liberties: of what the law is; and of all government, religious and secular, rules, regulations and statutes. People deciding the law establish their liberties, and, by that singular act in Trial by Jury, simultaneously decide which laws shall be enforced, and which behaviour is anti-social, forbidden, of criminal intent, and punishable.

Enforcement of injustice by the state is an illegal act: it is for the ordinary people at large represented by juries of indiscriminately chosen adult citizens to judge the justice of **every** act of law enforcement, including all regulations, by-laws, 'misdemeanours', 'on-the-spot-fines', and 'petty' rules.

However apparently insignificant the alleged infraction, the Constitution authorises that the accused shall **always** have the right to recourse to a Trial by a Jury of his or her peers, in order that **injustices**, whenever they occur, be annulled by fellow citizens acting as jurors. It remains, not for a person appointed by or representing government, but for **the jury** of ordinary citizens to decide if conviction or punishment would be deserved or would be unfair, and what constitutes a punishable act of mens rea. N.B. By common law, today's automatic fines, mandatory minimums and summary judgements are all **illegal**: citizens persecuted thereby have the right to elect a Trial by Jury and if found Not Guilty, are due Amnesty and Restitution.

From deepest antiquity to the present, the following remains the incontrovertible Fact for the Third Millennium, A.D.:

When the Jurors in Common Law Trial by Jury adjudge legislation and/or acts of enforcement to be unjust, antidemocratic, or arbitrary, then the said legislation and/or enforcement are unlawful: the prosecution of such legislation and/or the act of enforcement constitute tyranny, i.e., crime per se.

Citizen-juries educated and instructed to judge the justice of law and its enforcement, can be relied on to protect people from the state, when the state breaches correct behaviour in attempting to enforce injustices. It is for **this reason** that those who stand to gain from tyranny by the imposition of unjust 'laws', regard the genuine Trial by Jury as an obstacle to be undermined and destroyed. Untrustworthy at best, of outright criminal intent at worst, are those who, instead of restoring Common Law Trial by Jury to its true form, would discard it altogether; viz. e.g. commissars, politicians and bureaucrats of the European Union, whose antidemocratic 'constitution' installs the Stalinist, National Socialist (NAZI), communist and fascist system of trial-by-the-judge.

Trial by Jury has survived and been maintained only by the martial and willing self-sacrifice of many generations who, in the face of resurgent tyrannies, gave of their lifeblood that their contemporaries and we, their descendants, shall dwell within nations constituted upon the inherent Rights and high Principles of civilised free people in a state of Democracy. Even slightly to loosen the constraints which the constitutions, U.S. and Magna Carta, bring to the procedures of judicature, that is, to the Common Law Trial by Jury, to alter or undermine it in the smallest way, is potentially or definitely to prejudice the outcome of a prosecution by the government, i.e., the verdict, in favour of the prosecution. Such a false 'trial' is merely an outward show, a pretence, and is not definable as fair or just, and is no trial at all. Every tribunal or court everywhere which fails to conduct itself according to Common Law Trial by Jury has only the authoritarian outward semblance of authenticity. The findings of its tampered proceedings cannot legitimately be relied upon.

Legislators and judges are exposed to all the temptations of **money, fame and power**, to induce them to disregard justice between contesting parties, and to sell the rights and violate the liberties of the People. Jurors are exposed to *none* of these temptations. Jurors are not liable to bribery, for they are unknown to the parties until they come into the jury-box. They can hardly gain fame, power or money by giving erroneous decisions. Their office as juror is temporary. They know that when they have executed it, they must return to everyday life; but they rely on *their* rights being upheld by the judgements of jurors who will be their successors, and to whom they are an example. Further, the laws of human nature do not permit the supposition that twelve adult men and women taken by lot from the mass of the people will *all* prove dishonest. A jury insures to us—*what no other court does*—that first and indispensable requisite in a judicial tribunal: **integrity**.

The powers of juries not only place a curb on the powers of legislators and judges, but also imply an imputation on their integrity, impartiality and trustworthiness; and *these* are the reasons why legislators and judges have entertained the most intense hatred for juries, and, so fast as they could do it without alerting the People to the loss of their liberties, have now destroyed juries' power to judge on justice issues, and with it the Trial by Jury.

The Principle of our Western Constitutions' Trial by Jury is that it is the Will of the People represented by indiscriminately chosen Jurors, not the will of the court or the government, that must determine what laws shall be established and enforced [1]. History, and dispassionate reflection on the World today, teach no more certain lesson than this: Whenever and wherever Trial by Jury is not in place, or it is allowed by the insouciance of the population to be interfered with by government and its representatives, there tyranny and crime *inevitably* prevail. The (Western) tradition of Judaeo-Christian morality, *and* the *universal* natural common laws of equity and justice teach that Democracy, id est, the control by ordinary people of every aspect of government, is to be favoured over and when necessary fought for in resistance to the foible of humans established in authority always to suppress the Freedom of others.

As is visible everywhere, the less citizens' control there is of government, the more extreme the tyranny extant [2]. Men are slow to resist injustice inflicted upon others, and rebellion and civil war are the last extremities. Let us praise the wisdom of our forebears in finding in Trial by Jury so complete and unequalled a solution to eternal problems, which fulfils all that is required of a democratic justice system.

1 A laudable edict may express a tyrant's pretentions, but "a tyrannical statute always proves the existence of tyranny." See: Edward Gibbon, Chapter XXIX, Decline and Fall of the Roman Empire, Dent, London; Dutton, New York.

2 The converse is also true: the greater the tyranny, the less there is democratic control.

Restoration...

Governments are comprised of *human beings* and are *always fallible*. In individual cases or overall, governments may seek to, and do, discriminate and interfere arbitrarily in, political expression, personal and political affiliation, education, income, private possession and money, inheritance, taxation and duties, race, beliefs, the public, social and/or free market, free trade, in vitro and surrogatum fertility, genetics, freedom of speech, freedom of the (printing) press, customs, private practices, personal lifestyles, and religion. Government malevolently persecutes people for things that are not crimes, and as shown herein, generates and fosters the greater part of all *real* crime by the bias of its vested interests. Further, citizens are made to suffer judges' prejudices and incompetence.

To *lose* the legal controls which Trial by Jury gives to citizens, on exactly what the government may or may not do to the People, creates a lawless void which—*human nature ensures*—unscrupulous opportunists always exploit. Governments so empowered, incline towards dictating what people may and may not be, by force. *Without* Trial by Jury to guard the individual and thus, the entire population, the human predisposition for tyranny is exacerbated.

Governments at all times trend towards the tyranny of the enforcement of laws in which there is no justice. If they do not progress in this, it is because the constitutional, enforceable democratic control by the Trial by Jury stops them, or because they fear provoking mass reaction, rather than some intrinsic 'virtue'. As if any further evidence in support of this affirmation were necessary, the entirety of human History and Politics proves the point; and, quoted earlier in this Part, impartial citizens, judges, chief justices, politicians, and presidents concur.

Trial by Jury puts the forces of law and order under democratic control at the point of each and every act of enforcement. Trial by Jury gives a real degree of protection to good citizens who otherwise are always vulnerable to the brutalities of any state when it becomes venal, or deviates from democracy; or, whenever a prosecutor or judge has a tendency to incompetence or unfairness. Trial by Jury makes every citizen serving as a Juror a Safeguard of Justice and Liberty, reinforcing Democracy.

The façade which now replaces Constitutional Trial by Jury, *itself demonstrates* the unconstitutional character of Western governments, and exposes the corrupt illegalities and tyrannical practices routine in process of law within every Western nation today. By the protections intended under our Constitutions, English and American, government may pardon, suspend or moderate sentences; re-trials before a new jury may occur, and appeals take place; but, for every civil, criminal and fiscal instance of accusation, judgement on laws and other citizens' behaviour, is the ordinary citizen's domain, not that of government. Trial of the accused, not by the government's employees, but by a Jury of equal fellow citizens drawn indiscriminately from the country to have representation of minorities, requiring jurors' judgement on the law, facts and evidence; unanimity for conviction, and apportioning retribution where appropriate, remains indispensable to constitutional democracy. We forget the lessons of History at our peril.

Knowledge about Magna Carta, of the relevant law and history, combined with comprehension of the *nature* of Man, produce understanding of how and why the Trial by Jury has been broken down in practice; and of the unconstitutional illegal means by which this devastating dismantlement of Democracy has proceeded: premeditated denial of Trial by Jury's intended protection of citizens from the enforcement of unjust laws, is the result of unlawful manipulations by government. By the mens rea of great and petty despots undermining citizens' Trial by Jury, democracy is eroded and eventually utterly ruined. **This criminal government activity must be resisted and reversed**.

To most readers, it will be stating the obvious; but it needs to be made plain:

1— **Trial-by-the-judge is *inherently* illegal**: no government or court anywhere may *legally* 'deny', 'revoke' or 'legislate' away Common Law Trial by Jury which incorporates the Right of the citizen-juror to decide on the justice of law enforcement.

2— In order for the Trial to be by the Jury, as opposed to it being by someone else, the jury requires to judge on all aspects relevant to the case, including the law and the sentence, the facts and evidence, motive, and criminal intent if any.

3— When called to jury service in the trial of a fellow citizen, it is the individual juror's Duty to acquit as innocent any citizen who is tried under unfair or bad [i.e., illegal] laws, by pronouncing the verdict of Not Guilty to nullify the law which the juror considers unjust. 'Evidence' that the accused 'broke the law' is irrelevant to the verdict if the law itself is illegal: in these circumstances, the only just verdict possible is that of Not Guilty.

4— Similarly, any defendant tried under unjust law has the Right to expect his or her fellow citizens on the jury to acquit him or her as Not Guilty, and, for that purpose, to reveal such injustices to the jury.

5— Counsel for defence and the defendant have the Duty and Right to present in court the Whole Truth and evidence of the case to the jury; and to show any injustices in law and enforcement. Reviewing evidence, the jury alone decides what evidence is admissible.

6— It is the Duty of the judge (or convening officer) to instruct jurors to acquit according to the juror's conscience, any person whose conviction the juror judges would be unjust.

The jury's power to reject and annul bad law continues to be recognised, as in 1972 when the D.C. Circuit Court of Appeals ruled:

"The jury has an unreviewable and irreversible power to acquit in disregard of the instruction on the law given by the trial judge. The pages of history shine upon instances of the jury's exercise of its prerogative to disregard instructions of the judge."

Amongst many other most gravely criminal perversions of the course of Justice, in Britain following centuries of Unanimity, majority 'verdicts' replaced Unanimity. This occurred shortly after the Second World War, to facilitate producing false guilty 'verdicts' for the enforcement of money-motivated, unjust measures favoured by government.

Denial (or non-implementation) of citizens' Rights and Duty as Jurors, by governments or courts, negates Trial by Jury in particular and voids all 'due process' in general. This usurpation is a crime rendered the more detestable, for it desecrates the memory and defiles the sacrifice of men and women beyond number who gave their lives in the ongoing good fight for Liberty, to establish and re-establish just laws, constitutions and democratic procedures, such as that of the jury to judge on the justice of law in Trial by Jury.

It is a fact nowadays little-known within the United States, the continent of Europe and to a great extent within modern Britain, that at one time throughout Europe, all shared, and the people rigorously defended from government interference, their Trial by Jury Justice System. England (or Britain) is the world's oldest surviving example of this constitution, followed on by that of the United States of America. Both of these nations precisely embody that Trial by Jury Constitution formulated and adopted by all the Northern, or European, Peoples (also referred to as the Gothic Nations). Eventually, numerous other countries across the globe adopted this most natural and just constitution. The awareness that **all** Europeans once shared the constitutional ideal of the Trial by Jury has been eroded by insidious political miseducation. See "The Constitution Treatise," ISBN 9781902848747.

"DO-AS-YOU-WOULD-BE-DONE-BY:"
THE UNIVERSAL SENSE OF FAIRNESS.

In all times and places, from commonplace interactions and the experiences of life, **a sense of fairness** is acquired by children at a very young age, and possessed by adult humans (see Justice Sir William Jones: Jones on Bailments; and TRIAL BY JURY ISBN 9781902848723). This sense of fairness bestows on humans everywhere, i.e., universally, an understanding of what is called *natural law* and *justice*.

Natural law may be described as the Science of Justice. It is comprised of the Principles embodied in the basic components of Truth, Justice and Equity. The Universal Sense of Fairness is, like other *senses*, not imparted or taught to children by adults: it is not a case of "Let me tell you, children..." Certainly, the conscientious adult, teacher and parent will spare no effort in bringing young people into the advantageous awareness of how to behave in society; but this can be and frequently is perverted by prejudices and failures of character in grown-ups; or in the "thieves' kitchen," and so on.

The Sense of Fairness is *not* taught; but it *is* learned. The Universal Sense of Fairness is acquired almost intuitively. **Humans cannot avoid learning the principles of natural law**. Children *sense* that they do not like nasty things done to them and that other people *feel* exactly the same. They gather this from simple experiences of emotional and/or physical pain; from their receipt of petty injustices; and from assimilating the reactions of others to acts of unfairness inflicted against them.

The Universal Sense of Fairness is virtually infallible in teaching humans everywhere to understand natural law and justice. Children learn fairness even before they learn the language with which they can explain or define it. Indeed, it is necessary for people to be conscious of the sense *first*, in order to understand the true meaning of the words by which fairness is described.

Children learn that when one person has a sandwich, it is that person's possession, and others should not take it away from him without his assent. They come to understand further that the willing exchange of the sandwich for a toy or other object of desire, means that a 'transaction' of 'ownership' has taken place, and that the sandwich cannot *fairly* be reclaimed unless by another mutually agreed transaction.

Such are the fundamental principles of natural law, and they govern most or all of the greatest interests of individuals and society.

In this way, all people learn the constituents of **Equity** (i.e., fairness) and the commandment (i.e., rule of action) of natural law: the precept "do-as-you-would-be-done-by," or as it is often written, "do unto others as you would they do unto you." The **unwritten common law** of the People, formerly named **"the law of the land"** (Magna Carta, Article 39; see page 184), derives from and is founded on this pure sense. Based on the "do-as-you-would-be-done-by" **precept**, the common law is applicable **universally**.

It is the Sense of Fairness which endows humans universally with **conscience, the faculty or principle by which we distinguish right from wrong** in regard to our relations with others. Adults know when they are recipients of acts of unfairness or injustice; and similarly, they know when they do such wrong to others. Hence, all adult people qualify to be empanelled as jurors to judge both the justice of the law and of the intent, criminal or innocent, of the acts of others; and may likewise be judged by others in the common law's Justice System: Trial by Jury.

Equity is defined as moral justice and the spirit of fairness; which, to be *legal*, governments' written laws (statutes) are required to reflect. That is to say, *unjust* laws, i.e., embodying tyranny, cannot be enacted legally *anywhere* (cf. International Law; Crime against Humanity). Because statutes are fallible and imperfect written expressions, they require interpretation.

The *superiority* of natural law is witnessed, and confirmed, by the fact that the written law (statutes) must be interpreted by the natural. Because natural law and the Sense of Fairness are reliable and universal, *the judiciary is governed by* **the rule** that, for the *interpretation* and determining the meaning of the words comprising a written law, the language of statutes and constitutions shall be as closely as possible construed consistently with natural law. Whenever written law (statutes) cannot be construed consistently with natural law and justice, the written law infracts common law, rendering the statute abrogate and *illegal*.

Through this conception of fairness, adults know what constitutes justice, and what justice requires. Whilst outside of the jury situation, adults behave (whether fairly to others or not) according to what they consider to be in their interests, **within the jury**, when ordinary citizens know the facts from which a verdict is to be inferred, they arrive at the same conclusion or verdict, *unless* there is reasonable doubt ceded by the inconclusive nature of the evidence. Citizen-jurors are aware that they rely on *their* rights being upheld by judgements of jurors just such as they, to whom they are an example. So, whereas there is the strongest of incentives to judge truly and well, there exists no reason at all for disinterested ordinary citizens to render any verdict but the one which is fair and true.

Hence, regarding aspects of justice, equity and fairness in respect of people's treatment of one another, all adults are qualified to try and to judge each other's behaviour—with the obvious exception of government representatives and employees: prosecutors, judges, police and prison service, etc. These latter are remunerated and *feel themselves compelled to enforce* the legislation of their employer, the government, regardless of its potential injustice; because failure to do so incurs impeachment, punishment and/or expulsion from their jobs. These *inevitably* biased people cannot but make incompetent judgements on the justice or otherwise of their masters' laws. It must be stressed nevertheless, that the enforcement of injustice is a common law crime and where acts constitute enforcement or abetment of tyranny they are punishable under domestic and International Law. See ratified U.N. Principles, page 182.

Trial of an accused by a Jury of his or her peers (equals) is a central tenet of common law. Trial by Jury serves the people both as a system for the enforcement of just laws, and also, of paramount importance, as a constitution of itself in that it provides democratic and lawful control of the wayward measures and powers of abusive governments.

In apprehending **defining** attributes, note that within a **Democracy**:
firstly, the executive, legislatures, judiciary and all People are subject to, bound by, and judicable under, the law of the land, the universal natural and common law;
secondly, **the People**, as opposed to the government, **comprise The Supreme Legislature**: *common law is that law which is made by the People as enforced by Jurors in each Trial by Jury*; and,
thirdly, **common law**, which is known without being taught, which is learned without being written or read, which is the product of the People's Universal Sense of Fairness, Natural Law and Justice, which was known as "the law of the land," and of which Trial by Jury is the central tenet, constitutes the basis of proper civilisation, sine qua non.

196

Restoration...

Trial by Jury is an anti-racist, anti-sectarian, egalitarian measure, which militates on behalf of Good against Evil. Where practised, Trial by Jury envelops the entire adult population, cultivating and propagating those higher human concepts of natural justice, truth, social responsibility, liberty and equity, essential to civilisation, progress and the ongoing development of human cultures.

Since pre-historical time immemorial, juries of European people from all backgrounds, some literate, others not, have agreed on and enforced common law in the Trial by Jury, against injustices of all types: tyranny, murder, cruelty, bodily harm, rape, robbery, theft, etc. It serves the interest of the individual citizen and the People at large to do so. That is to say, the People reliably enforce just laws; and, only laws which are just are those which should and must be enforced. (Even and especially the covert undiscovered felon called to serve on a jury enforces the just laws, for not to do so would reveal his insalubrious character to the other jurors.)

However, if the justice of a law is not evident, and the sentence of punishment (being part of the law) cannot be accepted as justifiable and fair by twelve indiscriminately chosen adult citizens, then that 'law' is no law at all: it requires Jury Nullification and must not be enforced. When juries regularly reject (nullify) prosecutions of a statute, that statute requires legislative expunction.

With Trial by Jury holding sway, laws count for naught unless they be just. Thus the People are *served*, not ruled, by governments. Such government then cannot but embody truly democratic ideals and civilised aspirations. This type of government attracts, and is comprised of, representative democratic citizens; and no tyrant can attain power. At the behest of juries of ordinary citizens, the state is constrained into enforcing only just principles and democratic attitudes which accord with the People's judgement, such as those represented by common law: fraternity, liberty, egalitarianism, progress and justice.

By the diligent upholding of *this* Constitution, all tyranny is pre-empted. Not only are bureaucratic and fiscal injustices eliminated, but tyrants, great and petty, are emasculated. This enforceable democratic control by the People was constitutionally emplaced to extend equally over the historic and current 'religious' tyrannies, as to secular, which are suffered under man's inhumanity to man.

Thus, Constitutional Democracies founded on the Common Law Trial by Jury respond to, *but cannot initiate*, aggression, including wars so-defined. If Trial by Jury had remained operating throughout the European nations, whence it originated, the Hohenzollern and Hitler tyrannies would have been truncated, and the Holocaust and both World Wars averted.

Common law, legem terræ, which existed at Magna Carta's first enactment in 1215 A.D., must be differentiated from that which modern government has corrupted *by legislation*, which is "common law" *in name only*. Common law derives from the people's sense of fairness, natural law and justice: it is neither "government-made" nor "judge-made." It does not consist of case precedents (stare decisis) for juries decide the law (and sentence, if any) in each individual case, nor of judicial rulings, decisions or interpretations of statutes. When it is asserted to be any of the latter, this exemplifies government usurpation and tyranny at work.

NOTE: The Democracy Defined membership campaigns for RESTORATION of the constitutionally-correct Trial by Jury with Jury Rights, Duties and procedures, and the reversion of the judiciary to their correct functions: as convenors of courts, for arranging security, as counsellors, and for arranging retrials and appeals where relevant.

A Criminal Modus Operandi: Jury Tampering by Judges.

Nowadays, Trial by Jury **is precluded by judges' illegal intervention** to forbid jurors from judging on equity issues and on the justice of the law and its enforcement. **From this vile seed despotism is extant, all-pervading and visibly growing**.

The courts' current unlawful modus operandi is to facilitate the tyranny manifest in the judiciary's antidemocratic enforcement of partial statutes and regulations, which citizen-jurors *en masse* would otherwise emphatically annul.

The **motive** behind and explanation for judges' boundless treachery are the same today as they have always been… and they confirm that the indispensability of Trial by Jury is eternal: the judiciary is responsible, not to the People, but to the government; judges are dependent for careers, salaries and by impeachment, on the legislature: *to remain judges, they must reliably enforce unjust legislation.*

Judges regard themselves as, and are, *bound* to enforce the laws, even when doing so is an act of extreme injustice. Once a law has been passed and interpreted for enforcement by the courts, then, *unlike jurors*, in the routine of court cases judges are not permitted to dispute or judge the justice of law and its enforcement. To allow these compromised humans to dictate the law, i.e., trial-by-the-judge, utterly surrenders all the liberties, rights, property and money of the people to the arbitrary will of apostate politicians. Any person who would propose or support this system of enslavement and subjection of the People, suffers from dearth of education and knowledge of political history, or the stultifying lack of understanding of the *nature* of human beings—or from acute antidemocratic mens rea (criminal intent).

The infractions by modern judiciaries of the strictures of the U.S. Constitution, the U.K. Great Charter Constitution, of universal natural law and justice, and the Common Law, are epitomised, and the injustice of today's 'justice system' is demonstrated by judges' prevaricative misstatement of law (which they are all too fond of reciting) that "parliament/ congress makes law, and judges enforce it." Au contraire...

... a *just* system is the *only* one that is *legal*: trial-by-the-government-judge has always been unacceptable to people of probity. Viz. the reasoned advocation of the Trial BY JURY Justice System, by the chief justices, judges, lawyers and heads of state herein quoted. Under the Constitutional Trial by Jury Justice System, common law juries (*not* judges), try, reject or enforce the law.

Judges have participated in and overseen the criminal extinction of the lawful, the Constitutional, the democratic Trial by Jury. *Today*, as a citizen serving on a jury, it is unlikely the judge will tell you of your Duty to judge whether the law is just. Instead, expect the judge to instruct you that you may consider only evidence and facts of whether the Defendant broke the law. The judge might even tell you that you may not allow your opinion of the law, your conscience or the defendant's motives (however upright and justifiable), to affect your decision.

In flagrant jury-tampering by judges, no judgement by the jury upon the law is advised or permitted. This one-sided mistrial is illegal. It is against common law; it contravenes Human Rights' Articles; and breaks Constitutional Laws.

Compounding their **violation** of common law and **suffocation** of Justice, nowadays, arrant 'judges' do not permit defence lawyers to tell juries that it is a definitive and integral part of the Juror's function to judge the justice of law enforcement. Thus is Trial by Jury by judges **dismembered**.

A STATE OF TYRANNY.

Motives of power, money, self-interest and domination, from which derive governments' present-day destruction and denial of Trial by Jury, *continue unabated*, so the Democracy Defined Campaign can achieve RESTORATION only by citizens' political, civil and moral pressure. This necessarily makes The Campaign one of popular education; very much a mass movement.

What we have witnessed over the last generations has been the premeditated transformation of our democracies into totalitarian government. This has been brought about by the *mens rea* of politicians' and judiciaries' in their denying of Trial by Jury. Without the proper functioning of Trial by Jury, the despots' and plutocrats' accession to supreme power, and the total enslavement of the People to them, are unavoidable.

Consider some of the following breaches of common law and Constitution to which modern government resorts, in order to enforce its money-motivated statutes:

One can speculate *why* judges contravene the Constitution and civilised Standards, and do not instruct jurors of their constitutional, legal and moral obligations: i.e., the Jurors' Right and Duty to judge the justice of law enforcement; *why* judges perjuriously misinstruct jurors that they are not permitted to judge the law; and *why* judges decide what evidence may be heard in court, preventing juries from reviewing all evidence and deciding on its admissibility....

— disrespect for the ordinary citizen's ability to make fair judgements ?

— the judge is the willing servant of antidemocratic oppressive government ?

— unwillingness to part with his or her power to prejudice the verdict and produce the outcome desired by the judge or by his or her political masters ?

Whatever his or her motives, **the judge is _wrong_** not to instruct jurors of their Right and Duty to do justice: e.g., State of Georgia v. Brailsford, a supreme court forfeiture trial, the facts having been ascertained, U.S. Chief Justice John Jay instructed jurors that it remained only for them to judge the law itself, saying:

"The Jury has the right to judge both the law as well as the fact in controversy."

The modern judiciary have judicably [1] corrupted themselves beyond the pale, abetting and participating in abject tyranny with their perverted misconstruing and enforcing of criminogenic legislation.

The removal of equity and justice issues from trial by the citizen-jurors enables government, through the judge, to enforce *any* 'law', however unjust. Replacing Trial by Jury, Western governments' present system replicates that of Stalinist Russia and Hitler's Nazi régime. 'Trial' is no longer by jury, but *by judges*: the governing politicians' beholden employees. This uncivilised system, by which fascist, communist, and all primitive tyrannies thrive, is now in place in the United States, Britain, the European Union, and throughout all the former democracies of the West.

Where juries do continue to be empanelled (giving the *appearance* "trial by jury" will take place), in the courtroom—the very testing place of liberty—the People, i.e., the jurors, are forbidden from judging whether the law and its enforcement are just. Further, by judges' one-sided illegal intervention to exclude the overwhelming official Exonerative Evidence such as that which is assembled herein from being presented to the jurors, government suborns juries into false 'guilty' verdicts.

1 *Definition*, **judicable: that which may be impeached or tried by jury in a court of law.**

By disregard for Truth, Evidence, Constitution, Law, Justice, and denial of Trial by Jury, criminal government enforces every crooked subterfuge it introduces as 'law'. Hence, the political 'Prohibitions' exist, amongst innumerable illegal fiscal and criminal 'laws' and regulations. Every day in the West, criminal governments inflict abuse, extreme injustices, fines, forfeitures and incarceration on harmless people in their thousands.

Although documentary evidence is admissible in due process under provisions of criminal law in every modern nation, today in the West, to ensure Prohibition is prosecuted without the countervailing intrusion of Truth or Justice, **nota bene:** *lawyers, attorneys, solicitors and barristers are bound by a legally tenable obligation not to* "*dispute the legality of law.*" That is to say, to ensure the enforcement of whatever unjust legislation government passes, a government-contrived legal obligation bans attorneys, solicitors, lawyers and barristers from presenting evidence or defence which **exonerates defendants**, if it "*disputes the law.*"

We point out this crime, this disgrace, this contemptible species of inhumanity. There is no defence to the charge of lawyers acquiescing to the denial of their duty to find The Whole Truth and their profiting from, and being party to, the abuse and imprisonment of innumerable masses of innocent citizens. Consider the charges:

Fact 1: "lawyers cannot present defence or evidence which **exonerates defendants** if it disputes the legality of the law."

Fact 2: "lawyers must abide by the court's authority whenever judges rule out exonerative evidence." [1]

To emphasise this point in the cannabis context, the Empirical Exonerative Evidence shows: the 'law' is selectively inequitable (Part Three); is socially, medically and ecologically destructive unto homicide (Parts One to Six); is a premeditated criminal fabrication (all Parts); and it exposes the ulterior money-motive behind the fraud by which cannabis is Prohibited (all Parts). That defence counsel and defendant are forbidden from presenting this Exonerative Evidence is but one of the illegal techniques by which the tyranny protects and perpetuates itself.

Over years, literally billions accrue to law firms' personnel. In order to ply their lucrative trade (one can no longer dignify this morbid masquerade by calling it a 'profession'), nowadays lawyers blithely abdicate responsibility and utterly forsake honesty. *For gain*, lawyers subreptitiously [2] consent to this odious denial of the duty to find The Whole Truth. They abet the illegal dictates of politicians and compound their malfeasance by tacitly concealing the Jurors' Constitutional Rights and Duty to judge the law *and* to find the Verdict according to conscience.

The educated people who comprise the 'legal profession' are, by their acquiescence and continued participation in the unlawful, tyrannical, perverted processes of today, more to blame than any other group in society for the destruction of the Constitutional Justice System; *and for all the inevitably ensuing totalitarian injustice that results therefrom: the enactment and prosecution of fabricated, ex parte, financially-driven statutes; the abuse of innocent citizens; wrongful penalisation; and the mass incarcerations at the highest per capita rate in history.*

1 See The Illegality of the Status Quo; p. 26 of The Constitution Treatise ISBN 9781902848747.

2 *Definition*, subreption: concealment of evidence; the perjurious procuring of an advantage by concealing the truth.

Restoration...

To recapitulate: Obsequious for money, *the lawyer* adopts the perjury and subreption of not presenting evidence which exonerates defendants. It is not possible for anyone who is remotely au courant with the corrupt status quo, to deem as '*true*', and as '*counsel*' the word of these people who collude in and profit from the widespread enforcement of injustices against innocent citizens.

In shameful meek obedience, lawyers do not dispute the 'law' even when its enforcement is manifest injustice. Where the law is unjust and defendants are innocent of any crime (or mens rea), lawyers nevertheless 'advise' people to plead "guilty" and make plea bargains, rather than their pleading Not Guilty and electing to go to a Trial by Jury. *This comprises one major reason why Trials by Jury have become so infrequent. It also results in the West's largest prison population of all time*, consisting principally of citizens innocent of any crime. (See p. 152; on mens rea, criminal intent, Guilty or Not Guilty.)

The self-proclaimed Western bastions of 'democracy' are illusory. That which militaristic tyranny and the Twentieth Century's Great Wars of Aggression failed to ruin, is destroyed inimically from within, by parasitic individuals of insidious government.

If the correct form of Trial by Jury in which the jury judge on the law is not today *restored* (or, where not before emplaced, is not constitutionally adopted and implemented) then the judiciaries everywhere continue to be party to despicable pretence in place of just proceedings; and, on evidence herein, are judicable for, and culpable of, complicity in transnational tyranny, homicide, a multiplicity of crimes, and extreme oppression of citizens.

In myriad cases, citizens innocent of any real crime but charged under the illegal crime-producing War on Drugs subterfuge, would fare better by dismissing their lawyer and presenting a straightforward courtroom defence themselves in front of the jury, which is their right, with as much of the exonerative evidence as they can. Some have already done so with total success.

If a significant number of defendants were to take up this option of pleading Not Guilty, electing to go for a Trial by Jury and presenting their own defence, then the legal profession would either have to put up with losing the greater proportion of their phenomenally lucrative and easy paydays—or press hard for **restoration** of Constitutional Trial by Jury in which juries judge the law, and defendants and lawyers are obliged, in seeking The Whole Truth, to present such evidence as reveals an unfounded nature, inequity, and/or venal motive, of any modern statutes, and hence *the crimes* per se of the acts of their enforcement.

With defendants presenting defence for themselves, thus withholding from lawyers a major source of income, the legal professionals would have their prime, perhaps *only*, motivating impulse, i.e., *money*, compelling them to strive—for once on the side of Truth and Justice—for **RESTORATION** of the Constitutional Common Law Trial by Jury Justice System.

In the face of modern tyranny, state crime and corruption, *honest* members must forthwith free themselves from dependence on income from, and all association with, the scribes and pharisees of the legal profession. The correct course for every man or woman of probity, the only honourable way of proceeding for members of the profession, is to resist in wrath and indignation, and to refuse to accept the gains so ill-gotten; and campaign (with us) to right the wrongs.

Insincere, gravely wrong 'advice' and mendacity swiftly become the inscrutable, smooth practised habit of those who, *for lucre*, accept that they cannot tell the truth. Controlled by courts (judges) under threat of penalty, and as willing, paid participants in this massive Crime against Humanity, today's lawyers *cannot* give candid counsel or veracious defence; let alone be trusted to educate people truthfully about the principal Safeguard of Democracy: Jury Nullification in the Trial by Jury.

The lawyer's is the training which prepares the person for "the bench"—the judge who takes his pay from the government *only* as long as he or she reliably enforces politicians' inequitable deceptions dissimulated under the guise of 'law'.

It is a fact of life that degenerate humans can be found always and everywhere who will attempt to rule over the lives of others by illegal 'laws', to try to govern behaviour, religion, speech, etc., on the bias of personal taste or vested interests.

To obscure their shameful willing self-denial of the Duty to find The Whole Truth, the legal profession invents and spreads the fictions that "judges respond to the question of law and the jury only to the question of fact." These malicious misstatements of fact and law are contrary to common law, by which the legislature and judges are bound, and of which the Trial by Jury is mechanism of enforcement. They also contravene Constitutional law which installs the Trial *by Jury* Justice System, *not* trial-by-government-judges (*which is the meaning of their fictions*).

Today, to ensure the enforcement of the said illegal 'laws', judges knowingly exclude exonerative evidence, including expert scientific, legal, technical, academic, documentary, medical, philosophical, and that of grounds of equity ! and tell jurors to consider only that evidence which he or she (the judge) allows ! Thus, today, judges invalidate even their own pretence that "jurors try matters of fact."

Furthermore, by dictating the laws of evidence, that is, what evidence the jury may and may not hear and by ruling how jurors should weigh such evidence as the court chooses to permit them to hear, judges corruptly arrange and dictate the conclusion, the Verdict, to which juries must arrive. This criminal tampering by judges produces innumerable false guilty 'verdicts', penalisation and abuse of innocent citizens, and millions of man-years' wrongful incarceration.

In *every* country which aspires to Democracy and Justice, the Safeguard to protect citizens from tyranny is permanently installed and beyond removal; and *this* indispensable Safeguard is the Juror's Right and Duty to judge the law in Trial by Jury. Only in democracies is this check found. Where this Safeguard is tampered with or disallowed by undemocratic forces in power, *without exception*, tyranny is manifest in barbaric acts of persecution of members of the population.

It is beyond question to democratic men and women that the Jury's Right and Duty to protect people from persecution and the tyranny of unjust laws being enforced, must be re-instated and maintained *at all costs*, as an Absolute Right of all the People for All Time inviolable.

The Right and Duty of the juror to judge and, whenever necessary, nullify the law in Trial by Jury, are instituted as Constitutional Law by civilised nations specifically to annul tyranny. As seen in the practical experience of life today, *without* Trial by Jury, Democracy does not and cannot exist.

JURY NULLIFICATION IS A PRIVATE DECISION.

Jury Nullification is not an 'argument' which one presents; nor can it be 'disallowed'. A Right may be illegally denied and abused, but it is inherent to the life of every man and woman: it is never 'lost'.

One does not articulate Nullification in the court or the jury-room. It is a private decision: the legal and moral responsibility and duty of Citizen-Jurors *always* to prevent (i.e., nullify) the prosecution of a fellow citizen when conviction or punishment would be unfair. This is done by the Juror pronouncing the Not Guilty Verdict.

In the privacy of the jury-room, another juror may broach the topic of nullifying the prosecution on the grounds of injustice to the accused. If this is indeed the case, as many modern 'laws' and prosecutions are oppressive [i.e., illegal], then one owes spoken support to that juror. Otherwise, however, discretion is called for, because judges are known to dismiss the jury, pronouncing a 'mistrial', after jurors have informed the judge that other jurors have raised the subject of Nullification.

Jurors do not need to give a reason ever, to any person at any time, for refusing to render a verdict of guilty in the Trial by Jury.

Note the ruling of the U.S. 4th Circuit Court of Appeals, 1969 (herein on page 187), or Chief Justice Vaughan's ruling in upholding the acquittal of Quakers Penn and Mead, which pointed out that the court (trial judge) and the prosecution cannot know what evidence or reason is in the juror's mind by which he (or she) decides.

The educated good democratic person serving as a Juror adopts the overriding legal and moral duty to prevent injustice from being inflicted by the judge on the accused—one does not "ask" a lawyer, a Q.C. or the judge for permission to perform this duty. Educated citizens are aware that nowadays, the courts (judges) go out of their way premeditatedly to misinstruct Jurors and deny them their proper functions, especially that of judging on the justice of the law.

ILLEGAL "SELECTION" OF JURORS — JURY PACKING.

Today, because so many statutes which governments desire to have enforced are unfounded, partial, venal, and infringe upon people's lawful pursuits, rights and interests, citizens are 'interviewed' to exclude them from serving on juries if they admit that they would annul the enforcement of unjust laws. Nevertheless, the annulment of injustices against citizens is a moral and legal duty of the Juror's **definitive** of Trial by Jury.

People understand that the choosing of jurors *prejudiced* in favour of one party (litigant) or the other is against the common law fairness of Trial by Jury. At jury-selection interviews or by the use of questionnaires, the *ostensible* purpose of jury selection is to ensure that jurors are impartial and fair to both the defence and prosecution in judging on the facts and evidence. It would not be fair, for example, if a guilty dangerous criminal being tried, had friends, family and accomplices within the Jury !

Likewise, it is unfair and called '*packing* a jury' when the prosecution or court (judge) *selects* jurors who are predisposed to find guilt, regardless of whether this verdict would be unjust. Yet, prejudiced 'packing' takes place in countless cases to produce the verdict desired by the prosecution and government.

As shown herein, 'laws' can be, and are, illegal for a variety of reasons, such as their being inequitable [i.e., unfair], or unfounded [not founded in truth, or, technically incorrect], or prejudiced in favour of one party to the contravention of the human rights or legal interests of another. Moreover, as demonstrated by the Penn and Mead trial, to be found guilty, the accused has to have performed an act with *malice aforethought*, a criminal intention—not simply to have done something which is 'prohibited by legislation' but which is without guilt, is of no criminal intention, and is actually an act innocent of itself.

It is appropriate for people to be aware that jury packing and ex parte [i.e., one-sided] prejudice *by the court* (judge) comprise an unconstitutional and criminal modus operandi which itself exemplifies *mens rea*. Accordingly, when the potential juror is confronted by such disgraceful activities, the responsible citizen is duty-bound to take steps to defeat the criminal intentions of the court and prosecution, to redress the balance.

In order to *eliminate* your serving as a juror who would wish to uphold correct standards by nullifying bad laws and injustices, it is possible that at jury selection interviews you might be asked whether you know about Jury Nullification; or whether you would acquit the defendant if you did not agree with the law; or you think the potential penalties to be unfittingly harsh, and so on. If you consider such a process of 'Jury Selection' to be potentially or definitely prejudicial to the accused's receiving a fair trial, then you will consider it your moral obligation and legal duty to serve as a juror; and, to this end, **to thwart** any such interviews or procedures which stand in the way of your becoming a member of a jury.

To see that justice is done and to avoid being excluded from jury service, citizens are justified in responding at interviews or in questionnaires with discretion and intelligence, so that the prosecution and court have the greatest difficulty discerning, and therefore disqualifying, them. Generally, the less said the better. Do not volunteer your feelings and keep your responses to the very brief polite minimum.

GOVERNMENT FAILS THE PEOPLE
IN NOT APPRISING THEM OF THEIR RIGHTS AND DUTY.

Today, the state education system fails to teach people their most important secular adult duty: that of Juror in Trial by Jury. Hence, the raison d'être and rôle of The DEMOCRACY DEFINED Educational Organisation and Campaign for Justice (DD).

Jurors en masse operate in total absence of proper guidance and knowledge; rather, they are deliberately manipulated to produce verdicts desired by the government prosecutor. Jurors have an unimpaired sense of justice but, awed by the court's dominion and the misinstructions they receive, they do as they are told in the misguided belief that they must. The Democracy Defined Campaign hears all too frequently from or about tearful contrite jurors who are devastated to learn too late that they actively participated in tyranny and inflicted injustice because they followed the misdirection of the court. The Annulment-by-Jury Educational Campaign goes on**...**

Enlightened jurors do not go wheedling to the judge to ask whether he deigns to grant them the right to their own conscience **!** and begging 'permission'—when **it is their legal and moral DUTY** to judge on the justice of enforcement. In court, they do not kowtow when the judge misinstructs them, or tries to bully, or deny them their Rights and Duty to judge the law**...** Always remember the example of the upstanding citizens in the Penn and Mead case who set the standard for jurors and trials everywhere. Ref. The Commemorative Plaque (see page 189).

It is incumbent upon aware citizens to rectify the criminal status quo: there are countless trials-by-the-judge, i.e., false 'trials by jury', which are the modern corrupted activity of misgovernment where jurors do not know of, and are not instructed by the judge to do their duty to judge the law, the facts and decide on the admissibility of evidence.

It is encouraging to observe that there are also ACQUITTALS by responsible juries, which are examples of Jury Nullification. This has occurred in a variety of cases where the evidence against the defendant(s) has been overwhelming and irrefutable, but where the 'law' is the unfounded manifestation of ulterior motive. Such acquittals seldom receive veracious media coverage pointing out the Jurors' *duty* of Nullification whenever the Juror deems it appropriate.

Our constitutional freedoms are the achievement of morality, profound wisdom, civilisation and progress. Successive generations of our forebears unhesitatingly made the ultimate sacrifice for the sustainment of justice and these common law and constitutional freedoms. The gravitas of this is neither for the insouciant nor the faint-hearted: there is no place for appeasement, or the paying of respect where it is undue.

Our forebears knew that people are always slow to take action to resist injustice inflicted on others. As with the situation today, they experienced the fallibilities of the judiciary and tyrannical governments. With inspiration and sagacity, they responded by constitutionally emplacing the Trial by Jury [1] in which ordinary citizens make judgement in every case, civil, criminal and fiscal, on the validity of legislation and the fairness of its enforcement upon their fellow citizens.

Whereas formerly courts (judges) instructed jurors of their duties, including that of judging on the justice of the law, *nowadays*, judges go out of their way to misinstruct Jurors and deny them their proper functions, *especially* that of judging the law. Unless they are educated to their Duty *to nullify* injustice and prosecutions of unjust laws, citizens selected for jury-service cannot know of their Duty.

The Jury Nullification Principle of the Common Law Trial by Jury is not taught to Jurors or the general public because citizens would appropriately make unjust laws *unenforceable*. Educated citizen-jurors are aware of the unconstitutionality and injustice when judges automatically impose 'mandatory minimums'; or conduct interviews to exclude jurors who may nullify injustices; or preside over any process which denies Jurors' crucial functions in Trial by Jury. Educated Jurors deem it their absolute duty to nullify all such disreputable unreliable prosecutions.

1 **Exceptions only for cases of impeachment of judges and representatives.**

ARBITRATION AGREEMENTS

Only Trials by Jury can resolve lawsuits in which mens rea, i.e., a crime, is imputed by one party to another. Arbitration is acceptable—only where no party accuses another of malice aforethought or mens rea in a damaging act. Under the Constitution, the "Trial of all Crimes shall be by Jury (except cases of impeachment)." Magna Carta, The Great Charter Constitution, likewise installs the Trial by Jury for all (other than impeachable) crimes.

In all cases where a party is accused of a crime, only Trial by Jury is apposite; and where contracts or agreements are made to resolve disputes by 'arbitration' they are **voided** by the Constitutional Supreme Law. In the same way regarding health-care, negligence can be criminal where trained personnel act in such a way as is known likely to cause damages. Under the Constitution, *only* a jury in a Trial by Jury can legally decide the suit. Where a crime is imputed, judges judicably breach the Constitution who permit 'arbitration' to replace Trial by Jury.

The Subjection of Men and Rulers to the Principles of Justice.

In addition to the heads of state, presidents, prime ministers, and chief justices quoted, the following is further impartial appraisal of Magna Carta and the Common Law Trial by Jury, and by implication, of the U.S Constitution which also bases its Justice System on Trial by Jury. Sir James Macintosh (a Scot) says of Magna Carta,

"To have produced it, to have preserved it, to have matured it, constitute the immortal claim of England on the esteem of Mankind. Her Bacons and Shakespeares, her Miltons and Newtons, with all the truth which they have revealed, and all the generous virtues which they have inspired, are of inferior value when compared with the subjection of men and their rulers to the principles of justice; if, indeed, it be not more true that these mighty spirits could not have been formed except under equal laws, nor roused to full activity without the influence of that spirit which the Great Charter breathed over their forefathers."
Chapter Three of Macintosh's History of England. Emphasis added.

"The trial by jury ever has been, and I trust ever will be, looked upon as the glory of the English law. It is the most transcendent privilege which any subject can enjoy or wish for, that he cannot be affected in his property, his liberty, or his person, but by the unanimous consent of twelve of his neighbours and equals."
Emphases added. Book 3, Blackstone's Analysis of the Laws of England, p. 379.

Trial by Jury is the vital part of The Constitution, which places the liberties of the people **within their own keeping**. Of this Blackstone says:

"The Trial by Jury is that trial by the peers [i.e., equals] of every Englishman which, as the grand bulwark of his liberties, is secured to him by the Great Charter. The liberties of England cannot but subsist so long as this palladium [1] *remains sacred and inviolate, not only from all open attacks, which none will be so hardy as to make, but also from all secret machinations which may sap and undermine it."*
4 Blackstone, pp. 349-50.

Hume calls the Trial by Jury: *"an institution admirable in itself, and the best calculated for the preservation of liberty and the administration of justice that was ever devised by the wit of man."* Chapter Two of Hume's History of England.

Founded on and resulting from Trial by Jury, this British Constitutional Justice System earned respect worldwide as the finest and most democratic form of constitution and justice system ever devised; coveted by suppressed populations elsewhere.

For centuries since 1215, the English people have revered and called Magna Carta *"the Palladium* [1] *of the People's Liberties."* The Juror's Duty to judge the justice of law enforcement in Trial by Jury was the foundation of the People's sincere belief that all Britons never would be slaves; and that the United Kingdom, the United States, and the numerous post-colonial nations which constitutionally adopted the Common Law Trial by Jury Justice System, are *democracies*.

1 *Definition*, Palladium: any safeguard; a symbol, metaphorical or statuary, which represents the protection of the liberties and rights of man. Derived from Pallas Athene, Greek goddess of wisdom and war. Today, the world's most famous Palladia are the Trial by Jury, and the Statue of Liberty in New York harbour.
Ref. also Stuart: The Constitution of England. See TRIAL BY JURY for further references.

CONSTITUTIONAL TRIAL BY JURY IS THE ONLY PEACEABLE RESTRAINT OF ANTIDEMOCRATIC ILLEGAL GOVERNMENTS.

A. Governments **know** that if their laws are just, they have nothing to fear and they can have no (*good*) reason to prevent citizens from judging on their justice.

B. Consequently, the actions taken by courts and governments to prevent citizens from authoritatively judging the laws, can **only** be for the purpose of enabling government judges to enforce injustices.

Ergo: the *virulent* consequences of government denying or subverting Trial by Jury are predictable, premeditated and inevitable.

Today and throughout history, the veracity and accuracy of the aforegoing two statements and derivative logical conclusion are confirmed by the experience. The outcome of governments' violation and/or denial of Common Law Trial by Jury is that, today, as ever, local and national governments punitively enforce unjust laws and regulations on a routine basis.

Every aware adult understands the threat to their own security and well-being from despotism, and realises the vital necessity for The Democracy Defined Restoration Campaign.

"Among the Gothic nations of modern Europe, the custom of deciding lawsuits by a jury seems to have prevailed <u>universally</u>."
<u>Millar's second volume of The Historical View of English Government</u>. Emphasis added. See TRIAL BY JURY for further refs. concerning the pan-European Trial by Jury.

Apart from the British, European Peoples have, from the dismal causes of ignorance, servility and complacency, allowed unprincipled politicians to deprive them of Trial by Jury and its inimitable protections. The consequences of this political lawlessness could not be worse and are visible to all who care to look.

On the Continent, jury trials have been replaced by the illegal biased system of trial-by-the-judge. In Britain too, while politicians and their followers in law and media constantly tell people that they "live in a democracy," and to "get out and vote," the politicians put in place de facto trial-by-judges, exploiting the means by which democracy cannot exist and by which they assume power absolute. The commonest crime in Europe today is that of state-enforced injustice: it occurs incessantly everywhere.

Under Magna Carta and common law, citizens are presumed innocent until guilt is proven beyond reasonable doubt. What this means in practice is the following:

1.) The citizen cannot be stopped or detained at all by the police (no arbitrary arrest) unless evidence already exists to the commission of an offence.

2.) If such evidence exists, the police cannot detain a citizen for more than twenty-four hours without that evidence being brought before a court of law and *publicly* scrutinised. (No arbitrary detention. By common law, *wrongful* arrest, detention and penalisation are infractions; compensation becomes due to affected citizens; the state-employed and other personnel involved are accountable and suable.)

3.) Then, for a charge to be pursued, the evidence must be considered solid enough to convince *a jury*, who judges not only on the facts and evidence, but also on the validity and justice of the law and the sentence if any, in the subsequent Trial by a Jury of ordinary citizens (not state employees), the equals of the accused.

In contrast to the proper protection of citizens by common law, the Continental and "corpus juris" systems employ deceitful wording and false assurances about the "presumption of innocence." What is the truth and what they perjuriously claim are blatantly exposed: for, by the Continental systems the judge and/or police can detain a citizen for unlimited periods, weeks, months and years, without public trial and scrutiny of the evidence: *this* **is the presumption of** *guilt*.

The inhumanity and corruption that result from, and are encouraged by, the "corpus juris" type of law enforcement process are witnessed in incidents of injustice beyond number within every one of those states which have such systems. At any scale, to the individual or to the mass of people, injustice is cruel and always a crime.

Consider the innocent man wishing to obtain a plot of land on which to grow vegetables, who was maliciously accused of an "offence" by an adversary. The adversary took possession of the land whilst the innocent man was jailed and "under investigation" by the judge. Judges are frequently party to, and secretly receive benefits from, such crimes.

Consider the well-known cases of past and present national politicians keeping power by having judges incarcerate decent political rivals under trumped-up charges. This also occurs at local level. Corruption occurs everywhere when, instead of citizen-juries, state officials, i.e., judges, dictate the law. Any reasonably well-informed person can bring to mind examples from modern Russia, China, North Korea, Cuba, Argentina, Saudi Arabia, Syria, Iran, and other countries.

Whereas a generation ago the modus operandi of Western governments in relation to the citizen was arguably more legitimate, constitutional and democratic than those aforementioned, especially perhaps in regard to improving racial equality, nowadays alas, we Westerners must face the fact that politicians have completely overturned the balance. The evidence concludes that nowadays despotic oppression also pervades societies of the European Union and the United States.

Because these crimes against the People are perpetrated by state employees, that is, by individuals within the mighty apparatus of government, it becomes more and more difficult for innocent citizens to obtain justice, let alone redress from the state for abuses by the state's own personnel. Corruption becomes the 'norm', and injustice the way of life.

Instead of the state offering the opportunity to individuals to *serve* and do good for their fellows, *this* state attracts and offers gainful employment to people of the overbearing, intimidatory brutish type: it fosters carnality, crime, cruelty, inhumanity and sadism. Labour camps and prisons fill with droves of the innocent, while sisters, brothers, fathers and mothers, wretched beyond consolation, people a hate and fear-filled land ruined by despotism of the all-powerful state.

Citizen-jurors authorise and support Emergency Measures in a strictly wartime situation, but random or routine stoppage (which is a form of arrest) *without evidence or probable cause* is illegal and unconstitutional. Police thus abusing citizens perpetrate a criminal activity which obtains and deserves a punitive response from citizen-jurors (and especially so when, as today, police overstep their duty in order to try to obtain money by fines or to fulfil 'quotas').

Restoration…

By contrast, in the "corpus juris" modern police-state, the police can: stop, i.e., arrest, anybody at any time; for example, a pedestrian or a motorist, without evidence or probable cause; strip-search; blood/urine or breath-analyse; demand documents and indefinitely delay at their pleasure that innocent person from going about their legitimate business. This is without regard to the damages or inconvenience caused, and for which the citizen has no redress. Such abuses of state power are absolutely forbidden under common law and constitution.

None of this criminal misbehaviour by state employees can take place under the Constitutional Common Law Trial by Jury Justice System, which itself developed in response to the necessity of having to rein in the powers and eliminate the malevolent self-interested aims of statists [1] in positions of power. Only with the People's consent given through their verdicts in Trial by Jury does government have the executive power (i.e., of enforcement), and then only to execute in accord with the pronouncements of common law juries. Democracy *means* the People control government, not the other way around. The Trial by Jury Constitutional Justice System is the only way known to Mankind by which Democracy is achieved and maintained.

If readers ask what be the *cause* for the duplicity (albeit unclever) in the politicians' machinations by which they introduce 'Rights Conventions' and 'Bills of Rights' yet suspend Trial by Jury ?.... the answer is that the scheming politicians know exactly what they are doing, and the *cause* can be deduced from the *effect*…

Without Trial by Jury to protect the individual and hence the entire population, because *tyranny* remains within *the nature of man*, history repeats itself: what seems unimaginable (to some people) is the reality. Absolute social and political control of the People by the state is the *intended* result of systems which deny Trial by Jury, as previously imposed by tyrants and despotic political systems throughout European and world history.

There are always good citizens who adhere to an *other* outlook, way of life, economics, politics or religion, and good, freedom-loving men and women who disagree with the aims and procedures of government. However innocent or ordinary these people are, authorities fear them as rivals and regard them as political nuisances. They come to be treated as 'dissidents'. As with all the despotisms of history, ancient, medieval and current, whenever, rather than the ordinary citizens, the councillors, politicians and judges define what constitutes 'freedom' and what is 'the law', every word or act which incurs their displeasure becomes a 'crime'.

The raisons d'être for any of the inequitable and thus unlawful legislation (such as the U.S. Patriot Act), which replaces Trial by Jury with trial-by-judges or a 'no-trial' type of enforcement, are: the illegal elimination of dissent; and the organised establishment of tyranny. The *effect* of these systems is the empowerment of judges, and they 'entitle' the state to create an administration of systemised political prisons and forced labour camps for the detention and 're-education' of 'dissidents'. They mark the formal inception of the new pan-Western gulag state [2].

---

1 *Definition*, statist: one who believes in absolute control of the People by government officials in all aspects of life, social, economic and other (*as opposed to* the democrat, who believes in control of the government by the People, and, to achieve this end and protect the innocent from arbitrary government, justice being exclusively the province of ordinary citizens as jurors in Trial by Jury).

2 *Definition*, gulag: Russian acronym of a concentration camp for the detention and silencing of political prisoners. (N.B. All those held under the tyranny of unjust laws may be termed political prisoners.)

Munich Guarantees.

It is uniquely in the nature of jury trials that juries fulfil the function and purpose of law in a democratic society. These are to maintain Justice by protecting the citizen from injustice of all kinds, whether perpetrated by the state or by other citizens; and to uphold the freedom and legitimate interests of all. Under common law, the citizen is presumed innocent until hard evidence proves guilt and criminal intentions beyond a reasonable doubt in front of a jury of impartial disinterested fellow citizens. By the Continental and 'corpus juris' ex parte [one-sided] *mis*-trial system, when charged by a judge, Dutch, German, French, Italian, Spanish, etc., citizens are prejudged 'guilty' unless they can prove their innocence to the very judge by whom they are accused and detained, and whose personal interests are served by his being shown not to have been incorrect in bringing the accusation.

Apparently 'cultured', **judges past and present nevertheless 'justify' and enforce the most abject of legislation**, e.g. Nürnberg Race Laws; crime-generating intrinsically illegal 'prohibitions'; primitive 'religious' oppressions, etc. Without the Trial by Jury, no matter how many new 'Bills of Rights', 'European Conventions on Human Rights' or fabricated 'constitutions', when it comes to **justice** these legislative contrivances are *figments*: worthless, shaming pieces of paper—so many fine-worded "Munich guarantees." This is so because judges are governments' paid and bound obligants who continuously, unconscionably, and judicably enforce injustices and infract the laws and tenets which normal human decency and democratic constitutions emplace.

Every act of tyranny is a crime. By definition and in practice, tyrants are criminals. Even from a position of weakness, it is always wrong to make concessions to tyrants, for it prolongs and intensifies their criminality. *Appeasement* of tyrants is the criminal act of abetment of crime. It is insufficient for we Westerners (or indeed anyone) simply to 'denounce' the legislation and 'constitutions' of unthinking or criminal politicians. Instead, it is incumbent on all good and cerebral people everywhere **to press** their local and national political representatives to put in place that select constitution which alone secures Peace, Liberty and Justice: the Trial by Jury.

The Jury is the sole disinterested (i.e., non-governmental) constitutional body with the safeguard of a veto on unjust acts by the state. Explicitly installed by U.S. Constitution and Great Charter, the Jury's is the only *democratic* testing by the ordinary People of the country, i.e., "per pays," of the justice and validity of legislation; and the democratic judgement of every act of penal enforcement.

NOTES. I have coined "Munich guarantee" as an ironical epithet, not for that which is no guarantee, but for that which actually assures the *opposite* of what it purports to guarantee. Shortly before the commencement of the Second World War (September, 1939), following the German invasion of Czechoslovakia, British Prime Minister Neville Chamberlain visited Bad Godesberg to parley with Adolf Hitler, which resulted in the Munich Agreement (l'accord de Munich, September, 1938). France was already obliged by mutual defence pact to engage any foreign power attacking Czechoslovakia. Britain was similarly allied to France. After the indescribable slaughters of the First World War and decades of reduced expenditures on armament, the Allies' principal politicians were psychologically unready for the major armed conflict which, realistic observers warned, could only be avoided through strength, but would, by *weakness and appeasement*, become inevitable. See Winston Churchill's Nobel laureate for Literature opuses, in particular Volume One of The Second World War, "The Gathering Storm." All countries signatory to the Treaty of Versailles and/or members of the League of Nations had dishonourably allowed with impunity the German military occupation of the demilitarised Rhineland zone. This *appeasement* animated further criminal intentions. Following the subsequent German rape and dissection of Czechoslovakia, Chamberlain and others appeased the tyrant to emerge with this worthless *paper guarantee* promising *"peace in our time"*...

Restoration...

Let us all recollect the power of information as passed by the pen, the printing press and by word of mouth and now the world wide web. These are ultimately the means by which all causes succeed. It was the worthy literature of dissent which brought about the end from within of the tyrannical Soviet Union (viz. Sakharov, Sharansky, Solzhenitsyn, et al).

Knowledge and understanding of the past, of history, are valuable insofar as they lead us to form correct calculations about our present. Only by knowing the path whence we came can we discern the direction and gradient towards which we are inclined. The transitions of once-advanced communities from wealth to poverty, from knowledge to ignorance, from humanity to savagery, from freedom to slavery, can occur without dramatic events, as silent revolutions with minimal commotion.

Like statistics, facts by themselves are of no value and yield little meaning. Those employee-reporters, journalists and textbook authors who supply facts perform only the facile part of the writer's office. It is the writer's challenge and task to perceive and reveal the abstract truth when politicians, bureaucrats and others dissemble to conceal it. In politics, where ego, power and wealth are at the epicentre of transactions, human motive must always be taken into account when searching to expose the rich vein of verity from amongst the plain ore of facts, events and appearances.

The employee-editor of the news, information and education disseminated by the press, T.V. and radio media, is for obvious reasons bound to slant reportage and opinion in favour of the interests of those who are his (private or state) employers. At best this leads to gross distortion of truth; otherwise, to plain lies. Across Britain and Europe, party politicians and run of the mill journalists 'parrot' the delusive inventions of scheming legislators and writers, whose deceptions reveal that their authors, like their adherents, have never appreciated political rights and, while attaching themselves to the name of 'democracy', have never understood its definition and basis.

From this derives explanation for the fact that the philosophical and practical foundations of true democracy, i.e., the European and American People's common law and its central tenet, the Trial by Jury, are very rarely propounded today. By writings such as this, one seeks to right the balance.

Also see The DEMOCRACY DEFINED WEBSITE http://www.democracydefined.org/

The modern politicians care greatly for respect they maintain is due for their legislation which attempts social engineering by claimed political 'correctness'. Its attention to detail distracts to obscure the legislation's incorrigibility—i.e., its untruth and incorrectness beyond reform—which provokes widespread unrest, friction and violence. They should instead constitutionally emplace and leave citizen-juries to decide in each case, if indeed there be a case at all, to enforce only that which common law's common sense and fairness prescribe.

Politicians' partial laws, and the wrong rulings of their obsequious unprincipled career judiciary, are a tried and tested source of division, progressively increasing social turbulence by which ever harsher measures become engrained and complete loss of liberty inevitable. Abuse of Trial by Jury by politicians and judges is the embodiment of immorality, crime and constitutional decadence.

211

Our political 'leaders' and their camp followers undermine and destroy democracy while they allege with all enthusiasm to support it. As with all those of criminal inclinations, these people show complete indifference to truth, as much from a desire to conceal it, as from the incapacity to recognise it.

The names of 'liberty' and 'democracy' are misused by legislators as a pretext for suppressing everything which makes liberty valuable to the People: for politicians' measures obstruct and pervert the administration and course of justice; undermine tasteful values and the pursuit of excellence; stifle competition and oppose variety; discourage development of personal initiative, trade, skills, craft, and ordinary people's accumulation of property and financial independence. Vast taxation and resources are maladministered and squandered to produce nothing of authentic merit.

Like the misnamed Patriot Act, the U.K. Anti-Terrorist laws and the ludicrous (but dangerous) Euro laws, the new U.K. 'Bill of Rights' is a bad thing carefully formulated to deceive. Its authors are proud of the illusory 'liberty' which they make a show of deigning to bestow. They sacredly maintain the forms and formalities of legislative "freedom" while denying its substance. They do not understand and cannot see liberty as liberty, but as articles of institutionalised population-control law.

Already complex and mixed, our Western society is being propelled by its sordid political masters into a vortex of crime, mistrust and confrontation, concomitant with intermittent riot and violence. This is the familiar formula, the historically repeated environment which enables the demagogue to emerge and take control, with all the adverse results thereby entailed.

The U.S. Constitution's effective conceptual protections occupy a scant **8 pages** (followed by later Amendments) and similarly, Magna Carta's 63 Common Law Articles inexpugnably defending the People ***"in perpetuity,"*** **and,** ***"for ever,"*** * are rendered in ***only*** 7.
* See Magna Carta of the 15th day of June, 1215, Preamble and Article 63.

By contrast, modern legislatures shackle the population with *thousands* of pages of new restrictions and laws every year, of dubious intentions, committee-evolved double-talk, and outright despotism. After the trauma of World War II, great hopes were raised for the future of Mankind by U.N. member countries' recognition of the values scripted into the Universal Declaration on Human Rights (1948). Eleanor Roosevelt, respected widow of the U.S. president, in her speech to the U.N. assembly to inaugurate the Declaration, acknowledged *the significance of Magna Carta* by expressing the wish that the U.N. Declaration would become *"a new Magna Carta for the world."* Would that it were so !

One appreciates those good intentions voiced, but it must be understood now and for all time:

The significance of the *traditional* European constitution, that is, of Magna Carta and the U.S. Constitution, is in their installation of Trial by Jury's unique protection by its democratic legal empowering of ordinary citizens. This is acknowledged not only by those impartial intellectuals learned in the esoteric aspects of history and law (viz. the politicians, presidents, chief justices, academics and legal authorities quoted herein) but by all who have an understanding of human nature.

Restoration...

Legally and morally correct contents are subscribed by The U.N. Declaration, but tyranny bourgeons and justice remains unattainable without the constitutional emplacement and the full functioning of Trial by Jury. *Failure* of the U.N. Declaration and every other substantive (i.e., rights') charter, statute or legislation is *inevitable* unless the Common Law Trial by Jury is simultaneously installed as the exclusive mechanism of adjudication and enforcement. **Only** with Trial by Jury extant and operating as the sole Justice System for all causes, is there the sure means of the achievement of the civilised aspirations of good people.

The Americans and British have for so long enjoyed and been accustomed to political speculation and criticism of government that they cannot easily envisage the impending effects on them of the extinction of Trial by Jury. Real censorship of the writings of the press and similarly controlled reporting by other media are easily achieved by a wide variety of means in the coercive state, while at the same time the pretended protections of freedom of speech and press are proclaimed. Already today, reporting is rarely seen in mainstream media of the massive tyranny which is in place and of the crime and injustices by modern politicians.

The all-intruding despotism of Nineteenth and Twentieth Century statist theories which pervaded every social structure, mode of thought and education, gradually, but almost totally effaced the Westerner's singularly just nature and strength of character, which derived from and comprised the West's single greatest asset: the understanding by its citizens of Magna Carta and Trial by Jury's illuminating importance in the History of the World.

This phenomenon had in turn given birth to the U.S. and many other nations' Constitutions. Not since the achievement by Moses of the freedom of the Hebrews from Pharaonic bondage two and a half thousand years before Magna Carta's original enactment had such an emancipation been achieved, and nonesuch has occurred thereafter. Its present de facto eradication provides the most fateful augury, and embodies one of the worst and saddest events in Mankind's long catalogue of crime. Have the American and British people fallen so low as to allow this to happen ?

To counter the mendacity of self-serving corrupt politicians and officials, *and* the editors, journalists and media presenters employed and controlled to represent particular interests and views, may every person reading this book advise and transmit awareness to others.

From now on *beware* of and *denounce* every person who, from ignorance or self-interest, speaks well of any legislation or 'constitution' which denies or is not founded on the Citizens' Rights and Duties of the egalitarian Justice System of The Common Law Trial by Jury.

Always remember:

1.) It is dangerous naïveté to assume that the people who advocate, and already participate in intrinsically corrupt systems, are truthful, or unscheming; and

2.) It is of no avail to formerly contented free citizens, after they have been haplessly enfettered, to hear claims from those who persuaded adoption of the bonds that their intentions were for 'the best'.

RESTORATION AND UNIVERSAL ADOPTION OF TRIAL BY JURY IS THE SOLUTION AND WAY FORWARD TO A BETTER WORLD FOR ALL.

To a degree achieved by no other system of justice, Common Law Trial by Jury responds to Mankind's unceasing need: to enforce just laws; to uphold the innocent; to protect minorities; to nullify arbitrary government; and to reject injustice.

The power of government consists merely of the physical force which it brings to its support—of moral force, it has none. Western governments have decomposed into despotisms of the most primitive type. The proof of this derives from the fact that within the annual avalanche of legislation, there is hardly a single new law, regulation or amendment to law which would be welcomed by the whole populace and uniformly enforced by juries. Control of all governments by the overriding judgements and arbitration of citizen-juries is as much needed today as for any of the corrupt absolute dictators and monarchs of history whose inhumanity it was that produced the People's response: the creation and instalment of the Trial by Jury Justice System.

Politicians and judges have destroyed Trial by Jury: *politicians*, because they do not want citizen-jurors to curtail their money-motivated legislation; *judges*, because these powers aggrandise them on a permanent basis (jurors serve only momentarily, by comparison); and also because, to remain judges they must reliably enforce the unjust dictates of politicians on whom they depend for careers and salaries, and to whom they are subject by impeachment. The results of this felony by governments are witnessed in mercenary special interest legislation with numerous detrimental effects, such as: the engenderment of criminal acts comprising not less than 75 per cent of all crime in the Western world (official figures; Part Six); the interminable growth of Organised Crime; corruption of officials in positions of trust; an ethos pervaded by the misanthropy and brutality which characterise Prohibitionist-led societies; the haughty indurate attitudes of police and petty officialdom towards citizens; a crushing disincentive to Gross World Product; world poverty; famine; and the destruction and fatalities of Global Warming.

Today, rather than the citizen-jurors, while government judges run trials, *real* criminals do not receive appropriate retributive sentences, or go free, and harmless innocent citizens in their thousands are abused, fined and incarcerated. (See previous Parts.)

The juridical oath of office in no way binds judges to preside over this grisly charade which replaces Trial by Jury. Seen in precedential examples (e.g. Nuremberg Trials), following "orders" or the legislation of politicians is not an acceptable excuse for wrongdoing, *especially* tyranny. Such unquestioning allegiance never exculpates state executives who control proceedings which deny universal natural and common law; the Rightful; the just; the orthodox; the Dutiful; and the Constitutional.

Throughout the West, tyranny and kangaroo court are the reality. Today, the Rights and Duty of the jury 'exist' only in theory. In practice, these are but academic courtroom memories belonging to past generations who prized their hard-won Rights above life itself and whose leading judges (quoted herein) were people of unwavering rectitude. Trial by Jury is no more: in its place is a tidy but adulterated pretence with the trappings intact. In the U.S., U.K., Australia, Canada, New Zealand, Europe and many countries, the situation obtains wherein juries are now not allowed to judge on the justice of law. With Chief Justice Vaughan as their beacon and exemplar, contemporary judges everywhere must not consider themselves above just rebuke and, if the population awaken, arraignment; for their denial of jury Rights and Duty is not only the denial to the accused of Trial by Jury, it is always Obstruction of Justice and the denial of fair and proper trial.

Restoration...

It would be for the best if the judiciary itself publicly repents its present culpable activities and takes up the course of expiation; and resists that tyranny which precludes Trial by Jury. As citizens themselves, judges must bear their responsibility and assume the privilege or burden, if that it be, of upholding Justice, Liberty, citizens' Rights, and the Trial by Jury, at all costs to themselves. They must render unfalteringly steadfast service in the protection of tyrannised citizens, even, if needs arise, in the face of all manner of state threats and hostilities.

Without the Trial by Jurors to guard the individual and thus the entire population, the human predisposition for tyranny is unleashed: real power, subtracted from citizen-juries, devolves to every level of the state apparatus. From traffic warden, town clerk, or junior patrolman, to the justices, to the chief executive, all ranks are ceaselessly exposed to carnal and financial temptations: of utilising bullying, bribery, coercion and fear, over ordinary citizens, to flagitious advantage. Without exception, the resulting corruption is witnessed in (and definitive of) every tyranny.

Barbarian states, such as the Chinese communist or Soviet-style tyrannies, purblind intolerance and inhumanity (as also exemplified by the sebastomaniac 'religious' organisations and states [1]), are brought into being *inevitably* by disregard for and denial of the universally fair Trial by Jury Justice System. Truth, Knowledge, Justice and Liberty are suppressed in the statists' frozen, fearful society. Inexorably, the West is visibly metamorphosing into a cultural tundra and in the dismal process, is losing its moral ascendant of millennia. Only RESTORATION will reverse the morbid decline.

In a Constitutional Democracy, that is, a system of government controlled by the traditional European and Anglo-American type of constitution incorporating and based on Trial by Jury (be it in a republic or symbolic monarchy), it is the unalterable duty of government to uphold people's sovereign right to seek their own individually-defined self-fulfilment. Trial by Jury ensures that the government is controlled and society arranged so as to allow every innocent citizen unmolested tranquillity of existence and the pursuit of happiness.

In starkest contrast, the state-trial system psychologically detaches the personnel within its apparatus from the ordinary citizens. In this socially and mentally distorted environment, the reign of terror gestates. It adversely affects everyone, perverting those who govern and sorely oppressing the governed. All concentration-camp guards in the making: commissioners, politicians, bureaucrats, judiciary, police and prison service are thrust into a condemnatory brute overlordship of the ordinary citizen.

Let there be no mistaking the issue. There is no such thing as a 'benevolent dictator', which everyone learns to their cost who disagrees with the autocrat's will. Yet, in the totalitarian state, in each individual court-case, autocratic power over citizens is given to every judge. That is, in the totalitarian state (whether republic or monarchy, secular or 'religious'), despotic power is held over citizens by the state's judges: and citizens do not have the constitutional authority to annul injustices. Politicians and judges have the corrupting absolute power to decide people's liberty for them.

The result of allowing individuals or states to have such power over citizens is, without exception, always the same: democracy, decency, liberty, the cultivation of virtues and the pursuit of happiness are obliterated.

1 *Definition*, sebastomania: religious insanity.

THE DEMOCRACY DEFINED CAMPAIGN IS THE KEY.

"The great principle, that societies and laws exist only for the purpose of increasing the sum of private happiness," (see Macaulay, Essay on Machiavelli) and that *"Justice is the object of government,"* (see TRIAL BY JURY) are rules and morality lost on the unconscionably self-serving: the modern politician and judiciary.

Many citizens, righteously indignant with today's governments, find **the key** to their lawful and peaceful liberation from increasing tyranny by learning from this Campaign about RESTORATION of the Constitutional Common Law Trial by Jury Justice System. They join the Campaign and become **Educational Activists**.

What is the purpose of law (in a democracy or any state) if not to protect the citizen ? Increasingly, citizens all over the Western world are being *persecuted* by governments' employees for normal actions and everyday activities which are not crimes. This can only happen because governments have illegally denied the Citizens' protections ensured by the genuine Trial by Jury.

Juries of local citizens always have a natural regard for the compensation and care of victims of crime; and for the responsible protection of society from criminals. Under common law justice, the wrongdoer is required, according to the jury's judgement, to provide suitable recompense *directly to victims*, i.e.,, not to the government to whom fines are paid today. (For common law jury retribution, see TRIAL BY JURY, ISBN 9781902848723.)

The pernicious calumny that England (or Britain) has "no constitution," is promulgated today by individuals of parliament and judiciary, to obscure their routine violation of the 35 times ratified Great Charter Constitution by which they are bound and which installs the person's right to a Trial by a Jury of disinterested equals for every accusation or infraction. (See THE CONSTITUTION TREATISE ISBN 9781902848747.)

In order to enable governments (of any political background) to enforce unjust special interest 'laws' which would be otherwise be firmly annulled by Citizen-Jurors (i.e., made unenforceable by Jurors' refusal to find the undeserved 'guilty' verdicts), **governments conceal the Juror's Right to annul; this Right is also forbidden by judges; and our Jury Rights and Duties are deliberately not taught by the state education system**.

"There are more instances of the abridgement of the freedom of the people by gradual and silent encroachments of those in power than by violent and sudden usurpations."
James Madison, Fourth U.S. President [1].

Jury power is *indispensable*. Without it, *every* kind of injustice becomes enforceable and tyranny unstoppable (by peaceful means). **So, your country, your people, and THE DEMOCRACY DEFINED Campaign need YOU [2]**.

Amongst those who seek to 'govern', the instinctive subconscious challenges of domination and ascendancy obsess the psyche and control the behaviour of many (whether they understand themselves or not). They wish to rule and govern, not to serve and protect. They make pretence of being 'decent' to obtain votes at the infrequent ballot; but between times are a savage law only unto themselves.

1 **Virginia Convention on the ratification of the Constitution, 6th of June, 1788; 3 Elliot's Debates, p. 87.**
2 **Join us today. See Bibliography for details.**

Restoration...

Measured by the universally accepted values of equity, natural law and justice, these government people's ulterior agenda (exposed in Parts One through Six) reveals them for what they really are: generally and privately unscrupulous, acquisitive of money, fame, power and material possessions; dishonest and mendacious; disloyal, avaricious, covetous, licentious, faithless, proud and cruel. This should not come as a surprise though, for *only* such people could cause, participate in and tolerate the debasement of Trial by Jury.

In assimilating the aforegoing assessment, the reader will notice that there is nothing to distinguish between these 'politicians' and the common criminal or gangster; and yet, these are the individuals who we allow, and even select to run, or rather run down, our Western societies. To operate, they simply rely upon a façade of 'respectability'.

These people do not truly espouse virtues and values; rather they despise them: faith, hope, charity (love), prudence, honesty, selflessness, temperance, loyalty, fortitude, justice, liberty, service, generosity and real fairness to one's fellow man. Fortunately, the people at large know these virtues, and they have a firm hold on their minds. Otherwise, there would be nothing left to save of our Western culture. Nevertheless, more and more individuals from all strata of society succumb to the omnipresent malevolent influence of our decadent politicians and judges.

From society's putrescent 'top', the ophidian politicians' and judges' criminal macro-perversion and obstruction of the course of justice insidiously vitiate, invading and infecting the population, producing direst results at all levels. Led by the example of these self-serving ambitious ruthless degenerates, it is small wonder that Western society is visibly degrading, as seen in the deteriorating standards of behaviour and the fraught urban social flux.

The People would vehemently reject these crooks in government and the big political parties, if they but knew them for what they are. They would look for and find the valid alternative. So, while they can, the political gangs subvert the civilised precepts of salvation (of all Mankind) and, in order to strengthen their grip on power, replace them with their pernicious nonsense misnamed 'political correctness'. They erode and try to obliterate the wondrous concepts, commandments and accumulated wisdom of our great cultural heritage. They scoff at and ridicule the goodness of proven values for which generations of our finest forebears fought and died, but won and preserved for us. These abject contemporaries of ours presume to sow the wind—may they reap the whirlwind...

RESTORATION and Universal Adoption are indispensable to the well-being of the People and the Survival of Democracy. Let citizens unite to ensure RESTORATION of proper common law Trial by Jury. This would constrain judges and all due processes to function according to common law; and compel judges to instruct Jurors about, and to apply, the Right and Duty to judge the justice of law.

In a perfect world, Utopia, inhabited by perfectly incorruptible beings and where mistakes are never made, laws passed would be immaculate and no safeguards or checks upon them would be required. In a perfect world, of course, laws themselves would be superfluous. Democratic government generally attempts to enact legislation that is approved of by or is acceptable to the majority of the population. However, in the real world (not Utopia) majority assent of itself does not invest legislation with legitimacy or virtue, regardless of its support, e.g. Nürnberg Nazi Race Laws. If Trial by Jury had been operating in the Third Reich, the Nazi tyranny would have been truncated, the Holocaust and the Second World War pre-empted.

One of the most telling causes leading to the Abolition of Alcohol Prohibition in the U.S. in 1933 was that prosecutions for breaking the Prohibition on commercial activities of Production and Sale (smuggling and dealing) i.e., the 'decriminalisation' form of Prohibition controls, increasingly failed to obtain guilty verdicts. Juries *nullified* prosecution of what they deemed unjust law. In the last four years of Alcohol Prohibition, approximately half such trials (higher percentages were noted in parts of the U.S.) resulted in acquittal or hung juries, although defendants invariably had broken the law, often being apprehended *in flagrante delicto* ('red-handed').

Nowadays, to prevent a recurrence of Not Guilty verdicts being rendered by juries in the cannabis context, as happened with Alcohol Prohibition, judges instruct juries to uphold the 'law' and convict the accused whether or not jurors consider the law unjust; judges deny the defence exposition of inequitable aspects of selective controls; judges veto defence evidence, forbidding presentation of official documentary clinical exoneration of cannabis; judges exclude all disputation of whether the 'law' is legal. False 'guilty' verdicts are inevitably produced by judges' criminal tampering. This callous mistrial by government and government employees, **exemplifies**:

1.) *how government employees are never to be relied upon to prevent the enforcement of injustices*; and

2.) *conversely, how government employees are predictable in that they can be relied on to enforce government 'laws' however unjust*;

3.) *how every type of 'trial' or 'due process' everywhere, presided over or administered by government employees proves to be a corrupted façade*; and that

4.) *Trial by Jury is indispensable, requiring* Universal Adoption.

Without jurors' appraisal and approbation, *every* sentence is suspect and unlawful. The requirement for jurors' to judge on the law is inexpugnable. In every criminal, civil or fiscal lawsuit (everywhere), law and enforcement cannot be said to be legitimate unless the law and enforcement have been subjected to Trial by Jury.

Judged by the universally accepted civilised standards of the common law, the West, now bereft of genuine Trial by Jury, is in a state of Prohibition-induced degenerative 'free fall' (ref. A Closer Look). The mass of people will only realise that this was so, too late, on destructive impact if it hits bottom. But inertia can be overcome: the trend may be *reversed immediately* by re-establishment of particular cultural attitudes and practical procedures, *at the core of which is Trial by Jury*. Present-day loss of Common Law Trial by Jury is symptom and cause of gradual, but terminal, extinction of the benevolent culture which brought it into being.

RESTORATION of Trial by Jury to its true form in full vigour would be a profound Act of Survival, of self-preservation of the individual, the society, and the culture known as Democracy.

Being 'democratic' and 'civilised' is a state of existence not measured by material standards. (Tyrants are by definition uncivilised, but possess more than everyone else.) Trial by Jury is intrinsic to and justification for Constitutional Democracy as the civilised method of human organisation, embodying the Justice System without equal, a superior creation of Mankind. Trial by Jury is an inspiration of democratically advanced Culture. Its roots are as deep within us as the natural law of The Ten Commandments, at the base of every human concept of decency, fairplay and Liberty.

Those who undermine Trial by Jury and who do not actively support its Universal Adoption, abet tyranny, crime, and the law of the jungle; they vitiate Mankind's peaceful progress and the compassionate aspirations of human civilisation; they foster inhumanity, promote strife and personify injustice: they are the visible foes of all democratic people.

~

The Sentence of Curse and Excommunication

The following is of interest to Catholics and scholars of politics and history:

With publicity and self-congratulation, the U.K. government introduces a new 'Bill of Rights' *to obscure its tyranny and crime* of simultaneously producing legislation to remove the Right to a Trial by Jury from numerous categories of accused persons.

For a government to 'remove' or deny Trial by Jury, the principal, the unique and the only effective mechanism ever created by Mankind for peacefully protecting citizens from tyranny, demonstrates that the indictable ongoing *real* intention of government is to enforce tyranny. In Britain, as elsewhere, there is no (*good*) reason to suppress Trial by Jury: only corrupt intentions, mens rea.

NOTA BENE: Unless *unanimously* revoked by the Will of all the English People themselves, the constitutional authority of Magna Carta, The Great Charter of English Liberties, stands *forever* as the Supreme Law of the Land.

Magna Carta legally binds government and judiciary. The installation of Trial by Jury and the Common Law Articles imposed on governments by Constitutional Law Magna Carta were taken so seriously by all the People as to incur the most complete punishment and damnation known, Excommunication, upon every individual or government, who, from that moment on, at any time, breaches or in the smallest way undermines Magna Carta's strictures. Excommunication is a life-threatening modus vivendi of internal exile, spiritual damnation and social disgrace which separates the convict recipient from all familial, social and religious communication with other members of society.

At the 1253 ratification, all the legislative assembly, including Henry III, monarch, bishops and barons, ratified Magna Carta *and* The Sentence of Curse and Excommunication on infractors of Magna Carta. The Curse and Sentence were pronounced by Boniface, Archbishop of Canterbury. To read the Curse, see Statutes of the Realm, Volume 1, page 6; & Ruffhead's Statutes, Volume 1, page 20; & page 197 of TRIAL BY JURY ISBN 9781902848723.

Authors' note: This execration was pronounced by the Universal Catholic Church, i.e., before the 16th Century schism. "Vengeance is mine," saith the Lord, so we leave the richly deserved eternal damnation of our politicians' souls to those whose concern it be: but for their temporal Crimes against Peace and Humanity, and for the ruin of our societies, we hereby indict them and all their abject works.

In regard to Cannabis: The Facts, Human Rights and the Law,

1.) (i) As established by incontrovertible facts, law, evidence, reason, philosophy, equity, with the proper operation of Trial by Jury, juries would not have permitted the enforcement of the money-motivated Prohibitions.

Not only would more than one-in-twelve of the jurors at any given trial have found it impossible to find "guilt," but most juries, on being correctly allowed to peruse the official evidence (collated herein), would unanimously have found: A.) the 'laws' of commodity Prohibitions, the War on Drugs, to be unlawful, i.e., criminal; and B.) all the acts of related enforcement of this legislation to be crime per se.

(ii) With legislation of Prohibitions rendered a dead letter by citizen-juries, the crime engendered by Prohibitions, that is, the greater part of all peacetime crime since circa 1914 (Harrison Narcotics Act, etc.), would not have occurred.
(Ref. Prohibition: The Progenitor of Crime; Part Six.)

2.) (i) The inequitable Prohibitions would have been rendered unenforceable and abolished, were it not for the malfeasant connivance of the judiciary and lawyers in *denying* accused citizens Constitutional Common Law Trial by Jury. (Ref. Part Seven.)

(ii) Knowing common law juries would have rejected enforcement of all unfair 'legislation', governments would not have even contemplated its introduction.

(iii) As a result of governments' perversion of the Constitutional Justice System to render juries impotent to nullify enforcement of unjust, unlawful 'laws', today, many unjust civil, fiscal (taxation) and criminal 'laws' and 'regulations' are in place and illegitimately enforced. Had Trial by Jury been faithfully maintained by our political 'representatives', this persecution and suffering of millions of citizens would never have occurred. Politicians and judiciary bear the punishable Guilt for these injustices.

3.) If Jurors' Constitutional Rights and Duty had been maintained, this would have resulted in the nullification and rescindment of Prohibitions, including that of cannabis. Cannabis sativa provides the cheapest and most prolific source of fuel-energy. The judicable mens rea (criminal intent) of the politicians' crime of illegal denial of Annulment-by-Jury (Nullification) has resulted in Global Warming.
(Ref. The Cannabis Biomass Energy Equation; Part Two.)

4.) Apropos of Global Warming, Cannabis Prohibition is the racket of a government-corporate covert monopoly on fuel-energy.

Had cannabis remained legally accessible under normal competitive market conditions for production of relaxant-medication, paper, timber/tree substitutes, staple seed food, fibre, Dresden Cotton, textiles, concrete building material; and Mankind's cheapest resource to lubricants, plastics and fuel, Cannabis-Methanol, which is also non-polluting (no net increase of 'greenhouse' gases), *then*; in assessing the damage done to society and the individual by government, consider that since the time of:

A.) worldwide *misuse* of fossils as 'fuel' for electricity-generation, and,
B.) worldwide utility of the internal combustion engine for transport, that is to say:

Since the Nineteen-Twenties and 'Thirties, **<u>all the fossils commercially misused as 'fuel'</u> would have remained underground. Global Warming would today not be a problem...**

RESTORATION unites all honest people...

"The power of the Executive to cast a man into prison without formulating any charge known to the law, and particularly to deny him the judgement of his peers, is in the highest degree odious and is the foundation of all totalitarian government whether Nazi or Communist."
<u>Sir Winston Churchill</u>, 1874-1965, Author, Chronicler, Historian, Philosopher, Nobel laureate for Literature; Prime Minister of the United Kingdom; excerpt from a telegram from Cairo to the U.K. Home Secretary on November the 21st, 1943.

RESTORATION and Universal Adoption of Trial by Jury are the duty of every citizen who wishes to nullify tyranny in order to live in and pass on to our children a free civilised World.

The trial-by-judges technique of tyranny requires to be truthfully explained to populations everywhere, for the injustice it embodies, the servility it imposes, and the maelstrom of crime, corruption, misery and strife it always engenders. Given the choice, nowhere is this uncivilised mode acceptable, even to people in the rudest state of development; still less to citizens in a condition of relative enlightenment. Trial by Jury is relevant to every race, nation and society on Earth, bar none.

Trial by Jury is unique: there is no alternative and no substitute. Appeasement of tyranny leads to ultimate calamity. For all Time, each successive generation of men and women has to find the moral conviction, and courage, to save themselves. The Torch of Freedom is rekindled and passed on. Whatever its specious camouflage, resurgent tyranny must be recognised, exposed, and annihilated. The sooner, the better, for then the process of Resistance and Restoration is less sanguine.

Good people everywhere, when educated to the purpose and virtues of Jurors' judgement on the justice of law, reject the one-sided state-inquisitorial system and support Universal Adoption of Trial by Jury. Civilisation, sine qua non, *needs* constitutional emplacement of Common Law Trial by Jury. Funding requires to be allocated, education and emphasis given, swiftly to achieve Universal Adoption.

For many centuries right up to date, no system has been thought up, let alone emplaced, that approaches the efficacy of Common Law Trial by Jury in protecting citizens from crime and arbitrary government. History explains and present-day experience confirms: protection and justice cannot exist while due process remains the jurisdiction of state-employees.

No new 'Bills of Rights' are needed anywhere, when Jurors, backed by enforcement, decide which laws are just, and which government measures may not be enforced.

In Britain and the United States, legislation remains permanently subordinate to the discretion and consciences of Common Law Juries in all causes, civil, criminal and fiscal. This remains true, even if governments disband the vestiges of Trial by Jury and completely inflict the mistrials and miscarriages of justice of the state-trial system; for their actions are usurpations and their imposed methods are totalitarian and illegal.

The first act of Survival is to become *aware*: to forestall low motives in politicians and government employees who subvert Trial by Jury, and who thereby destroy the achievements and ascent of our Democratic Fathers. Let us anticipate **the awakening** of our Peoples to their Duty: **Resistance and Restoration**.

Without Trial by Jury in place, no dramatic event is required for democracy to be replaced by tyranny: men and women become enslaved by their insouciance to the ambitions, and plight, of others; and by allowing their minds to dwell on distractions. Roman Emperors knew well that sufficient "bread and the games" generally kept populations tranquil and subject to their bloody, capricious rule.

Are wage-slavery and materialism, video-voyeurism, professional 'sport' and the owned and controlled mass media, to be the "bread and games" of the Twenty-first Century ? or will good people awaken in time to save Trial by Jury and Western Democracy from the takeover of criminal opportunist arrogation ? No less is at stake. *Without* Trial by Jury's curtailment of tyranny, the state permanently offers an arena to the aspiring demagogue. In the age of mass media and electronic communication, control of the public consciousness is easier than ever. Be aware that even the word "government" malconditions the mind and subjugates the individual spirit.

Today, an unelected (generally concealed) plutocracy [1] served by self-seeking politicians and an unconscionable judiciary are the reality. The situation recalls the last stages of free Republican Rome as it metamorphosed into an autocracy. Suffrage (electoral voting) cannot avert that dread event (or one that parallels it) from recurring—only Trial by Jury can prevent this peacefully. Our Western democratic nation-states are falling prey to criminal government. Unlike the Romans, History gives us the benefit of hindsight. We need not repeat their mistakes. However, in this issue, the majority of the Western population is passive and completely *unaware*, because people are mentally self-manacled slaves of the newly materialist West. With their minds prepossessed and without a whimper, in the unblissful manipulated servitude of automatons and marionettes, individually, and thus the entire people, capitulate the last turrets of their ascendant culture of millennia, to the enemy within.

The upright citizen everywhere owes fundamental and supreme loyalty to moral and legal Principles, such as the Duties of Jurors in Trial by Jury, by which a civilised state is brought into being, and without which Justice is denied. May the People take action to redress this shameful extinction by politicians and state functionaries of democratic civilisation's greatest institution: the Trial by Jury.

Today, as throughout history, whenever the citizen's Jury Nullification Duty is suppressed by courts or despots, it is to serve a *criminal*, and frequently venal, motive of the government and others implicated. Nowadays, the intention of the denial of the Jury Nullification Duty is to establish despotic enforcement of money-motivated tax and drug statutes *and* to maintain hegemony over the supply of fuel-energy, which accounts for circa four-fifths (4/5) of the Cost of Production of Gross World Product; see Universal Re-Democratisation of Fuel-Energy Production in Part Two.

The legislation of the War on Drugs is untruthful, unfounded, inequitable and hence illegal. If this conspiracy is to succeed, government requires to perpetrate the illegal suppression of the proper functioning of Constitutional Trial by Jury, and especially its central tenet: Annulment-by-Jury (nullification). Otherwise, Juries will certainly come to annul the criminal Prohibitionists' War on Drugs subterfuge which is disguised as 'law'.

1 Plutocracy, government by the wealthiest members of society; also ref. p. 152.

Restoration…

Increasingly, this modern suppression of Trial by Jury has been intended to obliterate personal freedom-with-responsibility and re-form the mentality of the population: to subjugate people into subservience to the rule of the plutocratic minority. Politicians and parties who rely on **funding** are **always** susceptible to perversion, into following the interests and behind-the-scenes dictates of the few wealthiest people. This observation remains true even in the socialist-communist societies, for, where government controls the means of production and distribution of wealth [and that is the definition of socialism], the top politicians and government *themselves* become the embodiment of plutocracy. (Viz. Red China today.)

Petty tyranny, every act of oppression on citizens inflicted by individuals working for the state, is a microcosmic exemplification of Mankind's propensity to conflict and war. The question is raised whether the Orwellian doom is to be their lot, or whether good men and women will take tyrants down and save Democracy. Tyranny is in the nature of Man. Trial by Jury is the only effective measure known to Man, *pre-emptive* of tyranny. Tyrants' self-interested aims are not realisable and no tyrant can attain power. Constitutional Trial by Jury requires to be established through the United Nations' Organisation for simultaneous worldwide, i.e., Universal Adoption on a given date…

Only then do worldwide elimination of tyrannies and the Crimes against Humanity by politicians and governments, and permanent relative peace on Earth become feasible.

Had Trial by Jury been faithfully maintained and *Universally Adopted*, Twentieth Century History would have been of international Peace, of Fraternity, Prosperity, Justice, Liberty, Egalitarianism and Progress. The Hohenzollern and Hitler tyrannies, World Wars, the Holocaust, the Stalinist, Amin, Saddam Hussein, Pol Pot and countless other wars and oppressions, great and small, *could not have occurred*: such régimes of injustice cannot subsist alongside, and are nipped in the bud by, Trial by Jury.

If the exemplary human achievement of the Common Law Trial by Jury Justice System had been kept in place (for other nations of the World to emulate), the West would never have experienced much corruption and real crime; and, for centuries, tyrannies, local wars and extreme governments would all have been precluded. The World would have been a different and a better place in which to have lived, and the future would be looked forward to with confidence, pleasure, optimism and satisfaction.

The continuing illegal act by governments of denying and/or destroying Common Law Trial by Jury is the gravest of crimes which calls for utmost **Resistance**: all citizens have the Right and the Duty to take appropriate actions to terminate the crime and tyranny, and to achieve **RESTORATION**. Mankind will not, and cannot, find the psychological and social environment acceptable until Common Law Trial by Jury is Restored and Universally Adopted.

As to the future, without consummate **RESTORATION**, there are no bounds to the continuing inevitable future tyranny by Man of Man. Trial by Jury was the concept of and gift to us from our ancestors. Its **RESTORATION** is well within the wit and capacity of Humankind: Let the Third Millennium be aright with Universal Adoption.

~

RESTORATION: The Program.

RESTORATION is endorsed and supported by honest citizens, academics, authors, professors, doctors (of Medicine, Jurisprudence, Psychiatry, Physiology, Philosophy, Homeopathy), judges (U.S. & U.K.), Ecology and Economics' experts. In the Cannabis context, Restoration is comprised of Relegalisation, Amnesty and Restitution.

Relegalisation: legislation for the **Restoration** of the normal status of Cannabis to that which obtained before the introduction of any controls. (Ref. Parts One and Five of The Report.)

Amnesty, an act of oblivion: retroactive legislation containing explicit recognition that Prohibition of Cannabis was and is Tyranny, its enactment and every prosecution being the commission by the state, of Crimes; Crime Against Humanity, Crime Against Peace, of ex parte Tampering, Perjury and Subreption, amongst others, and that all acts of enforcement against, and penalisation of, solely Cannabis related activities were and are Malicious and Wrongful; the immediate unconditional release of all imprisoned solely for cannabis related activities; full pardon and the expunction of criminal records on Cannabis related activities. (Ref. all Parts.)

Restitution: retroactive legislation; the act of Restoring that which was taken away; return of Fines and refund of Costs (at current value); indemnification, reparations to make good for damage done; redress by monetary Compensation (as for other Wrongful Penalisation); **Restitution** also includes:

1. State-funded, mass public education to disperse essential knowledge and restore the esteem due Cannabis for its benign, life-saving, Health-promoting qualities as Personal Relaxant, as Preventive Measure, as Preventive Medicine and as Curative Medicament (ref. Parts One, Three & Four); public recognition, including at presidential and prime ministerial level, of Cannabis as the single safe Personal Relaxant, and recommended recreational substance of sensible choice. (Ref. Parts One to Five.)

2. **A.** State-funded, mass public education on THE CANNABIS BIOMASS ENERGY EQUATION (CBEE) formulation in THE REPORT of The FCDAE, which demonstrates Cannabis-Methanol (etc.) is the production-cost-free and completely non-polluting resource, and economical replacement for costly pollutant fossils misused as 'fuels', and uranium, in the generation of electricity and provision of fuels for all requirements, domestic, industrial and transportation; education on The CBEE to include dispersal of knowledge on how Cannabis RELEGALISATION and utilitisation contribute positively to world Ecology by the reduction of Global Warming and stabilisation of weather. (Ref. Part Two.)

   B. State-funded, mass public education on the numerous other market macro-economic applications of cannabis to compete with and replace inferior resources and products, cannabis being renewable, high quality, superior resource to, e.g. staple seed food; *production-cost-free* products: the Standard Fibre of textiles; Dresden Cotton ®; paper and card (replacing use of trees); economical superior lightweight 'mineralised' concrete building materials; *production-cost-free* resource to cellulosic polymers (plastics) and petro-chemical products; etc. (Ref. Part Two.)

3. The RESTORATION AND UNIVERSAL ADOPTION OF CONSTITUTIONAL COMMON LAW TRIAL BY JURY.

See The Form of Trial by Jury prescribed by Common Law and the U.S. Constitution, and defined by U.K. Constitutional Law Magna Carta, in TRIAL BY JURY: Its History, True Purpose and Modern Relevance. Also see Part Seven of THE REPORT.

A. (Universal) legislative instatement of Constitutional Common Law Trial by Jury, requiring all courts to participate in the full education of Jurors prior to and during trial, to ensure Jurors put into practice the Full Rights and Duty of Jurors to find the Verdict (not only on the Facts but also) specifically by making judgement on the justice of the law; including instruction so to do by the presiding judge.

B. Legislative instatement of the Defendant's Right and Defence lawyers' Right to dispute the legitimacy of legislation in front of the Jury, in seeking and presenting the Whole Truth. Jurors to judge on the admissibility of evidence. State-funded, mass public education on the aforegoing items. (Ref. Parts Six & Seven.)

4. The socially beneficial deterrent to recurrence of restrictions on Cannabis, by the execution of Due Process, whereby the Crime of Tyranny of Prohibition of Cannabis be terminated; and by which to bring before the public those responsible for the said Crime; and where appropriate, do justice. (Ref. all Parts.)

NOTA BENE:

I. (i) Having perused the historical and modern background (ref. TRIAL BY JURY; ISBN: 9781902848723) readers appreciate Common Law Trial by Jury has been the established system for settling civil, criminal and fiscal lawsuits for millennia, since before written history, throughout the Hellenic, Roman, Anglo, Saxon, Scot, Frank, i.e., French, German, Dane, Jute, Swede (all Scandinavian), Lombard, Russian, Pole, Dutch, Flemish, Schweizer i.e., Swiss, Gael, Breton, Manx, Cornish, Irish, Pict, Cymric i.e., Welsh, Celt, Norman, Viking, Visigoth (Spanish), Ostrogoth, Goth (modern Greek and Italian), Teuton, Marcomani, Allemani, Burgundian, Gepidæ, etc., races and nations of Europe. (For Origins of the Northern People, see Gibbon's Decline and Fall of the Roman Empire.)

Despite the gravest aberrances, Germanic, i.e., European/Gothic/Nordic Peoples[1] have a long democratic tradition: antecedent Trial by Jury in which the juror has the power, the Right and the Duty to judge on the justice of law in finding the Verdict, was guaranteed by <u>Emperor Conrad of Germany</u> two centuries before Magna Carta. To annul the tyranny of government enforcement of unjust laws, from time immemorial the Trial by Jury has been part of the law of the land, and was in use amongst the northern tribes and later, throughout the modern nations of Europe. The Anglo-Saxons and Normans were familiar with it before they settled in England. Various laws had been set down in writing but in re the law of the land, in Britain until Magna Carta the government was bound only by oath. Verbal contracts have never been easy to prove, still less to enforce. Citizens had no protection from governments bent on injustice, and no possibility of redress from oppression by the state. A commitment in writing takes on an altogether different aspect. Magna Carta acquired signed assent by the Head of State, entrenching into the Constitution of the Realm that every citizen facing prosecution would *always* receive the Trial, not by government employees, but *by a Jury of equal citizens who judge in every case on both the law and the facts, specifically for the purpose of ensuring that injustice to citizens, by representatives of the state and arbitrary laws, should never prevail.*

1 **See Edward Gibbons' Decline and Fall of the Roman Empire, for exposition on the Origins of the European/Gothic/Germanic Peoples, die Deutsche Bevölkerung.**

THE REPORT. CANNABIS: THE FACTS, HUMAN RIGHTS AND THE LAW.

Since before the beginnings of History, the People of the European, or Northern Nations, have never willingly surrendered to any Justice System other than Common Law Trial by Jury. Trial by Jury prevailed for so long because it is uniquely fair, the proven Just system. The democratic superiority and indispensability of Trial by Jury are acknowledged by *all impartial people*, from ordinary citizens to Heads of State, judges, presidents, and chief justices. Elimination of Trial by Jury by unthinking or corrupted politicians and bureaucrats represents a philistine regression to a state of primitive government totalitarianism over the *entire* Continent such as has never before existed, despite the repeated conquerings of tyrants and empires. Imposition by politicians and bureaucrats throughout the European Union of the intrinsically unjust, inherently illegal state-inquisitorial system, the 'trial' by government-employees, is an *absolute* tyranny anew on the European scene.

In Britain in particular, by Constitutional Law governing the way in which the People may be governed, no government, legislature or judiciary has legal authority: to deny or 'legislate' away the Right of the accused (for any alleged infraction of law or regulation), to a trial by a jury of peers in the People's Common Law Trial by Jury; nor to change the oaths, nor to impair or abridge the powers, rights and duties of Jurors to preside and judge both the law and the facts, and to decide on admissibility of evidence; to ascertain mens rea, if any, and to set the sentence.

In Europe, where TRIAL BY JURY is concerned, **Restoration** is the apt word: **"Among the Gothic nations of modern Europe, the custom of deciding lawsuits by a jury seems to have prevailed universally."** (Millar's second volume of The Historical View of English Government, p. 296 [1].)

In Germany, **"The Graff (gerefa, sheriff) placed himself in the seat of judgement, and gave the charge to the assembled free Echevins [jurors], warning them to pronounce judgement according to right and justice. The Echevins composed of the villanage (villagers) were still substantially the judges of the court."** (2 Palgrave's Rise and Progress of the English Commonwealth; 147-8 [2].)

1 & 2 See TRIAL BY JURY, for other examples and references.)

(ii) References to historical precedents and to European ethnic groups do not exclude people who have come from other parts of the world to make Britain, or Europe, their home. RESTORATION is based on Principles, universal fundamental truths upon which others are founded or from which they spring: Truth (Knowledge), Justice, Liberty, Fraternity, Egalitarianism; on natural law, natural justice, the common law, the Constitution, Human Rights, and the Trial by Jury. These concepts and RESTORATION are *inclusive to all* who cherish them.

(iii) Trial by Jury, prescribed by the U.S. Constitution and by U.K. Constitutional Law Magna Carta, and prescribed *universally* by the common and the natural law, is so significant a creation for the betterment of Mankind's modus vivendi, that grave problems now confronting the human race would not have accrued at all, had the Trial by Jury been universally adopted; and had Trial by Jury not been tampered with by governments in nations where it was once emplaced. (See GLOBAL WARMING: The Scientific Green Solution to this World Crisis; ISBN: 9781902848068.)

(iv) The Trial by Jury British Justice System is revered at home and respected abroad as embodying the finest and most democratic form of law enforcement ever devised. Intended also for enforcement of just laws and apportioning retribution, the extra, special virtue of Trial by Jury is in its duty-bound obligations on the citizen-*jurors to judge, by their own consciences*, in every individual criminal, civil and fiscal lawsuit, on: the *justice* of law and acts of enforcement; and, *to annul injustice*, i.e., Jury Nullification, to protect citizens from arbitrary government, *by pronouncing* the Not Guilty Verdict.

Trial by Jury is an anti-racist, anti-sectarian egalitarian phenomenon, which militates on behalf of Good against Evil. Where practised, Trial by Jury educates, cultivates and propagates those higher human concepts, natural justice, liberty and equity, essential to Civilisation. Liberty can best—and only—be ensured by Trial by Jury, for it constitutes the mechanism by which all other Rights are protected, and thus on which *all Rights depend*. The Trial by Jury Justice System is the foundation, and definitive, of true Democracy, sine qua non; and of the European and United States Culture; it is exalted, and was adopted by nations worldwide, constituting the sublime historic cultural legacy unique to the Empire of the British. Only people of real ignorance, or worse, of *mens rea*, deny or derogate this history, and blindfold citizens to Trial by Jury's universal common law Jurors' Rights. While *individuals* within Empire were fallible, far from discovering an ideal world and 'suppressing' populations, the secular Colonial Service and selfless missionaries found, and liberated peoples from repressive primitive quasi-religion, lapidation, etc.; ubiquitous sanguivolent tyrannies; economic unfreedom; slavery; suttee; and, in places, cannibalism.

Slavery embodies criminological aspects of Man's inhumanity to Man: violence; subjection; exploitation. Since before written history, Slavery existed in every society on Earth, and in a variety of forms persists today (ref. U.N.O. publications). In 1803, the British, *who were then nurtured in the liberating beliefs and societal ethos generated by their "palladium of liberties," i.e., the Trial by Jury*, abolished the Slave Trade throughout the British Empire. Then, in 1833, the British were the first to render possession of slaves illegal, by the Abolition of Slavery. **Inhumanity cannot subsist in an institutionalised or formalised way, in societies where genuine Common Law Trial by Jury is fully in place.** Conversely, all forms of exploitation, crime and inhumanity flourish in societies where Trial by Jury is undermined or denied. Trial by Jury protects and liberates, by emancipating every innocent individual from subjection. Future generations and historians seeking to understand our times that they may ameliorate their own, can gain nothing from the ubiquitous shallow accounts reflecting the almost universal untruth which surrounds us *today*. The unique Trial by Jury Justice System has been premeditatedly destroyed by malicious governments throughout Continental Europe, where it originated, and by despotic post-colonial régimes in general worldwide, and amongst the English-Speaking Peoples in particular, *directly* bringing the whole of Mankind, *and* the Ecosphere within which we all survive, to Crisis. The books of **The RESTORATION Trilogy** conduce to a shared objective: Restoration and Universal Adoption of Common Law Trial by Jury by all people and countries.

II. A. (i) Where a 'law' and its enforcement are illegal, as with the controls on cannabis, all people persecuted under its prosecution are due compensatory Restitution for their Grievance. Insistence on this Justice is essential—it is incumbent on all citizens to unite resolutely, to end the socially malignant and ecologically disastrous Tyranny of Cannabis Prohibition, which is a government-corporate duty, tax and profit-protection Conspiracy (Racket; U.S.). (Ref. Motive, THE REPORT, ISBN 9781902848167.) When the 'law' is wrong, i.e., illegal, it is weak, inconsistent and wrong not to insist upon consummate Restitution.

II. A. (ii) **Restitution *cannot apply to repayment of black marketeers' confiscated financial gains***: people's energies are required to be expended towards RESTORATION, in active **Resistance** to corrupt Prohibitions, not towards exploiting the illegal Prohibition and becoming partner to its crime. Nevertheless, by common law, import-export, cultivation, sale, etc., are innocent acts, never crimes: those penalised therefore are due normal compensation as for Wrongful Penalisation.

II. B. No Special Taxes Required for Implementation of Restitution:

(i) **Relegalisation** produces great savings to the Exchequer: the state expends huge sums annually on Prohibition propaganda and enforcement. Approximately half of all prisoners in Western jails are incarcerated for "drug" [sic] charges of which about 80 per cent are for cannabis related activities. Savings would also be made which are now spent on unnecessary police deployment, interdiction, prosecutions, Legal Aid defences, and on the courts. Relegalisation leaves vast sums available for Restitution.

II. B. (ii) In re Cannabis, on Health grounds, duty (sale tax), special taxes, trading licences, etc., can never be justified. Fiscal measures and all controls (i.e., Prohibitions) vitiate the herb's beneficial *life-saving* potential by *regular* use, to achieve mitigation, moderation and replacement of use of drugs: addictive, often-fatal pathogens alcohol, tobacco; toxic pharmaceutical drugs; heroin, morphine, etc. (Ref. Preventive Measure/ Medicine, in THE REPORT.) N.B. Fiscal measures are covert (illegal) schemes to protect government revenues and selected private Owners' profits, gained from sales of inferior and toxic products, by making benign Cannabis too expensive to consumers for regular use. (Ref. Parts Two, Three & Four of THE REPORT.)

(iii) Post-sale corporation and income taxes levied on profits from normal trade in commercial products of Cannabis would also render significant monies for Restitution. The number of Grievances to be processed is finite. Once Restitution has been made, savings described in II. B. (i), and revenues from tax on income and profits, continue to be available to the Exchequer for other social applications.

III. Democracy Re-Affirmed; Retro-Active Legislation.

A. (i) Common Law requires Trial by Jury to be the sole Justice System for settling all causes, civil, criminal and fiscal, i.e., all other systems, such as trial-by-the-state tribunals, etc., are one-sided and inherently illegal. Ref. TRIAL BY JURY, ISBN: 9781902848723.

(ii) To protect minorities, and for juries democratically to reflect the diverse views held in the country, Common Law requires Unanimity amongst citizen-jurors to find the guilty verdict. Thus, out of a jury of twelve, one citizen judging enforcement to be unjust suffices to find the defendant Not Guilty.

B. Reflections on a Precedent: Apropos of the **Precedent** of jury-nullification of Alcohol Prohibition law, circa *half* of trials not producing guilty verdicts made enforcement of the law untenable on grounds of Legal Equity, natural fairness and justice. (Ref. THE REPORT; Prohibition: The Progenitor of Crime; and: The Fallacy of 'Decriminalisation'.) Thus, one juror in twenty-four (circa 4 % of the adult population) judging a law to be unjust, is sufficient to render mandatory, the rescindment by government of any given 'law'. One-twenty-fourth (1/24) of the adult population deeming any prohibition or other 'law', to be unjust, renders the *'law'* antidemocratic, constitutionally void and abrogated: its enforcement is tyranny, i.e., crime per se.

By Common Law, and under the Constitutions of the U.S. and U.K., *in all due process, jurors' judgement on the justice of laws is required.* Where it can be shown 'trials' have taken place, in which, in the view of one-twenty-fourth of the adult population, the laws which have been enforced at those 'trials' are unjust, then judgement on the justice of those laws has not been forthcoming from the jurors at those (mis-) 'trials'; or, the jurors at those trials have been selected in such a way as fails to represent fairly the diverse views held amongst the population. Because constitutional law and Common Law Trial by Jury require judgement on the law by *representative* juries, all such 'trials' have been *mistrials*; all sentences pertaining thereto are Miscarriages of Justice; and all persecuted thereby qualify for Amnesty and Restitution.

Restoration...

N.B. Regarding numbers, judgement on justice does not derive from percentages. Enforcement of even a just law may be unjust in any given trial, where there was no criminal intent; or where sentences are harsh or savage; or, where sentences are prescribed by the government; or, where sentences are set by representatives or employees of the state (judges, magistrates, etc.). All sentences prescribed by the state are illegal, unconstitutional; and unlawfully interfere with the duties of the Jurors in Trial by Jury in each individual case, to judge the degree of responsibility, provocation, mens rea, and to decide fitting penalties. (Ref. The Form and Stipulations of Common Law Trial by Jury, in: Justice and The Constitution, Part Seven of THE REPORT.)

IV. A. Politicians and state-employees of the European Union and likewise of the United States, take note: Trial by Jury is irrevocably entrenched within the Great Charter Constitution of Britain, *and* the United States Constitution. Hence, (i) all forms of trial-by-government and trials wherein persons convening (presiding) are state-appointed (i.e., they are not answerable to, and not elected by, the citizenry), are ex parte (one-sided), and intrinsically illegal.

(ii) Every citizen disputing accusation *must always* receive the Common Law Trial by a Jury of equal adult citizens (not government representatives) drawn indiscriminately from the population, who judge on both the law and the facts. Legislatures have never received authority from the People to deny the accused the Right to Trial by Jury, nor to change the oaths, to alter the Duties, nor to abridge the jurisdiction of Jurors.

(iii) All trials everywhere, past and present, are illegally conducted wherein: Jurors are not educated into applying the aforesaid Rights and Duty; and also, are not formally instructed by the court (the judge) to include judgement on the justice of law and enforcement, in finding the Verdict. All such 'trials', are mistrials.

(iv) RESTORATION and Universal Adoption of the Common Law Trial by Jury for all causes, criminal, civil and fiscal, is predicated, explicitly binding judges to instruct jurors of their Rights and Duty to judge on the justice of law.

B. Following IV, A, by Common and Constitutional Law:
Where 'judges' i.e., convening court officers —
have *failed* to instruct the jurors to do justice; or,
have *misdirected* jurors that they should find the verdict only on facts (not on justice of the law); or,
whenever officers of the court or defence counsel or the defendant have been *disallowed* from instructing juries to judge on the justice of law; or,
whenever officers of the court or defence counsel or the defendant have been *disallowed* from disputing the justice of legislation; or,
where *jurors oaths have been tampered with*, i.e., to oblige jurors to enforce law as judges dictate; or, preventing jurors from judging on both the law and facts; or,
where jurors have been misinstructed that they may not allow their *opinion* of the law, or their *conscience* to affect their decision, these 'trials' too have been *mistrials*.

C.   Under the Constitution, the law charges all politicians, judges, prosecutors, government officials and employees, officers of the court, and others implicated, who so, and in any way, pervert and/or obstruct justice; these persons being accordingly indicted, to be brought before the public for justice to be done.

A Parting Thought.

Government may confer power but the esteem of the people can alone bestow authority. The legality, sine qua non, of all law derives from and serves Truth, Knowledge, Justice and Liberty. In the course of human affairs the achievement of ideals is given to few, if any, but the pursuit of them is all. In Mankind's dealings henceforth, as in the past, but few natural laws are needed to guide legislation, judicature, and behaviour in respect to others, so that Justice prevails. Two such unchanging precepts present themselves:

Do unto others as you would they do unto you.

Pursue that honourable life which cultivates a positive hatred for the causing of human woe.

— ADDENDUM —

<u>ARTICLES OF UNIVERSAL HUMAN RIGHTS.</u>

In the aforegoing Parts of THE REPORT it is seen that 'laws' or restrictions on cannabis are illegal and abrogate, being per se infractions of other laws, Common, Substantive, and Constitutional. In addition, as demonstrated in the aforegoing Parts, Prohibition of Cannabis breaches the following Articles of the 1948 Treaty, the Universal Declaration of Human Rights:

"Whereas it is essential, if man is not to be compelled to have recourse, as a last resort, to rebellion against tyranny and oppression, that human rights should be protected by the rule of law.

Article 1: All human beings are born free and equal in dignity and rights. They are endowed with reason and conscience and should act towards one another in a spirit of brotherhood.

Article 2: Everyone is entitled to all the rights and freedoms set forth in this Declaration, without distinction of any kind, such as race, colour, sex, language, religion, political or other opinion, national or social origin, property, birth or other status. Furthermore, no distinction shall be made on the basis of the political, jurisdictional or international status of the country or territory to which a person belongs, whether it be independent, trust, non-selfgoverning or under any other limitation of sovereignty.

Article 3: Everyone has the right to life, liberty and security of person.

Article 7: All are equal before the law and are entitled without any discrimination to equal protection of the law. All are entitled to equal protection against any discrimination in violation of this Declaration and against any incitement to such discrimination.

Article 8: Everyone has the right to an effective remedy by the competent national tribunals for acts violating the fundamental rights granted him by the constitution or by law.

Article 9: No one shall be subjected to arbitrary arrest, detention or exile.

Article 10: Everyone is entitled in full equality to a fair and public hearing by an independent and impartial tribunal, in the determination of his rights and obligations and of any criminal charge against him.

Article 12: no one shall be subjected to arbitrary interference with his privacy, family, home or correspondence, or to attacks upon his honour and reputation. Everyone has the right to the protection of the law against such interference or attacks.

Article 16 (3): The family is the natural and fundamental group unit of society and is entitled to protection by society and the state.

Article 21 (1): Everyone has the right to take part in the government of his country, directly or through freely chosen representatives.

(2): Everyone has the right of equal access to public service in his country.

THE REPORT. CANNABIS: THE FACTS, HUMAN RIGHTS AND THE LAW.

Article 26 (2): Education shall be directed to the full development of the human personality and to the strengthening of respect for human rights and fundamental freedoms. It shall promote understanding, tolerance and friendship among all nations, racial or religious groups, and shall further the activities of the United Nations for the maintenance of peace.

(3) Parents have a prior right to choose the kind of education that shall be given to their children.

Article 28: Everyone is entitled to a social and international order in which the rights and freedoms set forth in this Declaration can be fully realised.

Article 29 (2): In the exercise of his rights and freedoms, everyone shall be subject only to such limitations as are determined by law solely for the purpose of securing due recognition and respect for the rights of others and of meeting the just requirements of morality, public order and the general welfare in a democratic society.

Article 30: Nothing in this Declaration may be interpreted as implying for any State, group or person any right to engage in any activity or to perform any act aimed at the destruction of the rights and freedoms set forth herein."

~

The Parliaments and Congresses of all nations _signatory_ to the United Nations' Universal Declaration of Human Rights, are legally and morally bound to Abolish all Prohibitions, regulations and restrictions on Cannabis; to put an end to this tyranny and to redress all the injustices perpetrated thereunder. May all citizens take appropriate actions and continue ceaselessly to do so until this tyranny is expiated and permanently extinguished.

Readers are cordially invited to visit
The Democracy Defined Website
http://www.democracydefined.org/

Addendum.

Amicus Curiæ.

In legal parlance, amicus curiæ, which translates from the Latin as 'a friend to the court,' is the term given to describe a disinterested adviser, not a party to the case. An amicus curiae may proceed if requested or permitted to do so by the court.

In any prosecution, trial or case where charges are instigated against citizens for cannabis cultivation, trade, possession or use, whether or not the case is to be contested (i.e., whichever plea is entered by the defendant), it is fitting that in all countries, presiding judges, magistrates, members of the legal and educational professions, be reminded, or where in ignorance, be informed, of the empirical medico-scientific research-established Exonerative Facts and Evidence apropos of Cannabis; and of the untenable, illegal 'legislation' of its controls.

There is a significant semantical differentiation, in that the Clinical Empirical Evidence does not "dispute the law": the Empirical Evidence categorically abrogates the 'law'. By reading THE REPORT, legal counsel, defendants, teachers and parents from all over the world are learning the empirically-established medico-scientific reality of the harmless and beneficial nature of cannabis, and about the atrocious money-motivated criminality of its 'Prohibition'.

THE REPORT quotes legal grounds (national and international) which demonstrate numerous infractions of laws by the prohibition legislation, and which show all acts of its enforcement to be crime per se. All citizens persecuted thereunder are due Amnesty and Restitution (as for other Wrongful Penalisation).

NOTA BENE: The U.K. Criminal Justice Act provides for the presentation in proceedings of expert reports as evidence. Similar provisions in law exist in the U.S., Australia, Canada, New Zealand, the European Union, etc.

Any defendant anywhere who believes the contents of THE REPORT comprise documentary defence evidence relevant to his or her case, may present (i.e., send or hand in) THE REPORT to the court, together with a formal Letter of Application to the trial-judge, applying to the court (the judge) to authorise counsel to proceed as amicus curiæ in presenting the information collated by THE REPORT.

N.B. Courts do not accept E-Books, printouts, photocopies, etc. Courts require the genuine published article: the Publisher's textbook, current Edition ISBN 9781902848204.

In considering the defendant's formal Application for Amicus Curiæ, the court is duty-bound to peruse the evidence contained in THE REPORT, which exonerates defendants.

The purpose of presenting to the court THE REPORT accompanied by a letter applying for the court to appoint an Amicus Curiæ, is to draw to the judge's attention the Official Evidence of Exonerative Findings of Fact and Conclusions, the Circumstances and Res Gestæ collated in THE REPORT, which exonerate cannabis; vindicate the defendant; and counter-indict prosecution.

BIBLIOGRAPHY: Statements, Evidence and Exhibits.

ABEL, Ernest L., 'Marijuana: The First Twelve Thousand Years,' Plenum Books, N.Y., 1980.

ALLENTUCK, Samuel, & BOWMAN, Karl M., 'Psychiatric Aspects of Marijuana Intoxication,' American Journal of Psychiatry, Vol. 99, 1942.

BEAUBRUN, M. H., 'Cannabis or Alcohol: The Jamaican Experience,' in 'Cannabis And Culture,' Vera Rubin, Editor, Mouton de Gruyter Press, The Hague.

BENABUD, A., 'Psychopathological Aspects of the Cannabis Situation in Morocco; Statistical Data for 1956,' U. N. Bulletin on Narcotics, Vol. 9, no. 4, 1957, pp. 1-16.

BOCK, Alan W., 'Crimping Progress by Banning Hemp,' Orange County Register, 30th Oct., 1988.

Prohibition control(s) pseudo-legislation as corrupt duty, tax and profit protection-by-monopoly: exemplification of protected, undeserved profits of oil, petro-chemical and pharmaceutical corporations, whose dangerous, polluting and/or ineffectual products would be redundant were cannabis Relegalised; U.K. newspapers, The European, 21-27 March, 1996; and, Daily Mail, 23rd March, 1996.

CARTER, William E., Editor, 'Cannabis in Costa Rica: A Study of Chronic Marijuana Use,' Institute for the Study of Human Issues, 3401, Science Center, Philadelphia, PA 19104. ISBN 0-89727-008-8.

Channel Four (U.K.) public mis-information programmes and leaflet; March, 1995; disinformation by Home Office state-funded 'Institute for the Study of Drug Dependence' (sic); also, government-funded ISDD & 'Release', magazines, leaflets containing long-disproven derogatory fictions on cannabis.

CHOPRA, R. N., & CHOPRA, G. S., 'Treatment of Drug Addiction; Experience in India,' U. N. Bulletin on Narcotics, Vol. 9, no. 4, 1957, pp. 21-33.

COHEN, Sidney & STILLMAN, Richard, 'The Therapeutic Potential of Marijuana,' Plenum Books, N.Y.

COOPER, R. W., 'The Nuremberg Trial,' Penguin Books, Harmondsworth, Middlesex, England.

COTTS, Cynthia, 'Hard Sell in the Drug War,' The Nation, 9 March, 1992.

CRANCER, Alfred, et al, 'Comparison of the Effect of Marijuana and Alcohol on Simulated Driving Performance,' Science, Vol. 164, 1969, pp. 851-854.

DEMPSEY, J. M., 'Fiber Crops,' University Presses of Florida.

DEWEY, Lyster H., Botanist-in-Charge of Fiber-Plant Investigations, & MERRILL, Jason L., Paper-Plant Chemist, Bulletin 404, 1916, U.S. Department of Agriculture.

DOBLIN, Richard E., & KLEIMAN, Mark A. R., 'Marijuana as Antiemetic Medicine: A Survey of Oncologists' Experiences and Attitudes,' Journal of Clinical Oncology, Vol. 9, no. 7, July, 1991.

DOORENBOS, Norman, et al, 'Cultivation, Extraction and Analysis of Cannabis Sativa L.,' Annals of The New York Academy of Sciences, 191, December 31st, 1971.

D'OUDNEY, Kenn, 'Global Warming: The Scientific Green Solution to this World Crisis,' Scorpio Recording Company (Publishing) Ltd., Monomark House, 27, Old Gloucester Street, London, WC1N 3XX, England. ISBN: 978-1-902848-06-8.

D'OUDNEY, Kenn, & SPOONER, Lysander, U.S. Lawyer (barrister), 'Trial by Jury: Its History, True Purpose and Modern Relevance,' Scorpio Recording Company (Publishing) Ltd., Monomark House, 27, Old Gloucester Street, London, WC1N 3XX, England. ISBN: 978-1-902848-72-3.

D'OUDNEY, Kenn, 'The Constitution Treatise: A Treatise on Law, Constitutions and Democracy,' Scorpio Recording Company (Publishing) Ltd., Monomark House, 27, Old Gloucester Street, London, WC1N 3XX, England. ISBN: 978-1-902848-74-7.

DRESDEN COTTON, 1924 patent issued for Dresden Cotton, cottonisation of hemp process. Staatliches Material Prüfungsampt. This document combines with: BOERMANN, Professor Paul, Manchester Guardian, 1924. Cottonisation of hemp process renders cannabis fibre indistinguishable from cotton. Before Prohibition, cannabis came profitably onto the fibre commodities' market at less than half the price of the cheaper kinds of cotton.

Bibliography.

ECONOMIST, The, 2nd of April, 1988; see page 156.

FBI Serious Crime Statistics; cf: during Prohibition and then following Relegalisation of Alcohol in 1933; e.g. the halving of homicides following Relegalisation.

FRAZIER, Jack, 'The Great American Hemp Industry,' Access Unlimited, P.O. Box 1900, Frazier Park, California 93225.

FREEDMAN, H. L., & ROCKMORE, M. J., 'Marijuana, Factor in Personality Evaluation and Army Maladjustment,' Journal of Clinical Psychopathology, Vols. 7 & 8, 1946, pp. 765-782, 221-236.

FRIEDMAN, Milton, 'Capitalism and Freedom,' University of Chicago Press, Chicago and London. See also by the same Nobel laureate author: 'Why Government Is the Problem,' & 'The Tyranny of the Status Quo,' & with FRIEDMAN, Rose, 'Free to Choose,' (book, and the television series of that name, available on video) & with SCHWARTZ, Anna Jacobson, 'A Monetary History of the United States, 1867 - 1960.'

Authentic Common Law Trial by Jury requires judges formally to educate citizen-jurors on their Rights and Duties in finding the verdict, to judge the justice of law and of its enforcement, as well as the facts of the case, the admissibility of evidence, the moral intent of the accused (requiring malice aforethought to find guilt) and, where guilt is unanimously found, to take account of any mitigating circumstances and set the fitting sentence. To protect the People from arbitrary (i.e., illegal) laws and unjust acts of enforcement, The Democracy Defined Membership campaigns for RESTORATION and UNIVERSAL ADOPTION of Constitutional Common Law Trial by Jury. The Democracy Defined RESTORATION Campaign Information, Membership & and contacts are at WEBSITE www.democracydefined.org/
✻ Contact the Democracy Defined Campaign for information on how you can join in and help.

GIBBON, Edward, 'The Decline and Fall of the Roman Empire,' Everyman's Library, Dutton, N.Y.

Guinness Book of Answers, Guinness Publishing, Ltd., 33, London Road, Enfield, Middlesex, England. Encylopaedic compendium (one of many) confirming items of Evidence on Chemistry, Global Warming, and radioactivity.

HANEY, Alan, & KUTSCHEID, Benjamin B., 'An Ecological Study of Naturalised Hemp,' American Midland Naturalist, Vol. 93, Jan. 1975, University of Notre Dame, Indiana 46556.

Hawaii Natural Energy Institute, 'Methanol Plantations in Hawaii.'

'Hemp: Introduction of Chinese Hemp into America,' Bureau of Plant Industry, 1913 Yearbook of the U.S. Department of Agriculture.

HERER, Jack, 'The Emperor Wears No Clothes: Hemp And the Marijuana Conspiracy,' HEMP/Queen of Clubs Publ., 5632 Van Nuys Boulevard, Van Nuys, California 91401.

HERODOTUS, 'The Histories,' Fifth Century B. C., Penguin Classics, 27, Wrights Lane, London.

House Ways and Means Committee, U.S. Congressional Record Transcripts, Hearings on Taxation of Marijuana, 1937.

Indian Hemp Drugs Commission, Report of, 1893-1894, Simla, 1897.

JEFFERSON, Thomas, 'The Writings of Thomas Jefferson,' WASHINGTON, H. A., Editor, J. P. Lippincotts & Co., Philadelphia, 1871. N. B. In addition to Law and Human Rights, the Writings of Thomas Jefferson have further relevance in cannabis cultivation and Agronomics.

KABELIK, J., & KREJCI, Z. & SANTAVY, F., 'Cannabis as a Medicament,' U. N. Bulletin on Narcotics 12, 1960.

KNIGHT, J. A., 'Pyrolysis of Wood Residues with a Vertical Bed Reactor,' in 'Progress in Biomass Conversion' Vol. 1, Academic Press, N. Y.

KREJCI, Z. 'On the Problem of Substances with Antibacterial Action: Cannabis Effect,' Casopis Lekaru Ceskych 43, 1961.

LaGUARDIA, Mayor Fiorello, Committee on Marihuana; New York Academy of Medicine Empirical Studies: 'The Marihuana Problem in the City of New York, Sociological, Medical, Psychological and Pharmacological Studies,' Jaques Cattell Press, Lancaster, Pennsylvania.

LAPHAM, Lewis H., 'A Political Opiate: The War on Drugs Is A Folly And A Menace,' Harpers Magazine, December 1989.

LIPINSKI, E. S., 'Chemicals from Biomass: Petrochemical Substitution Options,' Batelle Columbus Laboratories, Ohio.

LOWER, George A., MECHANICAL ENGINEERING MAGAZINE, February, 1938, 'Hemp: The Most Profitable and Desirable Crop that Can Be Grown.'

MAGNA CARTA, The Constitutional Law. The British Library, Wetherby, Yorkshire, England. Also see: D'OUDNEY & SPOONER, 'Trial by Jury,' for in-depth analysis of MAGNA CARTA's strictures.

MUSIKKA, Elvy, 'See The Light: The Elvy Musikka Story,' Elvy Musikka, P. O. Box 7499, Hollywood, Florida 33081.

MUSTO, David F., 'The American Disease: Origins of Narcotic Control,' Yale University Press. Oxford University Press also.

NADELMAN, Ethan A., 'Drug Prohibition in the United States: Costs, Consequences and Alternatives,' Science, Vol. 245, Sept., 1989.

National Institute of Health (U.S.) Study: Tobacco; Lancet, Sept., 1983.

National Institute of Mental Health (U.S.) Empirical Studies, See: RUBIN, Vera, & COMITAS, Lambros, 'Ganja in Jamaica.'

National Institute on Drug Abuse (U.S. NIDA), Statistics on Alcohol. Ref. Part Three.

Old Bailey Commemorative Plaque, The Old Bailey Law Courts, London, England. Ref. Part Seven.

OSBURN, L., & OSBURN, J., 'Cannabis Hemp Seeds: The Most Nutritionally Complete Food Source on Earth,' 1993, Access Unlimited, P. O. Box 1900, Frazier Park, California 93225.

OSGOOD, R. V., & DUDLEY, N. S., 'Comparative Yield Trials with Tree and Grass Energy Crops,' Second Pacific Biofuels Workshop, University of Hawaii.

O' SHAUGHNESSY, W. B., 'Monograph on Cannabis Medicine,' 1839; 'On the Preparation of the Indian Hemp or Gunjah,' 1842; Transactions of the Medical and Physical Society of Bengal.

PACKER, Herbert L., 'The Limits of the Criminal Sanction,' Stanford University Press.

PHILIPS, V. D., KINOSHITA, C. M., NEILL, D. R., & TAKAHASHI, P. K., 'Thermochemical Production of Methanol from Biomass in Hawaii,' Hawaii Integrated Biofuels Research Program, Phase 2, Final Report, Hawaii Natural Energy Institute, August, 1990.

PONTE, Lowell, 'Radioactivity: The New-Found Danger in Cigarettes,' Reader's Digest, March, 1986.

POPULAR MECHANICS MAGAZINE, February, 1938; 'The New Billion-Dollar Crop,' &, the Ford Motor Co. Cannabis-Methanol fuelled and Cannabis-Plastic-Bodied Car; December, 1941.

PRINCE, R., GREENFIELD, R., & MARRIOTT, J., 'Cannabis or Alcohol ? Observations on Their Use in Jamaica,' U.N. Bulletin on Narcotics, Vol. 24, no. 1, 1972, pp. 1-9.

PRINCIPLES, United Nations' Resolution of the 10th of December, 1946. Ref. Part Six.

RANDALL, Robert C., Editor, 'Marijuana, Medicine and the Law,' Judicial Review of Cannabis Data. (See Vol. 2 for Decision of Administrative Law Judge.) Galen Press, P. O. Box 53318, Temple Heights Station, Washington DC 20009.

RIGGENBACH, Jeff, 'Repeal the Drug Laws to Help Fight Crime,' Orange County Register.

ROWELL, R. M. & HOKANSON, A. E., 'Methanol from Wood: A Critical Assessment,' in Progress in Biomass Conversion, Vol. 1, Academic Press, N. Y.

Bibliography.

RUBIN, Vera, & COMITAS, Lambros, 'Ganja in Jamaica: A Medical Anthropological Study of Chronic Marijuana Use,' U.S. National Institute of Mental Health; Empirical Studies; Center for Studies of Narcotic and Drug Abuse. Mouton de Gruyter Division of, Walter de Gruyter, Inc., 200 Saw Mill River Road, Hawthorne, New York 10532.
European availability from: Walter de Gruyter & Co., Genthiner Strasse 13, D-10785 Berlin.

SCHAEFFER, Jeffrey, ANDRYSIAK, Therese, & UNGERLEIDER, J. Thomas, 'Cognition and Long-Term Use of Ganja (Cannabis),' Department of Psychiatry and Biobehavioural Sciences, University of California School of Medicine, Los Angeles 90024. Copyright by the American Association for the Advancement of Science. Science, Vol. 213, 24th July, 1981.

Also: 'The Coptic Study: A Neuropsychological Evaluation; A Case History,' Neuroscience Associates, Inc., 6317 Wilshire Boulevard, Suite 606, Los Angeles, California 90048.

SCHLICHTEN Decorticator, The, 1916. See HERER, Jack; Appendix in: 'The Emperor Wears No Clothes,' Queen of Clubs Publishing, Van Nuys Boulevard, Van Nuys, Los Angeles, California.

SCHULTES, R. E. (Harvard University), 'Man and Marijuana,' Natural History, 82, Aug-Sept., 1983.

SCHUR, Edwin M., 'Crimes Without Victims,' Prentice-Hall, Inc., Englewood Cliffs, New Jersey.

SMITH, Adam, 'The Wealth of Nations,' Penguin Classics, 27, Wrights Lane, London W8 5TZ, U.K.

STERLING, Eric E., 'What Should We Do About Drugs ? — Manage the Problem by Legalisation,' and: 'The Bill of Rights: A Casualty of the War on Drugs,' Criminal Justice Policy Foundation, 2000 L Street NW, Suite 702, Washington DC 20036.

TASHKIN, Donald P., M. D., UCLA School of Medicine Pulmonary Studies, American Journal of Respiratory & Critical Care Medicine; Vol. 155, 1997.

United Nations' Declaration of Human Rights, The, 1948.

WHOLE LIFE TIMES, (U.S.) 'Would You Still Rather Fight Than Switch ?' mid-April/May, 1985.

WOLFE, Sidney M., M.D., & COLEY, Christopher, 'Pills That Don't Work,' and: 'Stopping Valium,' Public Citizen Health Research Group, 2000 P Street NW, Washington DC 20036.

ZINBERG, Norman E. (Harvard University School of Medicine), & WEIL, Andrew T., 'The Effects of Marijuana on Human Beings,' New York Times Magazine, 11 May, 1969.

ZINBERG, Norman E. & WEIL, Andrew T., & NELSEN, Judith M., 'Clinical And Psychological Effects of Marijuana in Man,' Science, Vol. 162, 13 December, 1968, pp. 1234-1242, and: 'Cannabis: The First Controlled Experiment,' New Society, 16 January, 1969, pp. 84-86.

The Authors express their gratitude to:

Astra d'Oudney, for her support and enormous help, which included innumerable perspicuous suggestions, proof-reading, indexing, and her Scroll design, and to

Elvy Musikka, for permission to quote her in Part Three, and to

Judy Osburn, for her diagrams, and to

High Times Magazine, for permission to quote from their interview with **Gordon Hanson**, in Part Three.

INDEX

247

— REVIEWS AND ENDORSEMENTS OF —

THE REPORT.
CANNABIS: THE FACTS,
HUMAN RIGHTS AND THE LAW.

"You have done a splendid job of producing a comprehensive summary of the evidence documenting that the prohibition of the production, sale and use of cannabis is utterly unjustified and produces many harmful effects. Any impartial person reading your REPORT will almost certainly end up favouring the re-legalisation of cannabis."
NOBEL LAUREATE PROFESSOR MILTON FRIEDMAN, Economics' Adviser to U.S. government; Author, video and TV series writer and presenter; Senior Research Fellow, Hoover Institution on War, Revolution and Peace; Professor Emeritus, University of Chicago.

"You represent a worthy part of the fight in many countries for the logical and beneficial use of cannabis. I thank you for that."
PROFESSOR PATRICK D. WALL, Author; Professor of Physiology, UMDS St. Thomas's (Teaching) Hospital, London; Fellow of the Royal Society; DM, FRCP.

"I am totally amazed at THE REPORT's quality and overall goodness."
DR. ANNE BIEZANEK, Authoress; ChB, BSc, MB, MFHom.

"A fine document."
U.S. JUDGE's letter to Authors.

"THE REPORT's thesis is sound."
U.K. JUDGE's letter to Authors.

"I <u>did</u> enjoy reading it. THE REPORT should contribute much."
THE HON. JONATHON PORRITT, Bt., Adviser to U.K. government on Environment; Author; Founder, Friends of the Earth; TV series writer and presenter.

PUBLICATIONS AND SUPPORT.

WEBSITE:
http://www.democracydefined.org/

Purchasing these books supports the not-for-profit DEMOCRACY DEFINED Educational Campaign for RESTORATION and UNIVERSAL ADOPTION of CONSTITUTIONAL COMMON LAW TRIAL BY JURY.

DEMOCRACY DEFINED textbooks militate on behalf of Political, Religious and Personal Freedom, Truth, Knowledge, Justice and Liberty, to promote the well-being of people everywhere.

THE REPORT. CANNABIS: THE FACTS, HUMAN RIGHTS AND THE LAW.
ISBN 9781902848204. FOREWORD by US government Adviser. Endorsed by eminent academics, authors, doctors, judges (US & UK). A book of The RESTORATION Trilogy.

TRIAL BY JURY: ITS HISTORY, TRUE PURPOSE AND MODERN RELEVANCE. Endorsed by academics, doctors and judges. A book of The RESTORATION Trilogy. ISBN 9781902848723.

GLOBAL WARMING: THE SCIENTIFIC GREEN SOLUTION TO THIS WORLD CRISIS. FOREWORD by a Nobel Prize winning Economist. Endorsed by academics, ecologists. A book of The RESTORATION Trilogy. ISBN 9781902848068.

THE CONSTITUTION TREATISE.
Endorsed by U.S. and European cognoscenti. ISBN 9781902848747.

THE DEMOCRACY DEFINED PUBLICATIONS ARE AVAILABLE DIRECTLY
FROM THE PUBLISHERS OR FROM
NORTH CAROLINA BOOK MANUFACTURER AND DISTRIBUTOR
LULU.
FOR "HOW TO ORDER" DETAILS,
SEE THE BOOKS ON THE RELEVANT PAGES AT

www.democracydefined.org

DEMOCRACY DEFINED BOOKS CAN BE STOCKED BY AND
OBTAINED FROM ALL BOOKSTORES, NEWSAGENTS AND LIBRARIES.

Publisher: SCORPIO RECORDING COMPANY (PUBLISHING) LTD.
MONOMARK HOUSE, 27 OLD GLOUCESTER STREET,
LONDON WC1N 3XX, ENGLAND.

TRADE ENQUIRIES CONTACT
SCORPIO BOOKS DISTRIBUTION ADMINISTRATION:
scorpiobooks@democracydefined.org